MYSTERY!

A CELEBRATION

STALKING PUBLIC TELEVISION'S
GREATEST SLEUTHS

MYSTERY!
A CELEBRATION

STALKING PUBLIC TELEVISION'S GREATEST SLEUTHS

RON MILLER

Foreword by
P. D. JAMES

Illustrations by
EDWARD GOREY

Edited by
KAREN SHARPE

KQED
BOOKS

SAN FRANCISCO

© 1996 by WGBH Educational
Foundation and KQED Books

Foreword © 1996 by P. D. James
All rights reserved.
No part of this book may be used or reproduced
in any manner whatsoever without the written permission
of the Publisher, except in the case of brief quotations
in critical articles and reviews.
For information, address:
   **KQED Books & Video, 2601 Mariposa St.,
   San Francisco, CA 94110.**

Publisher: James Connolly
Editorial Director: Pamela Byers
Editor: Karen Sharpe
Book design: Raul Cabra, Tin-tin Blackwell / Cabra Diseño
Researcher: Ellen Baskin
Editorial Assistance: Kim Haglund, Zoë Sharpe, Serena Marler,
         Mu'frida Bell, Trisha Feuerstein, Jefferey O'Rourke
Research Consultant: Nathan Hasson

Credits for all photographs, drawings, and review
excerpts will be found on page 299.

Mystery! is a trademark of the WGBH Educational
Foundation and is used by permission.

Books are available from KQED Books & Video
for quantity purchases for sales promotions,
premiums, fund-raising, or educational use.
For information, contact KQED Books & Video,
2601 Mariposa St., San Francisco, CA 94110.

Library of Congress Cataloguing-in-Publication Data

Miller, Ron, 1939-
      Mystery! : a celebration : stalking public television's greatest sleuths /
      Ron Miller ; foreword by P. D. James ; illustrations by Edward Gorey;
      edited by Karen Sharpe.
            p.   cm.
      Includes bibliographical references and index.
      ISBN 0-912333-89-8
      1. Mystery! (Television program) I. Sharpe, Karen. II. Title.
PN1992.77.M95M56 1996   96-42130
                                                         CIP

ISBN 0-912333-89-8

Manufactured in Hong Kong
10 9 8 7 6 5 4 3 2 1

Distributed to the trade by
Publishers Group West

DEDICATION

This book is dedicated to three important women in my life:
my mother, the late Evelyn L. Miller, who probably started all this by naming
me after British actor Ronald Colman and dragging me to every mystery movie
released during the 1940s; my wife, Darla, who never showed a jealous streak after all
the nights I neglected her while cozying up to Agatha, Phyllis, Ruth, Margery, Antonia,
Dorothy, Daphne, Josephine, Ngaio, Edith, Lynda, Paula, and all the other women
of mystery literature; and my intelligent and caring editor, Karen Sharpe,
who got me into this, then held my hand while I walked the tightrope
over the abyss of authorship.

—RON MILLER

For Zoë and Aisha, a great addition to the team—
especially as this experience means you now can understand
why Mom sometimes loses her sense of humor.

—KAREN SHARPE

TABLE OF CONTENTS

IX Acknowledgments

X   Foreword by P. D. James

XII Preface

PART I: SCENE OF THE CRIME

2   Setting the Scene

4   Wicked and Whimsical: Edward Gorey's Vision
    Replicating Gorey's World: **Animator Derek Lamb**

10 Amusingly Alliterative Host: Gene Shalit

11 Master of Menace to Mischievous Host: Vincent Price

13 Emmanently APeeling Host: Diana Rigg

15 Mystery! by Season

16 The Murders Begin: *She Fell Among Thieves*
    Once a Hero: **Malcolm McDowell**

PART II: THE INVESTIGATORS

22 Magnifying Glass Turned on the Investigators

THE VICTORIAN DETECTIVES

24 SHERLOCK HOLMES (*The Adventures of Sherlock Holmes*)
    The Real Doctor Watson: **Sir Arthur Conan Doyle**
    Fighting for the True Holmes: **Jeremy Brett**

36 SERGEANT CRIBB (*Sergeant Cribb*)
    Creator of Holmes' Counterpart: **Peter Lovesey**

THE ELEGANT DETECTIVES

42 HERCULE POIROT (*Agatha Christie's Poirot*)
    Mother of the Mystery: **Dame Agatha Christie**
    The Consummate Poirot: **David Suchet**

54 LORD PETER WIMSEY (*Dorothy L. Sayers' Lord Peter Wimsey*)
    Rebel with a Cause: **Dorothy L. Sayers**

62 ALBERT CAMPION (*Campion*)
    Writer from Childhood: **Margery Allingham**

68 Good Guys As Bad Guys

THE CIVIL SERVANTS

70 INSPECTOR MORSE (*Inspector Morse*)
    Classics Scholar and Detective Writer: **Colin Dexter**
    Acting on Morse's Behalf: **John Thaw**

82 COMMANDER ADAM DALGLIESH (*Death of an Expert Witness* et alia)
Queen of Crime: **P. D. James**
A Differently Defined Dalgliesh: **Roy Marsden**

94 DCI JANE TENNISON (*Prime Suspect*)
True to Her Subjects: **Lynda La Plante**
In Her Prime: **Helen Mirren**

106 INSPECTOR RODERICK ALLEYN (*Artists in Crime, Ngaio Marsh's Alleyn Mysteries*)
Flowering Tree of Mystery: **Ngaio Marsh**

112 INSPECTOR JULES MAIGRET (*Maigret*)
Literary Ladies' Man: **Georges Simenon**

THE PRIVATE EYES

118 SID HALLEY (*The Racing Game*)
Champion Steeplechase Jockey: **Dick Francis**

124 TOMMY AND TUPPENCE BERESFORD (*Partners in Crime, The Secret Adversary*)

132 ELLY CHANDLER AND DEE TATE (*Chandler & Co.*)
Driven by Social Issues: **Paula Milne**

THE TALENTED AMATEURS

140 JANE MARPLE (*Agatha Christie's Miss Marple*)
The Quintessential Miss Marple: **Joan Hickson**

148 JEMIMA SHORE (*Quiet As a Nun*)
Taking a Break from Biographies: **Lady Antonia Fraser**

153 The Classic Detective *by Carolyn Heilbrun (Amanda Cross)*

154 HUGO LOVELACE CHARTERS, GILES EVELYN CALDICOTT (*Charters and Caldicott*)

158 BROTHER CADFAEL (*Cadfael*)
Medieval Mystery Writer: **Ellis Peters**
Frocked Again: **Derek Jacobi**

166 FATHER BROWN (*Father Brown*)
Man of Many Literary Métiers: **G. K. Chesterton**

ON HER MAJESTY'S SECRET SERVICE

172 SIDNEY REILLY (*Reilly, Ace of Spies*)
Heroes, Anti-Heroes, Non-Heroes: **Sam Neill**

178 BERNARD SAMSON (*Game, Set and Match*)
Artist of Espionage: **Len Deighton**

IN A CLASS BY THEMSELVES

184 HORACE RUMPOLE (*Rumpole of the Bailey*)
Queen's Counsel: **John Mortimer**
Not to Be Confused with Horace Rumpole: **Leo McKern**

194 PARKER PYNE ET ALIA (*Agatha Christie Stories*)

198 OLIVER AND DIANE PRIEST (*Oliver's Travels*)

202 The Detection Club: The Crime Writers' Conspiracy

PART III: CASES FOR INVESTIGATION

206 Denizens of the Dark Side

THE DEEPLY DISTURBED

208 *MOTHER LOVE*
A Chilling Helena Vesey: **Diana Rigg**
A Man of Many Names: **Domini Taylor**

212 *DR. JEKYLL AND MR. HYDE*
Struggling with Two Sides: **Robert Louis Stevenson**

216 *A DARK-ADAPTED EYE, GALLOWGLASS*
The Dark Side of Ruth Rendell: **Barbara Vine**
Driven by Psychological Dramas: **Director Tim Fywell**

223 *DYING DAY*

THE PREDATORS

226 *SWEENEY TODD*

228 *PRAYING MANTIS*

230 *THE DARK ANGEL*
Like Characters in His Novels: **Sheridan le Fanu**

233 *THE WOMAN IN WHITE*

236 *BRAT FARRAR*
Doppelganger in Her Own Write: **Josephine Tey**

239 *DIE KINDER*

242 *MALICE AFORETHOUGHT*
A Mysterious Life: **Francis Iles**

RAISING REASONABLE DOUBTS

246 *REBECCA, MY COUSIN RACHEL*
Winning Writer Since a Teen: **Daphne du Maurier**

254 *THE MAN FROM THE PRU*

257 *CAUSE CÉLÈBRE*

259 *WE, THE ACCUSED*
Of Mysterious Parentage: **Ernest Raymond**

261 *THE LIMBO CONNECTION*

263 *MELISSA*

THE PARANORMAL

266 *MISS MORISON'S GHOSTS*

268 *SHADES OF DARKNESS*

PART IV: CASE CLOSED

274 Mystery! Trivia Quiz *by Ellen Baskin*

284 List of Photographs

286 Appendix A: Show Credits

296 Appendix B: Resource List

299 Credits

300 Index

ACKNOWLEDGMENTS

IT'S NO MYSTERY, REALLY, HOW A BOOK OF SUCH SCOPE AND MAGNITUDE AS THIS one gets done—only through the tireless dedication and tremendous generosity of a large number of individuals. From the mystery authors past and present who inspired the writers, producers, directors, actors, and behind-the-scenes personnel to create such marvelous television adaptations, to WGBH, who brought those programs to this country (most especially the late Joan Wilson and current Executive Producer Rebecca Eaton), to author Ron Miller, whose understanding of and love for the television mystery genre made this book a true celebration—to each of you, our heartfelt appreciation.

For coming up with the crazy idea of these celebration books, we are grateful to Mark Powelson, former vice-president of KQED. Thanks, too, to Pamela Byers of KQED Books for her support. Our gratitude, also, to the folks at WGBH (Karen Johnson, Marianne Neumann, Virginia Jackson, Danuta Forbes, and Anna Lowi), who entrusted their series to our scrutiny, opened their archives, and responded to urgent requests for yet more materials.

Then there is the dynamite team who made everything happen: Cabra Diseño (Raul Cabra, Tin-tin Blackwell, Scott di Girolamo, and Suzanne Scott), who blended Gorey's art and gorgeous type to capture the Mystery! sensibility; Ellen Baskin, who made the quiz so much fun and the appendices so thorough; Kim Haglund, who polished our style; Zoë Sharpe, who so capably assisted in just about everything; Nathan Hasson, who kept us informed and amused; Serena Marler, who picked up all kinds of errors; Mu'frida Bell, who found all the typos; Aisha Sharpe, who photocopied from Manhattan to Berkeley; Trisha Feuerstein, our terrific indexer, and Jeffrey O'Rourke, a great liaison.

And, finally, our appreciation to the many individuals who supplied us with the materials that made this book possible: P. D. James, who put aside Commander Dalgliesh to write the wonderful foreword; Edward Gorey and his attorney Gray Coleman, who generously allowed us to use the brilliant drawings that helped define the look of this book; Derek Lamb, who actually snipped off frames of his animated films for us to use; Diana Rigg, the late Vincent Price, and Gene Shalit, whose intros and extros add so much to our understanding of the series; Michael Shepley PR, particularly Ellen Fry, for help in arranging interviews and making their files available to us; Frank and Arlene Goodman, original publicists, whose archives were invaluable; Carolyn Heilbrun, for "The Classic Detective"; and all who allowed us to use excerpts from their publications.

For the marvelous photos, we are most grateful to many kind people: Laura Clark, Bobbie Mitchell, and Nicola Smith (BBC); Gilly Hartley and Colleen Kay (Thames); Elaine Collins and Kathryn de Belle (Granada); Shane Chapman and Penny McGuire (LWT); Nick Lockett and Barry Ledingham (Carlton UK); Esther Porter and Stephen Quirke (ITEL); Louise Fawkner-Corbett (Channel 4); Jon Keeble (Polygram); Kevin Brooks and Upali Samaraweera (Yorkshire); Ariane Sulzer (Administration de l'Oeuvre de Georges Simenon); and Michael Schulman (Popperfoto). For the Holmes postcards, our thanks to Deborah Nicholls of The Sherlock Holmes Memorabilia Company.

All of you are the real heroes of this Mystery! book.

—KAREN SHARPE

FOREWORD

〜

THE MYSTERY IS ONE OF THE MOST RESILIENT OF ALL POPULAR LITERARY FORMS; it is also the most paradoxical. It deals with the great absolute, death, yet in its clue-making uses the trivia of daily existence as the instruments of justice. At the nub of the plot are violence, murder, and destruction, yet the mystery is controlled and orderly, affording a familiar and secure structure within which the imaginations both of writer and reader can safely confront the unthinkable. It is written primarily for entertainment, yet it satisfies some of the most fundamental needs of the human psyche, providing reassurance, catharsis, and an affirmation of our cherished belief that we live in a rational and moral universe. Above all, the mystery tells a story and provides for us the satisfaction of excitement, suspense, and vicarious danger. It is no wonder that this popular form, at once cerebral and strongly visual, should be so successful on television.

Mystery! A Celebration is aptly named. It does indeed celebrate, through illustrations, photographs, reminiscences, commentary, and analysis, a television genre that has enthralled millions in every continent and culture. Here we can again encounter the detectives, amateur and professional, whose place is secure in the pantheon of great investigators, characters as varied as Miss Marple, the gentle but implacable spinster of St. Mary Mead; Brother Cadfael, medieval monk; Lord Peter Wimsey, debonair younger son of a duke; and my own Commander Dalgliesh. Here, too, we encounter the villains whose nefarious activities and final undoing have provided us with hours of satisfaction. They include some of the finest actors of the television screen, and the direction and production standards of the mystery as a genre are among the highest examples of television art. Here, too, we can enjoy interviews with many of the distinguished actors and writers who have made the televised mystery such a respected as well as a popular art form, and learn something of the problems, the challenges, and the satisfactions of their art. This is a book which is, indeed, a celebration, and one to which we will return with pleasure long after the first reading is over.

Many writers, myself included, have reason to be grateful to television. There is no doubt that the medium brings viewers to the books, and most of us gain an additional pleasure from reading a mystery that we have first seen on screen, or from watching what television has made of our well-loved detective heroes and heroines. Writers are frequently asked what they feel about the television versions of their books and how satisfied they are with the adaptations and the characterization. Most of us, I think, have our grumbles or small reservations. Television, a visual medium, is essentially different from the written word, and novelists have to accept that there will be some changes in their own conception of a story if it is to be successful on television. But all writers hope that producers and directors will be true to the spirit of the original work, will resist the temptation to make drastic changes to the story, and will use the author's dialogue whenever possible. The most successful mystery series, in my view, have been those which have been most faithful to the original novel. It may occasionally be necessary to drop a character; it should never be necessary to introduce a new one. But some of the best writing in televised mystery has been original work, not an adaptation. I remember with particular pleasure and admiration the work of Lynda La Plante whose female Scotland Yard detective, Jane Tennison, is so brilliantly played by Helen Mirren.

Another attraction of the mystery on television is, of course, the setting. Here again there is wonderful variety in the series illustrated in this book. We are taken into the gentle world of the English country village with Miss Marple, brilliantly played by Joan Hickson. We explore the colleges, streets, and pubs of Oxford with Colin Dexter's Inspector Morse. John Mortimer's Rumpole takes us into the very English world of the Old Bailey. With Brother Cadfael we are back in the Middle Ages, while Maigret takes us to France. With Dick Francis' Sid Halley we become familiar with the dangerous world of horse racing, and with Dorothy L. Sayers' Lord Peter Wimsey we enter the more peaceable, nostalgic England of the 1930s. Setting is immensely important to the mystery. It creates the atmosphere of menace, terror, or foreboding; influences plot and character; roots the sometimes bizarre events of the plot in the firm soil of a recognizable place; and in a television series often provides images of great beauty.

Mystery! A Celebration will give immense pleasure to millions of viewers who look forward to the excitement, entertainment, and suspense of some of the best of television, and will enhance our enjoyment of the genre, and of programs to come, by its review of some of the most remarkable series and performances in the art of television.

—P. D. JAMES, *1996*

PREFACE

My long journey to authorship of a book about PBS' Mystery! series probably began more than 50 years ago in the murky movie palaces that were strung out along First Street in San Jose, California, during the last few years of World War II.

Mom needed to get her mind off the war for at least a couple of hours each day, and the movies promised a cheap respite. She loved mystery movies, so she took me and my baby brother to any that came to town. I must have seen at least 500 between 1943 and 1947 and became a hopeless mystery addict—a natural development for any kid who saw Sherlock Holmes and Charlie Chan more often than he saw his commuter dad.

My mother doted on dapper, suave English movie stars and, in fact, named me after one: Ronald Colman. He didn't play detectives often, but probably was the best of all the Bulldog Drummonds.

Back then, the influence of British mysteries on Hollywood was enormous and there were innumerable American detectives who behaved like Yankee knock-offs of Lord Peter Wimsey and the rest of the debonair gentlemen sleuths from Blighty. Most had mustaches, slicked-down hair, and seemed to wear evening clothes 24 hours a day. William Powell's Philo Vance and Nick Charles are perfect examples. In my childhood, although the rise of hardboiled American private eyes like Hammett's Sam Spade, Chandler's Philip Marlowe, and Halliday's Michael Shayne had begun, they still hadn't pushed the British sleuths to the sidelines as they finally did in the more cynical post-war years.

That's why I still thought the king of all detectives, regardless of national origin, was Basil Rathbone's Sherlock Holmes. He literally held me spellbound. I was so excited by Rathbone's movie and radio Holmes that I turned to Conan Doyle's original stories at a very tender age to satisfy my craving for more, and by the time I was in high school, I'd read them all.

The influence of those formative years has been long-lasting. My exposure to all those detective movies turned me into a voracious mystery reader. When we bought our first television set in the early 1950s, I proceeded to catch up on any mysteries I'd missed as a kid. I've never lost my affection for the mystery genre, which now has broadened to include the suspense and thriller genres as well. All this surely helped make me a devoted fan of Mystery! when it went on the air in 1980. But there may have been some other mysterious force at work, too. In 1945, we had gone to see Val Lewton's *Isle of the Dead,* a spooky Boris Karloff thriller that took place on a cemetery island. There was a plague, so they were burying people as soon as they dropped. One was a cataleptic woman who slipped into a death-like coma and, by mistake, was put into her tomb alive. When she finally woke up and broke out of her coffin, her moans made my hair stand on end and I was cowering among the candy wrappers. As it turned out, that terrifying woman was played by Katherine Emery, whose daughter grew up to be Rebecca Eaton, the current executive producer of Mystery!. Call it coincidence, if you like, but I call it predestination.

For the past year, I've been totally immersed in the world of Mystery! and was grateful for the opportunity. My close scrutiny of Mystery! as a television critic during its first 16 seasons helped give me the confidence to try writing a book about it when my editor, Karen Sharpe, suggested such a project in the fall of 1995 and the producers of Mystery! at Boston PBS station WGBH gave us their blessing.

Before writing any of the essays included in this book, I read or re-read as many of the relevant mysteries as possible and screened or re-screened the actual programs. It's an approach I can highly recommend to serious fans. In every case, the result was almost always greater appreciation of the books, the television shows, or both.

By reading all P. D. James' Adam Dalgliesh novels in chronological order, for instance, I was able to trace the author's steady progress from a writer of old-fashioned detective stories into a thoughtful observer of late 20th-century society whose insights and ideas are today much more important than her clues. Filmed out of their proper order, the television adaptations lost that sense of sustained growth. Similarly, by screening more than 30 episodes of *Poirot* in just a few weeks, I saw how much an inspired production crew and a gifted actor like David Suchet can elevate material that might otherwise seem terribly dated today.

My voyage of discovery with Mystery! led me to fully appreciate the series' dedication to presenting a balanced selection of the various mystery genres, from "golden age" classic detective stories with characters like Poirot, Wimsey, and Campion to cutting-edge contemporary series like *Prime Suspect,* villain-driven thrillers like *Mother Love,* and incisive psychological mysteries like *A Dark-Adapted Eye.* Mystery! gives us the past, present, and perhaps the future of the mystery genre in a single venue.

In short, there is absolutely nothing like Mystery! anywhere on American television. It's a treasure trove for mystery freaks like us, which is a conclusion I'm sure you'll reach on your own as you read through this book full of memorable mysteries.

—RON MILLER, *1996*

I

SCENE OF THE CRIME

—

SETTING THE SCENE

ONE DAY IN 1979, HENRY BECTON, GENERAL MANAGER OF BOSTON PBS STATION WGBH, received the sort of phone call no public broadcaster ever expects. On the other end of the line was Herb Schmertz, head of corporate communications for Mobil Corporation, with an unsolicited offer.

"Henry, I've been thinking," Schmertz began. "If you were interested in putting together a series that was nothing but British mysteries, we'd be interested in funding it." In the late 1990s, with lean budgets for public television, such offers are practically unheard of, but even in 1979, they were exceedingly rare. Becton, who's still running WGBH, now as both general manager and president, wasted little time telling Schmertz to count WGBH in. And that's how Mystery! came into being.

Before Schmertz made that call, though, some important pieces had already begun to fall into place. First, Mobil, as the sole underwriter of WGBH's enormously successful Masterpiece Theatre ever since its inception in 1971, had enjoyed tremendous public relations benefits from that association. Mobil had still more money to invest in prestigious television programs and was looking for new outlets.

WIMSEY WAS THE INSPIRATION

At the same time, Becton, Schmertz, and Joan Wilson, the executive producer of Masterpiece Theatre, had noticed the tremendous viewer support for a series of Masterpiece Theatre adaptations of the Dorothy L. Sayers mysteries about Lord Peter Wimsey, starring Ian Carmichael as the stylish British detective.

Because there seemed to be a large number of similar programs available, there was a temptation to license other finely-crafted British mysteries for Masterpiece Theatre to capitalize on the Wimsey success story. But the consensus was that this sort of programming might begin to steer the distinguished series too much toward the specialized audience for mysteries and away from the more broadly-based following it had each Sunday night. That's when Schmertz came up with his notion for a "spin-off" of Masterpiece Theatre. It seemed an irresistible idea.

Joan Wilson and her staff combed through lists of mystery shows that were in production in England and might be available on short notice to help launch Mystery!, as the new series came to be called. One tantalizing prospect for Mystery! was *The Racing Game,* the first television series ever adapted from the novels of former world-class steeplechase jockey Dick Francis, whose mysteries were breaking onto bestseller lists all over the world. *Rumpole of the Bailey* had just gone into production and was another possibility. It was written by John Mortimer, who adapted Evelyn Waugh's *Brideshead Revisited,* one of the most elaborate miniseries ever undertaken by British television. Although *Rumpole* was basically a whimsical courtroom series that dealt with crime and only rarely with genuine mystery, WGBH nevertheless opted to take it. "We've always had the philosophy that we'd take what was well done and had superior characterizations rather than worry about whether or not it would fit the format," says Becton.

They also made another crucial decision: They would become investors in the production of *The Racing Game* and help share the financial risk in exchange for the right to show it first in the U.S. market. WGBH continues to invest production money in a majority of the Mystery! programs, including such enormous hits as the *Sherlock Holmes* and *Prime Suspect* series, and also helps develop them from their inception.

To the first season's schedule they added an offbeat series based on the novels of Peter Lovesey about Victorian-era policeman Sergeant Cribb, a new adaptation of Daphne du Maurier's *Rebecca*, and a wildly eccentric movie-length mystery spoof called *She Fell Among Thieves*. Together with *Rumpole* and *The Racing Game*, they suggested the many paths Mystery! would take.

While the schedule was being set, the WGBH team was rapidly moving forward with two other important parts of the package: a host and a snazzy opening. For the host, the idea was to follow the Alistair Cooke formula of Masterpiece Theatre, but with what Becton calls "its own quirky distinctiveness." They chose pun-happy Gene Shalit, resident film critic of NBC's *Today Show*. Meanwhile, Joan Wilson approached animator Derek Lamb about turning the macabre cartoon drawings of Edward Gorey into the opening and closing credits for the series.

Mystery! went on the air with *She Fell Among Thieves* on February 5, 1980, and after one of the quickest development cycles ever, a classic PBS series was off and running. Edward Gorey, *Rebecca*, and especially *Rumpole* were big hits. *The Racing Game* and *Sergeant Cribb* never caught on, but stayed on the Mystery! lineup until all the episodes had been run. Gene Shalit retreated back to commercial television and the mass audience that appreciated him best.

Current Executive Producer Rebecca Eaton, who took over after Wilson's death in 1985, believes the series has lasted so long because it hasn't tried to compete in violence with American crime shows, but instead gives viewers fascinating detectives to follow week after week. Whatever the reason, viewers have made Mystery! one of PBS' biggest hits, averaging 5 million viewers per week by 1990.

Wicked and Whimsical:

EDWARD GOREY'S VISION

SWOONING HEROINES IN LONG GOWNS, SINISTER MEN IN BOWLER HATS AND handlebar mustaches, dark figures playing croquet in a rainstorm—these are some of the unforgettable cartoon images that open and close each week's episode of Mystery!. And they're all mysterious escapees from the whimsically wicked world of Edward Gorey.

From the very first episode, Gorey's incredibly imaginative imagery, animated by Derek Lamb, has given the series its signature look. His skulking characters may seem to be up to no good, but look more closely and you'll probably realize Gorey is winking at you, like that skull in the tombstone in the opening credits. The message well may be: Enjoy what follows, but take it seriously at your own peril.

One of America's most eclectic—and eccentric—creative artists, Gorey is a writer who illustrates his ideas in a variety of mediums and isn't necessarily particular as to what form they take. Since the early 1950s, he has published more than 70 books of drawings such as *The Beastly Baby* and *The Curious Sofa* that bring his often macabre literary ideas to life. His illustrated versions of other people's works, including T. S. Eliot's *Old Possum's Book of Practical Cats,* are perennial bestsellers. A major retrospective of his work, *The World of Edward Gorey,* by Clifford Ross and Karen Wilkin, was published in 1996. His 1978 set designs for the Broadway revival of *Dracula* set him off as a stage designer, and his costumes for that show earned him a Tony award. His rare excursions into animation, including the short series of "Fantods" he did for Mystery!, have added to his enormous cult reputation. When he was in his late sixties, Gorey produced, wrote, directed, and occasionally even acted in his own community theater productions in the Cape Cod area, where he has lived and worked for years.

"[Gorey's] one of the few idols I've ever had in my life. So, when I saw him there in Boston and saw his set, I was very much impressed and awed. Gorey was unpretentious and put on no airs. It's funny he does all this ghoulish stuff because he has the kindest eyes."

—GENE SHALIT

IT ALL BEGAN WITH DRACULA

Born in 1925, Edward St. John Gorey was the only child of Helen and Edward Lee Gorey, a Hearst newspaperman based in Chicago. A precocious reader—Gorey says he devoured Bram Stoker's *Dracula* at the age of five "and I was scared to death"—he also began to teach himself how to draw. He later attended a few courses at the Art Institute of Chicago, but that's all the formal training in art he ever received. He graduated from high school in 1942 and was immediately taken into the Army, spending much of World War II as a clerk at the Dugway Proving Ground in Utah, mysterious site of the U.S. government's experiments in poison gas and bacteriological warfare. After the war, he majored in French literature at Harvard and earned his B.A. degree in 1950.

Though Gorey worked in mainstream publishing for a time (he was in Doubleday's art department for eight years), his real passion was creating his own bizarre stories and illustrating them. Then, as now, his ideas were often misinterpreted as "ghoulish," and he was turned down by publisher after publisher until *The Unstrung Harp* came out in 1953 and his reputation began to grow. Because many of his drawings were of children, he often was mistaken for an illustrator of children's books. Yet many publishers considered his books unsuitable for children because of what happens to some of the young characters. ("A is for Amy, who fell down the stairs," comes from one of his so-called "alphabet books.") Still, his darkly comic vision began to build a legion of fans of all ages and, in 1959, the great literary critic Edmund Wilson, writing in *The New Yorker,* hailed Gorey's work as "poetic and poisoned," and compared him to both Max Ernst and Ronald Searle.

Gorey may be the most over-psychoanalyzed of all living American artists. Critics have searched for deep meaning in his often obsessive crosshatching in the backgrounds of his drawings, in his subject matter, which often seems grimly preoccupied with death, or in his uneasy relationship with his doting mother as keys to understanding his art. Gorey neither helps nor hinders such inquiries and mainly seems bemused by them. His unusual lifestyle has only fueled the concoction of more psychological theories.

"In my little theater productions, I've discovered I can collaborate on my own terms. I do it by osmosis. I never tell anybody how to do anything. I sometimes scare everybody to death because they say, 'What are we supposed to be doing?' I just say, 'Figure it out for yourself. I just wrote it."

—EDWARD GOREY

CAPE COD'S EDWARDIAN ECCENTRIC

Tall and lean, Gorey wears a full beard, but is otherwise gloriously bald. He wears earrings and used to go about in long fur coats before his conscience got the better of him and he earned the blessings of animal rights activists by shedding his furs permanently. Gorey has never married and admits to no romantic relationships. He lives by himself in a rambling home in Yarmouth, on Cape Cod, that dates back nearly 200 years. When he's not working on the 100 or so projects he has outlined for himself, he's caring for his brood of six cats or indulging himself in one of his many special interests, mostly sedentary pursuits like watching old movies he has taped off his satellite dish or zoning out on his favorite television shows, such as *The X-Files.*

Though Gorey has heard himself called a recluse before, he really doesn't behave like one. For nearly 30 years, he attended every performance of the New York City Ballet until the death of his artistic idol, choreographer George Balanchine. He eats both breakfast and lunch each day at Jack's Out Back restaurant in Yarmouthport, where he happily signs autographs for the occasional fan who approaches him.

Often mistakenly labeled as "morbid," Gorey is in fact a rather cheerful individual, whose sharply pungent observations are laced with a ready wit. He's a superbly entertaining conversationalist who frequently enlivens a chat by humorously slipping into a falsetto voice or punctuating his remarks with a "turkey gobble" sound that one isn't likely to hear anywhere else. Gorey's long association with Mystery! began in 1979 when he was still riding the enormous wave of national publicity coming from Broadway's

Dracula, and he was sought to do the series' opening and closing credits.

QUESTION: *Did you take a very active role in the wedding of your art to the world of Mystery!?*

ANSWER: When we first started talking about it, I gave them a scenario for the credits, but they said, "Thank you, very much, dear, but this will take half an hour." I told them it wouldn't if they put it on at a reasonable rate of speed, but they didn't seem to care for that idea very much. So [animator] Derek Lamb or somebody concocted the final scenario and I had very little to do with it. Originally, I was going to draw all the backgrounds and every time I'd sit down to do them, someone would call at the last minute and say, "We've changed our minds. We're going to do something else." Ultimately, Derek Lamb was responsible for the whole thing.

What about your influence on the sets for Mystery!, which host Vincent Price used to call Gorey Manor?

This isn't terribly flattering to anybody, I'm afraid. I went up to Boston a couple of times, distributed bric-a-brac around, made suggestions and whatnot. Joan Wilson and I went around picking up things at flea markets and antique stores. Then they decided to abandon the three-dimensional set and go with flat drawings. So, I did a bunch of flat drawings, thinking the whole thing would be black and white and fairly austere. They kept calling me up and asking if I could do four more yards of wallpaper. Then I saw what they'd done with the first one or two. Well, I didn't throw a fit in public or anything, but I finally said I didn't think this was working out—and they've been faking me ever since.

At one point, though, Mystery! developed some short animated Gorey stories they called "Fantods" to use as fillers at the end of the shows, beginning in the third season. They were widely praised. What did you think of them?

I was very pleased with those. Joan thought that up. I had a great deal of fun making those. I went up for a couple of days to help. They had two men and two women to read the parts.

Which Mystery! series seems to fit most neatly into the world of Edward Gorey?

Any of the period ones do to some extent. I suppose the Agatha Christie stuff they've done is vaguely like some of my period drawings. I very much like the Tommy and Tuppence ones, the *Partners in Crime.* I quite admire Joan Hickson, but she's just a little too dark for Miss Marple. I'm old enough to love Margaret Rutherford's Miss Marple, even though I know perfectly well she wasn't Christie's idea of Miss Marple.

When did you first notice your trademark style of drawing emerging as your métier?

Probably when I was 20 or 21. I was just drawing and writing without any particular [focus]. When I finally was published, I was 28. I don't know if that pushed me in any particular direction. I don't think I had any ambition to do anything much. It was just what I did. But I pretty much stuck with it once it jelled. I would hesitate to say it was anything as strong as a métier.

What's the biggest myth about your work?

That it's gothic. Years and years ago, somebody wrote a very nice piece about me and referred to me as "American gothic." It sort of stuck.

Does it bother you when people lump you together with people who do "horror" like Stephen King or Charles Addams?

Yes. Only very occasionally do I try to shock in a mild sort of way. I'm very squeamish really. As for Charles Addams, I knew him. We had the same agent. I occasionally would have lunch with him. I was told he envied me because I had a more highbrow reputation than he did. I love Charles Addams' stuff. I suppose there's always the possibility somebody will come along and want to do the equivalent of *The Addams Family* movie with my stuff. Well, I'm not that rich, so I'd probably say, "Go ahead."

How did you get involved with the Broadway version of Dracula*?*

A very good friend of mine produced it and brought it back, and in that sense he was very smart, but I thought the whole *Dracula* thing was perfect nonsense. Since I was in on it from its inception, I think I can say with authority that I don't think anybody knew what they were doing. It started out on a stage that was on one of those raised platforms in a grammar school gymnasium in Nantucket. For some reason, it caught on down there. Artistically, it was a hodgepodge to end all hodge-podges. I knew nothing about set design. It was just one of those flukes that worked quite well. Of course, it made me a lot of money. It made everybody a lot of money. For some extraordinary reason, I was given a piece of the show.

You seemed a little surprised to get a Tony award for designing the costumes.

That was one of the more preposterous things. I did all of eight costumes and they were zilch, but everybody loved the sets. There was somebody else who deserved the set design award much more than I did that year, so they didn't feel like they could give that one to me. They gave me the costume award instead.

Dracula *wasn't just a passing flirtation with theater for you. Hasn't it become a real passion for you lately?*

I had another show that was an off-Broadway success [*Amphigorey, The Musicale*], but was one of the legendary Broadway turkeys that lasted one performance. In the last 10 years, I've done a lot of very local theater. I write, I direct, I design, I do everything. I even act if something happens to somebody in the cast. A lot of the actors I use are people who look like I might have drawn them. I even choose the music. That's really what I enjoy. People sometimes say it's such a pity this isn't going somewhere else and I say, "Well, where would it go?"

You're such a big movie fan, why haven't you made your own movie?

I have a silent movie script I wrote years and years ago for a budget of $50,000. I keep hoping somebody will call me up from Hollywood and say, "We just came across this, would you like to make it?" If somebody came to me and said, "We'll give you carte blanche to do a movie," I'd be thrilled. I have enough egotism to think I'd get through to the cameraman by osmosis.

Who are the typical Edward Gorey fans?

It ranges from dear little old ladies of 90 to rather distracted teenagers who some-times turn up at the door. I go to the same place for breakfast and lunch every day. Most of the people there are regulars, but every once in a while somebody will come up to the table and say, "I have a book of yours in my car. Will you sign it, please?"

And I'm thinking, "What is a book of mine doing in your car?" I'm nothing if not terribly amiable, though.

You already have more than 75 published books. What are your priorities for work these days?

Whatever has popped into my head. I also rely on serendipity a good deal. That's the trouble. It's gotten worse and worse. I have to write before I draw, so I now have about a hundred manuscripts that have to be illustrated. Well, obviously I'm not going to live long enough to do more than a few of them. I simply rely on my dear little unconscious to produce new ideas. I remember when I was much younger and had only published a couple of books, I thought, "Oh, dear, what if I never get another idea in my life?" But I've never had writer's block for more than two minutes. Now I have notebook after notebook filled with this, that, and the other thing—bits of plays, bits of books, drawings for nothing in particular. It's just mounting up.

Your work is often concerned with death. What's your own attitude toward death?

I hope it comes painlessly and quickly. I had a heart attack I didn't know I had until the doctor told me. That same week I discovered I had prostate cancer and diabetes, which was pretty much a downer. I figured I was going to be dead in a week, so I began to think about it a lot. But then the diabetes turned out to be very controllable and I get a shot in the fanny for the prostate cancer once a month, so I've had it for about two years. I'm good about taking my medicine and I eat fairly properly. I may not live forever, but I feel perfectly fine all the time.

When you look back at your career, are you content with what you've achieved?

There's some demand for my work, but it isn't exactly staggering. I have kind of an ardent little following, but the accent is on little. I know what it's like to be a very, very, very minor celebrity. My name turns up in a review of a book or something where they say it's very "Edward Goreyish" or something like that. That happens often enough, so I feel I've made a tiny mark somewhere.

> "I just saw a copy of a magazine in which somebody did one of those really in-depth psychological analyses of my work. I didn't recognize anything at all. I figure, why bother? As a child, I didn't walk in on an open coffin or anything."
>
> —EDWARD GOREY

SELECTED BIBLIOGRAPHY

The Unstrung Harp, 1953; *The Curious Sofa,* 1961; *The Hapless Child,* 1961; *The Beastly Baby,* 1962; *The Gashlycrumb Tinies,* 1963; *The Gilded Bat,* 1966; *The Epiplectic Bicycle,* 1968; *The Blue Aspic,* 1969; *Amphigorey,** 1972; *Amphigorey Too,** 1975; *The Doubtful Guest,* 1978; *Amphigorey Also,** 1983; *The Unknown Vegetable,* 1995.

* Source of illustrations for *Mystery! A Celebration*

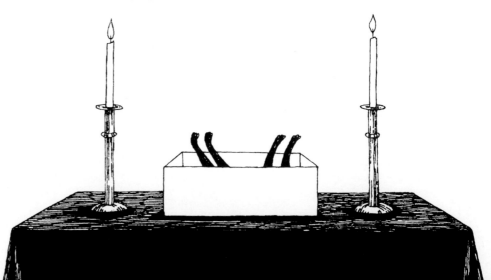

Replicating Gorey's World:

ANIMATOR DEREK LAMB

WHEN EDWARD GOREY WAS FIRST SHOWN ONE OF DEREK LAMB'S ANIMATED FILMS, he gave it what is perhaps his highest accolade: "It's so sinister," he said. So it was no wonder that Executive Producer Joan Wilson brought Gorey and Lamb together to create the titles for the new Mystery! series. Lamb, a British-born film and television producer/director/writer had done animation for WGBH for a number of years (*Eye to Eye, Piccadilly Circus*) and had created programming for such PBS staples as *Sesame Street, The Electric Company,* and *The American Dream Machine.*

But at first it seemed as though this was not a match made in...wherever. "Edward was in a huff," recalls Lamb, because he had been told that although the storyboard he had done would make a great 10-minute film, it was not suitable for 75-second credits. Some seven hours and a number of meals later, the meeting finally broke up with the understanding that Lamb would use for inspiration the brilliant drawings from Gorey's books and develop scenarios to be animated.

The animated sequences Lamb created so perfectly replicate Gorey's sensibilities—the camp tweaking the macabre, the humor suffusing the peril—as well as his drawing style that few realize Gorey didn't actually do them. And while initially both Gorey and Wilson had reservations about the tango music by Normand Roger that has since become Mystery!'s signature tune, both grew to love it.

While hesitating to say he actually got inside Gorey's head to create the animation, Lamb says he's "used to thinking in someone else's shoes," having previously adapted other people's cartoons and illustrations for animation, often overseeing a large team of animators. Lamb's films and videos have won numerous awards (Oscars for *Special Delivery* and *Every Child*—the "sinister" one—and Oscar nominations for *The Great Toy Robbery, The Shepherd,* and *Beadgame*), and have been screened at festivals all over the world. Over the years Lamb has held a number of teaching positions (at Harvard University, Rhode Island School of Design, McGill University) and has been working on a major project close to his heart—a series called *Karate Kids* for a Canadian-based organization called Street Kids International. The series' 30-minute animated adventure films capture stories of real marginalized children in different countries around the world and deal with health education issues such as AIDS and substance abuse. They have been released for worldwide distribution in 40 languages.

Whether capturing Edward Gorey's style or recreating the lives of street kids, Lamb says animation "is a medium that communicates so directly to the spirit and soul."

Amusingly Alliterative Host:

GENE SHALIT

IF THERE WAS GOING TO BE A MYSTERY!, THERE WOULD HAVE TO BE A HOST TO open the creaking door of Gorey Manor, welcome viewers, and try to make them comfortable with some of the murky goings-on they were about to see. The job fell to Gene Shalit, arts editor and film critic for NBC's *Today Show,* who turned up on the atmospheric set on the night of February 5, 1980, wearing a tuxedo and a twinkle in his eye.

"Good evening," he said, grinning like an usher at an Addams Family wedding. "We're about to set out on a series of entertaining mysteries—15 weeks of suspenseful, sophisticated, crafty conundrums that are darkly diabolical or amusing adventures with introductions that suddenly seem alarmingly alliterative." The series was called Mystery!, he informed viewers, and he was Gene Shalit. "That solves the first mystery," he said. "I'm wearing this tuxedo because it serves as a formal introduction and because I'm usually up so early and so early to bed that I rarely get a chance to wear one of these things."

MAN ABOUT ANYTHING

If the pun-happy, alliteration-addicted Shalit seems an odd choice today, some historical perspective may help. When the creators of Mystery! began looking for a host, Shalit was one of the brightest new stars of television's hottest morning show, the *Today Show,* which dominated the time period as no other network show had ever done before. He also was NBC Radio's so-called "Man About Anything," the commentator who aired on more stations on the network than anyone else. With his eccentric explosion of frizzy hair making him instantly recognizable anywhere, his genial, tongue-in-cheek style, and his ability to write stylish introductions the way Alistair Cooke did for Masterpiece Theatre, he was just what WGBH wanted. Plus, as the book reviewer for the *Today Show* before becoming their movie critic, he was not only familiar with but also a fan of the mystery genre.

Shalit set two primary goals for his introductions: to help viewers understand some of the peculiarities of the British programs and to do it as entertainingly as he possibly could. Shalit might still be hosting Mystery! if the experience had been all pleasure for everyone. He's now a little vague about exactly why he left, but he kept his day job, and is now the longest-running regular on the *Today Show.*

Master of Menace to Mischievous Host:

VINCENT PRICE

A YOUNG VINCENT PRICE LEARNED ALL ABOUT THE JOYS OF VILLAINY WHEN HE took his first curtain call on Broadway for *Angel Street,* in which he played a husband trying to drive his wife insane. Instead of applause, the audience greeted him with an enormous wave of boos and hisses. "It was the loveliest sound," he wistfully recalled nearly a lifetime later. Price built a career on such boos and hisses—and on the love of millions of moviegoers, who knew he was only kidding when he did all those awful things. He made a kind of pact with his fans: He'd scare the hell out of them, if only they wouldn't take him too seriously while he was doing it. That was the formula that made him Hollywood's new "master of menace" in the 1950s and helped him put up with all that the position entailed.

> "He was the sweetest scary man I ever met."
>
> —ACTRESS KATHERINE EMERY *about former co-star Vincent Price to her daughter, Rebecca Eaton, executive producer of Mystery!*

Born in 1911 in St. Louis, the son of a candy manufacturer, Price at first pursued a stage career after earning his bachelor's degree at Yale and a master's in theater at the University of London. When he finally reached Broadway in the 1930s, he was first cast as a leading man because of his height and good looks. But he was much more fun as the heavy, and it was only a matter of time until he made that his specialty, becoming the heir to Chaney, Karloff, and Lugosi for a generation of babyboomers. From *House of Wax* (1953) through *The Fly* (1958) to *The Abominable Dr. Phibes* (1971) and Roger Corman's Poe flicks, his chilling charm earned him legions of fans.

GENTLE GIANT OF GRAND GUIGNOL

Price became America's favorite mystery man, the gentle giant of Grand Guignol. That's why Executive Producer Joan Wilson couldn't wait to sign him up as the series' new host when Gene Shalit left in 1981. Price's first assignment was to introduce the BBC's new production of *Dr. Jekyll and Mr. Hyde,* an apt choice for a man who had run with Mr. Hyde's crowd for most of his movie career. Price loved hosting Mystery! and said so to virtually everybody he met during his eight years on the job. He became the program's walking, talking trademark. Price so clearly belonged at Gorey Manor that you often wondered if he wasn't a Gorey illustration come to life.

> "He was gifted with love—and he communicated that to everyone he met."
>
> —EXECUTIVE PRODUCER REBECCA EATON

His approach was to have fun with the genre and do a lot of winking at the audience. That's exactly what Wilson and her successor, Rebecca Eaton, wanted because it expressed the spirit of the show. He was their willing accomplice from the start. Price happily strolled through make-believe cobwebs, dodged dangling spiders, and ducked out of the way of nearsighted bats while doing his intros. It was all old hat to Price, who had become quite comfortable with haunted house chic by then.

Price came to Boston twice a year—once in the summer, once in the fall—to tape his "intros" and "extros" for the new season, which were drafted by a staff writer at WGBH, then reviewed by Wilson and, later, Eaton, with input from Price. Sandy Leonard, who wrote Price's commentaries for seven years and became a friend to Price and his wife, actress Coral Browne, says he and Price "seemed to be on the same wavelength." David Atwood, who directed Price for seven of his eight years, said the man was absolutely without pretension and was adored by the entire Mystery! crew.

A cultured man with diverse interests, Price was a renowned art expert—he was a big prizewinner in the art category on CBS' legendary television game show, *The $64,000 Question*—and a gourmet cook whose cookbooks had sold millions of copies. He could talk endlessly on those topics and many others. Those who worked with him say he was a champion storyteller and frequently used up his lunch hour spinning yarns for the crew or anyone who happened to drop by.

A SAD FAREWELL

Although in his seventies during his hosting stint, Price seemed able to call on an endless energy supply to handle the intensive shooting schedule. When he finally began to slow down, Price came to Eaton near the close of his eighth season and told her he thought the time had come to step down as host. "It was very poignant," Eaton recalls. "He was ill and I was worried that he was going to start looking frail on the air. I knew it was getting harder for him to do, but he never complained."

The final farewell party given for Price by the Mystery! production crew was a sad, emotional affair for everyone. "There wasn't a dry eye in the house," recalls Eaton, for whom the event was especially painful. Price had worked with her actress mother, Katherine Emery, and had embraced Eaton warmly when she took over as executive producer, saying, "You look just like your mother!"

Price kept in touch with many of his WGBH friends during the last few years of his life, including director Atwood and writer Leonard, who says he will never forget the last time he saw Price at his home in Los Angeles. His health already failing badly, Price took Leonard's hand to wish him a safe trip home, then added, "You know, we'll never see each other again." That turned out to be true. Vincent Price died not long afterward on October 25, 1993. He was 82.

Emmanently A Peeling Host:

DIANA RIGG

BEFORE BECOMING THE HOST OF MYSTERY!, DIANA RIGG HAD EXPERIENCED her share of murder and mayhem, theatrically speaking, of course. Her best-known venture was her portrayal of the mysterious Emma Peel in *The Avengers* from 1966 to 1968. But she has also had other close associations with the mystery genre, playing a number of different roles: the young journalist who uncovers the conspiracy in the movie version of Jack London's *The Assassination Bureau* (1969); the woman who marries secret agent James Bond in *On Her Majesty's Secret Service* (1969); Vincent Price's murderous co-conspirator in *Theatre of Blood* (1973); the nasty actress who becomes a murder victim in Agatha Christie's *Evil Under the Sun* (1982); Christine Vole in CBS' 1982 television remake of Christie's *Witness for the Prosecution;* and the coldly ominous Lady Dedlock in Masterpiece Theatre's murky and mysterious *Bleak House* (1985).

ART IMITATING LIFE

Many critics felt The Avengers *was a revolutionary show in many ways and that Rigg's Emma Peel—a name that was a play on the term* men appeal*—symbolized the emerging New Woman of the 1960s: strong, self-reliant, resourceful, yet still sexy. "There was a lot of truth in that," says Rigg, who led a fairly unconventional, free-spirited life at the time. "I was like that myself to a degree. It was a case of art imitating life."*

While Rigg feels Emma Peel has most to do with her being invited to be Mystery!'s host, Rebecca Eaton says it's because Rigg is "a woman of intelligence, wit, and style—all qualities our audience associates with Mystery!. She's a commanding actress with a dedicated following in this country."

A MYSTERY PLAYER, NOT A MYSTERY READER

Although she's not a mystery buff—she prefers biographies—Rigg says she feels quite comfortable introducing the mostly British television mysteries to an American audience, and is eager to act in another one like the critically-acclaimed *Mother Love.* Her role in that production won her a British BAFTA award, the equivalent of the Oscar and Emmy. Although she hosts Mystery! and appears in the occasional film or television movie here (in 1995 she played the housekeeper in CBS' eerie *The Haunting of Helen Walker*, a remake of Henry James' *The Turn of the Screw*), Rigg spends most of her time in her native England working as one of her nation's leading stage actresses.

Born in 1938, Rigg now believes her earliest glimmers of acting talent probably were shown when she was about 11, and her drama teacher encouraged her to do more acting. Her subsequent boarding school experience, she believes, forced her to retreat into her imagination a great deal, a resource she would later tap as an actress. She was not a great success as a classroom student, but shone in her stage performances and was accepted into the Royal Academy of Dramatic Art in 1955. By 1959, she had blossomed into a tall, handsome young woman with enough experience to land a job as an understudy for the Stratford season of the Shakespeare Memorial Theatre Company, where her colleagues included Vanessa Redgrave and Albert Finney.

When Peter Hall took over the company in 1960 and turned it into the Royal Shakespeare Company, he signed a number of unknown actors to five-year contracts, Rigg among them. She stayed with the famous company long enough to build a reputation as one of the nation's bright new stage talents, but at age 26 she gambled her acting future by agreeing to replace Honor Blackman as Patrick Macnee's right-hand woman in the popular British television spy romp *The Avengers.*

EMERGING "NEW WOMAN"

"It had tremendous impact on my career," she says. "Overnight I was a household word in England." When *The Avengers* was imported to America by ABC in 1966, it became a rage here, too. Rigg was a smash as the long-legged, sexy female spy in a black jumpsuit who lived independently, knew martial arts, and could take care of herself like no television heroine before her. Thirty years later, *The Avengers* remains the only British series to ever become a hit on U.S. prime-time commercial television.

Looking back, Rigg is happy she did *The Avengers,* but believes it may have had some long-term effect on how seriously she is regarded as an actress. She's much more likely to be hailed as Emma Peel by people in America than in Britain, but believes that's simply because the English have seen much more of her stage and other television work.

In the 1970s, Rigg made two widely-seen films, Paddy Chayefsky's *The Hospital* (1971) and *A Little Night Music* (1978). In between, she made *Theatre of Blood,* during which she became good friends with Vincent Price. (She was helpful in bringing Price together with fellow cast member Coral Browne, who later became his wife.) When the American television situation comedy, *Diana,* with Rigg as a sort of English Mary Tyler Moore, failed to make the ratings, she returned to England to concentrate on her stage career, which picked up considerable momentum over the next decade.

DAME DIANA STILL DOES MYSTERY!

In 1988, Rigg was decorated as a Commander of the British Empire (CBE) and in 1994 was named Dame Commander of the British Empire—the same year she won Broadway's Tony Award for Best Actress in *Medea.* She recently starred on stage in Bertolt Brecht's *Mother Courage and Her Children* and played Mrs. Danvers in a new version of *Rebecca* for Masterpiece Theatre. She travels to Boston once a year to tape all her intros and extros for Mystery! at WGBH during a concentrated period of a week or so.

Now that she has been hosting Mystery!, Rigg has noticed a significant change in what people say when they recognize her in the States. Though the occasional Emma Peel reference is inescapable, she now hears lots of warm, friendly compliments for helping bring all those wonderful mystery shows to America.

MYSTERY! BY SEASON
1980–1997

SEASON I (1980–1981)

She Fell Among Thieves
Rumpole of the Bailey—Series I
Rebecca
The Racing Game—Series I
Sergeant Cribb—Series I

SEASON II (1981–1982)

Dr. Jekyll and Mr. Hyde
Malice Aforethought
Rumpole of the Bailey—Series II
The Racing Game—Series II
Sergeant Cribb—Series II

SEASON III (1982–1983)

Sweeney Todd
Dying Day
Father Brown
Melissa
Quiet As a Nun
Sergeant Cribb—Series III
Agatha Christie Stories—Series I
Miss Morison's Ghosts
The Limbo Connection
We, the Accused

SEASON IV (1983–1984)

Reilly, Ace of Spies
Shades of Darkness

SEASON V (1984–1985)

Rumpole's Return
Rumpole of the Bailey—Series III
Partners in Crime—Series I
Praying Mantis
Agatha Christie Stories—Series II
*The Adventures of Sherlock Holmes—
    Series I*
The Woman in White

SEASON VI (1985–1986)

Death of an Expert Witness
My Cousin Rachel
*Agatha Christie's Miss Marple—
    Series I*
*The Adventures of Sherlock Holmes—
    Series II*
Charters and Caldicott
Partners in Crime—Series II

SEASON VII (1986–1987)

Shroud for a Nightingale
Brat Farrar
*Agatha Christie's Miss Marple—
    Series II*
The Secret Adversary
*The Return of Sherlock Holmes—
    Series I*
Cover Her Face

SEASON VIII (1987–1988)

Dorothy L. Sayers' Lord Peter Wimsey
*Agatha Christie's Miss Marple—
    Series III*
Inspector Morse—Series I
Rumpole of the Bailey—Series IV
The Black Tower

SEASON IX (1988–1989)

Cause Célèbre
*The Return of Sherlock Holmes—
    Series II*
Inspector Morse—Series II
*Agatha Christie's Miss Marple—
    Series IV*
Game, Set and Match

SEASON X (1989–1990)

Campion—Series I
Rumpole of the Bailey—Series V
Agatha Christie's Poirot—Series I
A Taste for Death
Inspector Morse—Series III

SEASON XI (1990–1991)

*Agatha Christie's Poirot:
    The Incredible Theft*
Mother Love
Campion—Series II
Agatha Christie's Poirot—Series II
The Dark Angel
Die Kinder
The Man from the Pru
Inspector Morse—Series IV

SEASON XII (1991–1992)

Devices and Desires
The Casebook of Sherlock Holmes
Artists in Crime
Prime Suspect
Agatha Christie's Poirot—Series III
Inspector Morse—Series V

SEASON XIII (1992–1993)

Maigret—Series I
Agatha Christie's Poirot—Series IV
Prime Suspect 2
*Sherlock Holmes:
    The Master Blackmailer*
Inspector Morse—Series VI
Rumpole of the Bailey, Series VI

SEASON XIV (1993–1994)

The Inspector Alleyn Mysteries—Series I
Agatha Christie's Poirot—Series V
Unnatural Causes
Sherlock Holmes: The Last Vampyre
Sherlock Holmes: The Eligible Bachelor
Inspector Morse—Series VII
Prime Suspect 3

SEASON XV (1994–1995)

Maigret—Series II
Agatha Christie's Poirot—Series VI
A Dark-Adapted Eye
Cadfael—Series I
Inspector Morse—Series VIII
*Ngaio Marsh's Alleyn Mysteries—
    Series II*
Rumpole of the Bailey—Series VII

SEASON XVI (1995–1996)

Gallowglass
Agatha Christie's Poirot—Series VII
The Memoirs of Sherlock Holmes
Inspector Morse—Series IX
Chandler & Co.
A Mind to Murder

SEASON XVII (1996–1997)

Oliver's Travels
Agatha Christie's Poirot—Series VIII
Original Sin
Inspector Morse—Series X
Cadfael—Series II

THE MURDERS BEGIN:

SHE FELL AMONG THIEVES

Based on the novel by
Dornford Yates

THE OPENING ATTRACTION OF THE NEW MYSTERY! SERIES
WAS A RATHER STRANGE AND WHIMSICAL CHOICE—A QUIRKY 90-MINUTE COMIC
ADVENTURE CALLED *SHE FELL AMONG THIEVES* ADAPTED FROM A NOVEL BY
DORNFORD YATES, AN AUTHOR LITTLE KNOWN IN AMERICA.

**PRODUCTION
COMPANY**
BBC

YEAR
1980

MAIN CAST
Vanity Fair
EILEEN ATKINS

Robert Chandos
MALCOLM MCDOWELL

Mansel
MICHAEL JAYSTON

Virginia
SARAH BADEL

Jenny
KAREN DOTRICE

Set in the French Pyrenees in 1924, Tom Sharpe's free adaptation of the novel amounted to a parody of international spy adventures. How free was it? Host Gene Shalit said Sharpe "kept the title, kept the characters, kept a couple of twists, and threw everything else away."

   With the zany animated Edward Gorey drawings setting the tone, followed by Shalit's pun-heavy introduction and an outlandish performance by Eileen Atkins as the film's comic villainess, *She Fell Among Thieves'* campy style might have left the impression that Mystery! was not a program to be taken seriously, especially not by the hardcore mystery fans expected to flock to the new series.

   Yet, in retrospect, the choice seems more inspired than it may have when Mystery! first opened for public inspection. For one thing, the star of *She Fell Among Thieves* was Malcolm McDowell, whose most recent film, *Time After Time,* had been a runaway hit and was also an outlandish adventure. In that film, McDowell played author H. G. Wells using his time machine to pursue Jack the Ripper into modern America. The other thing going for *She Fell Among Thieves* was that it was a big, expensive-looking film with the sort of production values PBS viewers had come to expect from its sister series, Masterpiece Theatre.

The program now seems a lost gem that perhaps wasn't fully appreciated for what it was at the time—a nostalgic nod to the Perils-of-Pauline school of cliffhanger, set against a backdrop of international intrigue that didn't seem so fanciful once the fact-based *Reilly, Ace of Spies* came along to illuminate the same period in espionage history. Sharpe, a popular British author best known for his farcical novels, had never written a screenplay before *She Fell Among Thieves,* but having done a great deal of research into the life of author Dornford Yates, he concluded that a farcical treatment would be the best way to approach the rather dated story.

In his adaptation, the bizarre Vanity Fair (Eileen Atkins) is a master criminal and former World War I spy holed up in her château in the French Pyrenees. Her evil plans are mostly concerned with stealing the £20 million inheritance her step-daughter Jenny (Karen Dotrice) will come into upon turning 21. Vanity's late hus-band, who may have been poisoned by her, left one loophole she's determined to utilize: If Jenny should marry before age 21, the inheritance goes to his widow instead. As the program opens, Vanity is trying to force a drugged Jenny through a wedding ceremony with Vanity's hand-picked stooge, Gaston (Jonathan Lynn), but nothing seems to be working.

At the same time, vacationing English gentleman Robert Chandos (McDowell) is fly-fishing in a stream below Vanity's Château Jezreel and hooks a dead body—another Englishman, who turns out to be one of Vanity's victims. Notifying the British consulate, he meets Mansel (Michael Jayston), a British agent on the track of Vanity Fair. They team up to bring her to justice and, ultimately, to rescue the imprisoned Jenny, a virginal beauty with the long, flowing blond hair of a fairy-tale princess.

Screenwriter Sharpe was amused by the colorful quality of Yates' make-believe world and that's what he and director Clive Donner placed as the backdrop for some incredible derring-do in *She Fell Among Thieves:* beautiful vintage luxury cars, stunning mountain settings, and a breathtaking château—located in Wales, not France. Thrilling escapes, fabulous feats, the venomous Vanity Fair with her diabolical plans—it was a stylish return to the classic Saturday morning serial, with a rather elegant Continental flavor.

While *She Fell Among Thieves* may not have been representative of the genuine mysteries to come, it most definitely was an attention-getter that introduced Mystery! with a bang.

CASTLES IN THE SKY

Author Yates, whose real name was Cecil William Mercer, actually built his own estate high in the Pyrenees and lived there until the Germans invaded France in World War II, spurring him to leave for Rhodesia. Best remembered in England for his **Berry and Co.** *and other books about the Pleydell family, Yates also wrote bold adventure stories involving castles with secret passages and wild chases along country roads in open-topped Rolls Royce roadsters. In real life, Yates was a dapper little man of Hercule Poirot proportions. Although he never actually saw action, Yates served as a British Army officer in both world wars and was known to friends as "Major Mercer."*

Once a Hero:

ACTOR
MALCOLM McDOWELL

As it turns out, *She Fell Among Thieves* pretty much wrapped up Malcolm McDowell's short run as a hero. "I've never been asked to play one since," says the actor who played plucky Robert Chandos, the dashing hero of *She Fell Among Thieves.* "I guess they just didn't like me playing those parts." After all, he had become an international star as the nihilistic student in Lindsay Anderson's modern classic *If...* and as the violence-loving youth in Stanley Kubrick's *A Clockwork Orange.* Though McDowell went on to become one of the screen's most reliable villains—he even got to finish off Captain Kirk in *Star Trek: Generations*—he admits it was especially gratifying to have a chance to play a swashbuckling hero like Chandos.

Having grown up on the derring-do novels of Dornford Yates, McDowell knew all about Robert Chandos before director Clive Donner asked him to play the part. He considers the Yates books "wonderful period stuff" and relished the idea of finally working with Donner, a director he knew and admired. "I'd just come off *Caligula*," says McDowell, who played the decadent emperor in the notorious X-rated movie, "and I was so sick of all that that I just wanted to play a simple, charming, innocent of the 1920s like Chandos. It was a purging of the soul." Besides the opportunity to finally play a good guy, there was another big reason why McDowell was attracted to *She Fell Among Thieves:* Donner intended to star Hollywood legend Bette Davis as Vanity Fair. McDowell thought it would be a wonderful experience to watch a great Hollywood star at work up close. The deal with Davis fell through, though, and McDowell now considers it divine providence.

"Well, she would have been a nightmare, of course," he says, 18 years later. He feels that way because he ultimately had the chance to watch his friend Lindsay Anderson direct Davis in *The Whales of August* and saw what an impossible martinet she could be on the set. "I can tell you now I'm bloody delighted Eileen Atkins got the part," he says.

Soon after he made *She Fell Among Thieves,* the British film industry pretty much collapsed and McDowell left for America to pursue his career. He now lives in Ojai, north of Los Angeles, where he works constantly in movies and television. In 1996, he played a Nazi villain in Disney's television movie *The Little Riders,* provided the voice for Czar Nicholas II in PBS' documentary series *The Great War,* and landed his first co-starring role in a weekly television comedy series, playing an acid-tongued college professor opposite Rhea Perlman in CBS' *Pearl.*

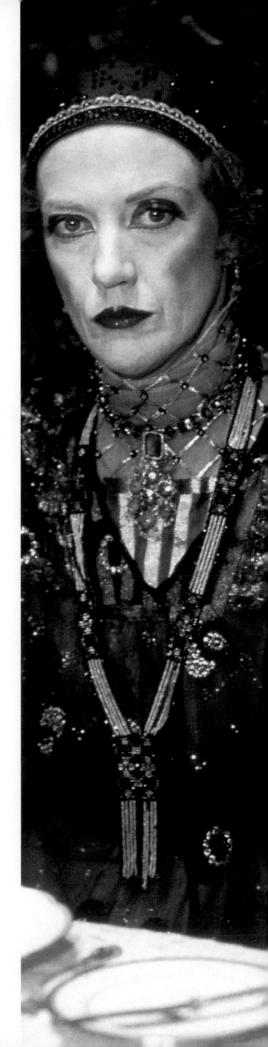

Vile and Venomous

VILLAIN
VANITY FAIR
(EILEEN ATKINS)

Cinderella never would have complained about her wicked stepmother if she'd spent a weekend getting to know the wickedest stepmother of them all—Vanity Fair. Played with unabashed gusto by British stage veteran Eileen Atkins, Vanity Fair was the first villain in the annals of Mystery!, and she remains one of the most memorable.

Despite her rather literary name, borrowed from the title of Thackeray's classic novel, Vanity's vanity is the least troublesome of her many dark qualities. In the story she's a master thief, a specialist in arcane drugs and poisons, a torturer without a shred of conscience, and a murderer many times over. Because her name keeps cropping up in messages intercepted by British Intelligence, Vanity is also suspected of being a ruthless espionage agent, a sort of cross between Mata Hari and the venomous queen from Walt Disney's *Snow White*.

Vanity is quite forthright, making no attempt to cover up her diabolical nature. "She'll marry the devil if I choose," she vows with regard to her stepdaughter's marital plans. When a degraded young actress threatens to upset her plans, she brandishes a branding iron and threatens, "You'll have no face. He won't know you from a bar of soap."

Atkins, the co-creator of *Upstairs, Downstairs* with actress Jean Marsh, was not the obvious choice to play this grotesquely comic creature. Best known as a serious stage actress and player in occasional television dramas and feature films (*Cold Comfort Farm,* 1996), she had never done anything quite so over-the-top before. But she was so entertaining as Vanity Fair that when time came for her to calmly sip her fatal glass of Château d'Yquem 1882 laced with deadly aconite, millions of appreciative viewers surely wanted to knock the glass from her hand.

THE
INVESTIGATORS

MAGNIFYING GLASS
TURNED ON THE INVESTIGATORS

HAVE YOU EVER WONDERED WHAT IT MUST BE LIKE TO LIVE WITH ONE OF YOUR favorite Mystery! heroes? For all their cleverness, most of these people aren't the type you'd want answering your ad for a roommate. Take Sherlock Holmes. The man does cocaine, for gosh sakes, keeps the room murky with pipe smoke, and sometimes even fires his pistols indoors for target practice. Hercule Poirot, though a neatness freak compared with the messy Holmes, would be just as trying. For breakfast, he requires two eggs of exactly the same size, side by side, and is beside himself if one half of his precisely groomed mustache is out of balance with the other.

These two aren't the only Mystery! detectives who might be hard to put up with. Inspector Morse, for instance, doesn't suffer fools gladly—or anyone else, really. The female sleuths of Mystery! wouldn't make much better companions. Miss Marple is a gossipy sort whose rock-solid composure makes the idea of her ever kicking up her heels too fanciful to take seriously. Jane Tennison of *Prime Suspect* is so work-obsessed that probably all she has time for is sleep during the few hours she's not in the squad room. If there's a message in all this, it might be that the detectives of Mystery! need to get a life.

Though they all share an ability to focus closely on the facts of the matter, their minds work in different ways. Morse and Albert Campion seem to leap to conclusions with a heavy reliance on intuition, while Tennison, Adam Dalgliesh, and Sergeant Cribb are likely to build to a solution by methodically gathering piles of information until they find the pieces that fit. Most of them need to be left alone during this process, which is hardly conducive to convivial relations with others. This may explain why so many of the Mystery! heroes are lonely, troubled, driven people who make enormous personal sacrifices.

VIEWED ACROSS TIME

Because Mystery! has drawn largely from the British traditions of the genre, it's interesting to look at the detectives from a contemporary American perspective. The British detectives of the 1920s and 1930s, for example, were solving crimes before the development of modern forensic science, before radical changes in the rights of defendants, and before the second world war erased many of the still-powerful elements of English class structure. So, why do they seem so nostalgically appealing? Perhaps we're weary of sordid cases involving drugs and perversity and abuse of children. Maybe we long for a time when we could assume the police were at least honest, if not too bright, and just in need of a "consulting detective" like Holmes or Poirot to solve the puzzle for them.

By looking at the investigators across time, we can see that Lord Peter Wimsey's cases are straightforward murders, almost hygienically clean compared with Adam Dalgliesh's. By comparing Miss Marple's cases with those of Chandler & Co., we see not only how much female detective characters have changed, but also how much more we know about them. We can consider the sociological implications, or we can just sit back and enjoy watching these detectives go about their work, which isn't such a bad idea either.

The VICTORIAN DETECTIVES

The famous consulting detective of Baker Street was still solving cases in the time of King George V— and so, presumably, was the man from Scotland Yard. But we remember them best as they were in the gas-lit time of Queen Victoria.

- **SHERLOCK HOLMES**
  THE ADVENTURES OF SHERLOCK HOLMES AND OTHER SERIES

- **SERGEANT CRIBB**
  SERGEANT CRIBB

SHERLOCK HOLMES

THE ADVENTURES OF SHERLOCK HOLMES

AND OTHER SERIES

Based on the stories by
Sir Arthur Conan Doyle

SERIES
The Adventures of
Sherlock Holmes
The Return of Sherlock Holmes
The Casebook of Sherlock Holmes
Sherlock Holmes
The Memoirs of
Sherlock Holmes

**PRODUCTION
COMPANY**
Granada Television

YEARS
1985–1996

MAIN CAST
Sherlock Holmes
JEREMY BRETT

Dr. John Watson
DAVID BURKE/
EDWARD HARDWICKE

Inspector Lestrade
COLIN JEAVONS

Mrs. Hudson
ROSALIE WILLIAMS

AT THE REICHENBACH FALLS IN SWITZERLAND, A PLAQUE
COMMEMORATES AN EVENT THAT NEVER TOOK PLACE, YET LIVES IN THE
MEMORIES OF MILLIONS. THE INSCRIPTION READS: "ACROSS THIS DREADFUL
CAULDRON OCCURRED THE CULMINATING EVENT IN THE CAREER OF
SHERLOCK HOLMES, THE WORLD'S GREATEST DETECTIVE, WHEN ON MAY 4, 1891,
HE VANQUISHED MORIARTY, THE NAPOLEON OF CRIME."

Each year, thousands of visitors to that spectacularly scenic spot pause to read the plaque and remember Sherlock Holmes, the most famous detective who never lived.

The overwhelming influence of Holmes and his creator, Sir Arthur Conan Doyle, on all the detectives who followed him is immeasurable. Agatha Christie often acknowledged her debt to Holmes for the creation of her equally brilliant and eccentric detective Hercule Poirot. Every keenly observant modern detective, from Inspector Roderick Alleyn to DCI Jane Tennison, works in Holmes' long shadow. Any loner with a loyal partner, like Inspector Morse with his Sergeant Lewis, is treading the turf of Holmes and Watson. When the introspective Adam Dalgliesh publishes a volume of poetry, he's taking after the even more introspective Holmes, whose many monographs on arcane topics helped build his formidable reputation.

In other words, by the time his creator had finished with him in 1927, some four novels, 56 stories, and 40 years after readers first met him, Holmes had pretty much done everything a detective could do. More than a century later, new investigators still pay their unspoken tribute to the great "consulting detective" of 221b Baker Street.

NO MYSTERY! WITHOUT SHERLOCK

That's why it was a foregone conclusion that there would be a Sherlock Holmes series on Mystery!. The inspired idea of having Jeremy Brett play the central character was originally suggested by Granada Television and was fully embraced by Joan Wilson, the first executive producer of Mystery!, who was then Brett's wife.

Brett was a well-known stage performer in England whom American viewers remembered as Freddy, Eliza Doolittle's suitor, in the Oscar-winning 1964 musical film *My Fair Lady* and as Max de Winter in the BBC's version of *Rebecca,* a highlight of the first Mystery! season. When first approached to play Holmes, Brett had his reservations. Firstly, he was concerned he had gotten the part because of his wife, but was assured that a compelling reason was because he bore a striking resemblance to the

Sidney Paget illustrations that accompanied the Holmes stories in *The Strand* magazine. But mostly, like millions of others, he thought Basil Rathbone "was the finest Sherlock Holmes there's ever been" and saw no reason to redo the Holmes stories. But after Brett took home an edition of Doyle's complete Holmes stories and read them thoroughly, he made a curious discovery. "I realized they hadn't actually ever done these stories as Doyle wrote them," he explained. "I think the only one Rathbone ever did that followed Doyle was *The Hound of the Baskervilles*." (A number of others were given contemporary spins and set in the 1940s.)

BECOMING HOLMES

After being costumed in black and made up in white-toned makeup, the tall, lean actor seemed transformed; he had become Holmes. From that point on, Brett became the official defender of Doyle's words. If he saw something in the scripts that didn't seem quite right, he immediately went to the original story to see how Doyle had handled it. "He carries this book—a copy of Doyle's complete works—around with him everywhere he goes," his amused Watson (David Burke) observed after filming the first 13 episodes. More than a decade later, Brett was still carrying that battered book, his Holmesian Bible, annotated with his countless notes.

His performance was almost universally hailed as the best new Holmes in a generation. Some critics went so far as to say he had become the *definitive* Sherlock Holmes. Dame Jean Conan Doyle, the author's daughter, told Brett, "You are the Sherlock Holmes of my childhood."

But viewers used to Rathbone's brisk, cheerful Holmes must have been quite startled by Brett's dark-hued portrayal, seen right from the first episode, *A Scandal in Bohemia*. In that episode, Watson arrives at 221b Baker Street to find a moody, irritable Holmes sitting alone in front of the fire. Nearby, Watson sees a hypodermic needle. "What is it tonight—morphine or cocaine?" Watson asks, disapprovingly. "I can strongly recommend a seven percent solution of cocaine," says Holmes. "Would you care to try it?" Ignoring Watson's lecture about the damage he's doing to his great intellect by using drugs, Holmes eventually gets around to his problem. "I abhor the dull routine of existence," he explains.

THERE'S NO ROLE LIKE HOLMES

Considered the role of a lifetime by many, the famous consulting detective has been portrayed by scores of well-known actors, including the following:

- John Barrymore
- Jeremy Brett
(he has said he's the 117th)
- Michael Caine
(with Ben Kingsley as Watson)
- Edward Fox
- Larry Hagman
- Charlton Heston
(Jeremy Brett played Watson)
- Raymond Massey
(with James Mason as Watson)
- Roger Moore
- Leonard Nimoy
- Eille Norwood
(who played him on film more times than anyone)
- Edward Petherbridge *(on NPR)*
- Basil Rathbone
- Ian Richardson
- Orson Welles *(on radio)*
- Nicol Williamson
(with Laurence Olivier as Moriarty, Robert Duvall as Watson)

For all Holmes' gifts, he's a lonely, unfulfilled man, a troubled soul. Brett knew the restless spirit was the key to Holmes, and so he gave the man a nervous energy that never relented. It shows in every action—from the quick little steps of his distinctive walk to his many dramatic hand gestures and sudden exclamations. Even in those episodes where Brett's own natural wit and wry humor glowed through the dark clouds around Holmes, his Sherlock is a man on a torture rack of his own creation.

A HOLMES FOR THIS GENERATION

Edward Hardwicke, who took over the role of Watson after the first 13 episodes, sees Brett's portrayal as being very contemporary. "I think every generation produces its own Hamlet and Sherlock Holmes," he says. "Jeremy was totally of his generation, with all the neuroses and complex stresses under which people live these days. Somehow he conveyed all that in that character."

The first series also was crucial for establishing Holmes as a man who was living his life almost entirely without the society of women. Holmes' disdain for women probably reflected Conan Doyle's own misogynist attitudes, but Holmes always explained that his heart was governed by his brain, and developing a relationship with a woman might "bias my judgment." Watson tells us on a number of occasions that Holmes had an aversion to women, maintaining, "Women are never to be entirely trusted—not the best of them."

Holmes' coldness to women, coupled with his monastic lifestyle and his obvious preference for male companionship, including the juveniles of his Baker Street Irregulars, has caused some Holmesian scholars to speculate Sherlock might have been homosexual. Billy Wilder's film, *The Private Life of Sherlock Holmes*, actually suggested that Holmes and Watson lived as gay men. "I don't think Holmes ever had sex at all," Brett once said when asked about it. "I think he got very hurt [by a woman] at one of the universities, either Cambridge or Oxford, and I think he must have had a very powerful mother. We all have to make up our own minds."

"Why all this devotion to a man who was intensely prejudiced, imperious, often bad tempered, thoughtless with people who might look to him for a little kindness, capable of an unmerited snub, grossly self-indulgent, arrogant, opinionated—and decidedly touchy about trivialities? Well, just because he is Sherlock Holmes. (And in our imaginations, we are Sherlock Holmes!)"

—VINCENT PRICE

HOME AWAY FROM HOLMES

221b Baker Street was always a fictional address, of course. But that doesn't keep fans from flocking to it or sending mail there for their beloved sleuth. The current resident is the Abbey National Building Society, headquartered in a large building whose address is 217-229 Baker Street. Fortunately there's a very kind secretary there whose main responsibility seems to be answering the large volume of Sherlock correspondence that arrives weekly—and has been for 50-odd years. Her letters say Mr. Holmes has retired to the Sussex countryside. Presumably, he's raising bees.

"In late Victorian England people believed in order, and the world was seen as possessing a mechanistic simplicity. How ripe, then, this scientifically inquisitive age was for the emergence of the 'consulting detective,' Sherlock Holmes. The proud Victorian principle of 'applied science' lent itself perfectly to Holmes' 'scientific method' of investigation, which culminated in his meticulous 'reason by deduction.'"

—VINCENT PRICE

THE ELEMENTARY WATSON

Holmes' relationship with Watson, though, is a crucial element of the great detective's personality. Holmes' sense of humor only comes out when Watson's around. The only warmth he ever shows is aimed at Watson. His need for Watson to share his activities is profound. Yet Holmes is often unmindful of Watson's feelings and scolds him when he fails to measure up to Holmes' standards. In *The Dancing Men,* Watson applies what he thinks is the Holmes method to a problem and pronounces the solution "absurdly simple." Responds Holmes, "Everything is absurdly simple when it's explained to you." (Incidentally, one thing Holmes clearly never said to the good doctor was "Elementary, my dear Watson." That was a Hollywood construct. But "elementary" does appear once in the Holmes canon—in *The Crooked Man.)*

There is one major difference between the treatment of Watson in the Mystery! series of Holmes adventures and other versions: He's not the detective's comedy foil, which Nigel Bruce, for example, clearly was for Rathbone's Holmes. The Watson played by both Burke and Hardwicke is a solid, reliable fellow of considerable intellect and no small amount of courage, as he would indeed need to be for Holmes to spend so much time with him. It's Watson's misfortune to be friends with an extraordinary man who always makes him look ordinary by contrast.

VICTORIAN VERACITY

The veracity Brett insisted on for his character was pursued equally diligently by the producers in their portrayal of Victorian England, especially its glaring contrasts. We see dung in the streets, choking fog from coal fires, raggedy urchins, and tumbledown tenements, as well as large, rambling mansions, velvet settees, and lots of taffeta and lace. The writers, too, maintained the Victorian pomp with its often puffy, florid prose.

They also kept a good balance between action and inaction. They left in those scenes where Holmes carefully studies a new visitor to his rooms then tells viewers, in extraordinary detail, what he has deduced about the person, because, as Brett said, "Those scenes underscore why Holmes is still unsurpassed as a detective." But the writers also built more action into stories by dramatizing some of the events that take place off the printed page. That resulted in some of the series' most exciting episodes, many of them filmed as two-hour movies, such as *The Hound of the Baskervilles, The Sign of Four,* and *The Last Vampyre.*

Despite Brett's insistence on being faithful to the original Sherlock Holmes stories, he did make one significant change. When he learned, to his surprise, that children all over the world were great fans of the stories (it seems Holmes appeals to children today as a sort of Superman, the way he did to children of the last century), he began to wonder how good an idea it was for them to see the world's greatest detective injecting himself with cocaine. He finally wrote Doyle's daughter asking permission to have Holmes kick the drug habit. She happily gave him the green light. So, in *The Devil's Foot* episode Holmes finally gets rid of his hypodermic needle by symbolically burying it in the sand. He never went back to the drug again.

LEAVING HOLMES

The series came to an end in 1995 because of Brett's deteriorating heart condition. But producer June Wyndham Davies says they really had filmed the best of the Doyle stories, and further production was problematical at best. The 41 Jeremy Brett Holmes adventures have been phenomenally successful all over the world. They play in repeat telecasts and are widely available on home video. This is all due to the mesmerizing authority of Brett's performance, the scrupulously authentic recreation of the Victorian period—and, of course, the genius of Doyle himself.

"Our aspiration to put our reason in control of our instincts and emotions is so deep and intense that we constantly pretend we are doing so. We almost never are, but Sherlock Holmes always is."

—REX STOUT,
creator of detective Nero Wolf

"Holmes, of course, will find the solutions because he believes, with architect Mies van der Rohe, that God is in the details. He will understand that RACHE scrawled in blood is a clue not that the killer's name is Rachel but that the word means 'revenge' in German. He will be drawn to a case by noticing how deep the parsley has sunk into the butter. Watson will marvel at his deductions until Holmes shows why they are elementary."

—STEFAN KANFER,
Time

The Real Doctor Watson:

AUTHOR
SIR ARTHUR CONAN DOYLE

SIR ARTHUR CONAN DOYLE, WHO CHRONICLED THE EXPLOITS OF SHERLOCK Holmes through four novels and 56 short stories, was the real Dr. Watson—a trained physician who gave up his medical practice when it became clear Holmes needed his attention more than his patients did. Moreover, Holmes paid a lot better.

Doyle was born in 1859, in Edinburgh, Scotland. His father was a civil servant whose real passion was his work as an artist; his mother had a family tree that could be traced all the way back to Plantagenet royalty. Young Doyle earned his medical degree from Edinburgh University in 1879 and began to practice medicine that year as an assistant to another physician. It's likely, though, that Doyle's natural yearning for adventure intervened almost immediately. He signed on as ship's surgeon for a sea voyage to the Arctic in 1880 and then to the West Coast of Africa. Readers of his vast number of short stories will notice that he put those early experiences to good use, since most of his stories are about robust, adventurous men in unusual, and often bizarre, settings. Doyle was a robust man himself—6 foot 2, weighing 210 pounds in his prime—and most resembled his other great literary character, Professor Challenger, hero of *The Lost World,* his famous novel about dinosaurs living on a remote jungle plateau.

A HOLMES-LIKE MIND

But Doyle also had the probing, endlessly curious mind of his greatest character, Sherlock Holmes, and created him in a three-week flurry of imaginative writing that produced *A Study in Scarlet* (1887). It was published in *Beeton's Christmas Annual of 1887,* and Doyle was paid only £25 for it—the only compensation he ever received for that much-reprinted story. Later, of course, he commanded more money from publishers than any other writer in the world—an amazing 10 shillings per word.

Doyle wanted to write a detective story because he was fascinated by the emerging field of criminal science and had been influenced by earlier fictional detectives, most especially Edgar Allan Poe's Inspector Dupin and Wilkie Collins' Sergeant Cuff in

The Moonstone. As the model for Holmes, he used his Edinburgh University professor, Dr. Joseph Bell, who had an incredible knack for diagnosing patients' ills by observing them closely when they first arrived at his office. Doyle never concealed the inspiration for Holmes and, in fact, dedicated his first collection of Holmes stories to Dr. Bell. Bell, in turn, wrote Doyle, saying, "You are yourself Sherlock Holmes—and you know it!"

Doyle did put much of himself into both Holmes and Dr. Watson. Holmes' low regard for women—often approaching misogyny—may have stemmed from Doyle's unsatisfying history with the opposite sex. His first wife, Louise, was diagnosed with tuberculosis eight years after they were married and, because of 19th-century fears about infection, Doyle was forced to be celibate until she died, even while carrying on an illicit romance with Jean Leckie. He married Leckie the year after Louise died and remained an outspoken foe of women's suffrage, as Holmes undoubtably also would have been.

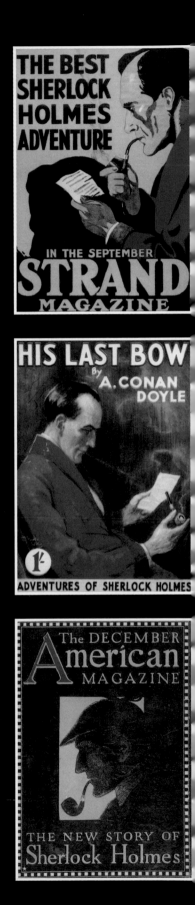

GREAT SENSE OF MARKETING

Doyle was never as enthralled with Holmes as his public was and resented the fact that his historical novels and serious non-fiction were never as popular as the Holmes stories. Yet he was enough of a businessman to bring Holmes back to life after apparently killing him off when the financial incentive became too tempting to refuse.

Although Doyle was knighted in 1902, ostensibly for having volunteered as chief surgeon in a South African hospital during the Boer War and for having written pamphlets supporting the British position, many feel the real reason was because he had promised the King he would bring Holmes back. When *The Strand* magazine published *The Final Problem*, in which Holmes and Moriarty plunge to their "deaths" from the Reichenbach Falls, tens of thousands of readers wrote to the magazine, begging Doyle to bring Holmes back. Some 20,000 readers canceled their subscriptions. Men wore black bands around their hats, and the country was in the deepest mourning it had experienced since Queen Victoria died. Surely Holmes' resurrection was well worth a knighthood.

Doyle later did all he could to cash in on the popularity of Holmes. He co-authored the play *Sherlock Holmes* with actor William Gillette and did other stage adaptations of Holmes stories. He cooperated with many silent movie adaptations and continued to write the stories until 1927, just three years before he died of a heart attack in Sussex.

In the last stage of his life, Doyle had become an enthusiastic supporter of spiritualism and lectured widely on the topic between 1917 and 1925, including several tours of the U.S. He always vowed to come back in spirit form. No one has ever spotted Doyle making a return visit, but if he has managed to slip back unnoticed, he surely must have been delighted to discover the world is still just as fascinated by Sherlock Holmes as it was when he left it more than 65 years ago.

SELECTED BIBLIOGRAPHY

Sherlock Holmes stories: *A Study in Scarlet,* 1887; *The Sign of Four,* 1890; *The Adventures of Sherlock Holmes,* 1892; *The Memoirs of Sherlock Holmes,* 1893; *The Hound of the Baskervilles,* 1902; *The Return of Sherlock Holmes,* 1905; *The Valley of Fear,* 1915; *His Last Bow,* 1917; *The Case Book of Sherlock Holmes,* 1927.

Other major works: *Micah Clarke,* 1889; *The White Company,* 1891; *The Lost World,* 1912; *The Poison Belt,* 1913; *The Land of Mist,* 1925; *The Maricot Deep & Other Stories,* 1929.

Holmes' Boswell:

SIDEKICK
DR. WATSON
(DAVID BURKE, EDWARD HARDWICKE)

Dr. John Watson was the boilerplate for all detective sidekicks, the Boswell who not only chronicled the adventures of Sherlock Holmes but also participated in almost all of them as helpmate, backup man, co-investigator, and sympathetic audience of one. He also remains the most maligned sidekick, pictured too often as a doddering old fool or a vehicle for comic relief rather than the loyal friend Conan Doyle meant him to be. Thankfully, the 41 Sherlock Holmes episodes gave only Doyle's authentic Watson—a decent, caring man who did what he could to keep Holmes off cocaine (*A Scandal in Bohemia*) and who would stand in for him at a moment's notice (*The Hound of the Baskervilles*), even if it meant getting thrown through a glass window (*The Three Gables*). If Watson ultimately profited from his accounts of Holmes' greatest cases, he surely earned the right to do so many times over.

There were two superb Watsons in the ten-year run of Holmes stories on Mystery!. David Burke played Watson during the first series then left to star with the Royal Shakespeare Company at Stratford. Burke has appeared in several BBC-TV productions, including *Henry VI, Parts 1* and *2, Richard III,* and *The Winter's Tale.* He also played Stalin in *Reilly, Ace of Spies,* and has since guest-starred in several Mystery! series. He was succeeded as Watson by Edward Hardwicke, son of the late Sir Cedric Hardwicke. Hardwicke has an extensive theater background, and his other television work includes *The Pallisers* and the *Lovejoy* mystery series. Since finishing the Holmes series, Hardwicke has appeared in such films as *The Scarlet Letter* and *Richard III.*

Fighting for the True Holmes:

ACTOR

JEREMY BRETT

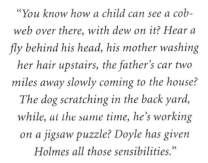

ON JANUARY 25, 1996, JEREMY BRETT APPEARED ON MYSTERY! FOR THE 41ST and final time as Sherlock Holmes. His normally slicked-back hair tousled, his face partly in shadow, Holmes loomed in close-up, a beatific smile on his face, and saluted his older brother, Mycroft, for solving the mystery of the Mazarin Stone for him. "Brother mine—bravo!" Holmes says. Though Brett once had brought Holmes back from almost certain death at the Reichenbach Falls, viewers knew he would not make a return appearance after this cameo: The 59-year-old actor had died four months earlier.

"Sir Arthur Conan Doyle, I believe, has been sent safely into the 21st century," Brett told his fans that year when he knew that because of his failing heart he'd never play the part again. "Anyway, it is done." The actor had played Holmes for ten years and found the journey both physically taxing and emotionally draining, once describing the experience as being "like a streak of lightning balanced on a magnesium tightrope." For years, he had searched Doyle's stories for an explanation of Holmes' gloomy nature but never found one, so he made up his own: A neglected child, raised by a nanny, Holmes seldom saw his parents, and withdrew into himself and his studies.

COMING TO HOLMES

Born Jeremy Huggins, he was the youngest of four sons, his father a decorated Army colonel. Though Jeremy had a speech impediment, he had a beautiful singing voice, a gift he always believed got him through his schooling at Eton. When his speech problem was surgically corrected in his teens, Jeremy was sent to London's Central School of Speech and Drama. The experience further fired his interest in acting, so when he later was sent to Cambridge, he rebelled and left to try for a career on the London stage instead, changing his surname to Brett, he said, so his efforts wouldn't embarrass his family.

As it turned out, his efforts embarrassed no one. Brett progressed to the National Theatre, where he blossomed under the inspired leadership of Laurence Olivier, and began to play a series of strongly romantic roles, followed by parts in international hit films, including King Vidor's *War and Peace* (1956) and George Cukor's *My Fair Lady* (1964). He was briefly married to actor Anna Massey, and they had a son, David, who remained close to him after the divorce. By 1982, Brett was still looking for that career-sustaining role that would define him as an actor. It turned out to be Sherlock Holmes.

Unlike Holmes (whom Brett referred to as "S. H." or "my deranged penguin"), Brett was a witty, garrulous man who could plunge into a room full of strangers and make friends immediately. Because, as Holmes, he dressed in black, funereal clothes so often, he wore nothing but light-colored clothes away from the set.

"My lasting memory of Jeremy will be of him laughing. There was always a lot of hilarity on the set, and Jeremy had a very infectious laugh," recalls actor Edward Hardwicke. "We had an understanding that the basis of the relationship between Holmes and Watson was having a great deal of humor between them."

DEVASTATING DEPRESSION

What Hardwicke and the others didn't know at the time was the extent of the pressure building on Brett. His second wife, Joan Wilson, the executive producer of Mystery!, had been diagnosed with cancer, and Brett began to sink into what his doctors much later diagnosed as manic depression. (Interestingly enough, many Holmes scholars feel that the great detective's drastic mood swings may have resulted from manic depression.) When Wilson finally died in 1985, Brett suffered a nervous breakdown and had to be hospitalized.

Brett was given drugs to control his depression, but the doctors weren't aware of his heart condition caused by the rheumatic fever he had contracted as a youth, and the drugs had a devastating impact on his heart. Brett finally rallied with the help of new drugs and returned to work to make the two-hour Holmes adventure *The Sign of Four,* which cheered him immensely. When Brett became ill again, he refused to let his health defeat him. He was encouraged greatly by his new friend and soulmate, Linda Pritchard, a former London bus driver 20 years his junior, whom he had met in 1988 when she enlisted his help in a marathon fund-raising run for cancer research. Brett presented her with a £3,000 prize he'd been awarded as England's "pipe smoker of the year," taking delight in knowing smoking was going to help fight cancer. Pritchard eventually moved into Brett's home to nurse him during his final year when his heart condition had finally been diagnosed and they learned he might have limited time left.

ACTING FOR LIFE

"The six final episodes were an act of incredible courage," says Pritchard. "He was so ill that he should have stopped working, but he felt so many other people depended on him." Though Brett had always scrupulously fought against any tampering with Doyle's stories, he had no choice but to agree to let *The Mazarin Stone* be rewritten so that Mycroft (Charles Gray), Sherlock's brother, could solve the case instead of Sherlock. After the series ended, he managed to do small parts in the feature films *Mad Dogs and Englishmen* and *Moll Flanders,* then accepted the fact that he'd never be able to act again. "Acting was his life," says Pritchard.

Brett died in his sleep on September 12, 1995, leaving behind a portrait of the great detective that went beyond where anyone else—including, perhaps, his creator—had ever taken him. "I think the great mystery will always be why he is so alive when he never existed," Brett said of Holmes in *The Armchair Detective.* "How can it be that a man who never lived has such identity? It is fascinating. It is . . . Conan Doyle's miracle." Surely it is also Jeremy Brett's miracle.

"Jeremy was an extraordinary actor to watch at work, amazingly expert technically, and was very, very good with other actors. I don't think he ever received the recognition he should have. He took Sherlock Holmes beyond even what Conan Doyle wrote, in the best possible way. That's his tribute, really."

—EDWARD HARDWICKE

"You realize who you're playing, don't you? One of the three most important men of the century—Churchill, Hitler, and Holmes."

—ALISTAIR COOKE
to Jeremy Brett

Inimitable Match for Holmes:

VILLAIN
PROFESSOR JAMES MORIARTY
(ERIC PORTER)

An immodest Sherlock Holmes once told Dr. Watson, "I cannot agree with those who rank modesty among the virtues." With that kind of ego, it must have been hard for the self-proclaimed master detective to admit that his phenomenal standing among sleuths owed a great deal to the formidable reputation of his most infamous adversary, the sinister Professor James Moriarty, played with brooding, beetle-browed force by veteran British actor Eric Porter. For his part, Moriarty had an ego nearly equal to Holmes, whom he considered "a mere amateur in the field of detection." Moriarty appeared in only two of the 41 episodes—*The Red-Headed League* and *The Final Problem*—yet intimidated Holmes more than any other villain he encountered.

Best known as Soames in *The Forsyte Saga,* Karenin in *Anna Karenina,* and Count Bronowsky in *The Jewel in the Crown,* the late Porter dipped deeply into his bag of actor's tricks to play an especially menacing Moriarty. Wearing long gray hair, slicked back over his ears, and a perpetual scowl, his Moriarty looks like a man whose stomach acid never stops bubbling. When he finally comes face to face with Holmes, Moriarty looks the famous detective over, studying Holmes' cranium especially carefully, and scornfully tells him, "You have less frontal development than I should have expected."

At their final struggle above the roaring Reichenbach Falls, it at first seems that Moriarty has taken Homes with him as he crashes onto the rocks below. Holmes' miraculous survival cements his reputation as a legendary crime-fighter, but the narrowness of his escape from death also ensures the professor's place in the Valhalla of villains.

SERGEANT CRIBB

SERGEANT CRIBB

Based on the novels by
Peter Lovesey

IF SHERLOCK HOLMES HAD EVER MET SERGEANT CRIBB OF SCOTLAND
YARD WHILE WORKING THE SAME CRIMINAL CASE ON THE FOGGY STREETS OF
VICTORIAN LONDON, IT'S NOT LIKELY THEY'D HAVE COMPARED NOTES.

Holmes, London's only "consulting detective," didn't hold the police in very high regard because too often he had solved cases they had abandoned as hopeless only to see the coppers claim the credit afterward. In fact, in *The Sign of Four,* we learn that Holmes "despises" the entire police force, a blanket denunciation sure to include his contemporary, Sergeant Cribb.

That probably wouldn't bother Cribb. Author Peter Lovesey created him as Holmes' exact opposite: a meticulous, not particularly imaginative detective who solves crimes the old fashioned way—by putting in the hours. Lovesey was willing to sacrifice charisma for credibility to make Cribb a realistic police detective of his era. If that makes Cribb what host Gene Shalit called "a comfortable plodder," Cribb probably wouldn't argue with that assessment.

Cribb first came to life late in the sixth chapter of Lovesey's first mystery novel, *Wobble to Death,* which was also the first Cribb story to appear on Mystery! in 1980. Lovesey made no effort to give Cribb sex appeal. Already in his forties, Cribb is described as a tall, lean man with a long nose and immense, bushy sideburns who, following the fashion of his day, is most often seen sporting a bowler hat.

A DOGGED DETECTIVE

In that first case, Cribb's style is clear: Look into everything with a jaundiced eye, take copious notes, and pile up the evidence until you have enough to point out the guilty party. He doesn't offer any great leaps of deductive logic, and he's about as colorful as boiled cabbage. But he's a hard-working, honest cop at a time when Scotland Yard is recovering from scandalous revelations about corruption on the force.

Lovesey's many books about Cribb (like Inspector Morse, Cribb doesn't use a first name) are concerned less with the details of the investigations than they are with the details of life in Victorian England. That's their great strength, and it was to be the great strength of the television series. In *Wobble to Death,* for example, Cribb (Alan Dobie) and his sidekick, Constable Thackeray (William Simons), turn up at the vast Agricultural Hall in Islington to investigate the puzzling death of an athlete who was one of the favorites in a grueling marathon walking race known as a "wobble." In these endurance races contestants fast-walk around an indoor track for six days and nights covering a total distance of up to 600 miles in front of a huge crowd of spectators, vying for prize money that's awarded for the greatest distance traveled within the allotted time.

**PRODUCTION
COMPANY**
Granada Television

YEARS
1980–1983

MAIN CAST
Sergeant Cribb
ALAN DOBIE

**Police Constable
Thackeray**
WILLIAM SIMONS

Inspector Jowett
DAVID WALLER

At first, the death of challenger Charles Darrell (Archie Tew) is believed to have been caused by an infection transmitted from the unsanitary track surface through the blisters on his bare feet. Toxicology reports, however, reveal a massive amount of strychnine in Darrell's system, accounting for the terrible convulsions he suffered before dying. Cribb and Thackeray learn that although small amounts of strychnine were used as stimulants in drinks supplied to the walkers, Darrell was given a huge overdose. Is his trainer guilty? What about the handlers for the favorite in the race? Or Darrell's sexy, promiscuous wife Cora (Bobbie Brown), who was seeing other men while her husband competed? Cribb slowly gathers information on these and other suspects, including the financially strapped race promoter.

VICTORIAN LIFE UP CLOSE

Since the colorful but grueling wobbles no longer exist, the *Wobble to Death* episode of *Sergeant Cribb* was a rare chance to see how they were run by promoters of the day. Other episodes of *Sergeant Cribb* provided close-up looks at other aspects of Victorian life: the music hall scene in *Abracadaver,* for example, bare-knuckle prizefighting in *The Detective Wore Silk Drawers,* and the macabre world of clairvoyants and seances in *A Case of Spirits.*

The great challenge, of course, was duplicating Victorian London on backlots and soundstages. Most of *Sergeant Cribb* was filmed in Manchester, where the crew made extensive use of authentic old halls and police stations, commissioning alterations and restoration work to make them conform to the period look whenever feasible. But the company did go on location in London once—to Madame Tussaud's famous wax museum for the *Waxwork* episode shown in 1981. While filming there, designers noticed the striking series of drawings from the *Police Gazette,* which then became the illustrations for the credit sequences of *Sergeant Cribb.*

Alan Dobie's Cribb is a rather sober, ferret-faced, no-nonsense cop whose attempts at humor are subtle at best. A respected stage actor in England, Dobie has played many classic roles in his television work, including Judge Brack opposite Diana Rigg in *Hedda Gabler*, the title role in Tolstoy's *The Death of Ivan Ilyich*, and Andrei in the BBC's 26-part version of Tolstoy's *War and Peace*. Though Cribb never became a big audience favorite, he occupies a unique position in the Mystery! canon as the only Victorian police detective who wasn't made to look foolish by some freelancer like Sherlock Holmes.

"[Cribb's] honesty is one of his crucial qualities since the series is historically set following a major British scandal that rocked London's Metropolitan Police Department in 1877. The case that touched off the scandal implicated two Scotland Yard detectives and was known as the 'Great Turf Fraud.'

The trial of these detectives naturally caused a public outcry and the Home Office set up a committee to investigate the detective department. The evidence of this committee made it clear that many changes would have to be made.

A young barrister assisting the committee visited Paris and made a thorough study of the French detective bureau. Back in Britain, he reported his findings to the committee. The result was the dismantling of the London detective department and the formation of a new division called the 'C.I.D.' (Criminal Investigation Department). To herald the change, Scotland Yard (with its dingy ramshackle swarm of buildings) was moved closer to the Houses of Parliament, and to distinguish it from the old Yard, the authorities decided it should be known as 'New Scotland Yard.'"

—VINCENT PRICE

"For atmosphere, the counterpoise of teacups and terror, coziness and crime, the Victorian mystery is supreme."

—PETER LOVESEY

Creator of Holmes' Counterpart:

AUTHOR

PETER LOVESEY

PETER LOVESEY MIGHT NEVER HAVE CREATED THE VICTORIAN-ERA POLICE detective Sergeant Cribb if his wife, Jacqueline, hadn't talked him into trying to write a mystery novel in 1970. She had read about a competition for the best first crime novel and urged him to try for the grand prize of £1,000. Passionately interested in track and field since a teenager, Lovesey had already published a non-fiction book, *The Kings of Distance*, about the careers of five great running stars between 1860 and 1960. It so happened that research for that book had turned up some fascinating information about the so-called "wobbles," so he took that as his starting point and created Cribb to unravel the ensuing mystery. The result was *Wobble to Death*. Lovesey wanted his detective to struggle to solve a crime; given the poor state of forensic science at the time, he thought this would make his character more believable. When his book won the award, Lovesey took off with a series of Sergeant Cribb novels, including several that were dramatized for television.

With his career as a mystery novelist established, Lovesey quit his day job—teaching English at high-school level—to write full time. One of the Cribb books, *Waxwork*, won the 1978 Silver Dagger award from the Crime Writers' Association, and Lovesey was awarded a Golden Dagger in 1983. He has also written other novels under his real name, Peter Lear, including *Goldengirl*, which was filmed in 1979. In recent years, Lovesey has continued to write historical mystery novels, including *Keystone*, set in silent-era Hollywood, and the "Bertie" series, in which Queen Victoria's son, Prince Albert solves crimes before he's crowned King.

SELECTED BIBLIOGRAPHY

Sergeant Cribb: Wobble to Death, 1970; *The Detective Wore Silk Drawers*, 1971; *Abracadaver*, 1972; *Mad Hatter's Holiday*, 1973; *Invitation to a Dynamite Party*, 1974; *A Case of Spirits*, 1975; *Swing, Swing Together*, 1976. Others: *Goldengirl* (as Peter Lear), 1977; *Waxwork*, 1978; *Spider Girl* (as Peter Lear), 1980; *The False Inspector Dew*, 1982; *Keystone*, 1983; *Rough Cider*, 1986; *The Secret of Spandau* (as Peter Lear), 1986; *Bertie and the Tin Man*, 1988; *On the Edge*, 1989; *Bertie and the Seven Bodies*, 1990; *The Last Detective*, 1991; *Diamond Solitaire*, 1992; *Bertie and the Crime of Passion*, 1993; *The Crime of Miss Oyster Brown and Other Stories*, 1994; *The Summons*, 1995; *Bloodhounds*, 1996.

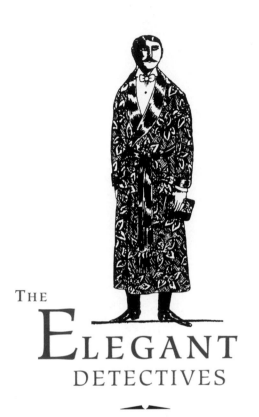

THE ELEGANT DETECTIVES

*They talk like elocution experts, dine like
epicures, and dress like peacocks from Savile Row.
If they weren't to the manor born, they wish they might
have been. They're the elegant detectives, who solve
foul murders without mussing their hair or
missing a luncheon date.*

- **HERCULE POIROT**
  AGATHA CHRISTIE'S POIROT

- **LORD PETER WIMSEY**
  DOROTHY L. SAYERS' LORD PETER WIMSEY

- **ALBERT CAMPION**
  CAMPION

HERCULE POIROT

AGATHA CHRISTIE'S POIROT

Based on the novels and stories by
Agatha Christie

IN AGATHA CHRISTIE'S *The Mystery of the Spanish Chest*,
COLONEL CURTISS, A SCAR-FACED MURDER SUSPECT, MAKES AN ENORMOUS
ERROR IN PERSONAL DIPLOMACY WHEN HE REFERS TO HERCULE POIROT
AS SIMPLY "A DETECTIVE." "I AM *the* DETECTIVE, MR. CURTISS,"
POIROT PROMPTLY CORRECTS HIM.

PRODUCTION COMPANY
London Weekend
Television

YEARS
1990–1996

MAIN CAST
Hercule Poirot
DAVID SUCHET

Captain Hastings
HUGH FRASER

Chief Inspector Japp
PHILIP JACKSON

Miss Lemon
PAULINE MORAN

Indeed he is. One can assume Poirot (David Suchet) was on to Curtiss (John McEnery) before the man even knew he was matching wits with the legendary Belgian detective. Poirot soon reveals Curtiss to be the vicious culprit who deftly plunged a keen-edged blade through a tiny peephole in a trunk, penetrating the brain of the man hiding within and killing him instantly. Poirot has the good taste not to gloat as the police haul Curtiss away, cursing "that bloody little Frog." "I am not a bloody little Frog," Poirot adds, presumably for the record. "I am a bloody little Belgian!"

A quick solution to a puzzling murder mystery is standard operating procedure for Poirot—and so is his facile sense of humor. He may be vain and egocentric, but he's also extremely observant—and one of the things he has observed over many, many years is the fact that he's the world's greatest detective. You have to expect a little egotism in one who knows he has no peer, *n'est-ce pas?* Fortunately, Poirot brags with such a disarming absence of guile that everyone ends up being charmed.

THE MOST-WATCHED MYSTERY! DETECTIVE

Poirot's engaging combination of a razor-sharp mind with rightful conceit has proved irresistible to viewers, who have made him the most-watched detective since Mystery! began in 1980. Poirot scores consistently high ratings and, through 1996, had made the most appearances of any detective: 45 separate adventures, many of them feature-film length.

That record is fully in keeping with Poirot's even more amazing record as a literary phenomenon. He made his debut as the hero of Agatha Christie's first novel, *The Mysterious Affair at Styles,* which was published in 1920 and immediately established her as a hot new mystery author. By the time Poirot's final case was chronicled 55 years later in her 1975 novel *Curtain,* Christie had written 33 novels about him and 55 short stories. Her Poirot books still sell by the millions annually, more than 75 years after the bloody little Belgian first appeared in print.

Obviously modeled on Conan Doyle's Sherlock Holmes, Poirot is an eccentric bachelor who has an able Watson-like assistant in Captain Arthur Hastings (Hugh Fraser) and a grudgingly respectful ally at Scotland Yard in the Lestrade-like Inspector "Jimmy" Japp, played by Philip Jackson, star of West End productions and films, and a

devoted disciple of Christie long before he played Japp. Yet Christie clearly didn't intend Poirot to be just Holmes with a foreign accent; she wanted to invent a character unique in the annals of detective fiction, as different from Holmes as David from Goliath.

A DIFFERENT KETTLE OF TRUITE AMANDINE

Hastings describes Poirot as "a quaint dandified little man" who limps badly and is so fastidious in his appearance that "a speck of dust would have caused him more pain than a bullet wound." A neatness nut, Poirot even arranges his medicine bottles by height in symmetrical rows. He's a gourmet diner who has the growing waistline to prove it. His image means everything to him, and he considers a carefully sculpted mustache a "work of art." Poirot needs companionship and relishes the society of others, even Inspector Japp, whom he invites to dinner when Japp's wife is away on a trip in *Hickory, Dickory, Dock*. He's a totally different kettle of *truite amandine* from Holmes, the disorderly, ascetic recluse.

When Producer Brian Eastman and actor Suchet set out to create a new series of Poirot mysteries for television in 1989, it was obvious they wanted to keep Poirot faithful to the spirit of Agatha Christie, which meant he must remain a warm and likable man. Suchet's ability to convey that amiability may be the major reason why this eccentric, old-fashioned character from a bygone age soared to heights of popularity in the new series. The stories still work wonderfully well as mysteries, but it's their affable sense of humor and the warmth of the relationships between Poirot and his ensemble that really make them so deliciously entertaining.

The gorgeous sets and settings also contribute to their appeal. Most of the stories are set in the striking art deco environment of England, circa 1936 (even though some of the original Christie stories take place much later in time). From the delightful art deco graphics that open each program to the breathtakingly beautiful silks and satins of costume and decor, the series perfectly captures the lushness of the period.

ELÉMENTAIRE, MON CHER HASTINGS

Much has been made of the Poirot-Hastings friendship, which often seems to resemble a master-apprentice relationship, with Hastings hovering about the older man, waiting for Poirot to drop a few crumbs of wisdom. Suchet, Fraser, and the writers have expanded upon that, having a great deal of fun with the needling sarcasm that true friends often use to show their affection for each other.

If one should come away with the notion Poirot thinks Hastings is a pathetic loser, that's far from accurate. He actually cares deeply for his old friend and considers him the rather dashing, handsome sort of upper-crust Englishman he might have enjoyed being himself. In his final words to Hastings in *Curtain*, the elderly Poirot's admiration for him is beyond dispute. He praises the bearing of the aging Hastings, calling him "très distingué," adding, "You know, my friend, you have worn well."

Departing somewhat from Christie's works, in which Japp appeared fairly infrequently, the series has greatly expanded the relationship between Poirot and the inspector. They first met while Poirot was still a policeman in Belgium, and they worked together on the Abercrombie forgery case. But Poirot's police career came to an end with the German occupation of Belgium in 1914. His refusal to collaborate made Poirot a prime target for imprisonment or worse. After dropping out of sight for two years, Poirot resurfaced in England to become a private detective, and ever since his arrival he and Japp have enjoyed a sort of friendly rivalry, matching wits in a long-running duel that is really no contest. Though they come from different classes and have only murder investigations in common, Poirot and Japp reach a rather warm state of détente in their television incarnations.

That was never more obvious than in the *Double Sin* episode. Hastings is anxious to attend a lecture by Japp on his "greatest cases," but Poirot belittles the lecture, questioning how many "great cases" Japp could take credit for when Poirot himself probably solved most of them. Yet that night Poirot secretly slips out to Japp's lecture—he's had the ticket all along—to hear what the inspector might say about him. At first, his worst fears are confirmed as he hears Japp complain bitterly about the intrusions of so-called "private detectives" into police business. But then Poirot is touched—and immensely gratified—to hear Japp tell the crowd there is one exception: his friend Hercule Poirot, the greatest detective of them all.

Basically insecure, Poirot needs to be praised as often as possible, and Japp's praise is sincere. After all, Poirot once challenged him to a crime-solving contest in *The Disappearance of Mr. Davenheim* and delivered on his promise to beat Japp to the solution without ever leaving his room.

Still, the show never lets us forget that Poirot and Japp are from different worlds and can't ever be as close as Hastings and Poirot. In *Hickory, Dickory, Dock*, for example, Japp wants to repay Poirot for feeding him while his wife is out of town, but also wants to show the little Belgian what real English food is like. He cooks a meal for Poirot and looks on with pride as he sets before him a plate of mushy peas and a deep-fried pig liver concoction called "faggots," with a steamed pudding called "spotted dick" for dessert. Japp looks crestfallen, but not entirely surprised, when a sickly-looking Poirot complains of allergies and asks for a bit of cheese instead.

FAGGOTS AND SPOTTED DICK

In Hickory, Dickory, Dock, *Hercule Poirot was invited to eat a traditional English meal prepared by Inspector Jimmy Japp in Japp's own kitchen. The repast began with* faggots, *an English delicacy made from pig liver, onions, breadcrumbs, and fat pork, which is all mixed together, then shaped into balls, wrapped in an animal membrane called a* caul, *then baked and served with gravy. The meal ended with* spotted dick, *a dessert that's essentially a steamed suet pudding dotted with currants or raisins. Cholesterol content: Herculean proportions!*

It's unlikely any actor but Suchet could play such essentially comic scenes without making us think of Poirot as a clown. Suchet walks the tightrope between comedy and drama with dazzling skill. He can amuse us by dancing the Charleston in one scene, then drag us back to the serious business of murder a few moments later without hurting Poirot's credibility. Furthermore, his strict attention to Poirot's physical look and his investment of genuine emotion into his performance has made Suchet's Poirot the definitive interpretation. His Poirot is a fussy and frequently ridiculous man who may be stuck in a permanent time warp, but a person whose great intelligence and humane outlook make all his eccentricities seem only minor distractions from his main worth. Though the television series takes place almost entirely in the mid-1930s, Poirot always dresses as he might have done in the pre-World War I days. Christie never changed Poirot's wardrobe, even though she took his character into the 1950s—unless widening pinstripes by two millimeters counts.

With the completion of the *Dumb Witness* episode in 1995, the filming of the *Poirot* series was finally halted. Yet for millions of people, Suchet's Poirot has become a staple of their television diet. At least two dozen more Christie originals exist that could be filmed, including the exciting and poignant *Curtain*. So perhaps the beloved little man will put on his hat, pick up his walking stick, twirl his mustache a few times, and come back to see us again one day.

> *"It was very much a watershed period of history. There were these elements of modernity set in a pre-war period which provided such a wonderful contrast. And when you combined this with a man, Poirot, who is interested in modern things but in terms of his dress and appearance is almost a pre-First World War figure, the contrast is even more striking. So 1936 became the driving force of the way we designed the series—the look of the costumes, the styles of architecture, and so on."*
>
> —PRODUCER BRIAN EASTMAN
> quoted in *Agatha Christie's Poirot: A Celebration of the Great Detective*

CLUES TO THE ORIGIN OF POIROT'S NAME

The following are perhaps some influences on Christie's decision for a name for her dapper detective:

• **Hercule Flameau** *(criminal turned detective) in G. K. Chesterton's works*

• **Hercule Popeau**, *a French detective in books by American author Marie Bellow Lowndes*

• **Jules Poiret**, *retired French police officer created by Frank Howell Evans*

• *poireaux—French for leeks*

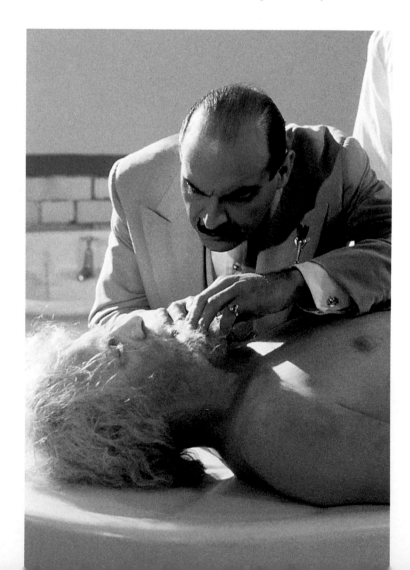

Dashing Sidekick:

CAPTAIN
ARTHUR HASTINGS

(HUGH FRASER)

Captain Arthur Hastings makes an early appearance in the Poirot stories as the narrator of Agatha Christie's first novel, *The Mysterious Affair at Styles,* in which Poirot is introduced. A retired Army officer wounded in World War I, Hastings is a hopeless romantic who falls in love frequently. He fancies himself a pretty fair detective, but doesn't have Poirot's power of concentration. For all that, though, he cuts a more dashing figure than his peculiar mentor— and knows it. Still, Hastings possesses considerable tact. In *Double Sin,* for instance, Poirot asks Hastings why so many people seem to be snickering at him. He's dressed, as usual, like a dandy, but is blissfully unaware of how ridiculous he looks. "I don't think they've ever seen anyone quite like you, Poirot," the loyal Hastings says. Hastings eventually marries and fathers two sons and two daughters before becoming a widower late in life.

Hastings was played by Hugh Fraser, a former rock musician who began his career in long-haired hippie roles in the 1970s. He later played Sir Anthony Eden in *Edward and Mrs. Simpson,* was in the epic Mystery! series *Game, Set and Match,* and has played classic roles for the Royal Shakespeare Company. While acting in television's *The Bretts,* Fraser met and married fellow cast member Belinda Lang, who plays Agatha Troy in *Ngaio Marsh's Alleyn Mysteries.*

"Poirot, like Holmes," he says, "is a lateral thinker, and one of Hastings' functions is to elucidate what is going on in Poirot's mind for the audience. I am certain, too, that it is a working relationship and that Poirot actually employs him."

Mother of the Mystery:

AUTHOR

DAME AGATHA CHRISTIE

IF SIR ARTHUR CONAN DOYLE, THE CREATOR OF SHERLOCK HOLMES, WAS THE father of the modern mystery story, then Dame Agatha Christie most certainly was its mother. Christie had the longest successful run of any mystery writer, publishing continuously for 56 of her 86 years. Her play, *The Mousetrap,* opened in London in 1952 and has been running ever since, breaking all records for the longest continuous theatrical run.

At the time of her death, she had sold more than two billion copies of her books around the world and was the largest-selling detective writer, male or female, anywhere. In her lifetime, only the Bible and the works of William Shakespeare had sold more copies. And her books continue to sell in the millions 20 years after her death. Even though Christie earned only £25 for her first novel, an American publisher paid $9.6 million after her death for the reprint rights to 33 titles.

There also can be no dispute about one other phenomenal Christie achievement: Her name appears on more Mystery! credits than any other author's— on a grand total of 75 separate programs. This includes 45 Poirot, 9 Miss Marple, 11 Tuppence and Tommy Beresford, plus 10 episodes of *Agatha Christie Stories*— quite an awesome representation.

DARED TO WRITE

Born Agatha Mary Clarissa Miller in 1890 in Torquay, a seaside resort in Devonshire, Christie wasn't the typical English girl of her day. She was the daughter of a successful American expatriate and a dreamy, creative-minded Englishwoman who encouraged her to be herself and do what she wanted in life. Christie never went to school but received intensive home schooling. Legend says she started writing her first mystery on a dare because she'd bragged that it looked quite easy.

Tall, bosomy, and strikingly handsome, the young Agatha had many suitors. She fell madly in love with handsome Archie Christie and married him in 1914, just before he went off to become an aviator in World War I. Christie finished *The Mysterious Affair at Styles* in 1916, and it finally was published in 1920, introducing the great detective Hercule Poirot to the world and starting the author on her long chain of successes. At about the same time, Christie started to lose a lifelong battle against obesity, which many felt eventually cost her the affection of her beloved Archie, who obviously failed to appreciate the greatness behind the girth.

She married for the second time in 1930, wedding Max Mallowan, an archeologist 14 years her junior whom she had met on the Orient Express. They had a successful marriage and shared many adventures together, including ones that later turned up in Poirot stories set in Egypt and other far-flung locales. In person, Christie was extremely shy, but she comes across as a warm, likable, vibrant, and exceptionally intelligent woman in the accounts of her close friends and relatives.

Agatha Christie received the highest honor bestowed on a woman in Britain when she was made a Dame of the British Empire in 1971. Her husband, one of the most distinguished archaeologists of his time, had been knighted three years before that.

A NEARLY UNSOLVED CHRISTIE PLOT

Perhaps Agatha Christie's most successful mystery plot was the one she began in 1930 when she created the elusive Mary Westmacott, author of romantic novels, and fooled the reading public with her for 19 years.

"Westmacott" wrote six novels—*Giant's Bread* (1930), *Unfinished Portrait* (1934), *Absent in the Spring* (1944), *The Rose and the Yew Tree* (1947), *A Daughter's a Daughter* (1952), and *The Burden* (1956). But it wasn't until 1949 that the author's cover was blown by a London newspaper columnist. Many critics believe Christie revealed much of her own outlook on love and marriage in these books, which have strong autobiographical elements, and didn't want the public to know whose private life she really was discussing.

During her life and after her death, debates have raged as to Christie's greatness. Critics around the world have sought to explain her enduring popularity in such cynical times, some ascribing it to her intricate mystery plots, interlaced with what may be the most brilliantly conceived clues ever devised by a mystery writer. Colin Dexter, who writes the Inspector Morse mysteries, feels that way. "Dear old Christie is much underrated," he says. "She had a wonderfully inventive mind."

Other mystery writers, like Ruth Rendell, believe Dame Agatha is overrated. She considers Christie's characters "cardboard" and her novels "remote from any recognizable social reality," and is tired of being dubbed the heir apparent to Christie.

Then there are others in the mystery field, including Hunter College (N.Y.) professor B. J. Rahn, who praise Christie's work principally for her character development. He argues that Christie was one of the first mystery writers to delve into the hearts and minds of her characters for motivation while most of her contemporaries concentrated on trying to puzzle their readers with tricky clues. John Mortimer, creator of Horace Rumpole, acknowledges Christie's limitations but assumes her popularity is due to her "enormous narrative skill" and her superb way of giving readers "pleasure and relaxation," a primary goal of many mystery writers.

One sure sign of her greatness is the fact that she's been so widely imitated over the past 75 years. Jessica Fletcher, the character Angela Lansbury played for more than a decade in the popular *Murder, She Wrote* television series, is patterned after Christie's Miss Marple. But all the imitation sometimes makes it difficult to see Christie's originality, her inventiveness.

Another possible rationale for Christie's continued sales in modern times is the absence of profanity and explicit sex in her writing. It's very likely, as Dexter feels, that millions of readers turn to Christie out of nostalgia for a time when detectives didn't wake each morning cursing a hangover and end each night in bed with a potential witness. While some believe the recent boom in Christie interest is a passing phase fueled by the Mystery! television shows, the many Poirot and Marple movies, and the critical re-evaluations they've spawned, others think Christie has a permanent lock on the world's imagination. Her open admirer, mystery writer and critic Julian Symons, has written that Christie's appeal will continue unabated into future generations because she is "the master conjurer of our time" who keeps seducing new crops of readers with a literary "sleight of hand" nobody has ever matched.

"Christie was a very religious woman, though not at all a proselytizer. She believed there was good, as well as evil, and that good would triumph. And therefore she presents someone like Hercule Poirot, who's sort of the spirit of good, a person who can come into a situation where evil has been committed . . . and by using his little gray cells, his God-given ability, is able to prevent that person from capitalizing on her evil action, or his evil action. He is the god in the machine. He comes forth for goodness and says, 'No, you will not get away with it, I will prevent you.' . . . She also believed that people who combat evil . . . don't necessarily look like Gary Cooper or John Wayne. They don't have to be . . . physically strong, macho people. They are people like Poirot [who] have a strong sense of inner certainty and morality, who are not interventionist in a certain way, but who, when called upon, will work for good."

—Christie biographer
Gillian Gill

MURDER BY THE BOOK

Agatha Christie is awakened one night in 1975 by the fierce barking of her dog, Bingo. Rising in alarm, she surprises an intruder in her country home: Hercule Poirot.

At least that's what happens in *Murder by the Book,* a British television drama by Nick Evans, which was telecast in the U.S. on the Arts & Entertainment cable network in 1990. It's certainly the most unusual program so far about the late queen of mystery. Under questioning by Christie (Dame Peggy Ashcroft), Poirot (Ian Holm) explains he is working on a most unusual murder case, which he's already solved, even though the murder has not yet been committed. The intended victim, you see, is Poirot himself—and Dame Agatha the potential killer.

The ingenious plot stems, of course, from Christie's legendary decision to kill off her famous detective because she'd finally grown tired of writing about him. She gave him a fatal heart attack in the book *Curtain,* which she wrote in the early 1940s, then locked away in a vault for publication only after her death. The drama becomes a duel of wits between author and character as Poirot attempts to discover why his creator wanted to write *finis* to his extraordinary career. The dubious answer: She is doing it for his own good, so some inferior writer won't try to keep him on the job after her death.

Christie finally let *Curtain* be published in October 1975, just a few months before her death the following January, and it became a bestseller.

"When Agatha Christie submitted her first Hercule Poirot novel in 1920, she ended it with a courtroom scene so filled with inaccuracies the publishers forced her to rewrite it. After that, she always asked an expert—a lawyer, a doctor, a dentist—when she wasn't entirely sure of her facts."

—DIANA RIGG

MAD WIFE DISEASE

The most famous incident of Christie's young adulthood was her mysterious 11-day "disappearance" in 1926. Her car was found abandoned along a public road in Surrey with her fur coat and overnight bag still in it. Foul play was suspected and a nationwide search commenced for the famous writer. It turned out she had taken an assumed name—actually, the name of her husband's mistress—and checked into a remote hotel. Her marriage ended after this unexplained disappearance, but most experts now believe she suffered a breakdown of some kind over her husband's infidelity.

SELECTED BIBLIOGRAPHY

Hercule Poirot stories: *The Mysterious Affair at Styles,* 1920; *Murder on the Links,* 1923; *Poirot Investigates,* 1924; *The Murder of Roger Ackroyd,* 1926; *The Big Four,* 1927; *The Mystery of the Blue Train,* 1928; *Peril at End House,* 1932; *Thirteen at Dinner,* 1933; *Black Coffee,* 1934; *Murder on the Orient Express,* 1934; *Murder in Three Acts,* 1935; *Death in the Air,* 1935; *The ABC Murders,* 1935; *Murder in Mesopotamia,* 1936; *Cards on the Table,* 1936; *Poirot Loses a Client,* 1937; *Death on the Nile,* 1937; *Dead Man's Mirror,* 1937; *Appointment with Death,* 1938; *Murder for Christmas,* 1938; *The Regatta Mystery,* 1939; *Sad Cypress,* 1940; *The Patriotic Murders,* 1940; *Evil Under the Sun,* 1941; *Murder in Retrospect,* 1943; *Murder After Hours,* 1946; *The Labors of Hercules,* 1947; *There Is a Tide,* 1948; *Witness for the Prosecution and Other Stories,* 1948; *The Underdog and Other Stories,* 1951; *Mrs. McGinty's Dead,* 1952; *Funerals Are Fatal,* 1953; *Hickory, Dickory, Death,* 1955; *Dead Man's Folly,* 1956; *Cat Among the Pigeons,* 1959; *The Adventure of the Christmas Pudding,* 1960; *Double Sin and Other Stories,* 1961; *The Clocks,* 1963; *Third Girl,* 1966; *Hallowe'en Party,* 1969; *Elephants Can Remember,* 1972; *Poirot's Early Cases,* 1974; *Curtain,* 1975.

Jane Marple stories: *Murder at the Vicarage,* 1930; *The Tuesday Club Murders,* 1932; *The Regatta Mystery,* 1939; *The Body in the Library,* 1942; *The Moving Finger,* 1942; *A Murder Is Announced,* 1950; *Three Blind Mice and Other Stories,* 1950; *Murder with Mirrors,* 1952; *A Pocket Full of Rye,* 1953; *What Mrs. McGillicuddy Saw,* 1957; *The Adventure of the Christmas Pudding,* 1960; *Double Sin and Other Stories,* 1961; *The Mirror Crack'd,* 1962; *A Caribbean Mystery,* 1964; *At Bertram's Hotel,* 1965; *Nemesis,* 1971; *Sleeping Murder,* 1976.

Tommy and Tuppence Beresford stories: *The Secret Adversary,* 1922; *Partners in Crime,* 1929; *N or M?,* 1941; *By the Pricking of My Thumbs,* 1968; *Postern of Fate,* 1974.

Other major works: *The Seven Dials Mystery,* 1929; *Mr. Parker Pyne, Detective,* 1934; *Witness for the Prosecution* (play), 1953; *And Then There Were None,* 1939; *The Mousetrap* (play), 1952; *Ordeal by Innocence,* 1958.

The Consummate Poirot:

ACTOR
DAVID SUCHET

POIROT'S LONELY HEART'S CLUB FANS

A woman wrote to Suchet saying she was recently widowed and very lonely. She told him she still sets two places for dinner in front of the television set for the nights Poirot is on. Suchet, who receives thousands of fan letters, says many are like this one.

BACK IN 1986, AGATHA CHRISTIE'S DAUGHTER, ROSALIND HICKS, WATCHED A British television series called *Blott on the Landscape* and was immediately charmed by the actor playing the eccentric handyman—a small fellow who wore a beret and sported a crisp little mustache. "He'd make a wonderful Hercule Poirot," she observed at the time. A decade later David Suchet isn't just a wonderful Poirot, he's the definitive Poirot, the one all others must be measured against from now on. He has played Poirot more times than any other actor and with infinitely greater accuracy.

BEATING THE CHRISTIE JINX

"Agatha Christie was quite famous for not liking any of the portrayals she'd seen during her lifetime," Suchet recalls. "I really wanted to put that right, so every endeavor on my part was to serve her memory." Suchet was somewhat intimidated by the fact that some of England's finest actors had tried the role, among them Charles Laughton, Francis L. Sullivan, Austin Trevor, Albert Finney, Peter Ustinov, and Ian Holm. Though Finney's Poirot in the 1974 Sidney Lumet film *Murder on the Orient Express* had been widely praised—Christie herself mercifully limited her criticism to Finney's mustache—he was one of the few actors the Poirot purists didn't crucify for blaspheming Christie's vision. Suchet hoped he might beat the Christie jinx.

Before Poirot, Suchet had starred in two widely seen series—*The Life of Freud* and *Blott on the Landscape*—and had been featured in numerous television shows, including *Reilly, Ace of Spies* and *Cause Célèbre* for Mystery!. He had also appeared in many feature films, from *The Falcon and the Snowman* to *Harry and the Hendersons*. Though he acquired a measure of fame from some of these roles, Suchet knew that few people recognized him from one role to another. As a member of England's Royal Shakespeare Company, he was able to disappear so completely into the characters he played that hardly anyone had any idea what he really looked like.

For Poirot, a number of theatrical aids helped Suchet become his character. Though Suchet is small in stature, like the literary Poirot, Suchet is much slimmer and had to be fitted with body padding to look the part. He was also given wing collars to make his neck appear fatter. But it was the waxed and sculpted mustache that really completed the transformation. "Typically, in the morning makeup, when Patricia Kirkman put that mustache on me, that's when I became Poirot," says Suchet.

Recognizing the importance of voice, he adopted a distinctive one for his character. While Suchet's natural voice is bell-clear and mellow, with a cultured English accent, he chose one for Poirot that is smaller, more precisely clipped in sound—and more French than the accent of an authentic Belgian.

Poirot's distinctive walk—tiny, light, quick steps—was developed after Suchet had tried several other approaches. Finally, he went back to Christie's own description: "A mincing gait with his feet tightly enclosed in his patent leather boots." Says Suchet, "That clinched it for me!"

To fully understand Poirot, Suchet literally read every word Christie had written about him. "Initially, I wondered why this egomaniac was so popular," says Suchet. "I searched and searched for the reason and finally discovered Christie always referred to the 'twinkle' in his eye. That's what I had to find. Otherwise, he would have been a real pain."

WOULDN'T MUSS UP HIS MUSTACHE

Suchet is clear on the subject of Poirot's sexuality: He's heterosexual, though he seems to become more asexual as he ages in the stories. He was once in love with a Russian countess, who claimed Poirot was the father of her child. In a Christie story that wasn't filmed, Poirot denies any such claim to fatherhood—and Suchet believes he was telling the truth. He doesn't think Poirot ever really got that far with any woman. "You can't imagine him doing anything like that at all. At least, I can't," says Suchet, who's married and a father himself. "It would have mussed up his mustache!"

Suchet thinks Poirot generates great respect for his brilliant deductive mind, but also immense sympathy for his vulnerability. "You felt a great sense of isolation with the man," he says. "He has emotions—and a great sensual side to his personality that he cannot release." Suchet is convinced that the lonely, sensitive aspect of Poirot came across to the television audience. "He seemed to touch people in an entirely different way," he says. "When I was filming, the women who came on the set would tell me it was extraordinary being in his company because he made them feel so safe."

In 1995, when the sixth series had been completed, Suchet learned from rumor that there would be no more. "I was very surprised because we were still reaching 11 to 11.5 million viewers in England. It's very popular in America, and it's been sold to 53 other countries. With about 12 million people watching in each country, you can multiply that and see there's a hell of a lot of people still watching and enjoying Poirot."

Suchet's fear that playing Poirot so long might cost him future roles has not come to pass. In 1996, he played the Jewish biblical character Aaron in the television miniseries *Moses;* the Arab terrorist leader in the big-screen thriller *Executive Decision,* and hard-drinking George opposite Diana Rigg's abusive Martha in a London stage revival of Edward Albee's *Who's Afraid of Virginia Woolf?.* He took no souvenirs with him from the *Poirot* series, saying he doesn't need such things to remember a grand, fulfilling experience. "My scrapbook is full of Poirot," he says. "If I have anything to treasure, it's the pleasure and gratitude that people have shown me personally in the portraying of that role."

"Who could I have as a detective? I reviewed such detectives as I had met and admired in books. There was Sherlock Holmes, the one and only— I should never be able to emulate him. There was Arsène Lupin—was he a criminal or a detective? Anyway, not my kind. There was the young journalist Rouletabille in The Mystery of the Yellow Room—*that was the sort of person whom I would like to invent.*

Then I remembered our Belgian refugees. We had quite a colony of refugees living in the parish of Tor. Why not make my detective a Belgian, I thought? There were all types of refugees. How about a refugee police officer? A retired police officer. Not too young a one . . ."

—AGATHA CHRISTIE,
from *Agatha Christie: An Autobiography*

LORD PETER WIMSEY

DOROTHY L. SAYERS' LORD PETER WIMSEY

Based on the novels by
Dorothy L. Sayers

TODAY THE VERY THOUGHT OF A DETECTIVE WHO WEARS A TOP HAT AND A MONOCLE AND GOES ABOUT WITH HIS PERSONAL VALET SEEMS LUDICROUS. IT WAS ONLY SLIGHTLY LESS LUDICROUS IN 1923 WHEN DOROTHY L. SAYERS CREATED LORD PETER WIMSEY, THE DEAN OF "GENTLEMAN DETECTIVES," AND HELPED USHER IN THE "GOLDEN AGE" OF THE DETECTIVE STORY.

Sayers' notion of a high-born, titled sleuth was a useful device for explaining how a private detective could gain access to so many people in high places in a structured, class-conscious society. And the fact that Wimsey often behaved like a twit and looked perfectly ridiculous probably didn't hurt his popularity with Sayers' great mass of ordinary readers, who may have accorded lords of the realm the requisite awe, but probably preferred to think of them as silly, privileged people whose feet seldom touched the ground.

How ludicrous was Wimsey? On the first page of *Whose Body?*, her first novel about him, Sayers tells us his "amiable" face looked as if it had spontaneously bloomed from under his top hat "as white maggots breed from Gorgonzola." That's some imagery for a newly-born detective hero! But, like her mystery writing colleague Agatha Christie, who had created an equally absurd-looking master sleuth in Hercule Poirot three years earlier, Sayers may have been consciously trying to distance Wimsey from his obvious inspiration—Conan Doyle's Sherlock Holmes—by making him Holmes' exact opposite. If so, the strategy didn't always work, especially when Wimsey himself, in that first novel, appraised himself in a mirror before going out and remarked, "Enter Sherlock Holmes, disguised as a walking gentleman."

LEAVING THE TWIT BEHIND

Happily, Lord Peter Wimsey gradually matured into something quite different from the young fop of that first mystery: a decent, fair-minded man who often used his superior intellect for the common good. Moreover, he soon enthralled hordes of devoted fans, who knew he possessed one of the keenest minds in mystery fiction and appreciated the fact that he was witty, convivial, and nowhere near the effete snob he seemed at first acquaintance.

The Wimsey who came briefly to Mystery! for three adventures in the fall of 1987 was the mature and attractive figure of the later period. The three Sayers novels adapted for Mystery!—*Strong Poison, Have His Carcase,* and *Gaudy Night*— were from the 1930s and concerned the years in which he meets, falls in love with, and woos mystery writer Harriet Vane. Lord Peter Wimsey was already familiar to American

PRODUCTION COMPANY
BBC

YEAR
1987

MAIN CAST
Lord Peter Wimsey
EDWARD PETHERBRIDGE

Harriet Vane
HARRIET WALTER

Bunter
RICHARD MORANT

audiences, having been seen on Masterpiece Theatre between 1973 and 1977 with Ian Carmichael in the lead role.

Though Carmichael's Wimsey was extremely popular with both critics and the public, a younger actor was needed for this much more romantic rendition of the famous detective. The BBC finally settled on Edward Petherbridge, a veteran stage actor from the Royal Shakespeare Company (RSC).

Petherbridge was a good choice for American audiences as well. He had recently been seen as Newman Noggs in the Mobil Showcase television production of the RSC's *Nicholas Nickleby* and had received much favorable publicity in the U.S. with an earlier one-man show. His 1986 appearance in Chicago with a series of plays from a National Theatre subcompany he headed with actor Ian McKellen was also well received. Though his post-Wimsey television performances have not been widely seen in the U.S., he did appear in one huge hit of the 1990s—NBC's 1996 *Gulliver's Travels* miniseries, playing one of the doctors who kept Ted Danson's Lemuel Gulliver in the lunatic asylum.

SILLINESS A COVER

Petherbridge had never read a Wimsey mystery when he was signed for the part and had only vague memories of having seen Carmichael's Wimsey on television. After reading the three books being adapted for the series and researching the character further, Petherbridge concluded Wimsey was actually a serious, intelligent man whose outward silliness often was just a cover-up for the uneasiness he felt in social circles since suffering from shellshock during his service in World War I.

That knowledge colored Petherbridge's performance, which many critics celebrated as "darker" and more serious than Carmichael's. Though many critics remained loyal to the Carmichael version of Wimsey, few failed to note that Petherbridge was a better physical match for Sayers' Wimsey. "I'm tall and slight like Wimsey," Petherbridge told one interviewer, "and I'm good at looking intelligent. Other actors give off more carnal qualities, but I'm afraid I have to work at them."

To further Petherbridge's resemblance to Sayers' Wimsey, the television producers had his hair dyed blond. Fortunately, Petherbridge had worked hard to lose his original Yorkshire working-class accent early in his acting career and didn't find it daunting to say lines like "Cheery-frightfully-o" in Wimsey's upper-class accent. His biggest problem: keeping the monocle from falling out of his eye because of the slippery makeup he wore for the cameras.

SAYERS' ALTER EGO

To play Harriet Vane, the producers went to another experienced RSC actor— tall, dark Harriet Walter, who had worked with Petherbridge in *Nicholas Nickleby,* playing Madeline Bray. She had been in a few feature films, including *The Good Father,* but was largely a new face for U.S. viewers. Walter sided with those who believe Sayers was portraying herself in Harriet Vane. She played Vane as a woman wrapped up in an inner struggle, jealously guarding the independence she had won with her writing career, yet recognizing her budding love for Wimsey and her longing for marriage and a family.

"I've had so many letters asking how do you keep in the monocle . . . it makes a change from 'How do you learn your lines,' I must say . . . The answer to both questions is, with great difficulty."

—EDWARD PETHERBRIDGE

"Sayers' attraction to Wimsey was no secret. Her colleagues used to laugh about her obvious infatuation. Ngaio Marsh said that when Sayers 'regrettably' fell in love with her own creation, she made 'rather an ass of both of them in the process.' Others were kinder. Rosemary Anne Sisson, who adapted our version, observes, 'It was a kind of daydream. Wimsey began as quite ordinary, and then grew into the man Miss Sayers never met— sensitive, mature, intelligent. And that's why I've no doubt Harriet Vane is Dorothy L. Sayers.'"

—VINCENT PRICE

In the first mystery, *Strong Poison*, Vane has been jailed on charges of murdering her former lover. Smitten with her, Wimsey vows to prove Vane innocent and openly declares his love for her. In their first face-to-face meeting, he shocks Vane by proposing marriage. In the second story, *Have His Carcase*, Vane goes on a brief holiday to Cornwall to recover from the rigors of her trial—and stumbles into a murder case, which Wimsey turns up to solve. For the final story, Vane attends a college reunion at Oxford and is asked to help solve a murder there. Naturally, her fervent admirer is called upon to use his detecting skills.

The Wimsey-Vane romance is probably the most famous in mystery fiction and was especially relevant in the 1980s, when, like Vane, many female viewers were struggling with decisions about career and possible married life.

MARRIAGE A NO-SHOW

Sadly, Mystery! viewers never got to see the payoff to this classic romance. Sayers wrote about the marriage in *Busman's Honeymoon*, which couldn't be filmed for Mystery! because Sayers had sold the film rights to Hollywood in the 1930s; it was turned into the 1940 film *Haunted Honeymoon*, but efforts to secure the rights for a new BBC-TV version weren't successful.

Even in the 1990s, Lord Peter Wimsey is still one of the most influential of all detective characters, and Sayers' novels about his most famous cases continue to be widely read by new generations. Though Wimsey's run on Mystery! was alarmingly brief, it would have been inconceivable for the man with the monocle to have been left off the series' roster of great detectives.

"In a [list] of least coveted acting roles, Lord Peter Wimsey, the noble criminologist, would probably appear close to top. Dorothy L. Sayers' monocled dilettante, who dabbled in crime-detection for intellectual thrills to enliven his parasitic upper-class lifestyle, is a hard man to view sympathetically in these more egalitarian times.

In Strong Poison, the first of a series of Sayers mysteries, Edward Petherbridge transformed this character into a fascinating phenomenon. Wimsey's brittle dialogue and vestigial emotions acquired the appearance of deep anguish. Heaven knows how he did it, but Petherbridge even contrived to invest the phrase 'cheery frightfully o' with an aura of neurotic sexuality."

—CELIA BRAYFIELD,
London Daily News

Rebel with a Cause:

AUTHOR
DOROTHY L. SAYERS

FREE-SPIRITED, UNCONVENTIONAL, ALWAYS CHALLENGING SOCIETY'S MORES, Dorothy L. Sayers might have found her antecedents among other like-minded women writers such as George Eliot or Collette—except each was unconventional in her own way. Sayers carried on a rather public love affair with one man and bore the child of another. At a time when young women were expected to just get married and raise children, Sayers pursued a college education from a university that wasn't even acknowledging women students. Later she forged an independent career as a novelist who could support herself in comfort.

Born in Oxford, England, in 1893, Sayers was the daughter of Henry Sayers, head of the Christchurch College Choir School and college chaplain—you don't get much more conventional than that. Fortunately, she took after her mother, Helen, who was livelier and had her own independent streak. Accounts of Sayers' youth suggest she was a lonely child. Though an excellent student, she was not popular with either students or teachers. Still, her academic accomplishments earned her a scholarship to Somerville College, Oxford, to study languages (she had learned Latin by age seven).

At that time, the university did not recognize female scholars and provided them only with "residence halls" where they might enroll for study. Sayers was a great success at Oxford, taking part in campus drama activities and enjoying herself immensely. Yet she wasn't able to earn a degree when she had completed her courses because Oxford hadn't officially ruled Somerville a part of the university. In 1919, she finally became one of the first female students allowed to go through formal graduation ceremonies at Oxford, where she took first honors in medieval literature. Sayers later used her Somerville days as background for *Gaudy Night*.

Sayers had worked briefly for a publishing house in Oxford and after her graduation went to work for Benson's advertising agency as a copywriter. Her most notable contribution there: the slogan "Guinness is good for you" for the famous Irish stout (it's high in vitamins). While dreaming up slogans for Benson's, Sayers was romantically involved with noted intellectual John Cournos, with whom she had a complex and stormy love affair. Both were trying to write novels at the time—Sayers was working on *Strong Poison*. In that novel Harriet Vane is accused of murdering her ex-lover Philip Boyes with a dose of arsenic. The murder may have been a bit of wishful thinking on Sayers' part: Cournos is assumed by many to be the role model for Boyes.

In 1923, Sayers took up with another young man, who dropped her after she became pregnant with his child. She decided to keep her pregnancy a secret from everyone including her parents—and succeeded because she was a large woman who had been putting on considerable weight even before the pregnancy. She took only eight weeks off work to give birth to a son, John Anthony, who was raised by her cousin Ivy, her closest childhood friend. Sayers provided support for her son and visited him frequently, but he never lived with her.

In her few interviews, Sayers often said she began writing mystery stories in order to earn money to indulge her hobby—collecting rare books, a passion she shared with Lord Peter Wimsey. By the late 1920s her books had become so popular that she was able to support herself from her literary earnings and give up her advertising job. Around the same time she married Arthur "Mac" Fleming.

WIMSEY TO DANTE

Sayers eventually lost interest in mystery writing, even though she was a founding member of the famous Detection Club and had served as its president. She intended to stop writing Wimsey stories after Lord Peter and Harriet Vane were married, but she wrote a few more volumes of Wimsey short stories and saw the couple through the birth of three sons. Her final Wimsey story was published in 1942 and was her last mystery of any kind.

The remainder of Sayers' career was devoted to writing theological essays, a new translation of Dante's *Divine Comedy,* and a series of radio plays on the life of Jesus Christ. Her disregard for conventional behavior hadn't abated: The religious plays were severely criticized because she had Christ speaking modern colloquial English. While working on a translation of Dante's *Paradiso,* she suffered a heart attack and died in December 1957.

"[Sayers'] erudite references, comedy-of-manners-like social commentary, untranslated French and Latin passages (many of them substantial), and complex characters made her the darling of overeducated pop-culturists. And that makes her work the perfect material for the PBS audience."

—CLIF AND SUSANNAH GARBODEN

SELECTED BIBLIOGRAPHY

Whose Body?, 1923; *Clouds of Witness,* 1926; *Unnatural Death,* 1927; *The Unpleasantness at the Bellona Club,* 1928; *Lord Peter Views the Body* (short stories), 1928; *Strong Poison,* 1930; *The Documents in the Case,* 1930; *The Five Red Herrings,* 1931; *Have His Carcase,* 1932; *Murder Must Advertise,* 1933; *The Nine Tailors,* 1934; *Gaudy Night,* 1935; *Busman's Honeymoon,* 1937; *In the Teeth of the Evidence* (short stories), 1939; *Hangman's Holiday* (short stories), 1942.

Resourceful and Resilient:

SIDEKICK
BUNTER
(RICHARD MORANT)

Bunter may appear to be a servant to Lord Peter Wimsey, but the version of him seen on Mystery! is definitely not the Jeeves stereotype of the snooty family retainer. Rather, he's a modern fellow more in the spirit of the 1980s, when the series was made, than the 1930s, when it takes place. Bunter was a sergeant under Captain Wimsey during World War I, when they formed a bond that would last a lifetime. Bunter functions as a mechanic and cook for Wimsey as well as valet—and has lots of other skills, including photography. It was Bunter's photos of footprints and fingerprints in the *Gaudy Night* episode that helped Wimsey solve the mystery. Bunter lives in a class-conscious society, so he knows his place, but he's regarded as a friend by Wimsey, not an employee.

Playing Bunter on Mystery! was Richard Morant, a veteran actor who first became a television star in England playing the bully Flashman in the BBC's *Tom Brown's Schooldays.* A well-traveled stage actor, he's one of the few who can claim to have done Shakespeare in repertory in war-torn Beirut.

"To Sayers, Bunter served as Wimsey's alter-ego. He was able to do the necessary things too improper for the aristocratic Wimsey: He can chat up a suspect's kitchen staff and charm them into spilling the beans, and occasionally break into music hall impersonations or vulgar songs . . . all, of course, in the line of duty.

And don't be deceived by the friendly patter between the two men. They each respect the strict codes established for servant and master, although Bunter doesn't hesitate, if pressed, to tell Lord Peter off . . . always in the most courteous way. It's a duo that owes as much to the medieval partnership of knight and squire as it does to P. G. Wodehouse's Jazz Age pair, Jeeves and Bertie Wooster."

—VINCENT PRICE

A Woman Ahead of Her Time:

COLLEAGUE AND LOVER
HARRIET VANE
(HARRIET WALTER)

Many mystery scholars say author Dorothy L. Sayers fell in love with her own make-believe detective and lived out her fantasies about him by creating Harriet Vane in her own image. Sayers never verified nor denied the rumors. Vincent Price, in his introduction to *Strong Poison,* cited all the obvious similarities: Both were mystery writers, both signed their name using a middle initial, both attended Oxford when few other women did, and both lived in the same Bloomsbury neighborhood.

Harriet Vane is essential to at least four Wimsey novels, starting with *Strong Poison,* in which Sayers characterized Vane as a strong-willed young woman who already has made her reputation as a popular mystery writer. She also made it clear that Vane is adamantly independent in her thinking and not at all afraid to defy conventional moral attitudes in England, circa 1930.

A college-educated woman, Vane supports herself without inherited wealth and lives a free-spirited, sexually-liberated life. She is a feminist ahead of her time who, while aware of her attraction to Wimsey, is most concerned that a romance with him might compromise her desire to continue her own career. That the successful and most unconventional Sayers patterned Vane on herself virtually guaranteed that she would be a maturing influence on Lord Peter Wimsey—which she definitely turned out to be.

Walter has been seen by American audiences in other Mystery! series, on Masterpiece Theatre, and in the film *Sense and Sensibility.*

ALBERT CAMPION

CAMPION

Based on the novels by
Margery Allingham

ALBERT CAMPION'S 1989 DEBUT AS THE NEWEST DETECTIVE IN THE MYSTERY!
STABLE OF ALL-STAR SLEUTHS WAS CONSIDERABLY MORE AUSPICIOUS
THAN HIS LITERARY DEBUT 60 YEARS EARLIER IN MARGERY ALLINGHAM'S
The Crime at Black Dudley.

In that 1929 novel (known in the U.S. as *The Black Dudley Murder*), Campion is neither the main character nor much of a hero. He is, in fact, what another character accurately describes as "just a silly ass," a goofy adventurer who is doing a job for a shady racketeer and inadvertently winds up helping the good guys out of a jam. He fares even worse in a 1956 feature of Allingham's 1952 novel *Tiger in the Smoke.* The British filmmakers tossed out Campion altogether!

Campion's first appearance on Mystery! put him in a much brighter spotlight. He is clearly the hero of that first two-part adventure, *The Case of the Late Pig,* and though effete and a tad starchy, he is far from a silly ass. Moreover, he is dressed to the nines in an impeccable gentleman's wardrobe, circa 1934, as the central figure in a handsome period production developed for the BBC by legendary writer/producer John Hawkesworth *(Upstairs, Downstairs, The Duchess of Duke Street, Danger UXB, The Flame Trees of Thika,* and *The Adventures of Sherlock Holmes).*

Helping to make the debut of Campion a special event for Mystery! fans was the fact that the sleuth was being portrayed by popular Peter Davison, an actor already well-known to sophisticated American viewers from his roles as farm boy Tom Holland in *Love for Lydia* on Masterpiece Theatre, as Yorkshire veterinarian Tristan Farnon in *All Creatures Great and Small,* and, most especially, as the fifth "doctor" (1981–84) in the long-running *Doctor Who* science-fiction series.

FROM SILLINESS TO SUAVITY

Hawkesworth and producer Ken Riddington wisely decided to start the television adventures of Albert Campion in the early 1930s when the detective was in a more mature phase of his career. By the time author Allingham got him to that point, he had shed some of his more egregious characteristics and finally was emerging as a suave gentleman sleuth who wouldn't suffer quite so much from the inevitable comparisons with Dorothy L. Sayers' aristocratic detective, Lord Peter Wimsey, whose literary debut preceded Campion's by six years.

Prior to that, Campion had been an unbearable twit who cracked insufferable jokes in a high-pitched voice and was barely tolerated by the gentry around him. Far from imposing, he presented a most unromantic, unheroic image of manhood. Allingham first described him on paper as "the fresh-faced young man with the tow-coloured hair and the foolish pale-blue eyes behind tortoiseshell-rimmed spectacles."

PRODUCTION COMPANY
BBC

YEARS
1989–1991

MAIN CAST
Albert Campion
PETER DAVISON

Magersfontein Lugg
BRIAN GLOVER

Inspector Oates
ANDREW BURT

The makers of *Campion* sagely gave him a deeper, more masculine voice, darkened his hair to a light shade of brown, and nudged him away from his silliness into suavity. But they couldn't very well dispense with the spectacles: They became his signature look and were used as his identifying "calling card" in the opening credits of the new series.

The glasses signify an intellectual man who addresses problems with a maximum of close scrutiny and perhaps a minimum of physical action. In that sense, Campion's eyeglasses do for him what spectacles did for movie comedian Harold Lloyd: alert audiences to his gentle nature and arouse their sympathy. They may also be a cosmetic affectation to fool his adversaries into seriously underestimating both his audacity and his mettle. In *The Case of the Late Pig*, Campion gets into fist fights and handles himself rather well, even when his hulking valet, the ex-thug Magersfontein Lugg (Brian Glover), is not there to help him out.

A MAN OF MANY ALIASES

If his spectacles are, indeed, an element of disguise for Campion, that fits his character neatly. Allingham created him as a blue-blooded aristocrat, the black sheep of a very highly-placed English family, who makes up the name Albert Campion to shield his true identity. Among his many aliases are Mornington Dodd, Tootles Ash, Christopher Twelvetrees, and just plain Orlando. Allingham never disclosed his true identity, though it seems any cut-rate detective might have found it out. Campion is Cambridge-educated, after all, and it seems likely he was registered there under his real name. Allingham permitted one clue to escape her cloak of secrecy: His real family name begins with the letter K. Yet when someone once surmises Campion might actually be the Duke of Kent, Allingham lets it be known his family is much closer to the throne than that!

That raises the question of what dreadful act Campion has committed to become the black sheep of such a family. He has enough money behind him to drive a spiffy Lagonda sports car, dress like a *GQ* cover boy, and keep a full-time manservant like Lugg. But he lives at 17 Bottle Street in a flat above a police station near London's Piccadilly Circus, rather than in more opulent digs in Mayfair, and he always seems to be working for pay on his various cases.

Though handsomely filmed, mostly in authentic locations in Essex and East Anglia, the Campion adventures never became wildly popular, and no more episodes were ordered after the 1990–91 season.

Hulking Ex-Thug:

SIDEKICK
MAGERSFONTEIN LUGG

(BRIAN GLOVER)

Magersfontein Lugg is the most unorthodox of the Mystery! family of sidekicks: a former burglar and ex-convict of hulking dimensions, shiny bald pate, and withering glare who usually dresses in black and wears a bowler hat. Lugg's official position is valet to detective Albert Campion, but bodyguard seems a more appropriate title. If he can't scare off the bad guys with his looks, he usually can handle them by shifting into his bone-crusher mode.

In the first Mystery! adventure, Campion seems rather inconsiderate of Lugg, at one point making him give up his seat to another passenger, leaving him to catch a bus back to the estate where they're staying. Most of the time, though, their relationship proceeds on much more equal terms, even though Lugg is portrayed as a lower-class Cockney who is, by definition, in a subservient role. Lugg is seldom deferential to Campion, and Campion bears Lugg's effronteries with customary good humor.

Lugg was played by former professional wrestler Brian Glover, who retired after 20 years in the ring to begin an acting career, after being encouraged by good reviews for his performance —as a wrestler, no less—in the Royal Shakespeare Company's *A Midsummer Night's Dream.* Glover has the distinction of being beaten up by John Wayne in *Brannigan* and has appeared in such films as *The Great Train Robbery, Quilp,* and *An American Werewolf in London.* In the 1990s he helped another television detective, playing the ex-wrestler landlord of private eye Anna Lee (Imogen Stubbs).

Writer from Childhood:

AUTHOR
MARGERY ALLINGHAM

MARGERY ALLINGHAM, THE CREATOR OF ALBERT CAMPION, LIKED TO TELL people that writing came as naturally to her as it would for "a shopkeeper's child to play at keeping shop." Little wonder, since Allingham grew up in a home where being able to express oneself by writing was taken for granted. Her mother wrote stories for women's magazines while her father was the editor of the *London Journal* and, later, a prolific writer of serials for pulp magazines. Born in 1904, Allingham had written her first story by the tender age of seven. The tale found its way into the children's column of the *Christian Globe* in 1912. Though her grandfather owned the paper, the family had high professional standards, so Margery's story made it on its own merits.

This early success was no fluke. Allingham kept writing throughout her youth, sometimes dazzling her teachers with her raw talent and prompting one teacher to accuse her of plagiarism! By 19, Allingham had published her first novel. Before that, though, Allingham earned her first real money from writing by doing short "novelizations" of current hit movies for a British cinema fan magazine. Some collectors might pay a pretty penny today for a 10,000-word Allingham version of *Nanook of the North* or one of her occasional epic magazine serials like *The Society Millgirl* or *The Eight Wicked Millionaires*.

At 23, Allingham married artist/writer Philip Youngman Carter, who had designed the cover for her first novel. He was her career adviser from then on, and Allingham freely admitted that he also was a collaborator for her subsequent novels. In fact, Carter actually completed her unfinished novel, *Cargo of Eagles*, after his wife's death and went on to write two more mysteries from her outlines. They lived most of their life together in the small village of Tolleshunt D'Arccy in Essex.

Beginning with her first Campion novel in 1929, Allingham wrote about her suave sleuth the rest of her life. Allingham's sister later revealed that Margery had altered Campion to be more like her real-life husband, Philip, and had patterned his courtship of Amanda Fitton after their own romance.

Literary critics most often praised Allingham's use of psychological motivations for her characters and her intellectual solutions to crimes. In real life, the author was a devoted fan of mystery writers Agatha Christie and Josephine Tey, but she refused to read any books by Dorothy L. Sayers, because she didn't want her development of Campion to be influenced by Sayers' very similar Lord Peter Wimsey, who had come on the mystery scene a few years before her own aristocratic detective. That didn't keep Allingham and Sayers from becoming good friends, though, and eventually neighbors.

Allingham was noted for her elaborate designs for gardens and widely praised for her civic work during World War II, when she helped relocate children from the German air blitz on London to temporary homes in her rural village, where she was a sort of

---

"Margery Allingham wrote her Campion stories in that rich period between the two world wars when readers were developing a taste for crime fiction of a higher quality. . . . Earlier crime writers could pen stories about the theft of the family jewels. But for the mostly female authors of the 'golden age' of detective fiction, a good murder was a minimum requirement. More than one was preferable. And not just any ordinary murder, either. Judging from most of the crime novels written between 1918 and 1935, English authors seemed to consider it impolite to bump off anyone below the rank of Earl. The scene of most crimes was usually a house with a name rather than a street address. And the most popular detectives were those with links to the Crown. . . . Middle-class readers enjoyed losing themselves in stories that took place in privileged settings: a country village or London's West End . . . And the works of almost all the crime writers 'between the Wars' seem to imply that only people with money were worth writing about. Most of the characters were of independent means—either born to wealth or at least on a modest pension. And rarely would a nine-to-five working man or woman appear—perhaps because it was important that all the suspects have enough leisure time to murder the victim. It's no surprise, then, that Albert Campion was a natural favorite among readers."

—DIANA RIGG

"Mrs. Miniver." She died in 1966, at age 62, unaware that her great detective would still be entertaining millions of new fans more than 30 years later.

SELECTED BIBLIOGRAPHY

Blackerchief Dick, 1923; *The Crime at Black Dudley (The Black Dudley Murder),* 1929; *Mystery Mile,* 1930; *Police at the Funeral,* 1931; *The Gyrth Chalice Mystery (Look to the Lady),* 1931; *Kingdom of Death (Sweet Danger),* 1933; *Death of a Ghost,* 1934; *Flowers for the Judge,* 1936; *The Case of the Late Pig,* 1937; *Mr. Campion, Criminologist,* 1937; *Dancers in Mourning (Who Killed Chloe?),* 1937; *The Fashion in Shrouds,* 1938; *Black Plumes,* 1940; *Traitor's Purse,* 1941; *The Galantrys,* 1943; *Pearls Before Swine (Coroner's Pidgin),* 1945; *The Case Book of Mr. Campion,* 1947; *Deadly Duo (Take Two at Bedtime),* 1949; *More Work for the Undertaker,* 1949; *Tiger in the Smoke,* 1952; *No Love Lost: Two Stories of Suspense,* 1954; *The Estate of the Beckoning Lady,* 1955; *Tether's End,* 1958; *Hide My Eyes,* 1958; *Three Cases for Mr. Campion,* 1961; *The China Governess,* 1962; *The Mind Readers,* 1965; *Cargo of Eagles,* 1967.

"We had this traveling library [in the small town where I grew up]. And we had a standing order for a dozen Agatha Christies and a dozen Margery Allinghams. Two strong men used to carry in all these books in a deep coffin."

—BRIAN GLOVER

"If you have an intelligent mind and you like to read and like to escape, then you require an intelligent literature of escape. I make no distinction between the novel and the thriller."

—MARGERY ALLINGHAM

GOOD GUYS AS BAD GUYS

PLAYING THE GOOD GUY CAN GET AWFULLY BORING YEAR AFTER
year, which is why so many of our favorite Mystery! heroes like to remind us they can
play villains, too. Here are some of their best efforts at earning boos and hisses.

JOHN THAW
(Inspector Morse) leads Sherlock Holmes on a merry chase as the sinister one-legged villain Jonathan Small in *The Sign of Four*.

PETER DAVISON
(Albert Campion) is the scoundrel Lance Fortescue in Miss Marple's *A Pocketful of Rye*.

DAVID BURKE
(Dr. Watson) has an extramarital affair with investigator Jemima Shore in *Quiet As a Nun* and orders wholesale executions as Soviet dictator Joseph Stalin in *Reilly, Ace of Spies*.

ROY MARSDEN
(Commander Adam Dalgliesh) puts on a long black cloak and scares the hell out of an English village as villainous John Stockton in Sherlock Holmes' *The Last Vampyre*.

CHERIE LUNGHI
is a madcap romantic heroine in Agatha Christie's *The Manhood of Edward Robinson*, but turns into the scheming, murderous Beatrice Manceau in *Praying Mantis*.

IAN HOLM
plays spy Bernard Samson in *Game, Set and Match* but is prosecuted for murdering his wife in *We, the Accused*.

LEO McKERN
(Horace Rumpole) thumbs his nose at justice as international criminal Basil Zaharov in *Reilly, Ace of Spies*.

PATRICK MALAHIDE
(Inspector Roderick Alleyn) plays a sleazy car salesman whom Inspector Morse tries to pin a double homicide on in *Driven to Distraction*.

JEREMY BRETT
(Sherlock Holmes) plays Max de Winter, who kills his first wife but pretends she drowned in a boating accident, in *Rebecca*.

THE CIVIL SERVANTS

*They put in long hours for slim wages
and endure some tiresome, bureaucratic bosses
who seldom appreciate their genius. They take an
awful lot of guff, these civil servants.*

- **INSPECTOR MORSE**
  INSPECTOR MORSE

- **COMMANDER ADAM DALGLIESH**
  DEATH OF AN EXPERT WITNESS, ET ALIA

- **DCI JANE TENNISON**
  PRIME SUSPECT

- **INSPECTOR RODERICK ALLEYN**
  ARTISTS IN CRIME,
  NGAIO MARSH'S ALLEYN MYSTERIES

- **INSPECTOR JULES MAIGRET**
  MAIGRET

INSPECTOR MORSE

INSPECTOR MORSE

*Based on the novels and characters
created by Colin Dexter*

FOR ANYONE RAISED ON A STEADY DIET OF AMERICAN PRIME-TIME
DETECTIVE SHOWS, THE ARRIVAL OF COLIN DEXTER'S *INSPECTOR MORSE*
ON MYSTERY! WAS CERTAIN TO BE A SHOCK. "I'M A QUITE DIFFERENT KETTLE
OF FISH," MORSE (JOHN THAW) TELLS HIS NEW AIDE, SERGEANT LEWIS
(KEVIN WHATELY), IN THAT FIRST PROGRAM.

It is a fair warning. Morse is often morose and cranky and, when he is, he'd rather stare at the bubbles in his beer than engage in casual conversation. His lack of normal social graces is so profound that Lewis looks positively dumbfounded when Morse asks him, in the *Twilight of the Gods* episode, how the wife and kids are doing. It is the first time in seven seasons that Morse has shown any interest whatever in Lewis' family.

Morse is definitely not a demographically correct sort of television detective. He's middle-aged with white hair, not the macho young stud favored by American advertisers. But then Barnaby Jones was an older guy with white hair, too, and he had a pretty long run. There's a big difference, though: You'd never catch Barnaby rushing off to choir practice right after cuffing a criminal, as Morse does in his very first television case, *The Dead of Jericho.*

Like Columbo and Spenser, Morse refuses to acknowledge his first name because it's so awful. If his nickname is any indication—in the *Deceived by Flight* episode, we learn the boys at school used to call him "Pagan"—one can hardly blame him.

UNORTHODOX IN EVERY WAY

Morse is a ruin romantically. It's almost a requirement for television detectives to be single guys with a roving eye, but most do a lot better with women than the bachelor Morse. Poor Morse has a terrible habit of developing crushes on women who turn out to be criminals before the episode's over. If the women don't hang themselves, they wind up behind bars.

Like Hercule Poirot, Morse is erudite to a fault, which seems just right for a policeman whose beat includes Oxford University and its Thames Valley environs. He loves opera, especially Wagner, knows a good deal about art, drama, and literature, and even attends lectures that have nothing to do with forensics or criminal psychology. But his erudition doesn't always serve him as well as it does Poirot. In that first mystery, for example, he develops a theory about a killer with an Oedipus complex after finding a copy of Sophocles' *Oedipus Rex* near the crime scene. Lewis, who's never heard of Sophocles, listens in rapt attention as Morse outlines his theory, then politely refrains from rubbing it in too much when Morse's theory collapses around him.

**PRODUCTION
COMPANY**
Zenith Production
for Central Independent
Television

YEARS
1988–

MAIN CAST
Chief Inspector Morse
JOHN THAW

Detective Sergeant Lewis
KEVIN WHATELY

Chief Superintendent Strange
JAMES GROUT

Max
PETER WOODTHORPE

Dr. Grayling Russell
AMANDA HILLWOOD

Morse's eccentricities don't always get him in trouble with the police brass, but he's certainly been reprimanded by "the super" enough times. Morse breaks his share of rules, including a fair number of fundamental ones. He lies on the witness stand in *Service of All the Dead* to help get a lesser sentence for a female suspect he fancies, and in *Driven to Distraction*, Lewis almost asks for a transfer because Morse insists on searching a suspect's property without a warrant. Fortunately, Morse usually doesn't get caught doing such things.

A CLEVER SOD

What bothers his superiors about Morse is his apparent lack of ambition to rise in the Thames Valley Police and his ineptness with office politics. "You're a clever sod," his boss, Chief Superintendent Strange (James Grout), tells him, while breaking the news that he's been passed over for the job of detective superintendent, "but you don't say the right things to the right people."

Strange and the others accept the fact that Morse doesn't mind being passed over. They figure he's gone as far as he wants to go by becoming a chief inspector. He likes to do his job, then head for the pub for a pint or two in peace. "At least you stop sulking when there's a beer glass in front of you," observes Strange. Unfortunately, the beer glass may be in front of Morse a little too often. He tends to swill down large quantities of the brew, which causes the rather straight-laced Sergeant Lewis to grimace from time to time.

"Of these three episodes of morose Morse (The Dead of Jericho, The Silent World of Nicholas Quinn, *and* Service of All the Dead), *the last is best—as if film noir had decided to visit the Middle Ages and put on a bloody show with an organ, a bell tower, and a crucifix. Perhaps because by then, like Detective Sergeant Lewis, we've accustomed and addicted ourselves to [Morse's] passionate flaws as well as his quirky brilliance, but also because we've spent so much time looking at odd-angled aspects of the action, in plate-glass windows and rearview mirrors and shiny surfaces of wood or metal, dismembered and reversed, that consciousness itself seems fractured.*

And if by then you've come to care for Morse as I do, read the novel. At the end of the book, the same thing happens to Morse that happened to Sammy and Rosie."

—JOHN LEONARD,
New York

LETTING LOOSE

Morse doesn't care to be lectured about his drinking and once even tells Chief Superintendent Strange to knock it off when Strange warns him he'd better not have any bottles hidden about the office. Despite all that, the television Morse still spends less time in the pub than Dexter's literary version did. Morse never denies being a drinker, but he tends to rationalize his drinking in various ways. In *The Silent World of Nicholas Quinn*, he's lunching with a woman who doesn't drink because she wants to be in "total command" of her faculties. "I like to let go," Morse tells her. "I always drink at lunchtime. It helps my imagination."

But it certainly doesn't help his physical fitness. Already squeamish for a cop, he's almost useless in any physical tangle with a suspect. In *Service of All the Dead*, we see Morse huffing and puffing his way upstairs to the roof of an Oxford church. Lewis takes one look at the inspector's ashen face and observes, "It's the beer." But Morse rudely retorts, "I'm scared of heights, you stupid sod!"

MAKING ALLOWANCES FOR MORSE

All of this may seem to make Morse a rather odd hero for a prime-time television detective series—and a most unlikely one to become by far the most popular of all television detectives during his long run in Britain. But the reason the English love him is the same reason he's enormously popular in America and in more than 50 other countries around the world: As with some crotchety, lonely uncle, we sympathize with him, respect his honesty, and root for his happiness. We make allowances for his bad moods and peevish behavior because he's such a vulnerable person, a romantic who wears his heart on his sleeve and is often hurt, a lonely man who compensates by playing his music too loud or having one more beer than he should.

When Morse turns away from a bloody crime scene with obvious distaste or jumps at the chance to skip out on witnessing a post-mortem exam, we sympathize. It may be unusual for a veteran cop to still have a queasy stomach, but it's more than that for Morse. He's a sensitive man who believes in respecting the dignity of death. His discomfort in such situations is something we readily appreciate because it's probably how most of us would feel in his shoes.

For all his personal shortcomings, Morse can show a disarming sense of awareness about them. It's one thing when a criminal suspect takes a dislike to him, but quite another when he knows he's irritating someone he respects. It wouldn't bother Morse, for instance, to know the murder suspect in *Driven to Distraction* thinks he's "a pain in the rectum area," but he's uncomfortable when he realizes his new colleague, the competent and attractive Sergeant Maitland (Mary Jo Randle), may share that view. "I do that," he admits in that episode. "I rub people up the wrong way."

He also acknowledges, from time to time, that he knows his lifestyle isn't what it ought to be. In *The Silent World of Nicholas Quinn*, Morse confides to Lewis that "My doctor says I should lose some weight, stop eating butter, start eating polyunsaturates, whatever they are. Not quite the same, though, is it, Lewis?"

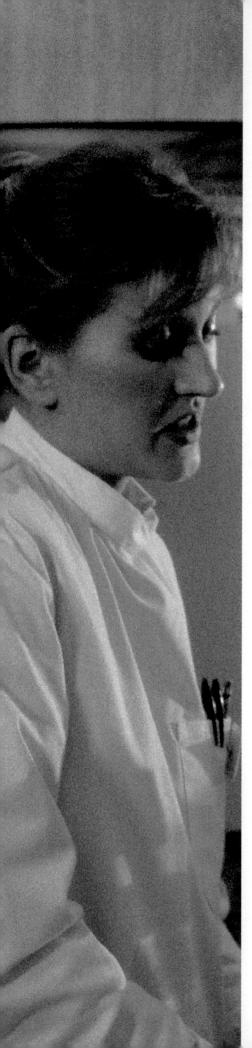

Unlucky in Love

Morse is a confirmed bachelor who likes women, and probably has had more unrequited schoolboy crushes than any other detective in the Mystery! canon. His closest call came many years ago when he was actually engaged to marry a woman named Susan (Joanna David), who ditched him at the eleventh hour and soured him on matrimony for good. Susan surfaced 20 years later as the widow of a murder victim in the *Dead on Time* episode, arousing Morse's interest anew. Again, the relationship went nowhere. Public displays of affection aren't Morse's specialty, but in *Fat Chance* he smooches a deaconess, Emma Pickford (Zoe Wanamaker), and in *Death of the Self* he is woefully smitten by glamorous opera star Nicole Burgess (Frances Barber), with whom he engages in at least one passionate kiss. So he's clearly not without certain skills. Then there's Morse's multi-episode flirtation with smashing female pathologist Dr. Grayling Russell (Amanda Hillwood), which seemed to show some promise. In *The Secret of Bay 5B,* Morse maneuvers her onto a dance floor, and we distinctly hear him ask her out on a date. But her interest in the inspector apparently is purely forensic, and he never gets his hands on her *corpus delecti.* Why doesn't he ever want to take a woman home to stay? Morse gave us the answer once: No woman could stand living with him because he plays his records too loud.

"Millions of women are attracted to TV's number one detective, Inspector Morse. They are charmed by his sad, baffled sensitivity, his brooding melancholy, and his cryptic vulnerability. He is both intimate and remote, but never menacing. He is both the thinking man's cop and the thinking woman's crumpet."

—MELANIE McFADYEAN,
Guardian

TRIBULATIONS OF THE FATHER/SON RELATIONSHIP

Unlike Morse, Lewis is young and healthy, and his life is well-ordered. He simply can't "hang out" with Morse because the inspector's style of life is so vexing and their interests are so different. In *Death of the Self*, Lewis accompanies Morse to sunny Italy, but can't seem to relax, even in the gorgeous splendor of Verona. He's not interested in opera, which preoccupies Morse, and he misses his family back in England.

The relationship between Morse and Lewis is a major reason why viewers were hooked on Inspector Morse. Although author Colin Dexter created Lewis as a man of Morse's own age, the series made Lewis young and a straight-arrow, fashioning a sort of father-son relationship that has become especially rich and endearing over the years. There are times when Morse treats Lewis with appalling insensitivity, and he is often very impatient with Lewis when the younger man doesn't get one of his sage remarks. In *Ghost in the Machine*, Morse observes, "There's too much *sang froid* all around." "*Sang froid?*" says the bewildered sergeant. "Cold blood, Lewis!" Morse barks back.

But Lewis holds his own over the years, earning Morse's respect for his quick, logical mind. He even one-ups Morse in the sarcastic remark department on the odd occasion. In *The Sins of the Fathers*, for instance, a guilty man vows to come out of prison someday and get revenge on Morse for bringing him to justice. "I shouldn't worry about it, sir," says Lewis. "By the time he comes out, you'll be long gone." "You're wasted as a copper, Lewis," says the startled Morse. "You should have joined the diplomatic service."

DEDUCTION VERSUS DETERMINATION

As a detective, Morse has a solid record of cases cleared, even though his approach is unorthodox. He tends to theorize more than is generally wise and he prefers intuitive deduction over the dogged police work that partner Lewis usually does for him. In *The Silent World of Nicholas Quinn*, crossword puzzle addict Morse explains his shortcomings as a puzzle-solver, and, by extension, as a police detective. "My weakness is guesswork," he says. "I leap to conclusions sometimes—usually wrong."

That weakness nearly undoes him in *Driven to Distraction*, when he orders car dealer Jeremy Boynton (Patrick Malahide) booked on suspicion of murdering a young woman, then has to release him for lack of evidence. Boynton is nearly killed when the victim's angry boyfriend attacks him. Morse ultimately has to grovel in front of Boynton, offering profuse apologies after finally catching the real killer, a vicious psychopath.

Still, Morse is hard to beat as a detective. He always solves the crime, one way or another, and always does it with fascinating style. In the mid 1990s, it appeared as if Thaw, Whately, and the others finally would abandon *Inspector Morse* for other projects, but the persistent demand for new episodes has kept them coming back to tackle just one more case or two. It seems unlikely that Morse's loyal fans will ever permit the inspector to retire from the force and just drive his classic Jag from town to town, in search of the perfect pint, while listening to his opera tapes.

Morse's Surrogate Son:

SIDEKICK
SERGEANT LEWIS
(KEVIN WHATELY)

Sergeant Lewis is like the son Inspector Morse never had, the younger detective who runs Morse's errands, absorbs his abuse, and, theoretically, soaks up his wisdom in repayment for all the grunt work. He's a decent sort, a husband and father and all-around law-abider who's there not only to give Morse a confidant and foil, but also to provide contrast to the eccentric inspector by reminding us what normal life is like.

Plainspoken and given to thinking out loud, Lewis often says things that jar Morse's fitful mind into a leap to the right conclusion. For that, he may earn a spontaneous "You've done it again, Lewis!" or "You've earned yourself a drink, Lewis," the closest things to compliments he's likely to hear from the inspector. More often, though, the response is "Not now, Lewis!" Still, Lewis suspects he may be the only junior officer Morse will tolerate as a partner, which he has to consider a source of some pride.

Lewis is played by Kevin Whately, who already was a star in England in the long-running British comedy series *Auf Wiedersehen, Pet,* before signing on as Morse's sidekick. He worked mostly in theater in the 1970s, then began doing television in the 1980s, including a six-week role as a truck driver in Britain's popular serial *Coronation Street.* He's married to actor Madelaine Newton, whom Morse fanatics will remember as the inspector's lady friend—until she became a murder victim—in the *Masonic Mysteries* episode.

Classics Scholar and Detective Writer:

AUTHOR
COLIN DEXTER

INSPECTOR MORSE WAS BORN UNEXPECTEDLY ONE RAINY DAY IN 1972 WHILE
Colin Dexter, a Latin and Greek scholar, was on holiday in North Wales. Dexter had read
all the worthwhile books he'd brought with him and was especially disappointed with his
selection of mysteries. He was sure he could write a better one, so he banged out the first
chapter of something he called *Last Bus to Woodstock.*

Even at that early stage, Dexter knew what sort of character he wanted for
Morse: a clever, cerebral sort of detective like Agatha Christie had envisioned in
Hercule Poirot, but with a much more down-to-earth personality. An Oxford resident since 1966, Dexter decided to place Morse there, solving crimes for the
Thames Valley CID. Dexter, like Morse, is a dedicated worker of crossword puzzles,
so as a name for his detective, he chose Morse after Sir Jeremy (C. J.) Morse, crossword luminary and chairman of Lloyds Bank.

Dreaming up Inspector Morse and getting him through his first chapter occupied
the rest of that rainy afternoon, but then Dexter put the four or five pages aside and didn't
think about Morse again for six months. When he finally went back to it, he decided it
wasn't bad, and began the long process of finishing the book at the unhurried pace
of a few hundred words a day. When *Last Bus to Woodstock* was published in 1975,
it found a public hungry for the classically complex plot—the hallmark of every
Dexter novel—and enthralled by the cranky, curmudgeonly Inspector Morse.

Though Dexter still refers to himself as only a part-time writer, his many
Morse books are all bestsellers, and Morse has been the most popular detective on
British television for most of the past ten years. Dexter is widely recognized by his
fans not only because of his many lectures and personal appearances for charity
but because, like Alfred Hitchcock, he always plays a cameo role in each of the Inspector
Morse shows. You can usually spot him in pub scenes, sipping a beer or glass of wine.
Dexter retired from teaching in 1987 due to health problems, but has continued to write
at his usual pace and to work at answering the large volume of fan mail he receives.

*"I've killed 71 people in Oxford, so if I
went in to see the police, they'd probably
arrest me for making Oxford the crime
capital of the European Community."*

—COLIN DEXTER

*"I usually wake up and cut the grass.
Sometime around mid-morning when
I get the feeling it's about time I wrote
something, I write for two or three
hours. I have no discipline whatsoever.
That's about as much as I can do."*

—COLIN DEXTER,
Houston Chronicle

QUESTION: *When you sit down to write a new Inspector Morse novel, does your mind's eye see the same man you created in 1972?*

ANSWER: I started writing about him when Morse seemed to be, emotionally, in his late forties or so. The old boy would probably be about 75 by now. Of course, everybody knows the police tend to retire after about 30 years in the business, if they go into it at 23 or 24. I've just written another book about him, and his physical deterioration continues because of his needlessly wanton, profligate lifestyle with the booze, cigarettes, and so on. I think it's only proper he should get a little bit of comeuppance for his disregard of all the rules of physical health.

In Last Bus to Woodstock, *you first describe Morse as "a lightly-built, dark-haired man," but the television Morse is stockier and white-haired. He also drives a Jaguar, not the Lancia you gave him. And Sergeant Lewis was about the same age as Morse when you created him. Do these changes bother you?*

The copyright of Morse is with me, so if anything appears to me to be off character, then I have the right to stop it. But, from the point of view of characterization, I think the television did me very proud. I think John Thaw was a wonderful choice. I've forgotten things like what color eyes Morse has in the first books anyway. These things aren't terribly serious to me.

Then has the television series influenced your writing at all?

Certainly in the case of Lewis it has. They made him about half the age I had him. Now whenever I write about Lewis, I'm vaguely conscious of the television image of Kevin Whately. If I had to do it over again, I think I'd probably do what television did and have that surrogate father-son relationship. It's quite sensible, really, and I think, at least on television, it worked better than having them be the same age.

In your parental view of him, what's Morse's primary quality, the essential thing that makes him Morse?

The one thing that doesn't come through on television: He has an A-plus brain. Fundamentally, the main thing I wanted to do with Morse was make him a clever fellow, that's all.

Your autobiographical input to Morse's character has been well documented—the love of ale, Wagner, crosswords, and so forth—but what traits did you purposely give him to distinguish him from you?

He's awfully mean with money, isn't he? Poor old Lewis, on a third the salary, has to buy nine-tenths of the booze. I hope that's not like me at all. He's very ungrateful and ungracious in his treatment of subordinates and fellow policemen. I hope that's not me either. He's a bachelor who doesn't want to get married, and I've been married for 40 years.

Could Morse still be Morse if he somehow fell in love and got married?

No, no, no, no! He definitely won't get married. But he meets a nice woman in the last book I've written, and that's fine. But he wouldn't commit himself to any long-term engagement, such as marriage, to any woman. He would think that'd be ridiculous. He values his independence too much. He likes the ladies, but not to the extent of sharing his life with them. Though he goes off with a lady at the end of the new book, the implication is it's just for a very pleasant weekend together.

Now and then, Morse seems a bit of a male chauvinist—and occasionally is taken to task for it by a woman. Do you consider him a misogynist?

I've never been terribly anxious to promote any of this political correctness or women's lib stuff. He falls in love with one or two, but usually the crooks, doesn't he? I don't think he has any profound views on feminism . . . He's to the left in politics and he's a Low-Church atheist. . . . But I don't take literature as seriously as all that. All I hope is that people will want to turn the page.

Many critics have written that the relationship between Morse and Lewis is the heart of the show. How important is it to you?

The relationship between the two is fundamentally important to both the books and the television show. Lewis is often cross and disappointed with Morse, but he's the only one Morse can work with and he feels greatly honored by that. He's not one of these monumentally stupid sidekicks. He's a very able policeman and often is of great help. But he doesn't have an incisive A-plus mind himself, and I think he's worried about that.

You're not known for hobnobbing with detectives to enrich your fiction. What research do you do and what do the local police think of your detective?

I don't do any police research. All I know about it is what I get from reading other people's novels. I make it up as I go along. I try not to get things wholly wrong, but I'm not one of those who knows anything about police procedures. The police smile at me vaguely and tell me I haven't the faintest idea about it. But I do a lot of charity work for them, so they're very gentle and kind to me.

We keep hearing that there won't be any more Inspector Morse *programs, and then another one turns up. How do you see the future for Morse on television?*

We're televising one this year and then we'll do another one next year. That'll take us to 31 episodes of two hours each, which is an awful lot. I think people will have had enough by then. I think when that point comes, that will be the finish.

NAME REVEALED

In Dexter's latest Morse book, Death Is Now My Neighbor, *the next to the last word reveals a mystery that has stymied readers, led bookmakers to place odds on its resolution, and forced the publisher to keep the galleys secret. The mystery? Morse's first name. And it is . . . you'll have to get the book.*

SELECTED BIBLIOGRAPHY

Last Bus to Woodstock, 1975; *Last Seen Wearing,* 1976; *The Silent World of Nicholas Quinn,* 1977; *Service of All the Dead,* 1979; *The Dead of Jericho,* 1981; *The Riddle of the Third Mile,* 1983; *The Secret of Annexe 3,* 1986; *The Wench Is Dead,* 1989; *The Jewel That Was Ours,* 1992; *The Way Through the Woods,* 1992; *Daughters of Cain,* 1994; *Death Is Now My Neighbor,* 1996.

Acting on Morse's Behalf:

ACTOR
JOHN THAW

IT WASN'T EXACTLY LOVE AT FIRST SIGHT BETWEEN ACTOR JOHN THAW AND Inspector Morse. In fact, Thaw still remembers his reaction when he finished reading Colin Dexter's novel, *The Dead of Jericho,* his first exposure to the detective he would play for the next ten years. "I don't really like this guy!" Thaw said to himself.

Thaw didn't think he matched the physical description of Morse in the novel, nor was he enamored of the inspector's wolfish attitude toward women, his drinking habits, or a few other unappealing qualities. What's more, feeling comfortable with a character was important to Thaw, since an actor can sometimes be trapped in a very long run if his show is a hit (Thaw had just finished playing another cop, Steely Jack Regan, in 53 episodes of the hit series *The Sweeney*). So Thaw went to producer Kenny McBain and director Alastair Reid with his concerns. They told him not to worry—that they had the same concerns, and so they were going to put a slightly different Inspector Morse on the screen, with the blessings of author Dexter.

SHAPING MORSE TO FIT THAW

And so began the evolution of a great television character. The various writers and directors who followed Reid and Anthony Minghella, the first writer on the series, all shaped Morse to fit Thaw's persona, so the actor's new identity would look as natural as possible. "I began to have little indications that this was right for me," says Thaw. "The very first thing was the music. I love music. . . . I often listen to music while I'm learning my lines. I thought that was a pretty good indication of what kind of guy Morse was. You have to relate every character to yourself, so I asked myself what it was about me—and therefore Morse, too—that finds solace in music. That became the key to his character for me."

When *The Dead of Jericho* debuted on British television in 1987, Inspector Morse was immediately embraced by viewers of almost every class. He soon became the most popular television detective in the United Kingdom, lifting Thaw to a new level of fame and making him so financially successful that he now modestly admits he needn't ever work again, if he doesn't like what he's offered.

Why did Morse have such wide appeal? Thaw thinks it is precisely Morse's imperfections that are the lure. "I think they recognize him as a fellow human being," says Thaw. "They see him not as a policeman, but as a man."

Thaw can relate somewhat to Morse's loneliness, having had a difficult childhood. He was raised by his father, a truck driver, from the age of six when his mother left home. By his mid-teens, though, he had found someplace he could call home—the theater. He was accepted by London's Royal Academy of Dramatic Art at age 16, and by 23, he had his first starring role in a television series, *Redcap*. After his second series, *The Sweeney*, became a hit, Thaw was established as a major star of British television.

CONFUSING IDENTITIES

Once he settled into playing the melancholy Morse, though, Thaw discovered that many people were beginning to confuse the identities of the character and the actor. Thaw doesn't drink, for example, so he's always turning down offers of the ale Morse tosses back with such relish. He's also married—to actor Sheila Hancock—and isn't interested in marriage proposals and other offers from affectionate female fans. Morse has the posh accent of a long-time Oxford denizen, while Thaw still has the considerably less posh Manchester sound of his youth.

Over the years, Thaw has increased his proprietary interest in Morse, making sure scripts take him where Thaw believes he should go. It was Thaw, for instance, who suggested doing episodes in Australia (*Promised Land*) and Italy (*The Death of the Self*) to vary the usual Thames Valley settings. Though he doesn't own a piece of the show, Thaw was granted the title of executive producer on the last few episodes.

"You could say I'm acting on Morse's behalf," he says. So when Thaw announced in 1993 (the same year Queen Elizabeth dubbed him a Commander of the British Empire) that the *Twilight of the Gods* episode would be his final one, it truly seemed as if that would be the end. He signed on to play a new character— a wealthy trial lawyer, the queen's counsel, who's married with two kids—in the series *Kavanagh, Q.C.*, which became a big hit.

KEEPING THE DOOR OPEN

Thaw didn't walk away from Morse because the character went sour on him. He simply felt Morse had done almost everything he could do and remain in character. He didn't want to stay with Morse so long that the public would abandon him or he would become stale in the role. "I've always made a point of doing something different between Morses," he explains, "whether it be theater, an offbeat role in another television film (the one-legged man in the Sherlock Holmes story *The Sign of Four*), or a feature film for Dickie Attenborough (*Chaplin*), just to do something fresh and different."

But Thaw kept the door open to do the occasional two-hour Morse film if he had the time and the script was right. He has done *The Way Through the Woods* and *The Daughters of Cain,* and says he'll consider others on their merits. He's very clear, though, that he never wants to play a Morse death scene. "One of the writers had the idea of blowing him up in *Twilight of the Gods*," Thaw says. "I wouldn't ever want anything like that to happen to him. If we ever end it for good, I'd like him to just walk away."

"*Only one college has refused to allow us to film there. Otherwise, everybody has been cooperative. But there have been stories in the British press where the University has expressed concern over the increase in tourism—100,000 more a year—since the series began. Seems all that walking on the grounds is wearing down the stone.*"

—JOHN THAW,
Daily News

COMMANDER
ADAM DALGLIESH

DEATH OF AN EXPERT WITNESS AND OTHER STORIES

Based on the novels by
P. D. James

SERIES
Death of an Expert Witness
Shroud for a Nightingale
Cover Her Face
The Black Tower
A Taste for Death
Devices and Desires
Unnatural Causes
A Mind to Murder
Original Sin

**PRODUCTION
COMPANY**
Anglia Television

YEARS
1985–

MAIN CAST
Adam Dalgliesh
ROY MARSDEN

DETECTIVE INSPECTOR ADAM DALGLIESH FIRST ENTERS THE WORLD OF MYSTERY ABOUT 50 PAGES INTO P. D. JAMES' 1962 NOVEL *Cover Her Face* WHEN HE IS SENT OUT BY SCOTLAND YARD TO INVESTIGATE A DEATH AMONG THE GENTRY AT AN ISOLATED, LUXURIOUS COUNTRY ESTATE.

Even then, his reputation precedes him. "I've heard of him," one of the suspects muses as the tall, dark, and handsome detective arrives at the crime scene. "Ruthless, unorthodox, working always against time. I suppose he has his own private compulsions. At least they've thought us adversaries worthy of the best."

Dalgliesh may indeed be the best Scotland Yard has to offer these days. His reputation for never theorizing ahead of the facts is legendary, yet his success at solving complex cases in record time is astonishing. He's more experienced than Detective Chief Inspector Jane Tennison, for instance, and much less trouble-prone. And he's the equal in every way of Inspector Morse, without the endearing imperfections. All of that may account for the string of promotions that have raised him to the rank of commander, in charge of a special unit of the Metropolitan Police that handles only the most "sensitive" murder cases. In fact, along the corridors of power at New Scotland Yard, the worst you will hear about Commander Dalgliesh is that he may be a little hard to know. He's an intense, rather solitary man whose taciturnity often is interpreted as intimidating aloofness.

A SENSITIVE POET

Those who have followed the career of Adam Dalgliesh for the past 35 years through James' nine mystery novels about him—and the nine television adaptations for Mystery!—know that behind his screen of diffidence lies a cultured man who is a widely respected author of serious poetry. He is an even-tempered, thoroughly decent human being who's extremely sensitive to the feelings of others.

Indeed Dalgliesh may be the most psychologically complex of all the detectives in the Mystery! family. He's a vicar's son who almost requires a degree of alienation to preserve his artistic sensibility, yet is also a man who once gave himself over so completely to the love of another person that he has never fully recovered from the pain of losing his young wife and infant son during childbirth. Consequently, of all the police detectives seen on Mystery! he's best able to relate to the pain of murder victims' grieving friends and families. His contemplative nature, mercifully free of quirks and affectations, and thoughtful approach to untangling the snarled threads of a homicide case make him unique.

Dalgliesh came to Mystery! in 1985 in a six-part serial adapted by Robin Chapman from James' sixth Dalgliesh novel, *Death of an Expert Witness*. Taped largely on location

in the remote fenlands of Norfolk in England's East Anglia, the show found Dalgliesh already promoted to the rank of Chief Superintendent of Detectives at Scotland Yard and trying to find the killer of a famous forensic scientist (Geoffrey Palmer) at a pathology laboratory in that eerie, marshy corner of England.

Like the books, each television program has been set in a small, confined world within the larger environment of contemporary England. For *Death of an Expert Witness*, it was the pathology lab. *Shroud for a Nightingale* takes place in a hospital and home for young nurses, *The Black Tower* in a nursing home on the Dorset coast, and *Devices and Desires* near the Larksoken nuclear power plant in north Norfolk.

SEXY AND SENSITIVE

As important as locale is to the shows, the key ingredient, of course, is the star. The producers ended their search for the perfect Adam Dalgliesh when they cast tall, lean Roy Marsden in the role. At the time, he was best known in the U.S. for his role as British spymaster Neil Burnside in the television series *The Sandbaggers*. Marsden captured the quiet strength of Dalgliesh while putting his own light spin on the character, filling in some of the areas James had left to the reader's imagination.

Marsden's Dalgliesh wears a mustache and is a good deal sexier than the one in the books, who has a love life, but rarely talks about it. He may not do anything overtly carnal, but Marsden has developed a large following among female viewers, who consider him extraordinarily sexy.

The shows have taken frequent advantage of Marsden's sex appeal, but without potentially embarrassing bedroom frolics. In *Cover Her Face* (1987) and *Unnatural Causes* (1994), he romances lovely Deborah Riscoe (Mel Martin), giving us a chance to see a more affable, loving Dalgliesh cuddling her on a sofa, hugging her on a seaside tryst, and even greeting her at his hotel room door, wearing his bathrobe, fresh from the shower. As a result, Dalgliesh seems so much more attentive and romantic on television that Deborah seems unduly hard on him when she finally decides to end their long affair, complaining that, "After all this time, I think he's forgotten how to commit."

In 1983, when producer John Rosenberg and director Herbert Wise started taping *Death of an Expert Witness*, there was no master plan for a series of dramas about Dalgliesh. P. D. James had not licensed all the Dalgliesh books to the production company (Anglia Television), so television rights had to be acquired, one by one, after *Death of an Expert Witness* turned into a huge hit and the demand for more Dalgliesh programs was clear.

Because they started with the sixth Dalgliesh novel, substantial changes were necessary in the adaptations of the earlier books to make them conform to the Dalgliesh viewers had been introduced to in *Death of an Expert Witness*. For example, the death of his wife and son takes place in the first television mystery, even though readers knew they had died many years earlier. Because Dalgliesh had been promoted to commander in the television version of *The Black Tower*, Dalgliesh couldn't go back to being just a superintendent when *A Mind to Murder* finally came to Mystery! So many changes in the original storyline were made for *A Mind to Murder* that author James actually was offended by it.

"Dalgliesh of Scotland Yard is a Scottish-born, balding, mustachioed, macho, but sensitive cop. He does a lot more for the Yard's image than Inspector Lestrade."

—MARVIN KITMAN,
Newsday

"So many of [James'] readers have clamored for more intimate information about Dalgliesh's personal life that she felt it necessary to respond: 'A serious love and sex interest in a mystery can endanger its unity as a novel, not to speak of the quality of its detection.'

And although, in a paraphrase of Jane Austen, James admits that mystery lovers seem to feel that 'an unmarried detective who is in receipt of a good income is in need of a wife,' she assures us that she is steadfast in her plans to keep him single."

—VINCENT PRICE

TAMPERING WITH THE TEXT

"We actually did go too far in the last one," Marsden said after the U.S. telecast of *A Mind to Murder.* "We changed who did the murder. In hindsight, I think it was a big mistake." Marsden had a couple of special reasons for thinking that. While filming the rewritten ending of *A Mind to Murder,* in which Dalgliesh chases the killer across mudflats and pulls him from certain death in a bottomless sinkhole, Marsden broke his thumb and wound up with his hand in a cast. While recuperating, he read James' new Dalgliesh novel, *Original Sin,* and was stunned to find the killer dies in a sinkhole! "We're going to have to alter the ending, because you can't have someone killed in the mud again," Marsden said as he prepared to tape the television version.

Yet for all the anguish in some corners over the changes television has made in James' stories, Marsden's Dalgliesh is very close to the classic detective of the novels, and the television programs have been, for the most part, beautifully crafted and skillfully acted. Each has been shaped into a special event, and the fans have responded accordingly, which is why Commander Dalgliesh is likely to stay on the job as long as P. D. James keeps dreaming up cases for him.

"We're not talking about Sam Spade here; we're talking about Hamlet and Lear and maybe Lao-tzu, in a three-piece suit with a mustache. As Dalgliesh, Roy Marsden is beyond reproach. He is a reproach to the rest of us who aren't so sad and wise and slump-shouldered under the weight of all that we know about iniquity and unfairness. He is weary, but he twinkles. He perseveres, as if he were writing a poem whose depressing coda he already apprehends. It never occurs to him that he shouldn't write this poem; he made that decision before we were born."

—JOHN LEONARD,
New York

Queen of Crime:

AUTHOR

P. D. JAMES

> "One of my own favorite mystery writers is Dorothy L. Sayers. She was a strong influence on me in my girlhood, and if I hadn't read her I have no doubt I would still have been a novelist, but I doubt whether I should have been a mystery novelist. It seems to me that she was one of the writers who elevated the mystery from a kind of sub-literary puzzle into a form which has serious claims to be regarded as a novel."
>
> —P. D. JAMES

IN ENGLAND'S HOUSE OF LORDS, SHE'S FORMALLY KNOWN AS BARONESS JAMES of Holland Park, of Southwold, County of Suffolk. Her close friends mostly call her Phyllis. But the rest of the world knows her as P. D. James, legendary "Queen of Crime."

The creator of Commander Adam Dalgliesh of the Metropolitan Police was born Phyllis Dorothy James in 1920, in Oxford, England. She was more than 40 years old before she published her first book—*Cover Her Face*—and discovered what it was like to have fans. Now she numbers them in the millions, partly owing to the enormous popularity of the television adaptations: All nine of her Adam Dalgliesh mysteries have been dramatized for television. Her novels about private eye Cordelia Gray—*An Unsuitable Job for a Woman* and *The Skull Beneath the Skin*—are now also arousing interest among television producers and may be coming soon to the small screen. Movie rights to her novels *Innocent Blood* and *The Children of Men* have been sold.

James' amazing success as a writer adored by the public and critics alike is all the more incredible because she started so late. Though she fancied the idea of being a writer almost from childhood, she was 38 before she began her first novel. A great fan of Dorothy L. Sayers' mysteries, James chose to make her first book a mystery, too. Since it was accepted by the first publisher she sent it to, she has never received even one rejection slip in her entire literary career.

James often blames her delayed start as a novelist on "the natural indolence of writers," but her very heavy workload in her early days as a wife and mother probably also had something to do with it. She married Connor Bantry White in 1941, and they had two daughters. But when White returned from World War II, he suffered from severe mental illness, and it became necessary for James to get the best job she could to help support the family. She earned a degree in hospital administration, and from 1949 to 1968, she was an administrator for England's National Health Service. In 1968 she became a principal (administrator) in the Home Office in the police department dealing with forensics. As it turned out, the jobs she held before she began writing supplied her with a great reservoir of knowledge that she later exploited in books like *Shroud for a Nightingale* and *A Mind to Murder,* which take place in medical facilities, and in all her mysteries that deal with criminal procedure.

By the time her husband died in 1964, James already had published her first two novels and was beginning to taste the success that eventually would permit her to give up her full-time job and devote more time to writing. She decided to use her maiden name, James, on her books because she believes women should work under their original family name. She decided to use her initials because they sounded slightly enigmatic and might "look good on the dust jacket." Each of her novels not only has increased her wealth and fame, but also has added weight to her literary reputation. Most critics now consider P. D. James' work to have transcended the mystery genre: Her full-bodied novels like *A Taste for Death* not only bring deeper, more thoughtful characterization to the mystery field, but also offer storylines rich in social context and significant ideas.

James' contributions to English culture and society have been immense. She has served as a magistrate, a governor of the BBC, a member of the Arts Council of Great Britain, and in 1983 was decorated with the Order of the British Empire (OBE). In 1991, she was made a lifelong British peer.

QUESTION: *Did you model Adam Dalgliesh on anybody you knew?*

ANSWER: No, I didn't. I gave him the qualities I admired: great intelligence, courage, compassion without sentimentality, a need for privacy. I wanted him to have an artistic interest, so I made him a poet because I think I understand at least the poetic impulse. I didn't want to deal at that stage with his love life, so I rather callously killed off his wife and newborn child. And there he was.

Dalgliesh is one of the least idiosyncratic detectives in the business. Did you make him that way on purpose?

When I created Dalgliesh, I think I had it in mind that he might be a character that would go through a series of books. In that case, I wanted a character who could develop, but who wasn't bizarre in the way that perhaps Poirot was. I think Agatha Christie got a little tired of Poirot and rather wished she'd made him not quite so eccentric. I learned a lesson from that.

I think, for example, of Dorothy L. Sayers and Lord Peter Wimsey. I have a great admiration for her books, and he's one of my favorite detectives. But the Lord Peter we first meet is very different from the Lord Peter of *Gaudy Night,* who's a historian, a scholar, and very different from the silly-ass-about-town. There was a huge development. If she had known how popular he was going to be, she might have made him a little different at the beginning. But who's to tell?

At the end of the first book, Cover Her Face, *Dalgliesh seems on the verge of a romance with Deborah Riscoe. You tell us, "He knew with heart-lifting certainty" that he would meet her again. He did, of course, but nothing ever came of it. Why not?*

"[The mystery] is an affirmation of a moral law that murder is wrong but men are responsible for their own deeds; and however difficult the problem, there is a solution. All this, I think, is rather comforting in an age of pessimism and anxiety."

—P. D. JAMES

"I'm very frightened of violence, I hate it, and I'm very worried by the fact that the world is a more violent place.... It may be that by writing mysteries I am able, as it were, to exorcise this fear. And I think this may be a reason why many people enjoy reading a mystery—that it is a way in which one can distance one's irrational fears ... including the fear of death, because although, paradoxically, a mystery has a violent death at the very heart of the novel, it does seem in some way to disinfect its terrors so that we can come to terms with it, perhaps to fictionalize it or to intellectualize it."

—P. D. JAMES

I did envision that he would see her again, but I don't think I'd worked out at that stage what exactly would happen when he did. But I don't think I was inventing a woman who would someday marry Dalgliesh. She really got very tired of his involvement with the job and never giving her any wholehearted commitment. I think one of the problems with Dalgliesh is his experience with total commitment to his wife, which ended with tragedy. He was deeply hurt and is very loath to commit himself again emotionally. He has that splinter of ice in the heart, and of course Deborah sensed that and went chasing off to America, didn't she?

Though you make it clear Dalgliesh has a love life, we never see him get very romantic in the books. Yet the television adaptations occasionally work in a love interest. What was your reaction to that?

That's one of the things about the television adaptation I don't approve of.

Have your readers pressured you to have Dalgliesh fall in love?

Well, I think lots of my readers—and I agree with them—feel it's time he got himself permanently settled with a wife. They rather feel, here's this poor man—well, he's not poor, of course—who's a very attractive man and very marriageable with a lot to give, so why can't we find him the right woman and get him settled down? At one time I thought he might marry Cordelia Gray, but I don't know. Lots of my readers would like him to marry Cordelia. There seem to be two schools there: Some who think she's not good enough for him and the people who feel he isn't good enough for her, so there you are.

You could always turn them into the Tuppence and Tommy of the 1990s.

Oh, no, no, no! I write reasonably realistic novels. If they did get married she'd have to give up her job running this rather amateur private detective agency. She wouldn't fit easily into being married to Dalgliesh. There are lots of interesting things she might do, but it would be difficult for her to carry on as an amateur private eye while she was married to a very eminent commander of New Scotland Yard.

Do you think you could get along comfortably with Dalgliesh?

I think he'd be quite difficult to work for because he doesn't stand fools for one moment. He'd be a very critical man to work for, but I have a very great respect for him indeed. He has great respect and affection for women generally. When he was made head of this squad to investigate crimes of special sensitivity he felt it was important to recruit a woman member and therefore recruited Kate Miskin, who I think is rather half in love with him.

Most critics seem to think the major change in Dalgliesh over the years is that he's become very introspective. Is he a troubled man?

I think over the years he's become increasingly aware of some of the ambiguities of his job. Murder investigations can cause great pain to people who are innocent, as well as to the guilty. Murder strips away all our defenses and exposes everybody's secrets. For the people involved, it's a very painful process. So, I think he is some-what introspective. We have to remember he is a poet. This provides a rather rich interior life for him, which partly accounts for his need for solitude and privacy.

Judging Dalgliesh from the books and the television shows, he seems to be a master of interrogation. Do you consider that one of his greatest skills as a detective?

He's very clever. Interrogation is a very great art, and I think Dalgliesh is very good at it with a variety of people. In the last book, *Original Sin,* he finds out vital information from the little girl, Daisy. He can respond to the young. He treats them with the same respect he treats adults. People do seem to want to confide in him.

Long-time fans of your books expect Dalgliesh to filter contemporary issues as well as criminal evidence through his keen mind. Has he become your spokesman on issues of the day?

I think that's probably inevitable. I don't think I'm a didactic writer. I don't set out to make points about social conditions, but if you're setting out to write a realistic book set ambiguously in the modern world, inevitably these questions are raised. I think they're fascinating, and often Dalgliesh has a view on them.

Is it possible that Dalgliesh and detectives like him are becoming almost mythic figures in modern fiction—lonely, ascetic, almost priest-like people that we trust and send out in search of the truth?

I think that's a very perceptive view. One can regard the mystery as a kind of modern morality play. It fulfills some of the functions the old morality plays used to fulfill. You usually have a rather settled community that's disrupted by this appalling crime and the detective comes in like an avenging god to set it right. It confirms our belief that we do live in a rational and moral universe. Where there's so much evidence that we seem to live in a chaotic, amoral, and vicious world, this is very reassuring.

If Dalgliesh were an American police detective, he'd probably spend much of his time slamming suspects up against the wall. Is there a cultural difference behind the sort of detectives the British create and the kind we Americans concoct?

I think there is a difference. We are a very long-established country, but more static in a sense. You are in many ways a more vigorous society. People are more on the move, and there's a higher level of violence, perhaps inevitably. You have the private eye who, in a sense, has his hands set against the police as much as he has against the villain. His morality is really only to be true and faithful to the man who's employing him. There's a greater suspicion, I think, in American crime novels, of official law and order. In the 1930s, in the British crime novel, you would never get a corrupt policeman. They might be rather inept or just foils for the brilliant amateur, but they were never corrupt. In America, you go far more for the private eye like Chandler's—knights striding down the mean streets. Some of the finest writing in the mystery has been done by Americans of what we call the hardboiled school: Dashiel Hammett, Raymond Chandler, Ross MacDonald. Writers of that caliber have had impact outside the mystery. They've certainly influenced British crime-writing, but theirs is a different world.

What does being a woman bring to your mysteries that wouldn't be there if a man had written them?

That's very difficult to say. I don't usually like to think of myself as a female writer. I like to think of myself as a writer. But nevertheless a woman must be writing as a woman. I think that one of the reasons why women excel at the mystery is their eye for detail, their fascination with personality and motive. We don't really deal so

much in violent events, explosives, firearms, or combat. It tends to be a gentler form of the mystery—the village or small town where the great interest is in the characterization, the motive, and the clues. That's a bit of an oversimplification, but I think women are good at understanding motive and human behavior.

You've generally been understanding of the changes made in your books in order to make them visual entertainment. But the 1995 adaptation of your 1963 Dalgliesh novel, A Mind to Murder, *had all kinds of characters and subplots added, along with an action ending in the mudflats that seemed very unlike anything you'd write. What was your reaction?*

They had great problems with *A Mind to Murder*. I was strongly disapproving of that. They should not have done that, and I didn't know they were doing that, so I have taken steps to see that they can't change the new one in that way. It was very well received here and had a large viewing public, but I was seriously displeased with it. I would not have signed the contract if I'd known they were going to make it in that way.

You and Ruth Rendell often are referred to as outstanding mystery writers who have transcended the mystery genre and are now considered among England's finest contemporary novelists. Do the two of you ever get together?

Ruth and I are great personal friends, but we write very different books. I think we've both been similarly rewarded. We're both doctors of literature of United Kingdom universities and we've both gained a lot of public approval.

But if you're the "Queen of Crime," doesn't that put you one up on Ruth?

(laughs) Well, I suppose then she'd have to be the "Empress of Crime."

With all you know about detective work now, how would you have done if you'd started out to be one as a young woman?

I think I would have been a good one. I'm not sure how good I would have been at plodding from door to door. I would find that rather boring, but I would have had to go through it. I would have been a good one once I'd reached senior level. I think it would have been a fascinating job.

> "P. D. James . . . has won accolades from readers and critics as one of that rare breed of respectable, middle-class British women who seem to have a knack for taking the fine art of murder and making it repellent and entertaining at the same time. . . . James' plots always revolve around a closed circle of suspects and the shocking, contaminating effect of violent death in a tightly-knit community."
>
> —VINCENT PRICE

SELECTED BIBLIOGRAPHY

Cover Her Face, 1962; *A Mind to Murder,* 1963; *Unnatural Causes,* 1967; *Shroud for a Nightingale,* 1971; *An Unsuitable Job for a Woman,* 1972; *The Black Tower,* 1975; *Death of an Expert Witness,* 1977; *Innocent Blood,* 1980; *The Skull Beneath the Skin,* 1982; *A Taste for Death,* 1986; *Devices and Desires,* 1989; *The Children of Men,* 1992; *Original Sin,* 1994.

A Differently Defined Dalgliesh:

ACTOR
ROY MARSDEN

ACTOR ROY MARSDEN HAS SPENT THE BETTER PART OF THE LAST 15 YEARS IN A challenging—and sometimes frustrating—search for the elusive essence of Adam Dalgliesh. "I think his interior life is one of extreme loneliness," says Marsden. "He finds his only happiness and fulfillment through work."

That's one of the reasons why Marsden has found it so difficult to feel entirely comfortable as the introspective Dalgliesh, a man whose need for privacy has been a defining characteristic since author P. D. James created him in 1962. Though he has taken on Dalgliesh's role in nine acclaimed Mystery! productions, Marsden finds the emotionally reticent detective a daunting person to get to know. "I'd desperately like to see the occasional emotional outburst in the character," he explains. "That's what's so fascinating about Inspector Morse, for instance—his emotional nature. He's a man who, in his despair, turns to drink, so you actually see the decay of the human being."

But Dalgliesh isn't decaying and, in fact, has risen to a position of considerable authority within London's Metropolitan Police. He has remained in perfect control of himself from his first television adventure through his latest. Even the tampering by various adapters of the original James novels has not substantially altered his carefully constructed persona. "There are areas of the man that are difficult to bend," says Marsden, who has worked closely with the writers of the television shows for years to maintain his character's core personality.

> "I think I'm fond of Dalgliesh, but I'm certainly not in love with him. I never have any fantasies about him; I'm not sure I'd like to work for him. I think he has a splinter of ice in the heart, but I have an immense respect for him and of course, I do like him very much. I don't think you create a detective and carry him on through a series of books unless you have an affection for him."
>
> —P. D. JAMES

SHAPING DALGLIESH

One area the writers have tried—without success—to improve has been Dalgliesh's romantic life. Marsden sees it as "a real dilemma" but is now resigned to remaining a sexually inactive character. "He's a man who's looking for a companion, a friend," he says, "but I don't see him as someone who's sexually energized."

Yet Marsden is far from disenchanted with Dalgliesh, a character whose subtlety makes his positive qualities stand out all the more. Indeed, Marsden finds much in him to admire. "He has real compassion," says Marsden. "He struggles very strongly with the class system in this country, which is still deeply entrenched."

That's not quite how James defined him. In the books, says Marsden, who grew up in London's impoverished East End and is a political liberal, Dalgliesh is very much the class-conscious conservative, even when he's behaving compassionately. "He's much more of a Tory on the printed page, but on television he's apolitical."

ACTOR AND AUTHOR SOMETIMES AT ODDS

At times, the relationship between Marsden and P. D. James—he calls her Phyllis—seems a testy one because they share a proprietary interest in Adam Dalgliesh, yet don't often see eye to eye on much of anything, especially Dalgliesh's character. "We don't necessarily have a whole lot in common," he says. "There are huge differences in our outlook on life—our politics, our view of how human beings ought to behave, and how society ought to be managed. Yet she's the most thoroughly charming and enjoyable person, and I do enjoy her company."

Marsden hasn't always been that politic. He frequently says he has little interest in detective stories per se and that he "had to struggle" with the first James novel he read. "I couldn't visually find the character at all," Marsden says, explaining there was very little physical description of Dalgliesh in *Death of an Expert Witness*, the first James book to be filmed. When he asked James for more, Marsden says she simply said she saw Dalgliesh as "tall, dark, and handsome."

Marsden says he decided to fill in the blanks himself. When he noticed that most of the mounted policemen in London wore mustaches, Marsden elected to give Dalgliesh one. "It was the one thing Phyllis disliked," says Marsden, "because she thought mustaches were 'common.'"

Because James also has given Dalgliesh almost no idiosyncratic personality traits, Marsden sought in vain for some visible clue to his life away from crime scenes. He finally concluded Dalgliesh might enjoy rowing for exercise—he pictured him as a lonely sculler in his one-man craft—and made him a member of the Leander Rowing Club by wearing the club tie in his scenes.

RESEARCHING REAL-LIFE DALGLIESH

Once Marsden began investigating the realities of police work, he found the intellectual pursuits and discipline with which James had invested her character were common among the upper ranks at Scotland Yard. "I was taken around to meet the real commanders, who are all on one floor at Scotland Yard," he recalls. "One of them was a finalist in the Leeds piano competitions, one of the finest in the world. Another was the leading expert on the Lakeland poets. Another wore a blue cornflower in his buttonhole every day. There was a quality of intellectualism and epicene behavior that I found very surprising. The fact was Phyllis had hit on something that was very clearly thought-out and truthful."

Yet Marsden believes the reason he isn't able to care about Dalgliesh to the degree that he did his earlier character, British spymaster Neil Burnside of the acclaimed series *The Sandbaggers,* may be the fact that the Dalgliesh novels were not filmed in the proper chronological order, which upset the careful pattern of character development James has managed over 35 years in print. "He's an interesting character," says Marsden. "When the character is no longer interesting, I won't play him. I delight in playing him when the story's good, and if we make a two- or three-hour film every 18 months, that just means people won't think of me as that actor who always plays the same character."

"I've had hundreds of letters over the years from people complaining that I look miserable. Well, it's hard to be the life and soul of the party when you're looking at dead bodies all the time."

—ROY MARSDEN,
TV Register

DCI JANE TENNISON

Prime Suspect

Series created by
Lynda La Plante

JANE TENNISON STORMED ONTO THE AMERICAN TELEVISION LANDSCAPE IN JANUARY 1992, WITH A FULL HEAD OF STEAM. SHE WAS MAD AS HELL AND WASN'T IN A MOOD TO BE IGNORED—NOT BY HER SUPERIORS AT THE SOUTHAMPTON ROW POLICE STATION AND CERTAINLY NOT BY MILLIONS OF VIEWERS WHO IMMEDIATELY REALIZED THEY WERE WATCHING SOMETHING NEW AND UNIQUE, NOT ONLY FOR MYSTERY!, BUT ALSO FOR THE WHOLE TELEVISION MEDIUM.

The occasion was the premiere of a four-part series called *Prime Suspect,* written by Lynda La Plante with a blistering realism rare in even the best crime shows—and a distinct feminist sensibility. In the early minutes of that first episode, Detective Chief Inspector Tennison (Helen Mirren) is shooting off angry sparks because Chief Superintedent Kernan (John Benfield) has assigned a man to run the investigation of a grisly murder. He has bypassed her even though she was in line to handle the next big murder case. She chokes on his explanation that it may not be "the right time" for her. "When is the right time?" she fumes. "Look, I'm the only officer of my rank who's continuously overstepped, sidestepped, or whatever. What do I have to do to prove myself?"

FIGHTING THE GOOD FIGHT

It was a question that resonated powerfully through 1992 America where headlines about a "feminist backlash" were growing more common. Millions of ambitious, talented women like DCI Tennison were smashing their heads against the glass ceiling. Like Tennison, many had marched through the doors other women had wedged open for them in the 1980s, yet sexism still blocked them from real authority.

Tennison was immediately real to most young adult female viewers—and overwhelmingly sympathetic. She was fighting the same battle and also living with the same compromises they were. But *Prime Suspect* wasn't just a show for women. Jane Tennison also won over millions of male viewers who admired her tenacity—and her professionalism. No matter how they might feel about the women's rights movement, many men could see the basic injustice in denying such a capable person the respect she had earned. She was even playing by the men's rules: fighting for her rights without relying on sex appeal, tears, or court orders.

ISSUE-FILLED AND NERVE-BENDING

Prime Suspect's focus on difficult social issues of the 1990s became a hallmark of the first three series. Racism takes center stage in *Prime Suspect 2,* which is about the murder of a black girl in a black district and that community's resentment of white police investigators.

PRODUCTION COMPANY
Granada Television

YEARS
1992–1994

MAIN CAST
Detective Chief Inspector Jane Tennison
HELEN MIRREN

Detective Chief Superintendent Mike Kernan
JOHN BENFIELD

Detective Sergeant Bill Otley
TOM BELL

Detective Inspector Tony Muddyman
JACK ELLIS

Detective Inspector Frank Burkin
CRAIG FAIRBRASS

Detective Inspector Brian Dalton
ANDREW WOODALL

AWARDS
Emmy for outstanding miniseries
(*Prime Suspect 2 & 3*)
Peabody
(*Prime Suspect 2 & 3*)

Homophobia is the issue of *Prime Suspect 3,* which has Tennison working with the Soho vice squad on murder among the young male prostitutes known as "rent boys." In each series, Tennison gets involved in the issue on a personal level—as a victim of sexism in *Prime Suspect,* through a love affair with a black cop in *Prime Suspect 2,* and as the supervisor of a cop who's tormented by his secret gay orientation in *Prime Suspect 3.*

Yet the *Prime Suspect* shows enthralled even those viewers who were blissfully unaware of the issues being played out on the screen. That's because they're first and foremost nerve-bending, suspense-filled police shows, usually focusing on a desperate search for murderers. The result was an enormous audience for the first *Prime Suspect*—more than 12 million viewers, one of the largest audiences for any Mystery! program of the past ten years.

Prime Suspect twice won American Emmys (1993, 1994) as the season's best miniseries. Mirren won an Emmy in 1996 for the *Scent of Darkness* episode (seen on Masterpiece Theatre). The series generated many projects for writer Lynda La Plante, including development deals at CBS and NBC, and a deal to write a *Prime Suspect* feature film. It fostered an obvious American imitator during the 1994–95 season—CBS' *Under Suspicion*—and inspired production companies in both England and the U.S. to work more independent Tennison types into their crime shows. Finally, it encouraged PBS to shift the *Prime Suspect* franchise to the network's big Sunday night drama showcase, Masterpiece Theatre, starting in 1995 with the fourth in the series, *Prime Suspect: The Lost Child.*

Why all the excitement about a female police detective? After all, DCI Tennison was hardly the first: A string of policewomen stretching from Casey Jones in *Policewoman Decoy* (1957) through Pepper Anderson on *Police Woman* (1974–78) to Katy Mahoney in *Lady Blue* (1985–86) had preceded her. *Cagney and Lacey* (1982–88), a female "buddy show" adored by feminists, was one of the few shows that tried to deal with the real, often mundane, day-to-day problems of women trying to make careers in police work.

PUSHING THE ENVELOPE

But *Prime Suspect* took a giant step past even *Cagney and Lacey* by pushing the envelope of realism. Before Tennison, the generally acceptable model for such characters was the leggy blonde in her early thirties, who probably could have found work as a cover girl if she hadn't stumbled into this exciting job with the coppers. In vivid contrast, Tennison turns out to be a chain-smoking workaholic in her late forties who cuts her hair short so she won't have to mess with it in the morning and wastes little time on looking good. At times, she seems a monument to gender assimilation—a woman who has worked among men so long that she's begun to think and act like one. The result is a lot of rough edges unfamiliar to television viewers on a female hero.

In a pub scene in the first *Prime Suspect,* for instance, a male customer sees Tennison having a drink and tries to pick her up. Pepper Anderson might have swapped wisecracks with him and gently put him off, careful not to hurt his feelings. Tennison could care less about his feelings. "I'm busy now," she snaps. "Sod off!" When Kernan tells her the administrative consensus is that a serial murder case is too much for

"It's not the beauty of the subject, the surroundings, and the actors that I'm trying to heighten, but, if you like, the reverse—the ugliness, the inarticulacy of life. It's people's flaws that give them character and depth and make them resonant. This is not a nicely crafted period drama where everything is rounded off."

—DIRECTOR JOHN STRICKLAND

"Jane Tennison is someone who absolutely and uncompromisingly doesn't do anything that you could call feminine. She is a character who has rejected manipulation which, historically, is the way that women have gained power. You hate it, but you know that it's the only way to achieve your ends. Women are taught to smile, to be pleasant, to be charming, to be attractive—'you're a darling, thank you so much.' They get their way like that. Jane Tennison doesn't do that. She doesn't say please. She's more at ease with her circumstances. She has won certain battles, and is a lot more relaxed with her position."

—HELEN MIRREN

her to handle, Tennison doesn't say, "I heartily disagree," but looks him in the eye and says, "That's a load of bullshit!" It's hard to imagine tough old Cagney and Lacey responding to their boss quite that way. As the series goes on through *Prime Suspects 2* and *3*, Kernan and the others at Southampton Row station begin to understand there is little this resourceful, competitive woman can't stomach, including the most brutal murders and the most depraved sex crimes.

THE PRICE OF SUCCESS

Though *Prime Suspect* portrays DCI Tennison as a woman who successfully forces herself up through the power structure, it also shows the price women often have to pay for that success. Since she has to work longer and harder to prove herself to her skeptical male supervisors, Tennison has no life outside her obsessive devotion to her career. That's clear in the first *Prime Suspect* as she systematically wrecks her relationship with live-in boyfriend Peter Rawlins (Tom Wilkinson). Tennison's so tied up with work that she's never "there" for him, literally or figuratively. She's late coming home to meet Peter's little boy when he pays an important first visit to their flat. Peter is recently divorced and has problems of his own, but Tennison can't make time for him on her crowded agenda. When he finally leaves her with an outburst of bitter words—"It's all you, isn't it, Jane? You, you, you, you!"—she looks hurt, but hardly surprised.

She doesn't find any more time for her blood relations, either. After agreeing to be the first female detective interviewed on television's *Crime Night* program, she remembers a prior commitment. "Oh, bugger!" she says, "That's dad's birthday night." Nevertheless, Tennison scoots home from the studio late for the birthday party, then forces everybody to watch the tape of her interview over again after they've just watched it live. Worse yet, she lights into her aged father for screwing up the taping of the big event, completely oblivious to the fact she's screwed up his birthday.

CUTTING OFF

Though Tennison can show compassion to crime victims and their families, she's just as likely to forget it. At one point in the first *Prime Suspect*, Detective Inspector Frank Burkin (Craig Fairbrass) loses his temper when she presses a murder victim's father too relentlessly. "Jesus Christ, let the man cry," Burkin finally blurts out. "He's heartbroken!"

In *Prime Suspect 2*, Tennison argues with her black lover, Detective Bob Oswalde (Colin Salmon), when he breaks up with her for treating him "like some black stud." "That's just not true," she tells him, but then says, "I hope I can rely on you to be discreet." "You really are something else, aren't you?" Oswalde says, suspecting she may not want it known she has been to bed with a fellow officer, especially a black one.

Tennison has few close friends, which is probably just as well because she wouldn't be able to spare them much time. She often seems a pathetically lonely woman when she isn't caught up in a murder case and surrounded by her troops. In *Prime Suspect 2*, we see her hugging a stuffed animal, alone in her flat, as she plays back her telephone messages.

Yet these unflattering glimpses of her aren't there to make us dislike Tennison. They simply serve to humanize her, so we're sure to understand this isn't some supercop who always gets it right. There's also another subtle, but significant point being made: She isn't any more profane, insensitive, or self-absorbed than the cops she works with, yet they're put off by a woman behaving in a manner they take for granted in a man.

CRACKING THE GLASS CEILING

For all her shortcomings, though, Tennison is a crackerjack detective who usually wins the respect of the men who work with her on a murder case. That means a great deal to her, as it would to any leader. The closest she ever comes to tears is not when she's nearly taken off the serial murder case in the first *Prime Suspect,* but rather when she learns every single man in her department has signed a statement saying they don't want her taken off the case.

The net effect of watching DCI Tennison grow more real, more respected, and more capable before our eyes is the knowledge that a woman of quality can sometimes succeed in even the most hostile atmosphere, if her character is strong enough—and the glass ceiling cracks a bit. By the time she left Mystery! for Masterpiece Theatre, Tennison had become a Detective Superintendent and was on her way up the slippery ladder to Scotland Yard, standing alone as the television policewoman all others will be judged against from now on.

True to Her Subjects:

AUTHOR

LYNDA LA PLANTE

IF ACTOR LYNDA LA PLANTE HADN'T BEEN SO CONVINCING PLAYING BAD GIRLS
and tarts, there might never have been a *Prime Suspect.* Trained as a Shakespearean actor,
La Plante expected more than a string of tart parts after winning a scholarship to the
Royal Academy of Dramatic Art at age 16 and acting with England's best in both the
Royal Shakespeare Company and the National Theatre. But the fiery redhead was
so impressive playing sexy bad girls that she quickly was typecast and couldn't
break out of that mold in either television or stage productions.

     That's why La Plante decided to give up her acting career in 1983 and take up
writing for a living. She scored an early triumph with the wildly popular British
miniseries *Widows* in 1983, a six-episode thriller that immediately marked her as a
major new talent among British television writers. Though she continued to get
writing jobs, La Plante then hit a fallow period of six years in which nothing she
wrote under contract actually was put on the air. That all changed when the first
Prime Suspect became a huge hit on British television in 1991, winning the BAFTA
award for best series, then repeating its enormous success in the U.S. on Mystery!
the following year.

     Since then, La Plante has written the storyline for *Prime Suspect 2* and the
script for *Prime Suspect 3,* which she also worked on as associate producer. She has
written a feature film version of *Prime Suspect* for Universal, which is still in development. She wrote the novels *Bella Mafia* (which CBS is turning into a miniseries),
Framed (which was a 1992 miniseries starring Timothy Dalton), *Entwined, Cold
Shoulder,* and its sequel, *Cold Blood.* She also created the British prison series *The Governor.*

     Busy on both sides of the Atlantic, La Plante has homes in London and East
Hampton, New York. She talked about the origins of *Prime Suspect* during a San Francisco
stopover on a U.S. promotional tour for the U.S. edition of her novel *Cold Shoulder.*

QUESTION: *Because* Prime Suspect *exposed the problems women face with sex discrimination in the workplace, many assume you started with that cause and created Jane Tennison to
embody it. Is that how it happened?*

> *"What [Agatha Christie] was going
> for with Miss Marple—the little old
> doddery lady—was the mind, the nimble
> mind in a woman. A woman's mind is
> very different from a man's. We're very
> fast at organization and also usually
> incredibly observant. . . . Women are
> very predatory creatures, and they size
> up things very quickly, whereas a male
> doesn't. A male detective has to learn
> that. Whereas a woman's had it since
> she was a tiny little tot."*
>
> —LYNDA LA PLANTE,
> *At Random*

ANSWER: That wasn't it at all. I didn't start out championing anything. The first thing I did for television was *Widows,* which was about women whose men were blown to smithereens trying to pull off a very dangerous robbery. So, they team up and do the robbery themselves and get it right. *Widows* became this huge success. After that, everything they offered me was the same thing: They wanted four strong women bank managers, four strong women athletic coaches, and so on. I kept saying, "No, no, no, I don't want to do another *Widows.* I've already done that." But they rejected everything else.

That went on for years. . . . Then I started doing this series on paratroopers for the BBC, starring all men, but they dropped that, too. The script editor left the BBC in a row over that and went to Granada Television. She called me up and . . . said they were looking for a new series with a female star.

My brain went on automatic pilot. I told her I'd been working on a series about a woman homicide detective in London. She asked why I thought that was interesting, so I told her it was "because she's not like any other detective you've ever seen on the screen. She's a woman and she's very high-ranked." When she asked me what it was called, I told her *Prime Suspect.*

How far along had you actually developed the Prime Suspect *story when you talked with her?*

I hadn't done a thing. I made it up on the spot. When she called me back later and said Granada was "very, very interested in *Prime Suspect,*" I asked myself, "Now what do I do?"

Well, what did you do?

I quickly rang the London Metropolitan Police and said I wanted to do a show about a female police officer. They said that was fine. But when I told them I needed to find a plainclothes woman detective, age 35 to 40, who had a high rank and who could lead a murder inquiry, they started passing me from department to department to department. Eventually, I discovered there were only four in the whole of England.

You were finally introduced to DCI Jackie Malton. How important was she to the process of creating the woman we saw on screen?

The first *Prime Suspect* was all Jackie. I couldn't have done it without her. Because I was with her, I was taken inside to see the real police at work. Right away I thought, "How could so many writers of detective stories have gotten it so wrong!" The real people can't watch the television shows because they're all rubbish, so I paid particular attention to the facts all the time. I just wanted to put it right. If people have given me that much of their time, I want them to approve of whatever I do.

You created Jane Tennison as a woman so obsessed by her work that her personal life is a shambles. Did DCI Malton show you that, too?

That's Jackie's story. She can't have a relationship with anybody. They have a very high level of divorce in the police, particularly in those pressure-point jobs like hers.

How important was it to you to deliver a powerful message about sex discrimination in the police department?

If you want to hear about that, ask her, not me. I saw her cry, saw her angry, saw her shortchanged, but that's what made it real. I just put it on the page. Even Jackie didn't speak out right away. But one of the English reviews said the discrimination issue had been overemphasized. That's when she came out and went on the attack. It became such a discussion point with the police themselves. You know, they now use *[Prime Suspect]* as a recruitment film. It's unbelievable.

Once you resolved to write a very honest and authentic story about what it's like to be a woman in an all-male homicide unit, did you have to fight to keep it real?

They wanted me to drop her age. I said, "No. She's 40, and she couldn't get that far without being that age." They said she should show more emotion when she sees a dead body. I said, "Why? A doctor doesn't cry every time somebody's wheeled into his surgery. This is her job." I'd been rejected too many times to start doing *Murder, She Wrote*. For the first time in my life, I dug in my heels. I wanted to protect Jackie. I couldn't take up six months of this woman's life and then trivialize it.

How did you feel about casting Helen Mirren to play DCI Tennison?

They had a list of three people for the lead, and one of them was Helen Mirren, so I said go for her. Helen was the right age, she's naturally sensual, . . . and she has the "weight" as an actor. I owe a lot to Helen Mirren. I wrote the part, but she added a lot of qualities to it.

How early did Granada realize it had a potential blockbuster hit in Prime Suspect?

At first, they had so little confidence in it that they only had me write the first hour. They finally put my script in "flexipool," which was a system where the networks would pool all their leftover scripts in a heap, so everybody could look at them. Then weird things started to happen. I started getting calls from Anglia, from London Weekend Television, and from other companies, offering me jobs and throwing money at me. That's when Granada finally realized it might be sitting on something good.

After writing the first Prime Suspect, *someone else wrote the screenplay for* Prime Suspect 2, *following your outline. You came back to write* Prime Suspect 3, *but haven't been involved with the series since. What happened?*

I don't own Jane Tennison or *Prime Suspect*. I'm just a writer for hire. It sounds churlish to complain because, without that television company, I wouldn't be where I am today. But you can't help the anger. Take *Prime Suspect 2*. They used all my research, all my contacts. The story was all blocked out, every character. . . . There was even dialogue. . . . I first learned how little a writer means to a network when it won the Emmy. Did they mention my name? Not once.

The next Emmy [for *Prime Suspect 3*] was very emotional for me. I was associate producer on that one and had worked with the real "rent kids" [sexually exploited children whose lives were dramatized in the story]. I wanted to go back to them and say, "See, this is what we got!" Then, on the steps of the Emmy theater, the executive producer took the award out of my hand and said, "That doesn't belong to you. That belongs to the producer." That's when I walked.

They came back to me later and said they wanted to do *Prime Suspect 4*. I told them to go ahead without me. I've had nothing to do with it since.

In Her Prime:

ACTOR

HELEN MIRREN

IN THE OPENING MINUTES OF THE FIRST *Prime Suspect* SERIES, DETECTIVE Chief Inspector Jane Tennison finds herself pushed to the back of an elevator at the Southampton Row police station, surrounded by male detectives who act as if she isn't even there. It was a defining moment for the series, because it symbolized the problem Tennison was going to face when called upon to take command of those same detectives in a complex murder investigation. It also turned out to be a symbolic moment in the career of Helen Mirren, who was about to elbow her way out of the crowd of other mature British actresses and into the international spotlight.

As DCI Tennison, Mirren was universally acclaimed by critics and viewers, and her unforgettable performance earned her a BAFTA award and a host of other honors. Mirren was born Ilyena Lydia Mirren in 1946. Her father, a Russian émigré, worked as a civil servant. Though hampered by poverty, both parents were very bright and interested in the arts, exposing their daughter to theater at an early age. At 12, Helen saw an amateur production of *Hamlet* and was enraptured. Her family tried to discourage her from joining the theater, pointing her instead toward a teaching career. Nevertheless, at 18, she joined the National Youth Theatre, which assembled youngsters on their school holidays and put on shows in London's West End. By then, Mirren had blossomed into a radiant blond beauty and was cast as Cleopatra in *Antony and Cleopatra*. Because of the high visibility of the production, many national critics attended, and Mirren got superb reviews. As a result, she was summoned by the Royal Shakespeare Company, though she had never spent a day in drama school. Soon Mirren was generating raves for her performances in *Troilus and Cressida, Hamlet,* and other plays. She made her film debut in *Age of Consent* (1969) as a beguiling free-spirited beach waif who poses nude for artist James Mason.

Mirren's signature in her earlier films was her willingness to try almost anything, from music hall tap-dancing in *The Fiendish Plot of Dr. Fu Manchu* (1980) to the limitless perversity of *Caligula* (1979). The performance that made critics really take notice was in *The Long Good Friday,* as gangster Bob Hoskins' girlfriend. Since then, the acclaim has only mounted in fervor. She won the Cannes best actress award for *Cal* (1984), a BAFTA for *Prime Suspect,* an Oscar nomination for *The Madness of King George* (1994), a 1995 Tony nomination for *A Week in the Country,* and an American Emmy in 1996 for the *Scent of Darkness* episode (seen on Masterpiece Theatre) of *Prime Suspect.*

The following interview, by Amy Rennert, is excerpted from the book *Helen Mirren—Prime Suspect: A Celebration* (KQED Books, 1995).

QUESTION: *Before* Prime Suspect, *you were known in this country primarily for playing sexually voracious characters in your film roles. How eager were you to portray Detective Chief Inspector Jane Tennison?*

ANSWER: This is a role I have been waiting for. Certain roles are exactly right I'm exactly the right age and the right mentality—I don't have to pretend to be anything other than what I am. Actresses complain about there not being enough strong roles for women. This is the kind of role they are seeking.

You've done three Prime Suspect *series and three* Prime Suspect *movies for television. Any worries about being typecast?*

There's a danger in coming back to character roles because you can get stuck with them. They kind of wrap you in their octopus-like arms, and you can't struggle free. I know that sounds like actor talk, but it's true. This is the first time I've done someone more than once—I've always deliberately avoided that—but Jane really is a wonderful contemporary character. You only have to look at the material you usually watch on television and in cinema to realize how little good work there is.

Tennison isn't a completely likable character, but audiences root for her. How would you describe her?

She is a driven, obsessive, vulnerable, unpleasantly egotistical, and confused woman. But she is damn good at what she does, and totally dedicated. I also see her completely participating in life. She's very much alive.

Do you like her?

Yes and no. I enjoy disliking her. She isn't always a nice person. She can be selfish and driven. Those aspects are actually quite attractive in that they are forceful and dramatic. We're accustomed to seeing neurotic or hysterical women characters—victims—but we rarely see a woman whose faults are directly related to her strengths. The only way to change the perception that women have to be consistently perfect is to show that we're not. I know that it is important to project an attractive image, but male actors have been allowed the freedom to play a broad range of character types and have us care about them. It's time women claimed that right for themselves. I hope this is a turning point in the way people view female characters.

Do you believe film, theater, and television play a major part in speeding up the social process?

I do. I get a big response from women in many different professions who like that *Prime Suspect* is political without being propagandist. It just shows the world the way it is. And I'm glad that my character has inspired some women to be more confident and

"*I'd been through the same thing [as Tennison] in a small way when I was much younger. Things have changed since, but in those days a film set was a very macho, male-oriented environment. It was pretty brutal. You often were one of only two or three women among 60 men.*"

—HELEN MIRREN

"*In [Jane Tennison], television has one of its all-time great heroines, if so noble a superlative can be used to describe a character who, in essence, is so supreme a bitch. . . . A British writer suggested that she is the kind of person who manages to compress all of the anxieties of her day into the movement of her hand as it combs back her cropped hair. Often she barks at her underlings as if she were in charge not of the vice squad but of Buckingham Palace, and her eyes are always on her career. First thing on the first day in her new office she says, 'Right, Sergeant, I'm not going to take any crap from you.'*"

—ROBERT SULLIVAN
Vogue

optimistic. But I think getting women into politics as quickly as possible is what's needed most, because there they have tremendous visibility. I've always said that Mrs. Thatcher was one of my great heroines; but whenever I say that, especially in England, I have to immediately dissociate myself from her politics, which I loathed. Her politics actually drove me out of England. I found them that repulsive.

Could you talk a little about your early family life?

I grew up with a brother and a sister in a small seaside town, Southend-on-Sea. The town was like the Coney Island of London, only not quite as wild. It's very working-class, or lower-income, as you call it in America. I was incredibly foolish as a child, always having fantasies, never very practical.

And what did you dream for yourself?

I wanted to be an actress from a very early age. I didn't quite know why, but I used to lie in my bed looking out the window at night at a particular configuration of stars, and I would see this huge letter A in the sky. It was enormous, and it was the last thing I would see before going to sleep. For me, it represented Acting, and it represented America. That was another dream, that I would go to America one day.

What is it that drove you to be an actress?

My desire really came from Shakespeare. I found his stories so much more interesting than the Rock Hudson and Doris Day movies that would come to my little town.

You've portrayed all the great Shakespearean women—Ophelia, Lady Macbeth, Cleopatra. Do you want to return to Shakespeare?

Some of the roles I could do again. It's good to go back to a role because there's so much in Shakespeare, and you never get it right. [Laughs] But there are very few good Shakespearean roles for women my age, and so many fabulous male roles. There's such inequity.

The same can be said for the movies and television. There aren't many leading roles for women your age. That's why Tennison is such a breakthrough character. It's wonderful—and very unusual—to see a beautiful, forty-something woman on the screen in such a major role. Your character doesn't seem afraid to show her age.

With Tennison, you see everything. If you don't like it, too bad. It's so much better to think like that. It's the advantage that male actors have—they don't have to bother with mascara and worry so much about how they look. It's disappointing to me that so many American actresses are obsessed with good looks. They believe they have to be perfect. I mean, please. Life's too short. Agewise, you have to move on. I think we have to say, "Yes, we do get older," because we do. And I don't mind saying how it is, if you know what I mean. The amazing thing is that audiences don't mind, either. Audiences are constantly underestimated and insulted by American producers.

It sounds as if both you and your character have come up against authority figures who are a little out of touch with the real world.

Yes. Tennison is fighting a world that has its rules. You cannot flank, and you can't sail off directly into the wind. You will only get blown back. So you have to tack against the wind, and you have to be very, very clever. Women want to be as much like men as possible, because if they look obviously different, they get a lot of flak. I know it sounds trivial, but cutting my hair short for the role was the most difficult preparation. With each snip I got more into character. For some reason, there's this idea that powerful, intelligent women have to have short hair. Look at the clothes that policewomen wear—very tailored dark suits and ties.

They're supposed to fit into a masculine world, but not too much, because that has other traps.

Right. In many ways, we've underplayed how much women in powerful roles have to give up. It's incredibly difficult for them. In England a woman was sacked from her job for being too bossy. For being too bossy! She was the head of a health organization, and her patients loved her.

Several years ago, an English survey indicated that 90 percent of those polled would choose to have a male detective investigate if one of their loved ones were murdered. Do you think Prime Suspect *might affect the results in a new poll?*

Definitely.

Would you rather have a male or female detective assigned to a case?

Now, I would say I wouldn't mind either way. Ten years ago I used to think of the police as the enemy. I had absolutely no confidence in them, male or female. And I've always been nervous around them; whenever one was following me, I'd get sweaty palms. But doing the series has given me more respect for the cops—an informed kind of respect, not blind admiration.

How have the police responded to the series?

They like it. The police love to see themselves on television—when the camera is turned on them, they are on their best behavior. What they don't like to see is a real-life documentary that's been secretly filmed.

I'm a bit surprised that they enjoy watching the series, since the cops on Prime Suspect *are not always portrayed in a favorable light. Corruption and cover-ups are often part of the story.*

One of the great things about the series is that it is fairly critical of the police. The biggest response I've had is from people in the streets, often young black guys, who say, "Hey, you're that lady cop. Keep up the good work. It's fab!"

What has changed now that the format is a two-hour movie and creator Lynda La Plante is not involved?

With the three miniseries, we really had time to explore the texture of the characters and do wonderful character development. You aren't really able to do that in the two-hour format. Lynda created such an extraordinary life force—an amazing invention. But I do think there has been great consciousness of not shifting the terrain and continuing in a way that is faithful to her original creation.

American and English viewers alike seem to agree that Prime Suspect *is great television. The ratings have been sky-high in both countries. Do you get a similar response from fans?*

When we first did the series, we didn't know if it was going to fly in America; we thought maybe it was too English. But the reaction has been similar—the only noticeable difference is that American audiences are much more vocal and more

"[Police inspectors] are extremely observant, much more so than actors. They have to be; sometimes it's a question of survival. I was observing [the two women inspectors hired to teach me policespeak and body language] observing me. When I tried on the costume for the part in the mirror, I folded my arms because you have this idea that you've got to look strong, and one of these policewomen said, 'Incidentally, we never fold our arms, it's a defense action.' They have to be conscious of these things."

—HELEN MIRREN

"I never really liked Jane Tennison's brutality or her selfishness, and I don't like her job and could never be involved in a profession like it. But I do approve of the way she walks on men and uses them, which is just what men often do to women. I think women are just as capable of that as men. And I think the fact that she could be unlikable is one of the reasons she was popular. Sometimes being a female character is a bit like being a black character. You're treated with kid gloves. You can't be selfish and greedy unless you're like Joan Collins in Dynasty. *You can't be an ordinary, flawed person."*

—HELEN MIRREN,
Independent

INSPECTOR
RODERICK ALLEYN

ARTISTS IN CRIME

Ngaio Marsh's Alleyn Mysteries

Based on the novels by
Ngaio Marsh

RODERICK ALLEYN CAME TO MYSTERY! IN 1992 AS A DISTINCTIVE NEW
KIND OF DETECTIVE FOR THE SHOWCASE—A SORT OF HYBRID OF THE TWO TYPES OF
DETECTIVE THAT HAVE ACCOUNTED FOR THE BULK OF PROGRAMS IN THE SERIES:
THE ELEGANT ARISTOCRAT AND THE WORKADAY COP.

Like Dorothy L. Sayers' renowned Lord Peter Wimsey, "Rory" Alleyn is a blueblood aristocrat, the doting son of the Dowager Duchess of Devonshire, a glib old lady who's always
happy to help out her odd duck of a son by letting him use her large country estate as a
waystation during the course of his many murder investigations. That roots Alleyn firmly
in the so-called "golden age" of British mystery—the 1920s and early 1930s—when
Sayers, Agatha Christie, Margery Allingham, and so many others introduced their man-
nered and elegant sleuths, then turned them loose on clue-heavy murder cases.

But New Zealand author Dame Ngaio Marsh, who created Alleyn in 1931, gave
him a fundamental conceptual difference that immediately set him apart from Wimsey,
Campion, and the rest: He works for a living, on salary, like most of us, as a detective
inspector at Scotland Yard. And that seems to place him in the front ranks of the detectives who would lead a new trend toward the modern "police procedural" novel, a course
that would eventually turn most mystery writers into "crime writers" and make their
novels more factual, more realistically plotted, and more involved with recognizably
human characters.

STRADDLING TWO ERAS

What astute Mystery! viewers soon realized is that Chief Inspector Alleyn is a transitional
detective who's passing from one era into another. Indeed, by the time Marsh had finished
with Inspector Alleyn, he seemed to have much more in common with Ruth Rendell's
Inspector Wexford and P. D. James' Commander Adam Dalgliesh than he had with the
"golden age" sleuths he resembled at the start of his career. A sensitive, caring Inspector
Alleyn solves his cases through dogged police work, slowly piling up evidence until he
has the culprit nailed.

Producer George Gallaccio saw great potential in Inspector Alleyn because he
could function both as a modern cop who utilizes modern techniques to catch criminals,
and as a romantic hero from an earlier period destined to find the clever, independent,
modern woman who might become his partner in life—in this case, well-known painter

PRODUCTION COMPANY
BBC

YEARS
1992–1995

MAIN CAST
Chief Inspector
Roderick Alleyn
SIMON WILLIAMS/
PATRICK MALAHIDE

Agatha Troy
BELINDA LANG

Inspector Fox
WILLIAM SIMONS

Agatha Troy. In fact, Gallaccio found Troy so compelling that he had her added to several stories in which she didn't originally appear.

"I wanted to capitalize on that character," Gallaccio explained when the series premiered. "She's so strong. I certainly didn't want her relegated to the kitchen or her studio, so I've put her into books that Ngaio Marsh didn't." In the novels Marsh permitted Alleyn and Troy a passion-free, but tantalizingly romantic courtship, then arranged a marriage that pretty much took Troy off active duty. Marsh wasn't keen on creating another husband-and-wife detective team like Tuppence and Tommy Beresford or Nick and Nora Charles.

We first meet the pair in *Artists in Crime,* when Alleyn (Simon Williams) is trying to forget the horrors of war by enjoying a vacation cruise. On board he meets a lovely painter but soon is called back to duty to help solve the murder of a glamorous artists' model (Siri Neal), who had been posing for a group of artists under the supervision of . . . the shipboard artist Agatha Troy (Belinda Lang) at her studio in the country.

As Alleyn digs into a complex series of relationships between the various artists, he discovers what appears to be a blackmail plot. Though he doesn't want to, the already-smitten Alleyn also has to consider Troy a potential suspect in the murder. The situation is not unlike the meeting of Lord Peter Wimsey and the woman who eventually becomes his wife—mystery writer Harriet Vane, who is a suspect in the murder of her former lover in the novel *Strong Poison.*

> *"While the beau monde may privately frown on Inspector Alleyn's line of work, his distinguished pedigree invariably opens the doors of England's grandest houses—giving him entry into a world that Ngaio Marsh knew well. Swept into the whirl of country-house weekends and lavish garden parties, she absorbed the nuances of fashionable English society: where the drinks should be placed, what time dinner should be served, how to dress in the evening.*
>
> —DIANA RIGG

A WELL-GROUNDED INSPECTOR

Williams played Alleyn—the *y* is silent, by the way—as a courtly, but well-grounded individual who appears neither a snob nor the black sheep of his titled family. He has few of the eccentricities of the early Wimsey or Campion, though he does have a rather unadvanced sense of humor and likes to call his colleague Inspector Fox by the nickname "Brer" Fox. Two years after *Artists in Crime,* Inspector Alleyn returned in the person of older, more taciturn Patrick Malahide, who starred in five episodes. Malahide, a veteran stage performer, used former English Prime Minister Anthony Eden as the role model for his portrayal of Alleyn. "He has to be truly elegant—someone who has a top-class, well-tailored look, but done with sobriety," Malahide told interviewers. "He's far too much of a gentleman to wear anything that looks too overtly expensive." That touch of logic is a key to understanding Alleyn, who wears his good breeding with grace and dignity but has no trouble consorting with his colleagues from humbler backgrounds.

Reprising the roles they played in *Artists in Crime* were William Simons (not to be confused with Simon Williams) as Detective Inspector Fox, who also had played Constable Thackeray in the *Sergeant Cribb* series on Mystery!, and Belinda Lang, who played Troy as a strong-minded modern woman, which she felt made her a perfect match for the often intense Alleyn.

"Neither of them is prepared to compromise," Lang said in promotional interviews. "She can be a bit frightening [because] she's so strong. When she and Alleyn meet, I think they recognize their similarities, but they dance round each other. They're quite cagey about their relationship." Alleyn and Troy eventually married, but Mystery! viewers never got to see it: No additional episodes were telecast after the five with Malahide.

Artist in Crime:

SIDEKICK/INAMORATA
AGATHA TROY
(BELINDA LANG)

Agatha Troy is much more than a sidekick to Inspector Roderick Alleyn. An independent woman, she's a well-known artist with her own career, who's also his inamorata, automatically placing her closer to his heart than Watson was to Holmes or Hastings to Poirot. Marsh described Alleyn's first sight of Troy this way: "She wore a pair of exceedingly grubby flannel trousers, and a short gray overall. . . . Her face was disfigured by a smudge of green paint, and her short hair stood up in a worried shock, as though she had run her hands through it. She was very thin and dark." Not the most enticing image, but it worked just the same. Inspector Alleyn was completely smitten.

Troy frequently draws Alleyn into puzzling cases, and it's her observant eye that often helps him get to the bottom of them. In *Final Curtain,* she suspects a murder and prods the inspector to check into the case. In *A Man Lay Dead,* she overhears a quarrel that provides a vital clue. In *Death in a White Tie,* a blackmailer picks the opening of Troy's exhibit at the Winchester Galleries as the site of his payoff.

Belinda Lang came to the role with a well-established television following from two earlier British series—*Second Thoughts* and *2.4 Children.* She had to practice her painting all during the filming of the Alleyn mysteries, doing sketches of her fellow actors and, on weekends, of husband Hugh Fraser—who also was pulling sidekick duty as Arthur Hastings in the Hercule Poirot mysteries.

Flowering Tree of Mystery:

AUTHOR
NGAIO MARSH

DAME NGAIO MARSH OFTEN SAID SHE DIDN'T ESPECIALLY LIKE DETECTIVE NOVELS and rarely read them. But perhaps that's because she had already read all her favorite ones by Dorothy L. Sayers. Marsh acknowledged a certain debt to Sayers, whose Lord Peter Wimsey clearly was the pattern for Marsh's Inspector Alleyn. Though Wimsey was a private detective and Alleyn a civil servant, both were aristocrats, both fell in love with and married independent women who rather strongly resembled their creators, and both behaved like insufferable twits in their earlier mysteries. The Alleyn novels from the late 1930s on tend to be less "Wimseycal" as Alleyn begins to evolve into a more likable, more thoughtful detective who seems more like P. D. James' Adam Dalgliesh in the embryo stage.

Marsh was born in 1899 at Christchurch, New Zealand. The name *Ngaio*, which she went by through most of her life, is Maori in origin. Pronounced "Nye-oh," it's variously translated as "flowering tree," "light on the water," or "little tree bug." Her father was English, but her mother was from a British colonial family that had come to New Zealand from the West Indies 45 years before she was born. Though she created one of England's most popular detectives, Marsh didn't set foot in England until she was nearly 30.

AN ARTIST BEFORE CRIME

Originally, Marsh had planned a career as an artist and at 16 entered art school, where she attended a stage play and became enthralled by the theater. For the rest of her life, her main interests were art and the theater, not mystery writing. Her affinity for those subjects shines through her Inspector Alleyn mysteries. Many take place in theater settings, and of course her main female character, Agatha Troy, is a painter.

In 1928, Marsh went to London to stay with a friend—a visit that extended to four years. During that time, she found work as an actor, a fashion model, and a newspaper correspondent, sending accounts of her travels back to readers in New Zealand. She also helped her friend open a handicrafts shop and, while struggling to make a go of the shop, began writing her first novel. Though she returned home in 1932 when her mother was fatally ill, Marsh had fallen in love with England and divided her time between both countries through most of her adult life.

Marsh wrote 32 Inspector Alleyn mysteries, many of them bestsellers. She was highly regarded as a literary stylist and one of the last great practitioners of the so-called clue-driven "golden age" genre of British murder mysteries. She also wrote a number of plays for stage, radio, and television. Queen Elizabeth made her a Dame of the British Empire for her great contributions to theater as a writer, producer, and director. She died in New Zealand in 1982.

SELECTED BIBLIOGRAPHY

A Man Lay Dead, 1934; *Enter a Murderer*, 1935; *The Nursing Home Murder*, 1935; *Death in Ecstasy*, 1936; *Vintage Murder*, 1937; *Artists in Crime*, 1938; *Death in a White Tie*, 1938; *Overture to Death*, 1939; *Death of a Peer* (English title: *A Surfeit of Lampreys*), 1940; *Death at the Bar*, 1940; *Death and the Dancing Footman*, 1941; *Colour Scheme*, 1943; *Died in the Wool*, 1945; *Final Curtain*, 1947; *A Wreath for Rivera* (English title: *Swing, Brother, Swing*), 1949; *Night at the Vulcan* (English title: *Opening Night*), 1951; *Spinsters in Jeopardy*, 1953; *Scales of Justice*, 1955; *Singing in the Shrouds*, 1958; *False Scent*, 1959; *Hand in Glove*, 1962; *Dead Water*, 1963; *Killer Dolphin* (English title: *Death at the Dolphin*), 1966; *Clutch of Constables*, 1968; *When in Rome*, 1970; *Tied up in Tinsel*, 1972; *Black As He's Painted*, 1975; *Last Ditch*, 1978; *Grave Mistake*, 1978; *Photo Finish*, 1980; *Light Thickens*, 1982.

"One of Ngaio Marsh's trademarks as a mystery writer is the bizarre deaths she dreamed up for her characters. One poor soul was packed into a bale of wool; another was done in by a booby-trapped piano. But very few of her victims were dispatched with poison, as Sir Derek O'Callaghan was in The Nursing Home Murder. *"Marsh had feared poison since childhood, when her imagination was inflamed by a line from one of her father's favorite ballads—'a cup of cold poison lay there by her side.' The song so terrified the little girl that she burned the sheet music in the fireplace. 'To this day,' she wrote, 'on the rare occasions that I use poison in a detective story, I am visited by a ludicrous aftertaste of my childish horrors.'"*

—DIANA RIGG

INSPECTOR
JULES MAIGRET

MAIGRET

Based on the novels by
Georges Simenon

CHIEF INSPECTOR JULES MAIGRET OF THE PARIS POLICE IS THE ODD
MAN OUT IN THE FAMILY OF MYSTERY! INVESTIGATORS. HE'S THE ONLY RECURRING
DETECTIVE WHOSE SERIES DOES NOT TAKE PLACE IN ENGLAND.

In a way, that's a tribute to the international appeal of Belgian author Georges Simenon's pipe-smoking French detective, who already had fostered a publishing legend by appearing in 84 novels and 18 short stories, selling more than 500 million copies in 55 different languages before he made his debut on Mystery! in 1992.

Maigret always was a distinctive detective from the time Simenon dreamed him up during a 1929 vacation in the Netherlands and hastily wrote the concept down on the back of an envelope. Simenon conceived him as a big, burly man, but one who solved crimes in a thoughtful, methodical manner, without taking part in gunfights, car chases, or brawls in dark alleys. Moreover, Maigret was the sort of detective who not only understood the criminal mind, but also could feel empathy for many of the people he tracked down. In fact, it's often said that Maigret found redeeming qualities in nearly all the lawbreakers he brought to justice.

MAIGRET IN MANY TONGUES

Though there were already a number of film Maigrets—Charles Laughton played one in *The Man in the Eiffel Tower*—the new Mystery! series needed an all-new Maigret. So the producers turned to one of England's finest stage actors, Michael Gambon, a veteran star of the Royal Shakespeare Company and the National Theatre who was probably best known to American audiences as the star of Dennis Potter's acclaimed series *The Singing Detective,* for which he won the British equivalent of an Academy Award.

Gambon had the essential rumpled look, big, thick build, mustache, and shrewd eyes. Suited up in trilby hat and overcoat, a pipe jammed in his mouth, he could easily be imagined stalking criminals through the Paris underworld. The Gambon interpretation of Maigret was that of a compassionate, nonviolent man who likes his work, even the part of it that requires associating with criminals. "He likes criminals," Gambon observed during the filming. "He finds good people boring."

The producers decided to forgo fake French accents in the shows and instead have the mostly English cast speak naturally, just saying a few French phrases here and there. That was fine with Gambon, who speaks no French and had to be coached even to say

**PRODUCTION
COMPANY**
Granada Television

YEARS
1992–1994

MAIN CAST
Chief Inspector Maigret
MICHAEL GAMBON

Madame Maigret
*CIARAN MADDEN/
BARBARA FLYNN*

Sergeant Lucas
GEOFFREY HUTCHINGS

Inspector Janvier
JACK GALLOWAY

Inspector Lapointe
JAMES LARKIN

"England's Granada Television chose wisely in making Michael Gambon its Maigret. His deceptively benign smile and hulking, square-jawed somberness convey the sort of weariness you'd expect from someone who'd made a career of exploring the dark side of human behavior."

—HOWARD ROSENBERG,
Los Angeles Times

113

those few French phrases properly, but it may have caused some casual viewers to wonder when the English took over Paris and threw all the French people out.

Another imposing challenge presented itself: The company's designers couldn't find enough sectors in Paris that still resembled 1950s France, the period covered by the series, so Budapest stood in for the City of Light. But even if Paris didn't look or sound exactly right, the stories were quite authentically Maigret. In *The Patience of Maigret*, for instance, the inspector has to sort through the suspects in a Paris apartment block to find the killer of a wheelchair-bound gangster. In *Maigret and the Burglar's Wife*, the inspector comes to the aid of a petty burglar who discovers a dead body while breaking into a house. In *Maigret Sets a Trap*, the inspector cleverly uses newspaper publicity to lure a Montmartre serial killer into striking again.

Altogether, Mystery! presented 12 *Maigret* episodes over two seasons. Mme Maigret was played by Ciaran Madden in the first six and by Barbara Flynn, who later starred in *Chandler & Co.*, in the second six. Many episodes also featured top British actors and fellow Mystery! players in guest roles, among them Catherine Russell *(Chandler & Co.)*, Edward Petherbridge *(Dorothy L. Sayers' Lord Peter Wimsey)*, and Joanna David *(Rebecca)*.

BUDAPEST STANDS IN FOR PARIS

The producers filmed in Budapest because the City of Light was just too modern to resemble Paris of the 1950s. But the dark, crumbling atmosphere of Budapest was just perfect, with its "dingy 1920s atmosphere and wonderful shabby courtyards, balconies, and staircases," says production designer Chris Wilkinson. "We found huge apartments empty since World War II."

Naturally, some changes had to be made. Wallpaper had to be imported from England, and street signs, advertising posters, cars, books, and magazines—even a special brand of beer—had to be shipped in from Paris. Many of the street structures were built from scratch (the onion-domed advertising carousel, a "pissoir"), while some were altered slightly (Maigret's favorite watering hole, the Brasserie Dauphine, was originally a Hungarian cafe), and a number were pressed into service just as they stood (the city's train stations and a bridge, because according to Wilkinson, they're "straight from the Eiffel school of architecture"). Even the local KGB office played a role—it became the minister's office in *Maigret and the Minister*.

Literary Ladies' Man:

AUTHOR
GEORGES SIMENON

GEORGES SIMENON, THE CREATOR OF CHIEF INSPECTOR MAIGRET, MIGHT have been an even more fascinating subject for a television series than his famous Parisian police detective. Born in Liège, Belgium, in 1903, Simenon landed a job covering the police beat for his local newspaper at age 16. By the time he was 20, he had left for Paris and begun his career as a fiction writer, knocking out adventure and romance stories for pulp magazines. In all, he published more than 300 of them, all under pen names.

Simenon seemed to do everything with singular intensity. When he began writing his first Maigret novel in 1929, he had a complete manuscript at the end of four days. He wrote an average of 80 pages per day and managed to turn out 18 more Maigret novels at the rate of one a month before taking his first break. Later, he settled into a routine of six novels per year, spending two weeks on each. By the time he retired, he had written 84 Maigret novels, 100 other novels, and countless short stories.

SEXUAL EXPLOITS AS "RESEARCH"

The author's love life was equally hectic. Simenon boasted in his memoirs that he had made love to more than 10,000 women in his lifetime—often engaging in sex three or four times in a single day. But it was just research, *vous comprenez:* "Women have always been exceptional people for me, whom I have vainly tried to understand," he said. "It has been a lifelong, ceaseless quest. And how could I have created dozens, perhaps hundreds, of female characters in my novels, if I had not experienced these adventures?" Simenon had a passionate affair with the legendary chanteuse Josephine Baker and even served as her secretary and fan magazine editor. He finally broke off the relationship when he realized it was cutting into his writing time. Simenon was married twice, the first time at age 20. His second wife, whom he divorced in 1955, was widely quoted as saying he had exaggerated his love-making prowess and probably had only slept with a mere 1,200 women.

INSPECTOR INSPIRED BY REAL ONES

Simenon is generally believed to have based the Maigret character on police detectives he knew in his hometown—and on his father. Another influence on the character was a Paris Police Commissaire named Guillaume, who impressed Simenon with his ability to extract information from suspects without resorting to violence.

After World War II, Simenon served as the Commissioner for Belgian Refugees in Paris, but he wasn't especially comfortable there and finally moved to the U.S. Paris may have lost its charm for the author when he was accused of being a Nazi collaborator. From 1946 to 1955, Simenon lived in America, often in colorful fashion, running briefly with the Hollywood crowd. His second marriage fell apart after he moved to Switzerland in 1955, perhaps due to his love affair with his wife's maid. He officially retired as a novelist in 1973 at age 70—and died in 1989, before ever seeing the *Maigret* series for Mystery!.

SELECTED BIBLIOGRAPHY

The Strange Case of Peter the Lett, 1931; *Maigret's War of Nerves,* 1931; *Maigret in New York's Underworld,* 1947; *Maigret Afraid,* 1953; *Inspector Maigret and the Burglar's Wife,* 1955; *Maigret Sets a Trap,* 1955; *Madame Maigret's Own Case,* 1959; *Maigret and the Killer,* 1969; *Maigret and Monsieur Charles,* 1972; *Maigret and the Bum,* 1973; *Maigret and the Apparition,* 1976; *Maigret and the Black Sheep,* 1976.

FILM COLLABORATOR

Charged with being a Nazi collaborator during the final days of the second world war, Simenon was placed under house arrest. But he was released after three months when no proof of the charges could be found. Still, he continued to hear criticism from people who felt he shouldn't have sold film rights to his stories to a film company that then inserted Nazi propaganda into them.

THE PRIVATE EYES

*A famous jockey who can't race
anymore, a frolicsome husband and wife team,
and a pair of inquisitive 1990s women looking
for exciting new careers. What else could
they become but private eyes!*

- **SID HALLEY**
  THE RACING GAME

- **TOMMY AND TUPPENCE BERESFORD**
  PARTNERS IN CRIME, THE SECRET ADVERSARY

- **ELLY CHANDLER AND DEE TATE**
  CHANDLER & CO.

SID HALLEY

THE RACING GAME

*Based on the novel Odds Against
by Dick Francis*

SID HALLEY IS A YOUNG MAN WHO TRULY KNOWS THE THRILL OF
VICTORY AND THE AGONY OF DEFEAT. BUT WHEN THE MYSTERY! AUDIENCE FIRST
MEETS HIM IN *THE RACING GAME*, HE IS CERTAIN THE VICTORY PART IS ALL
IN THE PAST AND IS RESIGNED TO SPENDING THE REST OF HIS LIFE LEARNING
TO LIVE WITH THE AGONY.

**PRODUCTION
COMPANY**
Yorkshire Television

YEARS
1980–1981

MAIN CAST
Sid Halley
MIKE GWILYM

Chico Barnes
MICK FORD

Jenny Halley
SUSAN WOOLDRIDGE

Charles Rowland
JAMES MAXWELL

Halley had been a champion steeplechase jockey and one of the most famous athletes in England until a racing accident ends his career, mutilating his left hand. Unable to cope, Halley has become increasingly sullen and withdrawn, slipping into a steady downward spiral of self-pity that has wrecked his marriage and threatens to finish him off as a productive member of society. But during the six episodes of *The Racing Game*, spread over the first two seasons of Mystery!, viewers were able to witness his redemption. In these shows, Halley regains his dignity by finding a new calling—that of private detective.

Created by Dick Francis, one of the world's top-selling contemporary mystery writers, Sid Halley represents a milestone in the history of Mystery!. As the series' first authentic modern detective, he gave Mystery! instant credibility with hard-core gumshoe aficionados who had patiently waited through a tongue-in-cheek spy parody, a whimsical courtroom series, and a neo-Gothic romance before finally getting a legitimate nitty-gritty detective series.

Working with four of England's best television dramatists—Terence Feely, Evan Jones, Leon Griffiths, and Trevor Preston—Francis mined his own 1965 bestseller, *Odds Against,* for plots they could use to concoct a six-episode series about the Halley character. The first episode, also called *Odds Against,* reached the U.S. audience at the same time Francis' second Halley novel, *Whip Hand,* was turning into an enormous bestseller.

A WORK-IN-PROGRESS

In that first episode, the crucial element that makes Halley a great literary character, rather than just a superb detective hero, is already present: his vulnerability. As a detective, Halley is a work-in-progress. His painful adjustment to losing the thing he had lived for—horse racing—gives him the sensitivity to understand the pain of others. By helping his often desperate clients, he finds new meaning for his life. Halley's gradual discovery that he has the inner strength to master a difficult new trade makes him a rarity in the realm of detective fiction—a real person with realistic problems who just happens to be a detective.

It's territory Francis knows intimately. He, too, was a national champion jockey who basked in the glow of near-universal praise, then had to give up racing while still a young man. Like Halley, Francis refused to be put out to pasture after his retirement from the racing game. Instead, he took the opportunity to start a new career as a novelist. He created his own literary genre—the horse racing mystery—and now has a string of more than 30 bestsellers dating back to 1962.

CRIPPLED IN SPIRIT

When Mystery! viewers first see Sid Halley (Mike Gwilym), he is brimming with pent-up hostility. In a flashback, we see where it began—the nightmare moment when he is thrown from his mount in the heat of a race, then feels the blazing agony as the horse's hoof comes down on his hand. Ashamed of the maimed hand, he keeps it tucked in his jacket pocket, a symbol of his new persona as a "cripple." But there are indications that Halley may have been crippled in more profound ways even before the accident. He's riding not only for prize money and glory, but also to overcome the damaging psychological effects of a childhood marked by poverty in a working-class Welsh family. His marriage to Jenny Rowland (Susan Woodridge), an English blueblood, has been a disaster. In a series of intense scenes between them, it seems obvious he had had little time for her—or for anyone else—when he was racing.

Since his accident, he's unable to see himself in anything but a self-pitying way. His father-in-law, retired Admiral Charles Rowland (James Maxwell), realizes the young man needs shock treatment to get him back on his feet and bullies him into taking on a special task for him—investigating a series of damaging accidents at a rural racetrack that's the proposed site of a new commercial development.

WITH A POKER IN THE BOILER ROOM

In the story's exciting climax, Halley uncovers a plot to destroy the main building at the racetrack by blowing up the huge steam boiler. Seized by bête noire Howard Graves (Gerald Flood) and his cronies, Halley is left in the boiler room to die, but not until after Graves wrecks what's left of Halley's crippled hand by striking it repeatedly with a poker while his decadent wife watches in a state of obvious sexual arousal. In subsequent episodes Halley's hand is amputated and he's fitted with a myo-electric "bionic" hand that further aids his return to a full-functioning life. Helped by his old friend Chico Barnes (Mick Ford), a martial arts instructor, he builds up a solid reputation as a private eye who specializes in cases involving horses and England's high-stakes racing world.

Filmed in and around some of England's top racecourses, *The Racing Game* featured a number of leading British actors in guest roles—and a few of the racing world's top jockeys. Producer Jacky Stoller called on the services of author Francis as a consultant and put together an advisory group of experts to ensure the series' authenticity. Gwilym, a popular stage actor who also starred in the television version of *How Green Was My Valley,* spent a full year playing Halley, which meant learning to ride and to do all other complex actions with just one hand. He also had to master the use of the authentic bionic hand for close-up scenes.

By the time *The Racing Game* ended its run in the second season of Mystery!, Sid Halley had regained his self-respect and was on his way to building a reputation in detection nearly as formidable as the one he once had as a jockey.

THE LONG, ELECTRONIC ARM OF THE LAW

To play one-armed detective Sid Halley Mike Gwilym was fitted with a modified version of a real artificial arm developed in Germany. The "myo-electric" prosthesis is activated by muscle impulses and can pick up a fragile egg or crush a beer can. In the modified version, Gwilym inserted his hand into the hollowed out arm and touched the electrodes with his fingers, triggering the gripping mechanism. He had to practice holding his shoulder at an angle to make the artificial arm appear the same length as his other arm because it actually was five inches longer.

Champion Steeplechase Jockey:

AUTHOR
DICK FRANCIS

DICK FRANCIS WAS A FAMOUS MAN LONG BEFORE HE WAS A BESTSELLING novelist. In fact, if he had never written a single book, his name still would be revered by the English—for being one of the most celebrated steeplechase jockeys of his era.

Born in Tenby, Wales, in 1920, Francis grew up around horses and was an exceptional horseman at a very early age. By 15, he was helping his father run his hunting stables. After service as a bomber pilot with the RAF in World War II, Francis decided to try his luck as a jockey and in 1946 began what was to become a distinguished career in the grueling field of steeplechase racing. By the time Francis retired in 1957, he had won 345 races, finishing second 285 times and third 240 times. In 1953 and 1954, he was the National Hunt Champion and raced under the colors of England's Queen Mother for four years.

At one point, Francis predicted he'd always be remembered as "the man who didn't win the National." That was a reference to his most unusual—and frustrating—race, the 1956 Grand National. Francis was riding Devon Loch, the most celebrated mount in the Queen Mother's stable, in what many still consider his most strategically brilliant race. Suddenly, disaster struck: With a comfortable lead, 30 fences behind him and only about 10 strides remaining to the finish line, Devon Loch suddenly fell flat on his belly. Francis later surmised that Devon Loch may have been spooked by the tremendous roars of the largest, most enthusiastic crowd he'd ever experienced—just as his victory seemed imminent.

Although that fall was more psychologically than physically painful, the many falls Francis had experienced over his career had begun taking a physical toll, and he announced his official retirement a few months after the Grand National. Suddenly, like Halley, he faced the dilemma of finding a new career to replace the one that had consumed his life for so many years.

Encouraged by friends who knew his knowledge of racing was matched by few, Francis went to work as a racing columnist for the *Sunday Express* in 1957 and published his autobiography, *The Sport of Queens*, which revealed his talent as a narrative writer. In

"The first thing I found was that a racehorse has no back—just a knobbly backbone. You can't spread your legs and hold on. You are balanced miles from the ground, legs tucked under you, like a peg on a clothes line. I was introduced to this grey horse, who was pawing the ground at the time. He knew immediately that I hadn't a clue, and horses don't suffer fools gladly.

It was an eight-horse field, with seven professional jockeys and old muggins me in green silks with face to match. The jockeys were friendly—after all, it was a bit of a novelty for them. The one piece of advice they gave me was, 'Don't get ahead of the field.' I found out why only too soon.

A racehorse will go like the wind if you give him his head, but he doesn't want to stop. Unless the jockey is experienced, the horse will go on until he either runs out of steam or falls over."

—MIKE GWILYM,
TV Times

1962, he published his first novel, *Dead Cert,* about an investigation into the mysterious death of a famous steeplechase jockey during a race. Applauded by critics and the racing gentry, it started him off on a long string of more than 30 international bestsellers, all connected in some way to the world of horse racing.

Francis is married and has two sons. He now spends most of his time at his home in the Cayman Islands near Jamaica in the British West Indies. Though he considers himself the author of "adventure stories," Francis has been a fixture of the literary world's mystery scene for a generation and has won both the Edgar Allan Poe and Golden Dagger awards.

QUESTION: *What was your reaction when you learned that Mike Gwilym, a young Shakespearean actor, was the first choice to play tough little ex-jockey Sid Halley in* The Racing Game?

ANSWER: Jacky Stoller, who was the producer of *The Racing Game,* said they'd decided on someone they thought could play the part and asked if I'd like to meet him. Well, I went to the Aldwych Theatre in London, where he was playing Troilus in *Troilus and Cressida* as a member of the Royal Shakespeare Company. He played the part very, very well. So, I went backstage to meet him, and he was very nice. Indeed, my wife and I made great friends with him. I remember the first time he came and stayed with us. I asked him if he'd like a drink, and he asked for a scotch and soda. When I gave him his drink, it was just like I was handing the drink to Sid Halley. I thought, "Yes, he'll play the part, all right."

Though Gwilym had a real jockey double for him in the risky racing scenes, did you have to teach him how to make his horseback scenes look authentic?

He mixed a lot with my wife and me and our sons, and our talk was always about the racing scene. He learned a lot about it. He had ridden a bit as a child, but Yorkshire Television sent him to a riding establishment somewhere to bring his riding up to scratch a bit more. He rode quite well enough for the scenes he played.

Have the two of you kept in touch?

He went abroad and became somewhat of a recluse. No one seems to know where he is. The last I heard he was somewhere in Spain.

Is Sid Halley mostly you or did you base him partly on someone you knew in real life?

He was made up of a number of people. I never adapt a character from one person I know. There was part of me in him, but all my characters are slightly autobiographical. I don't ask them to do anything I wouldn't do myself.

But Sid is a most unusual detective because he has a severe disability and eventually has a hand amputated. Did you draw on real-life experiences of anyone for that aspect of his character?

I had the insight of someone who was very close to me—my wife. She had polio in 1950, when our first son was on the way. She was in an iron lung for five to six weeks. Like Sid Halley, she had to readjust her way of life after she came out. If you saw her today, you wouldn't realize she had been a polio victim. My wife and I went to the Artificial Limb Center in London and did a lot of research there on people being fitted with new limbs. One was an officer from the Egyptian Army. He'd had his hand blown off. He was so scared of using his new hand. That's how I painted Sid Halley to start with. He wasn't scared, but was just embarrassed for other people to see him with this hand.

How active a role did you play in the making of the series?

I did the storylines for the series. Otherwise, I didn't take a very active role. I did go to a number of the tracks where they filmed it, but I didn't have a lot to do with how they did it.

Weren't they originally going to film 13 episodes of The Racing Game? *What happened?*

They had planned to do 13. I'm sorry they didn't go on past the first six. At the time, Yorkshire Television was having a big problem with strikes. The executives decided to scrap all the series they had going at the time, and mine was one of them. Jacky Stoller was heartbroken, and I was, too, for her sake, because the first six had been very well received, especially in England.

So many of the incidents in Odds Against *and the second Sid Halley novel,* Whip Hand, *suggest corruption in the racing world. Did that make it difficult to film on real racetracks?*

They shot at several different tracks. I get very good cooperation worldwide with the people who run the tracks. Wherever I go, they always make me feel welcome, and the track is the first place they take me.

How did you happen to start writing mysteries?

When I was a jockey, I traveled a lot. When I was traveling about, I always liked to read the sort of books I write now. Although I'm called a mystery writer, I like to consider myself an adventure story writer.

Many fans feel you've transcended the mystery—or adventure—field to become a major contemporary author because of your insight into character and social issues. Are you happy to hear that?

When I first started writing, my books were reviewed by the racing correspondents. My books were published in the winter, so when the bad weather came, they all needed something to write about. I'm reviewed more by literary critics nowadays, and they treat me rather well. That pleases me more.

Very few people have become famous in two entirely different professions. Is there anything a jockey and a novelist have in common?

There are 12 fences in a two-mile race. When you're riding in toward a fence, you squeeze your horse and try to get him to take off at the right spot and gain a bit of ground on your opponent. It's the same when you're writing a book. When you're getting toward the end of a chapter, you've got to get it to such a pitch that the reader can't put it down. He's just got to go on to the next chapter. So many people tell me they enjoyed my new book and read it last night in four or five hours. And I think, "My God! All that work gone in just four or five hours!"

"Actor Gwilym took a few tumbles but wasn't ever seriously hurt. The stunt man who rode for him in the opening credit sequence of each program was not so lucky. What we'll see on the screen in Horsenap *actually happened without any clever editing. The fall was planned, but apparently the stunt rider got his instructions muddled and fell off the wrong side of the horse—and was trampled and severely injured. Needless to say, there was no 'Take 2'—so that's the accident you see."*

—VINCENT PRICE

SELECTED BIBLIOGRAPHY

Dead Cert, 1962; *Nerve*, 1964; *For Kicks*, 1965; *Odds Against*, 1965; *Flying Finish*, 1966; *Blood Sport*, 1967; *Forfeit*, 1968; *Enquiry*, 1969; *Rat Race*, 1970; *Bonecrack*, 1971; *Smokescreen*, 1972; *Slayride*, 1973; *Knockdown*, 1974; *High Stakes*, 1975; *In the Frame*, 1976; *Risk*, 1977; *Trial Run*, 1978; *Whip Hand*, 1979; *Reflex*, 1980; *Twice Shy*, 1981; *Banker*, 1982; *The Danger*, 1983; *Proof*, 1984; *Break In*, 1985; *Bolt*, 1986; *Hot Money*, 1987; *The Edge*, 1988; *Straight*, 1989; *Longshot*, 1990; *Comeback*, 1991; *Driving Force*, 1992; *Decider*, 1993; *Wild Horses*, 1994; *Come to Grief*, 1995; *To the Hilt*, 1996.

TOMMY
AND
TUPPENCE BERESFORD

➤━

PARTNERS IN CRIME

THE SECRET ADVERSARY

*Based on the novel and stories
by Agatha Christie*

SHORTLY AFTER THE END OF WORLD WAR I, CHILDHOOD PALS
TOMMY BERESFORD AND PRUDENCE "TUPPENCE" COWLEY MEET BY ACCIDENT
AT THE EXIT OF THE DOVER STREET SUBWAY STATION IN LONDON AND
RENEW A FRIENDSHIP THAT WAS TO HAVE A PROFOUND IMPACT ON THE MYSTERY
GENRE FOR GENERATIONS TO COME.

**PRODUCTION
COMPANY**
London Weekend
Television

YEARS
1984–1987

MAIN CAST
Tuppence Beresford
FRANCESCA ANNIS

Tommy Beresford
JAMES WARWICK

Albert
REECE DINSDALE

Inspector Marriott
ARTHUR COX

That chance meeting takes place in the early pages of Agatha Christie's second novel, *The Secret Adversary* (1922). Out of work and nearly out of funds, Tuppence and Tommy need to find jobs fast but want their work to have some of the excitement they had come to expect during the war years. A few pages later, they form a partnership they call The Young Adventurers, Ltd. and soon are hired to help the British government track down a vital secret document—a case that puts them in immediate peril at the hands of spies and Bolshevik terrorists. Headed for marriage by the end of that book, the Beresfords go on to become the whimsical pair of detectives now known as the "partners in crime."

SEMINAL GUMSHOE COUPLE

Tuppence and Tommy didn't know it at the time, but they were making literary history as the first internationally popular, zany, crime-solving married couple, forerunners to a host of other eccentric, upper-class husband-and-wife detective teams that eventually included Nick and Nora Charles, Pamela and Jerry North, and Jonathan and Jennifer Hart. Though Tuppence and Tommy never were as popular as Christie's immortal sleuths Hercule Poirot and Miss Marple, the author never lost interest in them and their merry brand of deduction. They are, in fact, the heroes of the final novel she wrote, *Postern of Fate,* which found the Beresfords in their seventies, still busy flushing spies and saboteurs out of their beloved England.

Tommy and Tuppence finally came to PBS in the 1984 with a ten-episode series adapted from *Partners in Crime,* Christie's 1929 collection of shorter adventures featuring the Beresfords, followed two years later by *The Secret Adversary.* Actually, the series represented a triumphant return to the screen for Tuppence and Tommy. They were, in fact, the first Christie characters to ever appear in a movie: a 1928 German film called *Adventures, Inc.,* based on *The Secret Adversary.*

Though 75 years have passed since Christie dreamed up the Beresfords, their influence is still felt every time a television station reruns an old *Thin Man* movie or an episode of *McMillan and Wife.* Christie's daffy couple served as the blueprint for nearly all the male-female detective teams that followed.

BATTLE OF THE SEXES

Constantly competing to see who can solve a case first, the Beresfords originated the atmosphere of comical banter and gender-based rivalry that has characterized all their imitators. Their ongoing battle of the sexes probably begins in the early pages of *The Secret Adversary,* when Tommy assures Mr. Carter, their government boss, that they can handle the job because he'd "look after" Tuppence and she resentfully snaps, "And I'll look after you!"

That friendly competition was in full swing some 60 years later when *Mystery!* presented the *Partners in Crime* series for the first time. In the first episode, *The Affair of the Pink Pearl,* the Beresfords are investigating the apparent theft of a priceless pearl from a wealthy American woman during a dinner party at a British estate. Tuppence shrewdly discovers that the aristocratic British hostess has a prior record of kleptomania, but that turns out to be a red herring—it's Tommy who solves the case a few minutes later, deducing that the French maid had filched the gem and hidden it in a hollowed-out cake of soap.

Tuppence saves face in their next case, *The House of Lurking Death,* by observing needle marks on the arm of a woman who survives a poisoned meal that has killed their client, Lois Hargreaves (Lynsey Baxter). She decides that the killer has built up an immunity to the poison by injecting herself with small doses, enabling her to avoid suspicion by eating the same meal that kills Lois.

The couple's rivalry is punctuated by the cheerful sniping that enlivens their partnership. In *The Sunningdale Mystery,* the Beresfords check in to a golf resort to investigate a murder on the links. Arriving with her usual load of hatboxes and luggage, the relentlessly chic Tuppence tells Tommy, "You talk and I'll unpack." "But that will take ages," he complains in a jab at her excessive wardrobe. "Not if you stick to the point," she snips, in a dig at his endless digressions.

"References to the occult crop up frequently in Agatha Christie's stories. In the 1930s, fashionable people were interested in spiritualism. They ended elegant dinner parties by bringing out a Ouija board, or holding a seance. The author was no stranger to this form of entertainment. While growing up, she'd read the stories of Edgar Allan Poe. As an adult, she researched mysticism and dream interpretation, and was fascinated with 'madness,' a word she used to describe a range of emotions."

—DIANA RIGG

Tuppence is the fifth daughter of a clergyman. She tells Tommy she made up her mind to "marry money" quite young and assures him "any thinking girl would!" She spent the war years in London, doing clean-up work in an officers' hospital and driving for a British general, but complains she never met any rich men. Young Tommy seems quite idealistic in contrast. Wounded twice in the war, he reached the rank of lieutenant and has an edge in maturity, though it isn't always so evident in their later adventures. The primary assets Christie gave them were quick minds and youthful exuberance.

Handsome James Warwick was cast as Tommy and lovely Francesca Annis as Tuppence (she had played the ravishing Lillie Langtry in the popular Masterpiece Theatre series *Lillie*). Stylishly dressed by costume designers Linda Mattock and Penny Lowe in often breathtakingly original 1920s period outfits, the couple simply can't be ignored whenever they enter a scene.

The Beresfords officially become sleuths in *The Affair of the Pink Pearl*, taking over a nearly bankrupt firm called The International Detective Agency, run by one Theodore Blunt. Tommy assumes Blunt's identity and dubs Tuppence "Miss Robinson," assigning her the job of "confidential secretary." With them from the start is their clerk, the boyish Albert (Reece Dinsdale), an elevator operator and incorrigible mystery movie addict, whom Tuppence befriends in *The Secret Adversary*. None of them really knows anything about crime-solving, but they feel confident they'll succeed at it because they've read hundreds of murder mysteries and know how all the great detectives work.

"Agatha Christie, some say, made more money from murder than any woman since Lucrezia Borgia."

—ROBERT A. MCLEAN,
Boston Globe

> *"Where did this 'upper middle-class British housewife' (as Christie liked to call herself) come up with her hundreds of sinister plots? She claimed that she thought of them most often while eating apples and soaking in her old-fashioned footed bathtub. (Years later, she mourned the replacement of her old tub, claiming she was no longer able to derive quite as much inspiration from the newer, more modern fixture.)"*
>
> —VINCENT PRICE

That attitude gave Christie the opportunity to parody almost all the contemporary mystery writers of the 1920s, many of them fellow members of the legendary Detection Club, which Christie belonged to for years. The *Partners in Crime* episodes on Mystery! retained some of her original in-jokes. The big problem for modern viewers, though, was the fact that hardly anyone read writers like Anthony Berkeley in the 1980s, so few realized that the Beresfords were parodying his sleuth, Roger Sherringham, in *The Clergyman's Daughter*, or the detectives of such writers as Baroness Orczy, A. E. W. Mason, and Freeman Wills Crofts in other episodes.

VIEWING THE BERESFORDS WITH MODERN EYES

Some present-day critics suggest Christie unconsciously veered into sexism by making Tuppence a clothes-horse and a gossip whose cases were more likely to be solved by "woman's intuition" than deductive logic. In his on-air wrap-up to the episode *The Unbreakable Alibi,* Vincent Price reminded Mystery! viewers that Christie once said, "Men have much better brains than women." Price conceded that feminist critics of Christie's female characters, including Tuppence Beresford, might have a point, but he also suggested Tuppence may have been a woman ahead of her time, making her own mark in a male-dominated field rather than staying home to iron her husband's shirts.

It's also important to remember that Tuppence and Tommy were born fully grown in the 1920s and reflected the attitudes of their period. Bearing that in mind, there's still reason for even hard-core feminists to appreciate the Tuppence we see in *Partners in Crime.* In *The Sunningdale Mystery,* for instance, Tuppence tells Tommy off for automatically assuming the killer was a woman just because a hatpin was the apparent murder weapon. "You're notoriously old-fashioned," she tells him, pointing out that the female suspect wears her hair bobbed and would have no reason to carry a hatpin. Instead, she explains, it seems to her the killer was a man who used a hatpin because he wanted male investigators to instantly jump to the wrong conclusions. Needless to say, she turns out to be right.

"Christie made her killers bump off their victims in an interesting variety of methods: a kitchen skewer thrust into the base of the skull; a poison dart from a blowgun; even a deadly ukulele string around the neck. One of my favorite murder methods that she devised was a chess set: The white bishop was electrically wired to a power line in the apartment below. The victim went to make his move, and zap! Christie. . . . confessed that she knew nothing about pistols and revolvers, which is why she killed off her characters with other instruments—or with poisons. . . .
One of Christie's most ingenious killings takes place when a character is listening to the radio while examining a glass bulb which is, unbeknownst to the unfortunate victim, filled with an exotic and lethal poison gas. The tenor on the radio hits a particularly high note—the glass shatters. . . . During World War I, the fledgling novelist had volunteered for service in a hospital dispensary and there first became interested in poisons. During the second world war, Christie again volunteered for hospital dispensary work."

—VINCENT PRICE

"James Warwick and I are very well suited to the parts. I'm more impetuous and extroverted. He lets me chatter on, and eventually he'll come to the same conclusion, but by a more laid-back route. I remember one day when we were shooting Partners. *We were in a railway carriage rolling up and down a short piece of train track. It was supposed to be a steam train, so there was a prop man outside. . . . His job was to blow smoke, so the camera would see steam streaming past the windows.*

"We were sitting there playing a scene, and I thought that the amount of smoke outside was slightly excessive for one steam engine. Then I noticed that part of the field outside was burning. I told James, and he just said, 'No, dear, the field can't possibly be on fire.' I shrieked, 'Yes it can! Yes, yes, yes!' I jumped up and down like a lunatic. James finally peered through the smoke and saw the fire. He leaped up and led everybody out, cast and crew alike. He set up a chain of buckets, and they tried to fight the fire. I stayed inside the carriage in my makeup, yelling orders out the windows. The fire brigade came eventually and put it out."

—FRANCESCA ANNIS,
Philadelphia Inquirer

A LIBIDINOUS LEADING LADY

Modern female viewers of *Partners in Crime* also should be amused to notice how much more sexually liberated Tuppence is than Tommy. In *The Sunningdale Mystery*, Tuppence is aroused to friskiness by the plush surroundings of their room at the golf resort and asks Tommy, her mind on the bedroom, if they can skip dinner and retire early. He misses the point, telling her he doesn't feel particularly sleepy. Clearly, he hasn't a clue as to what they'd do lying awake in that luxurious bed. "We'll think of something," she says, coyly.

In *The Clergyman's Daughter*, Tuppence gets a certain gleam in her eye as soon as she sees the inviting four-poster bed their host has assigned them for their first night in a house supposedly haunted by a poltergeist. Though Tommy seems wary of what might happen, Tuppence gaily remarks, "I'm very much afraid four-posters always have an effect on me. I couldn't possibly spend an uneventful night in a four-poster."

Even outside the bedroom, Tuppence seems much more adventurous than her mate. In *The Ambassador's Boots*, Tommy's life is even saved at the climax by Tuppence and her female friends from the beauty parlor. Though Tommy brags that Tuppence "taught me how to tell a peroxide blonde from a natural one," it's obvious she has a lot more left to teach him.

Perhaps that's why Tommy seems so deliriously happy to be with his frolicsome wife at the conclusion of every case. She promises him, in the closing pages of *The Secret Adversary*, that marriage can be a haven, a refuge, a state of bondage, and all kinds of things, but that mostly she thinks of it as a sport. "And a damned good sport, too!" he agrees, happily looking forward to the fun they'll be having over the next generation or two.

"Agatha Christie introduced an adapter of detective stories into a book just once. He was illegitimate and overweight or, not to put too fine a point on it, a fat bastard. His father and his mother were murderers and so was he. You draw in your breath a bit smartish. When Miss Christie brings one up from the floor you certainly know, as your teeth fall tinkling around you, that it has connected.

Call me over-sensitive, but I don't think she was fond of adapters. She wasn't all that keen on actors either. Three turn up in her books as murderers and the rest are only just this side of certifiable. I would deduce that she had not found the dramatizations of her books a wholly happy experience and, indeed, some of the films were very peculiar indeed."

—NANCY BANKS-SMITH,
Guardian

ELLY CHANDLER
AND
DEE TATE

CHANDLER & CO.

Series created by Paula Milne

UNTIL PAULA MILNE'S *CHANDLER & CO.* MADE ITS DEBUT IN EARLY 1996,
MYSTERY! VIEWERS HAD NEVER SEEN PRIVATE DETECTIVES DOING THE DIRTY,
UNGLAMOROUS KIND OF SLEUTHING THAT PUTS FOOD ON THE TABLE
FOR MOST OF THE WORLD'S REAL PRIVATE EYES.

In the four episodes that introduced the series, we see Elly Chandler (Catherine Russell) and partner Dee Tate (Barbara Flynn) sneaking into bedrooms to catch couples *in flagrante* and combing through records to find a person's whereabouts. There isn't a single shooting, stabbing, or poisoning—the usual Mystery! fare. In fact, there isn't a single body dead of anything other than natural causes.

Yet *Chandler & Co.* provided several mysteries for Dee and Elly to solve in the intriguing area of their specialty: marital infidelity. Those cases also gave the show's creator, writer Paula Milne (*Die Kinder, The Politician's Wife*), a golden opportunity to delve into contemporary social issues—AIDS and sexism, for example—in a way that Mystery! seldom has before.

EXPERIENCING INFIDELITY TO INVESTIGATING IT

The idea of going into detective work is inspired by Elly's sad experience of discovering the infidelity of her own husband, Max. Suspicious of him, she hires private detective Larry Blakeston (Peter Capaldi), who provides her with evidence that Max is cheating on her. Quickly filing for divorce, she faces the challenge of starting her life over again in her early thirties after seven years as a homemaker. Elly's closest friend and staunchest supporter is her older sister-in-law, Dee Tate, who has turned a cold shoulder to her brother over what he has done to Elly. Married to successful barrister David Tate (Struan Rodger), Dee has a teenage son and daughter, but is beginning to long for something meaningful to do with her life now that her children are nearly raised.

That leads the two women to consider going into business together. Their first thought is to work for Blakeston in some apprentice capacity, but that plan doesn't get too far, because he's phasing out his detective business and turning full time to work as a security consultant and provider of high-tech equipment. "Couldn't you just open a flower shop instead?" he asks. But Larry likes both women and harbors special feelings for the attractive Elly. So he agrees to give them a few minor cases to work on while breaking them in to the science of tailing people and showing them how to use such tools of the modern gumshoe as bugging devices and

PRODUCTION COMPANY
Skreba for BBC

YEAR
1996

MAIN CAST
Elly Chandler
CATHERINE RUSSELL

Dee Tate
BARBARA FLYNN

Larry Blakeston
PETER CAPALDI

David Tate
STRUAN RODGER

surveillance cameras. Once they learn the basics, Dee and Elly start running an ad in the yellow pages, and Chandler & Co. is born, much to the distress of Dee's husband, who thinks his wife is getting into something extremely unsavory—and potentially dangerous.

Though most of their cases seem mundane, they often lead to poignant—and sometimes dramatic—conclusions. In the *Family Matters* episode, the wife of a prominent British union leader hires Dee to provide evidence that her husband is involved with another woman, who she suspects may even be having trysts in her home while she's away. The wife gives Dee the key to their house so she can bug the place while the husband's at work, but Dee is there only a few minutes when the husband arrives with his girlfriend and starts undressing her. Hiding on an upstairs landing, Dee gets photos of the couple in the throes of passion and gives them to the wife. The next day, Dee is shocked to find the photos displayed in a London tabloid, along with a photo of her as the private eye who exposed—literally—the union official. Immediately, the Tate home is surrounded by press crews and tabloid reporters—and Dee learns how much damage her detective work can do to her own family relationships.

In *Those Who Trespass Against Us*, Elly poses as a rather mature college student while she tries to track down a minister's daughter who has deserted her father for an unknown man she met on campus. Ultimately, Elly discovers the daughter has been living at her father's vicarage all along, dying from AIDS. The father was really using Elly to track down the person who infected her, a man his daughter refuses to identify.

In that episode, Milne uses the AIDS mystery as a way to have Dee and Elly address their own attitudes about casual sex—Elly as a sexually active newly single woman, and Dee as the mother of a son who's reached the age when sexual exploration is very likely. Many of the cases give Milne and her writing staff similar opportunities. In the AIDS episode, Dee works a case that's a classic example of role reversal: A wife whose travel business has done extremely well is suspected of adultery by her husband, who has become a "Mr. Mom," taking care of the children and preparing the meals. The investigation is a way of turning the spotlight on marital relationships from a new angle.

SENSITIVE ISSUES AND HUMOROUS SITUATIONS

Though sensitive issues are the basic currency of *Chandler & Co.*, the series also depends heavily on its humor, especially when the rookie sleuths fail abysmally— but amusingly. In one case, they plant a transmitter in a garden to relay recorded conversations back to them, but the family dog digs it up and brings it to its startled master. They never seem to master the use of a crossbow-like implement for planting bugging devices in the exterior walls of buildings—and repeatedly have to sneak in to retrieve the little arrows. They're also apt to come face to face with the occasional naked husband as they try to capture him fornicating on film. "Who the hell are you?" one such startled man asks Elly when he finds her, camera in hand. "Jehovah's Witness," she replies, rather feebly.

Throughout the series we see Dee and Elly confronting very real situations that many women face: a child acting out because Mom suddenly has a new career (Dee's studious daughter begins cutting classes); the difficulty of fully letting go of an ex-husband who continues to tell lies one still wants to believe (Elly's ex says he wants to get back together with her, but it's only because his finances are in total ruin); the fear of embarking on the first post-marital affair after a long period of monogamy (though attracted to Larry and he to her, it takes Elly a while to finally become his lover, which happens, presumably, after the last episode). The dialogue between the two women is also very real as they struggle to solve problems for one another and together find their way in the new work world.

Barbara Flynn is a veteran British actor who played Mme Maigret in the *Maigret* series and was Monica Height in *The Silent World of Nicholas Quinn* in the *Inspector Morse* series. She also was Judith Fitzgerald, the wife of the criminal psychologist played by Robbie Coltrane in the popular British series *Cracker.* Catherine Russell also appeared in *Maigret,* as Marthe Jusserand in the episode *Maigret Sets a Trap.* Peter Capaldi has appeared in such films as *Local Hero* and *Dangerous Liaisons* and played the drag queen Vera Reynolds in *Prime Suspect 3.*

Driven by Social Issues:

WRITER
PAULA MILNE

PAULA MILNE, THE CREATOR AND CHIEF WRITER OF *CHANDLER & CO.*, IS ONE OF the most sought-after screenwriters currently working at the "top end" of British television. Trained as a painter, she broke into television as a BBC script reader, graduated to a "relief editor" job on the hit series *Z Cars,* and created the first series of *Angels* episodes. She then developed a growing reputation as the author of hard-edged, often controversial dramas, including the political thriller *Die Kinder,* shown on Mystery! in 1991; the acclaimed political drama, *The Politician's Wife,* shown on Masterpiece Theatre in 1996; and, most recently, *The Fragile Heart,* a trilogy about Western skepticism toward alternative medicine in other cultures.

Milne also has written Hollywood feature films, including *Mad Love* (1995) and a new version of Daphne du Maurier's *My Cousin Rachel,* as yet unfilmed. She considers *Mad Love* her formal initiation into the Hollywood system: Five other writers later were brought in to work on her original script, a violation she referred to as a "rape," though acknowledging that as it had happened to Scott Fitzgerald and Raymond Chandler, it was likely that it would happen to her.

New Line Cinema is developing an American film version of *The Politician's Wife,* but Milne decided not to work on it because she had the feeling it might turn into "a bit of tosh." CBS also tried to coax Milne into writing a network movie, but she balked when she saw all the commercial interruptions she'd have to make room for in the second hour. The witty Milne is married to a doctor and is the mother of four children. She writes at her home in Wimbledon.

QUESTION: *What inspired you to create* Chandler & Co.?

ANSWER: I was in the States, doing some work in Hollywood feature films. I was in a hotel watching television, and there was some item on about how surveillance equipment was used mostly in the private sector by detectives, with no national secrets involved. I thought that was interesting. I suppose I'd always thought it was

just used by the CIA. I came back to London, got the yellow pages out, and called a few detective agencies to see what kind of equipment they used. I had no ideas about a series then. I was just interested in the equipment and the fact that it was used privately for people spying on each other. Then I started just going out with the detectives to see how they used this equipment and what sort of cases they did.

Where did you get the idea of having two women running a detective agency?

One of the agencies I visited was run by a woman named Lindy who had two women operatives, and I noticed they did things very differently. It seemed such an unlikely job for a woman. At first I thought I'd make the detectives in my series a man and a woman, but then I thought it would be too much like *Moonlighting.*

Can women like Elly and Dee, with no special training, really become detectives in England?

It's not like *Cagney and Lacey*—you know how they got into it: They joined the bloody police force. It's completely easy in England. There are no licenses here. You can just hang up a sign.

Where did you get the idea for surveillance expert Larry Blakeston?

In order for [Elly and Dee] not to look like two fumbling housewives going out poking microphones in the wrong direction and not knowing what they're doing, I needed someone experienced to help them. So I went to some of these so-called "spy shops" and found some pretty weird guys who had worked as croupiers in the south of France, done this and that, then wound up in these weird shops selling spy equipment. The idea for him came out of that.

Chandler & Co. is unique among the detective series on Mystery! because Elly and Dee do basic, real-life detective work and never get involved in murders. Was that done on purpose?

That was a definite imperative . . . to see if you could hold an audience when the stakes were the death of a relationship, not the death of a person. I wanted to see if it was possible to engage an audience with low-key but truthful stories and make the mystery grow out of the mysteries of human nature.

As a result, Elly and Dee often get involved in stories that seem to have more to do with human relationships than crime. Did you find that happening in real detective agencies?

The real detectives I observed did have quite a few very human-interest sort of things happen. In fact, 60 percent of detective work is still for marital cases. Before they changed the divorce laws in England, you had to prove adultery to get a divorce, so people hired detectives to collect evidence. I assumed not many people went to detectives for that anymore, but they do. That's interesting if you consider that they don't have to get proof of adultery anymore. They just want to know for their own peace of mind, the men clients as well as the women.

Are women better suited to handle these often very sensitive marital cases than men?

I think so. They not only deal with clients differently, but they also ask such different questions. I remember what happened with one of the male detectives I was observing. A woman client came in and said she thought her husband was having an affair because he no longer wore sensible white boxer shorts. . . . After she left, he started laughing and said, "Bloody hell, the poor guy just changes his boxer shorts, and his wife thinks he's having an affair." It turned out the husband *was* having an affair. When I went around with the women detectives, there was a similar case where a woman walked in with no tangible evidence her husband was cheating on her except for a change in his behavior—and the way he related to the children. She said he seemed "sad" with them, which I thought was an extraordinary way of putting it. We followed him and bugged him, and it turned out he was seeing prostitutes— three or four every lunchtime. The detective, Lindy, was really kind and supportive to this wife. She got her into her office and told her what she'd found, then put her on to a counselor, promised to keep in contact with her, and so forth. I don't think that male detective would have done that. He'd have just said, "Well, it happens, luv; that's what men are like. Can I have my check?"

Some very amusing things happen to Elly and Dee while they're learning, on the job, how to be detectives, like the time the client's dog digs up the bugging transmitter they plant. How much real humor is there in detective work?

Not a lot. But, since there weren't going to be murders, car chases, poisonings, and the like in the series, I wondered how I was going to get the buggers to watch. You've got to have something like humor, but I wanted it to have that Frank Capra kind, not in-your-face humor. As for the dog, that's a true story.

Elly's own husband cheated on her, and now she finds out, as a detective, that it's not that uncommon. Does that make her more or less cynical about marriage?

More. She started off pretty cynical anyway. What she does with Larry is start a relationship that's purely sexual, without emotion. I was never able to realize the potential of that, because we lost the actor who played Larry.

How did that happen and why did you stop making Chandler & Co. *after only 12 episodes?*

The BBC waited so long to put the first series of six on the air that they overran the actors' options. Then the show was a huge success, and we couldn't get most of the actors back. Peter Capaldi, who played Larry, Barbara Flynn, who played Dee, and her entire family were gone. So, I rewrote the second series and brought in another woman as the victim of a stalker, then made her the second detective with Elly. Susan Fleetwood played the part through the second series. Unfortunately, Susan then died of cancer, so I decided not to do any more.

It's likely Chandler & Co. *will be remembered as a detective series that used the mystery genre to explore contemporary issues. Was that what appealed to you as a socially-committed writer?*

One of the sort of good things about it was that you could look at an issue like AIDS and make it user-friendly by using the genre to make people look at the issue without bias. Still, you can't explore issues at any great depth in a series like that, because it's not a sole-author show like *Die Kinder* or *The Politician's Wife,* which had a strong imperative to investigate certain things.

The
T ALENTED
AMATEURS

They didn't train at the police academy and they seldom report any earnings from detective work to the tax man. They're not even listed in the yellow pages under Sleuths. The only things they have in common are their intelligence and maybe a little more free time than most of us have. They may be amateurs, but are they talented!

- **JANE MARPLE**
  AGATHA CHRISTIE'S MISS MARPLE

- **JEMIMA SHORE**
  QUIET AS A NUN

- **HUGO LOVELACE CHARTERS AND GILES EVELYN CALDICOTT**
  CHARTERS AND CALDICOTT

- **BROTHER CADFAEL**
  CADFAEL

- **FATHER BROWN**
  FATHER BROWN

JANE MARPLE

AGATHA CHRISTIE'S MISS MARPLE

Based on the novels by
Agatha Christie

LATE ONE AFTERNOON IN THE ENGLISH VILLAGE OF ST. MARY MEAD, THE VICAR'S
WIFE, GRISELDA CLEMENT, BEGINS TICKING OFF THE NAMES OF THE "OLD BIDDIES"
SHE IS EXPECTING SHORTLY FOR "TEA AND SCANDAL." HER LIST OF LOCAL
GOSSIPS ENDS WITH "THAT AWFUL MISS MARPLE." "I RATHER LIKE MISS MARPLE," HER
HUSBAND, LEN, OBSERVES. "SHE HAS, AT LEAST, A SENSE OF HUMOR."

He might have warned, though, that she's also a lady who comes to stay. Introduced in that rather offhand fashion in Agatha Christie's 1930 novel *The Murder at the Vicarage*, Miss Jane Marple is now in her seventh decade as the world's most popular elderly spinster sleuth. First described by Christie as "a white-haired old lady with a gentle, appealing manner," Miss Marple was already 70 in 1930 and must now be nudging her way into the record books.

BACK BY POPULAR DEMAND

Christie rather backed into the job of making Miss Marple a star. She was almost a peripheral character in that first mystery, even though she cracked the case for the police. However, she was adopted by an adoring public, and Christie quickly moved her to top billing in 12 more novels and a dozen short stories. Many mystery fans believe Miss Marple eventually eclipsed even Hercule Poirot in terms of all-around appeal.

Whatever you think of her—and the vicar's wife thought she was "the worst cat in the village"—Miss Marple is clearly one of the great detective characters in all of mystery fiction. She has been played on screen by a variety of accomplished actors, from Margaret Rutherford and Gracie Fields to Helen Hayes and Angela Lansbury. Now, thanks to the fabulous series of Marple stories starring Joan Hickson on Mystery!, she's an immortal among the television sleuths as well, being seen all over the world.

The Mystery! series of Marple cases began in 1986 with *The Body in the Library* and continued with eight more cases over four seasons. It ended only when actor Hickson decided to retire; the producers decided to end the series rather than continue with a new actor who might cloud the memory of Hickson's incandescent—and scrupulously authentic—rendition of the role.

Jane Marple's enduring appeal is not hard to understand. She represents every one of us who has ever felt overlooked and unnoticed behind their quietness. She politely refuses to push herself on anyone. The very essence of Miss Marple is her unobtrusive manner, which masks her keen eye and shrewdly analytical mind so thoroughly that the police more often than not shoo her out of the way when they really should be unrolling a red carpet for her.

PRODUCTION COMPANY
BBC

YEARS
1986–1989

MAIN CAST
Miss Jane Marple
JOAN HICKSON

Detective Inspector Slack
DAVID HOROVITCH

FORENSIC INTUITION

In *A Pocketful of Rye,* for instance, a policeman scoffs at Marple's notion that a series of killings is somehow linked to a nursery rhyme. "I think the old gal's got an attic to rent," he mutters, but lives to regret his remark when Marple ultimately names the killer. Once the cops do know what she's capable of, though, they're likely to hail her as vigorously as does Chief Constable Col. Melchett (Frederick Jaeger) in *The Body in the Library,* when he learns a friend has summoned her to examine the murder scene at Gossington Hall. "I've often held that Miss Marple has what I would call forensic intuition developed to the point of genius," he says.

Later, when Detective Inspector Slack (David Horovitch) insists her intuition can't compare with standard police procedures, Melchett underscores his endorsement even further. "Let me give you a piece of advice," he tells Slack. "That old lady is tougher-minded, more cynical, and just plain cleverer than most barristers you'll meet in what I hope is going to be your long and no doubt distinguished career."

His opinion is seconded later by another Marple admirer, Sir Henry Clithering (Raymond Francis), a retired police inspector, who notices Miss Marple sitting quietly nearby and observes, "There she sits, an elderly spinster. Sweet, placid—so you'd think—yet her mind has plumbed the depths of human iniquity and taken it all in the day's work. It's extraordinary. She knows the world only through the prism of that village and its daily life. By knowing the village so thoroughly, she seems to know the world."

ST. MARY MEAD A MICROCOSM

Sir Henry is very close to the secret of her genius, all right. Miss Marple's deductive method is to look for "village parallels" in any murder case and to draw her conclusions from them, once she finds the ones that apply. Her method has been condemned from the very beginning by many skeptics, including her own nephew, the novelist Raymond West, who tells his aunt in the first Marple novel that her St. Mary Mead is nothing but "a stagnant pool." Miss Marple sees no insult there. "Nothing, I believe, is so full of life under the microscope," she tells her haughty nephew, "as a drop of water from a stagnant pool."

For the series, Miss Marple's 1930s cases were moved forward to the late 1940s and early 1950s, where most of her later cases took place. It makes no significant difference to Marple, who dresses about as frumpily as she always did and still seems to be knitting the same amorphous something or other she was working on in 1930. Otherwise, her personification by Joan Hickson is dead-on accurate to Christie, especially when compared to the corpulently comic Margaret Rutherford Marple, the imposingly robust Angela Lansbury Marple, and the pint-sized and oddly Americanized Helen Hayes Marple.

Hickson's Marple is haltingly respectful of authority, but if you watch her body language, you understand she's a patient woman who's biding her time, waiting for the mostly male blowhards to let up for a moment, so she can slip in a few pungent thoughts. Her eyes are brightly intelligent, and she seems to hold her energy in reserve for those moments when she really needs it, as in *Sleeping Murder,* when she saves her own life by spraying insecticide in the eyes of the villain who's about to throttle her.

Miss Marple is almost placid to a fault. She walks among murderers without showing any signs of fear and looks upon the most grisly of murder scenes without flinching. Hickson plays her as if she's so involved in her mental concentration that truly frightening circumstances fail to register. Her only signs of any distress seem to come over trifling things. At worst, she might clutch her purse with both hands and mutter, "Oh, dear; oh, dear!" She reserves her greatest dismay for herself—for having failed to see a clue.

Christie, who patterned her sleuth after her great aunt and her grandmother, often said she never intended to tell Miss Marple stories all her life, which is probably why Marple wasn't such a lovable character in *The Murder at the Vicarage.* But she was so offbeat that readers wanted more anyway. In her subsequent books, Miss Marple's gossipy nature faded into the background and her neighbors seemed to like her and hold her in awe.

By the 1950s, Miss Marple had grown quite frail and was even under doctor's orders not to tend her beloved garden, her regular observation post for keeping up on village gossip. St. Mary Mead also had changed, the open fields filling up with new housing and even a supermarket. Still, Christie never put Miss Marple to rest, as she did Hercule Poirot, which is a sure sign she was as fond of Miss Marple as were her readers.

That's why it's possible to imagine Miss Marple still walking the paths of St. Mary Mead in those sensible shoes of hers, scouting out the latest gossip while keeping her eyes alert for signs of any overlooked dead body that might be lying under a neighbor's hedgerow.

"In her books, the question 'Whodunit?' always takes precedence over the more interesting 'Whydunit?' The criticism of her stories is not that they take place in pleasant houses in sleepy English villages, but that they show no interest in the criminal mind. Christie's criminals are not human beings driven by passion or terror to forget their humanity, but pieces to be moved so cleverly on the board that we fail to guess that, in fact, Colonel Bodgers did it with the blow-pipe in the bathroom.

Another result of the chessboard approach to detective stories is that the crime becomes a sort of abstraction, an opening gambit which engages only the pawns. Murder is an extremely squalid and messy business, a fact appreciated by such writers as P. D. James. In Christie's novels it seems almost as harmless as horticulture, it is something that happens to surprise the reader and add a slight frisson *to any part of the story where interest starts to flag. No doubt that was the way her audience preferred to read about it, just as in court during a murder trial no one wishes to look for very long at the photographs taken in the morgue."*

—JOHN MORTIMER,
New York Times

"In the novel version of Nemesis, Miss Marple makes reference to Shakespeare. She tells godson Lionel that if she were staging Macbeth, *she wouldn't have the witches cackling and dancing about. Instead, she'd only have the three old hags look slyly at one another. That way, she says, 'The audience would feel a sort of menace just behind the ordinariness of them.'"*

—VINCENT PRICE

"*What also comes to light in the BBC dramatizations is the accuracy of P. D. James' categorization of Agatha Christie as 'a literary conjurer.' Distraction of the observer's attention is paramount— not just with the author but with her murderers, too. Like her, they specialize in diversionary devices: The body in the library isn't the one it's assumed to be; poison-pen letters deflect suspicion from a poisoner; a murder is loudly announced so that a killing can be quietly palmed off on people; the nursery-rhyme rigmarole of A Pocketful of Rye camouflages a vital murder among a sequence of irrelevant ones.*"

—PETER KEMP,
Times Literary Supplement

The Quintessential Miss Marple:

ACTOR

JOAN HICKSON

IN 1946, AGATHA CHRISTIE ATTENDED A PERFORMANCE OF THE LONDON stage adaptation of her Hercule Poirot novel *Appointment with Death* and was intrigued by the actor who was playing the small part of a spinster in the production. A few days later, the author sent the actor a complimentary letter. "I'd like you to play Miss Marple one day," she wrote.

The actor was Joan Hickson, who was then barely 40 and didn't consider it such a great compliment to be seen as the ideal actor for the role of a somewhat crotchety spinster in her seventies. Nothing ever came of it in Christie's lifetime, though Hickson played several scenes with actor Margaret Rutherford in *Murder, She Said* (1961), the first of Rutherford's four Miss Marple movies.

Hickson and Rutherford were great friends; in fact, Rutherford was godmother to Hickson's son. Yet Hickson never went to see any of Rutherford's Miss Marple films, even though she was in the first, and never rendered her opinion of Rutherford in the role. Christie, however, thought Rutherford was totally miscast and hated all her Marple films. She argued Jane Marple should be "slender and fragile," while Rutherford "always looked like a warmly-bundled English bulldog."

INTIMATE KNOWLEDGE OF JANE MARPLE

Today, of course, Hickson is widely reckoned to be the best Miss Marple of them all, though the actor, who retired from the role several years ago, never subscribed to the idea that she was the quintessential Jane Marple. In fact, when she finally was asked to play the role in the 1980s, Hickson felt there were many who could play Marple better—and already had. Such self-effacement reminds one not a little of the queen of self-effacement, Jane Marple. Hickson did find one Miss Marple rather disappointing—that of Helen Hayes, who she felt was unsuited to the role because she was an American.

Hickson already was a veteran character actor when Christie saw her in that 1946 stage production. Born in 1906, she made her stage debut in 1927 and played her first role in London's West End in *The Tragic Muse* in 1928. She was in films from the early 1930s on and can be seen in several classic British films, including *Seven Days to Noon* (1950), the 1959 remake of *The Thirty-Nine Steps,* and *Theatre of Blood* (1973), the latter with two future hosts of Mystery!—Vincent Price and Diana Rigg. As comfortable in comedy as she was in drama, Hickson probably scored her biggest hits on stage in Peter Nichols' black comedy, *A Day in the Death of Joe Egg*—she reprised her role with Alan Bates in the 1971 film version—and the comedy *Bedroom Farce.* When England's National Theatre brought *Bedroom Farce* to Broadway, Hickson won a Tony Award for her performance. Among her many other television roles are Mrs. Varden in *Barnaby Rudge* (1960), Madame Drosdov in *The Possessed* (1969), and Miss Havisham in *Great Expectations* (1981).

In later years, Hickson became acquainted with Agatha Christie and was a devoted reader of her books. Still, she has always insisted that she did no special research to play what is now her most famous role. She felt she knew Jane Marple intimately and needed to do nothing more than put on the Marple wig and those "sensible" shoes to bring her to life. "I admire Miss Marple enormously," she has said. "She's got great integrity, she's as straight as a die, and she believes so much in justice, and I think that's remarkable. I think she's a wonderful woman. I wish I were more like her, really, because I think her outlook on life is really splendid, don't you?"

Some Marplisms

"I may be what is termed a spinster, but I know the difference between horseplay and murder."

"Nothing is ever as it seems."

"Very nasty things go on in a village, I assure you. One has the opportunity of studying things there one would never have in [a large city]."

"Gentlemen are sometimes not quite so level-headed as they seem."

"I believe in evil, everlasting life, and, oh, yes—goodness."

"Most crimes, you see, are so absurdly simple. . . . Quite sane and forward— and quite understandable— in an unpleasant way, of course."

"Some of the best murderers are women—especially in an English village. You turn over a stone and you don't know what will crawl out."

"Burglary is so violent nowadays. There used to be a certain grace and decorum about it."

JEMIMA SHORE

QUIET AS A NUN

Based on the novel by
Antonia Fraser

STYLISH JEMIMA SHORE, THE RENOWNED BRITISH TELEVISION REPORTER
AND "CHAT SHOW" HOST, BEGINS MOONLIGHTING AS AN AMATEUR SLEUTH WHEN
SHE BECOMES PERSONALLY INVOLVED IN A MURDER CASE THAT NOBODY
ACTUALLY KNOWS AT FIRST IS A MURDER CASE.

It happens in *Quiet As a Nun,* a three-part adaptation of Lady Antonia Fraser's best-
selling 1974 novel that first introduced Jemima Shore, who solves murders when she isn't
busy chasing ratings at Megalith Television, also known as just plain MTV.

The strange case starts with a newspaper article about the alarming death of a nun
named Sister Miriam, who has committed suicide by starving herself to death, locked in
an ancient and rarely used stone tower at a Catholic convent school, Blessed Eleanor's
Convent in Sussex. Reading that bizarre account shakes Shore to the core because Sister
Miriam used to be Rosabelle Mary Powerstock, her classmate at the same school.

Shore (Maria Aitken) finds it hard to believe Sister Miriam would even consider
taking her own life. She also considers it incredible that anyone could stay hidden long
enough to die by starvation. Wouldn't someone have missed her in such a busy place? Her
reporter's curiosity aroused, she decides to visit the convent for the first time in 20 years.

A LOT OF BLACK CROWS

Her decision is bewildering to her lover, Tom Amyas (David Burke), a liberal member of
Parliament, who can't begin to associate the trendy, sophisticated, and worldly Jemima
Shore he knows with a convent school. "You're not a Catholic," he says. "I can't imagine
you in a convent. Never cared much for nuns. Can't tell one from another. They're like a
lot of black crows."

That point of view is not so different from the way Shore saw them herself at age
15 when she was placed in the school by her parents, even though she was a Protestant.
Her return to that world proves to be more than a jarring bit of nostalgia. Before she's a
few steps out of her Volvo sports car, a frightened nun rushes up to her as if to tell her
something crucial, then as quickly retreats without saying a word. Mother Ancilla (Renee
Asherson) also has some shocking news for Shore—Sister Miriam left behind a note,
saying simply, "Jemima will know." Know what? So mystifying is it all that Shore readily
agrees to Mother Ancilla's request to stay on at the convent to help get to the bottom of
the mystery, especially when she begins to suspect that her own recent report on plans
for a large public housing project on land adjacent to the convent may be connected in
some way with her friend's death.

**PRODUCTION
COMPANY**
Thames Television

YEAR
1982

MAIN CAST
Jemima Shore
MARIA AITKEN

Mother Ancilla
RENEE ASHERSON

Sister Boniface
SYLVIA COLERIDGE

Tom Amyas
DAVID BURKE

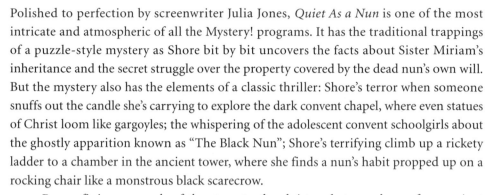

Polished to perfection by screenwriter Julia Jones, *Quiet As a Nun* is one of the most intricate and atmospheric of all the Mystery! programs. It has the traditional trappings of a puzzle-style mystery as Shore bit by bit uncovers the facts about Sister Miriam's inheritance and the secret struggle over the property covered by the dead nun's own will. But the mystery also has the elements of a classic thriller: Shore's terror when someone snuffs out the candle she's carrying to explore the dark convent chapel, where even statues of Christ loom like gargoyles; the whispering of the adolescent convent schoolgirls about the ghostly apparition known as "The Black Nun"; Shore's terrifying climb up a rickety ladder to a chamber in the ancient tower, where she finds a nun's habit propped up on a rocking chair like a monstrous black scarecrow.

By confining so much of the story to the cloistered atmosphere of an ancient convent, Fraser creates a compact world within a world, peopled with some fascinating characters, among them a heavy-footed nun who races her little car around the country lanes of Sussex like a Grand Prix finalist; a poetry-spouting nun whose every other word seems to be from Shelley, Wordsworth, or Joyce; and the doddering Sister Boniface (Sylvia Coleridge), who seems to constantly be passing out without much advance notice. But the most fascinating of them all is Jemima Shore herself, the tall, slim, leggy redhead, whose ever-present turtleneck sweaters made an impressive 1970s fashion statement throughout her television adventure.

Shore's debut in *Quiet As a Nun* signaled the arrival of a whole new kind of sleuth on the mystery scene—a liberated and independent female who's still defining herself in terms of her generation of equality-oriented women. She isn't sure what she's ultimately going to wind up with by striking out on the often lonely path she's chosen, but she knows she doesn't want the traditional woman's role. Whatever future awaits Jemima Shore, it will be of her own making.

FRASER'S FANTASY

While she most assuredly spoke to the new generation of female readers, Shore represents Fraser's effort to imbue a female detective with her personal fantasies, making her everything Fraser herself is not in actuality but might be under other circumstances. Shore ends up made partly in Fraser's own image, but with a rather significant modification: Lady Antonia has been married twice and has borne six children, while Shore is still zero for zero in both categories, quite by choice. Like Shore, the author also attended a Catholic boarding school after being raised as a Protestant. While Shore is the mistress of a married member of Parliament in *Quiet As a Nun,* in real life Lady Antonia was married to Sir Hugh Fraser, a well-known member of Parliament, whom she left to live openly with playwright Harold Pinter. (They were married three years later and are still together.) So, one might say the author knows Shore's turf quite well.

Fraser's decision to write a detective novel came after she'd already established herself as a major biographer of historical figures. She wanted to examine the influence of enormous media fame on a personality, so she made her protagonist a television superstar and patterned her after her close friend Joan Bakewell, the 1970s British equivalent of Barbara Walters or Diane Sawyer. In Shore's case fame makes her a very special kind of detective. She can't very well watch quietly from the sidelines, gathering clues unobtrusively like a dowdy Miss Marple, because she's instantly recognized wherever she goes. But Fraser has turned that into an asset for Shore—her popularity loosens many lips and often gets her into places closed to the general public.

The name Jemima Shore was, itself, a kind of in-joke, a combination of the sacred and the profane. Jemima is a name of 17th-century Puritan origin, while Fraser took the surname Shore from Jane Shore, the dissolute mistress of Charles IV. Although *Mystery!* didn't show any further Jemima Shore adventures after *Quiet As a Nun*, a 13-week series of one-hour adventures called *Jemima Shore, Investigator,* was shown in England after the success of *Quiet As a Nun.*

Taking a Break from Biographies:

AUTHOR
LADY ANTONIA FRASER

Lady Antonia Fraser already was well established as one of England's most respected historical biographers when she published *Quiet As a Nun* in 1977 and suddenly became a best-selling mystery writer. She did it as a lark—a break from the laborious research required by her biographies. But the enormous success of *Quiet As a Nun* created a demand for more Jemima Shore stories, leading her to write a whole string of best-selling adventures.

Born in 1932, Fraser began writing as early as age 14, first poetry, then romantic short stories. She earned her M.A. degree from Lady Margaret Hall at Oxford and embarked on a career as an author of non-fiction books, beginning with the 1963 publication of *Dolls.* Her reputation was made with the biographies *Mary, Queen of Scots* (1969), a bestseller, *Cromwell, the Lord Protector* (1973), and *King James VI of Scotland* (1974).

"I enjoy writing biographies very much, but it's a terribly laborious job," she said. "When I write a thriller, I can sit in a deck chair or in a hotel room and jot it down to my heart's content. With a biography you need so much clobber (files, books, and reference materials) and you have to spread it all around you constantly."

Since she created Jemima Shore, Fraser has divided her loyalties between her mysteries and her biographies and other writings, which have included the television plays *Charades* (1977) and *Mister Clay* (1985). She has honorary doctorates in literature from both Hull University and the University of Nottingham.

SELECTED BIBLIOGRAPHY

Quiet As a Nun, 1977; *The Wild Island,* 1978; *Jemima Shore's First Case,* 1980; *A Splash of Red,* 1981; *Cool Repentance,* 1982; *Oxford Blood,* 1985; *Your Royal Hostage,* 1987; *The Cavalier Case,* 1990; *Jemima Shore at the Sunny Grave,* 1991; *Political Death,* 1994.

THE CLASSIC DETECTIVE

THE DETECTIVE STORY PROVIDES THE INTELLECTUAL DELIGHT OF ADMIRING—
and trailing after—a single individual of such skill, subtlety, and persistence that he or
she can figure it all out and, in the end, apportion blame or redemption. This is just
what God is sometimes thought to do, though usually not in fewer than 300 pages.
When Rex Stout declared that 'people who don't like mystery stories are anarchists,' he
understood the yearning for order that dominates detective fiction. . . . The methods
used by the detectives may vary from the driest of ratiocinations to the highest flights of
intuition, but it is the presence and the personality of the detective that continue to
delight us. We welcome a universe in which such persons operate and prevail. We want
to know how they came to be, and what happened after their deaths.

To the ranks of these detectives have been added the creations of women writers
(Christie, Sayers, Ngaio Marsh, etc.), and most pertinently, perhaps, women themselves.
Although in the 1930s in England, female sleuths were appearing at the side of detectives
like Sayers' Wimsey and Marsh's Roderick Alleyn, the ladies were both secondary in the
finding of solutions and chastely in love with or married to the detective.

Now women have been freed to step out into the wider world of detection. In part
this is due to cultural conditioning—women are traditionally prepared for nurturance and
the defense of the young and helpless, and detection is in part an extension of that enduring role. But women have been aided as well by the change in sexual mores. For a long
time women detectives had to be virgins, and while Christie's spinster Miss Marple may
know all the old reasons for sexual passion, today's kinky crooks may well have motives
that could never be understood by a virgin. Now that celibacy is out of fashion, women
detectives can be more complex—and knowing. Angela Lansbury's Jessica Fletcher, for
example, is a widow, and hardly blinks when told of orgies or mad nights of love.

But what of Dashiell Hammett, Raymond Chandler, Ross MacDonald? These
American tough guys sought murderers as part of a society inured to murder. They walked
the mean streets alone without mean hearts, as Chandler said, but were hardly able to do
more than revenge one death out of many and drink away their sorrows while stanching
their latest wounds. One might go in for gender distinctions and call this the male mode.

Time has done little to erase this strict division between the macho lower world
and the effete vicarages of Christie and her colleagues. Even today, the male writers
waver between detection and suspense but stick pretty firmly with gore and the bumping
off of one's enemies for obscure reasons. It is women, and a few Englishmen such as Dick
Francis, who still embrace the classic detective form. Their protagonist is the good man
or woman, whose primary life work is not sleuthing, who struggles to subdue evil and
rescue the virtuous, rarely beats up and never—heaven forfend—kills anyone.

Above all, this classic detective promises us redemption without mysticism, faith
without dogma and ritual, comfort in this life and the fun of putting together all the clues
we know our world contains but which we lack the grace to discover, to read, or to interpret.

—PROFESSOR CAROLYN HEILBRUN, A.K.A. AMANDA CROSS,
excerpted from "Who Dunit? The Mysterious Appeal of the Mystery," *Harper's Bazaar*

HUGO LOVELACE
CHARTERS
AND
GILES EVELYN
CALDICOTT

CHARTERS AND CALDICOTT

Based on the characters created by
Frank Launder and Sidney Gilliat

THERE'S NO MORE ECCENTRIC SERIES IN THE HISTORY OF MYSTERY!
THAN *CHARTERS AND CALDICOTT,* A SIX-EPISODE SERIAL THAT WRITER KEITH
WATERHOUSE CREATED BY RESURRECTING TWO MINOR COMIC CHARACTERS
FROM ALFRED HITCHCOCK'S 1938 SUSPENSE THRILLER *THE LADY VANISHES* AND
PLOPPING THEM DOWN IN THE MIDDLE OF A MURDER MYSTERY.

Actually, it was nothing new for the characters, who have been popping up in the oddest places for nearly 50 years. In Hitchcock's classic film, Charters and Caldicott were a pair of cricket-loving Englishmen in their mid-thirties, returning from a trip to the Tyrol on the same train with a young woman named Iris Henderson (Margaret Lockwood). Iris has stumbled onto a spy plot involving the disappearance of another passenger, elderly Miss Froy. The Englishmen are the only other passengers who remember seeing the missing woman, but they'd rather not tell anybody because they're afraid the train will be delayed and they'll miss seeing a crucial cricket match in Manchester.

Charters and Caldicott were put into *The Lady Vanishes* as comic relief when the screenplay was adapted from Ethel Lina White's 1936 novel *The Wheel Spins,* which has no such characters. But the pair got such big laughs that they were brought back two years later in Carol Reed's 1940 thriller *Night Train to Munich,* which was based on another novel that had done quite well without the presence of the two gentlemen.

STICKY WICKET

While casting about for ideas a generation later, novelist/playwright Waterhouse, who's best known for *Billy Liar,* thought it would be a great idea to revive Charters and Caldicott in a whimsical mystery serial, and the BBC agreed. In the show, Charters (Robin Bailey), a lifelong bachelor, and Caldicott (the late Michael Aldridge), a widower, are now in their 60s and retired from their jobs, which involved "doing something or other" in the British Government's Foreign Office. They're in the habit of meeting the first Friday of each month for lunch and a movie. One day they stop off at Caldicott's flat to settle one of their frequent disputes about cricket statistics—and find the corpse of a woman there. It's a situation host Vincent Price aptly describes as "a sticky wicket."

PRODUCTION COMPANY
BBC

YEAR
1986

MAIN CAST
Charters
ROBIN BAILEY

Caldicott
MICHAEL ALDRIDGE

Margaret Mottram
CAROLINE BLAKISTON

Inspector Snow
GERARD MURPHY

Jenny
TESSA PEAKE-JONES

It turns into a full-fledged mystery when they learn the dead woman may be the daughter of an old pal who is recently deceased. But then another young woman turns up, claiming to be the old friend's daughter. By the time they figure out who's who, six hours have gone by, more bodies have piled up, and they've driven fussy Police Inspector Snow (Gerard Murphy) to distraction.

Aldridge was a familiar face to Mystery! followers from his appearances in *Malice Aforethought*, the *Mystery of the Blue Jar* episode of *Agatha Christie Stories*, and as Count Orlove in *Reilly, Ace of Spies*. Bailey—he's the one wearing the mustache—was best known as Gerald Maitland in Masterpiece Theatre's *Upstairs, Downstairs*. In 1996 he turned up as an eccentric writer in the British detective series *Dalziel and Pascoe*.

"From Wilkie Collins to Arthur Conan Doyle to Agatha Christie, the best tales of detection have featured other eccentric characters with remarkable abilities to absorb all sorts of supposedly useless knowledge. Proceeding rationally, they are indefatigable generalists, interested in everything. In today's advanced universe of specialists, surrounded by the very latest in technological ingenuity, Sherlock Holmes and Miss Marple are apt merely to seem quaint. Their logical assumptions don't necessarily apply to an assertiveness-trained world in which gentlemanly conduct is, more often than not, considered a sign of weakness.

Charters and Caldicott is bent on having it both ways, poking a bit of fun at its two impossibly fussy heroes while, at the same time, making it clear that touches of elegance and honor have disappeared from our lives, replaced largely by what looks suspiciously like grubby greed."

—JOHN J. O'CONNOR,
New York Times

Public School Chaps

"A *public* school in England is the equivalent of a *private* prep school in America. I think some confusion may come from the term *public*. Unlike in America, where the education system is called public because it derives financial support from government funds, schools in England are called 'public' for a very different reason. The British public school derives its name from the fact that centuries ago, certain gentlemen thought it preferable to have their children educated in a group away from home, rather than by private tutors. So the term *public* in England applies in the sense of group (rather than solo) education.

There is no strict definition of public schools, though it has become clear what they are, and what a public school boy is. He is a boy, like both Charters and Caldicott, who attended one of the Great Schools—Eton, Harrow, Rugby, Charterhouse, Winchester, Westminster, Shrewsbury, and perhaps one or two others.

Even Americans can usually recognize the public school stereotype, especially on television or in the movies. There's that tone of voice, a look, a particular kind of accent, a way of laughing, a use of certain phrases, or even just a vague, unspoken sense of something superior. It's the difference between the boy, or man, who was at a public school, and the rest. The difference which sets Charters and Caldicott apart from, say, Inspector Snow—definitely a grammar school type."

—VINCENT PRICE

"Part of the enjoyment of Charters and Caldicott, it seems to me, is its wealth of British slang expressions. Most of them are perfectly understandable in context, but they do illustrate the truth in what Oscar Wilde tells us: 'The English have really everything in common with the Americans, except of course language.'"

—VINCENT PRICE

BROTHER CADFAEL

CADFAEL

*Based on the novels and characters
created by Ellis Peters*

IF THERE IS A DEFINING MOMENT FOR THE CADFAEL MYSTERIES,
IT MAY COME IN THE *MONK'S HOOD* EPISODE WHEN THE CANNY SLEUTH
BROTHER CADFAEL BRINGS SHOCKING NEWS TO THE FAMILY OF A
HEALTHY MAN WHO HAD SUDDENLY COLLAPSED AND DIED AT HIS DINNER TABLE.
"THIS IS NO ORDINARY DEATH," SAYS CADFAEL. "MASTER BONELL DIED
OF POISON, TAKEN IN FOOD RECENTLY EATEN."

He doesn't reach that conclusion by peeking over the shoulder of the forensic pathologist assigned to the case nor by quickly scanning the results of toxicology tests. They didn't have those in the 12th century. He figures it out by sniffing the distinctive aroma of an oily toxin around the dead man's mouth, by observing the staining of his lips, and by listening to witnesses' descriptions of the dying man's agonizing symptoms.

In the village of Shrewsbury, England, circa A.D. 1140 or so, Brother Cadfael functions principally as a medicine man who runs his own apothecary shop, cultivating the plants and herbs from which he makes medicines himself. But his job doesn't end there. He's Quincy, M.E., in a cowl, a kind of two-fisted Father Brown with carnal knowledge. He's what Sherlock Holmes might have been if born 750 years earlier and bottle-fed on a good deal more of the milk of human kindness than Conan Doyle ever gave him.

In fact, one can imagine Holmes learning a great deal at Brother Cadfael's side. In *The Sanctuary Sparrow,* for instance, Cadfael carefully extracts three different specimens of herbs from the clogged nostrils and bloated lips of a corpse recently fished from a nearby stream. Find the place where these rare plants grow together, he avows, and you will know where the murder was committed.

Cadfael is a Welshman who took up the sword in the First Crusade and fought his way to Jerusalem and back. He has seen and done it all before deciding, at age 40, to devote the rest of his life to God's work. He hopes he might make a start at cleansing the bloody stains off his immortal soul by joining an order of Benedictine monks at the Abbey of St. Peter and Paul. While atoning for his sins, he also becomes England's first master detective.

HERETICAL HOLY MAN, WORLDLY WISE MAN

First introduced by mystery writer Ellis Peters (Dame Edith Pargeter) in her 1977 novel *A Morbid Taste for Bones,* Brother Cadfael became an instant literary sensation, inspiring a number of imitators to invent their own medieval sleuths and simultaneously building an enormous following for what his creator called the *Cadfael Chronicles.* Historically the earliest, Cadfael also may be the most unique of all the detectives in the Mystery!

**PRODUCTION
COMPANY**
Central Independent
Television

YEARS
1995–1997

MAIN CAST
Brother Cadfael
DEREK JACOBI

Brother Oswin
MARK CHARNOCK

Abbot Heribert
PETER COPLEY

Prior Robert
MICHAEL CULVER

Brother Jerome
JULIAN FIRTH

Hugh Beringar
*SEAN PERTWEE/
EOIN MCCARTHY*

family—a wise, thoughtful, and sometimes heretical holy man who uses classic investigative techniques to solve crimes in an era when anything resembling science was called witchcraft and accused men often "proved" their innocence by beating up their accusers with sword or cudgel.

Cadfael was handsomely filmed in Hungary, where a mock abbey was built in a natural setting that resembled the 12th-century Shrewsbury as Peters described it in her meticulously researched novels. Cast as Cadfael was Sir Derek Jacobi, one of England's most revered stage actors, best remembered by U.S. television viewers for his incandescent performance as the stuttering Roman emperor in *I, Claudius*. Though he doesn't quite resemble Peters' shorter, rounder, and older Brother Cadfael, Jacobi brought a vigor, strength, and earnest humanity to the character that made him immediately credible—and enormously likable.

"[When Cadfael] joined the holy order of the Benedictines, he entered a tradition that began with Saint Benedict, the father of Western monasticism. As a young man, Benedict was so disgusted by the decadent culture of Rome that he abandoned his studies to devote himself to God and sought solitude in the mountains. Though he had renounced the world, the world wouldn't return the favor, and he soon found himself with a flock of disciples— so many, in fact, that he later established 12 monasteries. Benedict died in 583, but his order flourished, and half a century later, it gained a foothold in England, where it stood unrivalled for the next 600 years."

—DIANA RIGG

INTERVENING FOR THE INNOCENTS

In nearly every Cadfael mystery, the monk intervenes on behalf of the innocent party, often in the very nick of time. Like Perry Mason, he has an uncanny ability to pick clients most in need of a discerning eye and a forceful advocate. His friend and frequent ally, Undersheriff Hugh Beringar—played by Sean Pertwee in the first series, Eoin McCarthy in *Cadfael II*—tells us Cadfael "seeks goodness in the blackest of hearts," and often finds it.

Cadfael's greatest asset is his worldly wisdom. Unlike so many of the other monks, he knows the human heart because he still has one of his own. In *Monk's Hood*, Cadfael comes face to face with Richildis (Mary Miller), the sweetheart he left behind for the Crusades, now an aging widow with grown children. Though they long for each other, he explains he has given himself to his present life and, now in his sixties, cannot turn back. After he saves her son from the gallows, she stands ready to give Cadfael the prize he once sought as a robust young lover, but Cadfael settles for a chaste kiss, telling her, "To part with friendship is a reward greater than I could have hoped for."

Yet in *The Virgin in the Ice* in the second series, Cadfael discovers a "reward" from another early liaison that drains the color from his face: He has a full-grown son by Mariam, the Saracen widow he once dallied with in Antioch. Discreetly, he never lets the young man know that he's his father. Another time, when Cadfael is asked if he ever misses "human love," he replies, "I've fought many battles and I've been gravely wounded," but "nothing wounds so much as a love that was lost."

"I have one sacred rule about the thriller. It must have morality. If it strays from the side of the angels, provokes total despair, takes pleasure in evil, that is an unforgivable sin. I am not very good at villains."

—ELLIS PETERS

These aren't the usual musings of a 12th-century Benedictine monk—and Cadfael is frequently reminded of that fact by his most severe critics within the abbey, Prior Robert (Michael Culver) and his weasel of a flunky, Brother Jerome (Julian Firth). They consider him a troublemaker who must be watched at all times.

To be sure, Cadfael has some ultra-liberal attitudes. In *The Sanctuary Sparrow*, a fugitive minstrel and a servant girl wonder if they've committed an act of unforgivable sacrilege by having sex in the abbey. "Where there is natural love," Cadfael observes, "I find it hard to consider a place too holy to house it." Spoken like a liberated cleric of the flower power generation. In *The Leper of St. Giles*, Cadfael ventures the opinion that "the senses are the gateway to the soul" and suggests "we should celebrate them more often." When he's reminded that that might be considered a rather eccentric attitude for a man of Christ, Cadfael owns up to the philosophy that guides him at the abbey, saying, "Sometimes I like to put the sand of doubt into the oyster of my faith."

If all this suggests Cadfael is poised for sainthood, it's well to remember that, by his own admission, he has spent years covered in the blood of his enemies without a flicker of conscience. The reformed Cadfael also is far from immune to fits of bad temper, especially when his clumsy aide, the gawky Brother Oswin (Mark Charnock), cracks a heated cooking pot by rinsing it in cold water or dribbles toxic rubbing oil onto a basket of hard-to-find herbs. In such moments, Cadfael can sound remarkably like Inspector Morse giving poor Sergeant Lewis a royal going-over for some minor infraction.

Still, notwithstanding his occasional bad temper, one could only wish there were more Cadfaels in the world today, holding coroner's inquests, investigating homicides, even sitting in judgment on defendants brought before the bar. Taking his inspiration from the word of his God, Brother Cadfael looks for the truth by ignoring the obvious and finds it within his fellow man. "Man beholds only the outward appearance," he tells us. "God looks upon the heart."

"From London to Tokyo, Athens to Sydney, the Benedictine sleuth has crossed language barriers as well as the centuries to win a global readership, largely because his creator has endowed him with universal human qualities that indeed make him 'the person next door.'"

—Publishers Weekly

> "[Brother Cadfael has] really
> made me think about what I believe.
> I say that I created him, but he's
> been busy creating me."
>
> —ELLIS PETERS

SELECTED BIBLIOGRAPHY

A Morbid Taste for Bones, 1977; *One Corpse Too Many,* 1979; *Monk's Hood,* 1980; *Saint Peter's Fair,* 1981; *The Leper of Saint Giles,* 1981; *The Virgin in the Ice,* 1982; *The Sanctuary Sparrow,* 1983; *The Devil's Novice,* 1983; *Dead Man's Ransom,* 1984; *The Pilgrim of Hate,* 1984; *An Excellent Mystery,* 1985; *The Raven in the Foregate,* 1986; *The Rose Rent,* 1987; *The Hermit of Eyton Forest,* 1987; *The Confession of Brother Haluin,* 1988; *A Rare Benedictine* (short stories), 1988; *The Heretic's Apprentice,* 1989; *The Potter's Field,* 1990; *The Summer of the Danes,* 1991; *The Holy Thief,* 1992; *Brother Cadfael's Penance,* 1994.

Medieval Mystery Writer:

AUTHOR

ELLIS PETERS

(EDITH PARGETER)

THE PEN NAME ELLIS PETERS, LIKE BROTHER CADFAEL, WAS THE INVENTION OF Dame Edith Pargeter, a quiet but industrious novelist and historian who lived virtually her entire life in Shropshire, not far from the Welsh border and the village of Shrewsbury where her fictional, crime-solving monk labored at the Abbey of St. Peter and Paul. Pargeter wrote her first book, a historical novel called *Hortensius, Friend of Nero,* in 1936 while working as a pharmacist's assistant, a job with some similarities to that of her medieval monk. Then 22, she was anxious to earn a living as a writer and continued to write novels while in uniform as a member of the Women's Royal Navy Service (WRENS) in World War II. She wrote both novels and medieval history works, but began to indulge her passion for the mystery genre after the war, writing a number of contemporary thrillers, including the Inspector Felse series. One of her novels, *Death and the Joyful Woman,* won a 1962 Edgar award and was adapted for American television as an episode of *Alfred Hitchcock Presents.*

In 1959, Pargeter adopted the pen name Ellis Peters for her mysteries, keeping her real name for her historical works. Then, in 1977, she merged the two streams of her literary life by publishing the first Brother Cadfael novel, *A Morbid Taste for Bones,* which became a booming bestseller. Pargeter was made a Dame of the British Empire in 1993—at the same time her Brother Cadfael, Derek Jacobi, received his knighthood.

When she died in 1995 at age 82, 20 Brother Cadfael volumes were in print, and more than 9.5 million copies had been sold worldwide. Pargeter always believed in the principles Cadfael stood for and made it a goal to create a hero who would counter the influence of anti-hero culture in the world. Long before her death, her most beloved character had fulfilled her promise and become an international cult hero whose spiritual values and devotion to justice made him one of the mystery genre's most enduring positive role models.

Frocked Again:

ACTOR
DEREK JACOBI

As an actor Derek Jacobi is used to spending many months in front of a camera wearing a frock and sandals. That was his costume for the stammering Emperor he played in *I, Claudius* on Masterpiece Theatre seventeen years before his Brother Cadfael role. Worried after the Claudius stint that he wouldn't get any other work because "they would think all I could play was ancient Roman emperors," Jacobi moved ahead several centuries and across a few countries to play the melancholy Dane in an Old Vic Production of *Hamlet*. That performance reportedly inspired Kenneth Branagh to become an actor; it also led to the formation of the Jacobi Cadets, an all-woman fan club. Although Jacobi says theater is his "first love," he has appeared in several films, inluding Branagh's *Henry V*, in which he played the Chorus, and Branagh's *Dead Again*, in which he was a villain.

Jacobi attended Cambridge University, studying history and taking part in drama productions with fellow undergraduate Ian McKellan (Anthony Skipling in Mystery!'s *Dying Day*). He subsequently joined Sir Laurence Olivier's National Theatre, where he was to understudy Jeremy Brett (Mystery!'s Sherlock Holmes) in a series of plays until Brett was cast by Warner Brothers in *My Fair Lady*, at which point Jacobi inherited the roles. Though he says it took a while after Claudius "to get around London without someone shouting 'Hail Caesar' to me," these days he is perhaps more likely to be hailed with "My good brother." Frockless, he solves another kind of mystery when he reprises his Tony-nominated role of Alan Turing in *Breaking the Code* on Masterpiece Theatre in 1997.

FATHER BROWN

FATHER BROWN

Based on the stories by
G. K. Chesterton

THE CLEVER LITTLE CATHOLIC PRIEST CALLED FATHER BROWN MAY BE
THE MOST BELOVED OF ALL CLERICAL SLEUTHS BECAUSE HE SEEMS SO BENIGN—
EVEN TO THE CULPRITS HE SNARES WITH HIS AGILE MIND.

That's the image intended by English author G. K. Chesterton, who figured his priest might be much more effective as a detective if nobody suspected he knew which end of his cassock was up. Like Agatha Christie's inconspicuous Miss Marple, who came along 20 years later, Father Brown was purposely sketched in shades of modest coloration and given what his creator called "the harmless human name of Brown."

PROGENITOR OF GUMSHOE PRIESTS

With "a face as round and dull as a Norfolk dumpling" and "eyes as empty as the North Sea," he carries no tools of the shamus trade, only a shabby umbrella. Yet Father Brown has left an indelible impression on the detective genre, obviously inspiring any number of amateur ecclesiastical gumshoes, some as recent as Harry Kemelman's Rabbi David Small, Ralph McInerny's Father Dowling, and television's Father of Hell Town, Noah "Hardstep" Rivers, the streetwise priest played by actor Robert Blake. He also was among the first of the literary sleuths to go without a first name, though Chesterton once referred to him as the Reverend J. Brown of St. Francis Xavier's Church, Camberwell, which suggests he at least had one.

The good priest had been on television before (in a series starring Heinz Roemheld) and in film (*Father Brown, Detective*, 1934, with Walter Connolly, and *The Detective*, 1954, with Alec Guinness). In the Mystery! series he was played by the respected English actor Kenneth More, who died four months before the U.S. airing. Best known to PBS audiences as Jolyon from *The Forsyte Saga*, More had been a major presence on stage and screen (*Doctor in the House, The Longest Day, The Battle of Britain*).

Mystery! presented Father Brown in four adventures. In *Three Tools of Death*, he informs the police that the man they've charged with the murder of a famed philanthropist can't possibly be guilty; in *The Head of Caesar*, he comes to the aid of a young woman who's being blackmailed; in *The Eye of Apollo*, he investigates a cult of sun worshippers; and in *The Secret Garden*, he travels to Paris to solve the mystery of a headless body found in a garden.

In two of the cases, Father Brown joins forces with the notorious Flambeau (Dennis Burgess), an aristrocratic Frenchman who once was a gentleman thief but has reformed himself so completely that he's now a detective and frequently assists Father Brown in discovering the facts of a crime.

PRODUCTION COMPANY
ITC Entertainment

YEAR
1982

MAIN CAST
Father Brown
KENNETH MORE

Flambeau
DENNIS BURGESS

Set in the 1920s, the series stuck firmly to the Chesterton formula: Father Brown is a lovable absent-minded parish priest whose interest in solving crimes springs from his natural involvement in the troubles of his parishioners. His calling brings him into contact with all sorts of people—rich and poor, ordinary and extraordinary, suffering and thriving, who give him plenty of grist for his sleuthing.

"Some people are drawn to crime; in my case, crime seems to be drawn to me."

—FATHER BROWN

"One of [Agatha Christie's] favorite contemporary mystery authors was her friend, G. K. Chesterton. She described his Father Brown stories as 'never to be forgotten, and always reread with pleasure.' It should come as no surprise, then, when Tommy and Tuppence apply the methods of Chesterton's detective priest in The Man in the Mist.*"*

—VINCENT PRICE

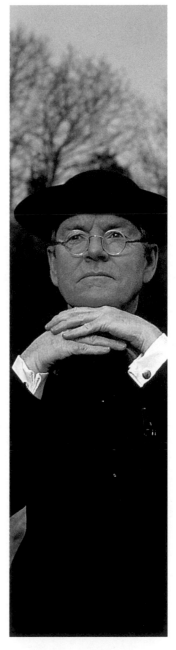

PATTERNED AFTER A REAL PRIEST

A jovial sort, he likes nothing better than the challenge of solving a crime. "After all," he says, "puzzles are the only passion permitted in the priesthood." Ellery Queen went so far as to rank Father Brown with Edgar Allan Poe's August Dupin and Arthur Conan Doyle's Sherlock Holmes as "the three greatest detectives in literature." Chesterton's detective-priest was unique, said Queen (a pseudonym for Frederic Dannay and Manfred B. Lee) because "he views wrongdoers as souls needing salvation, not criminals to be brought to justice." Chesterton patterned Father Brown after a real clergyman, his friend Monsignor John O'Connor, who often corrected flaws in Chesterton's reasoning during their conversations, displaying an unusually keen mind. Chesterton once overheard a couple of Cambridge students discussing how unworldly a certain priest was—and came up with the idea of creating a clerical sleuth as clever as Monsignor O'Connor, but who generally left the impression he was as naive as the priest the students had described. That inspiration ultimately led Chesterton to write 51 much-anthologized and collected Father Brown stories, which have remained popular over the years because of their literary quality and the ingenuity of their plots.

"I try to get inside a man . . . thinking his thoughts, wrestling with his passions, till I have bent myself into the posture of his hunched and peering hatred. Till I am really a murderer. And when I am quite sure that I feel like the murderer, of course I know who he is."

—FATHER BROWN

> "[Chesterton] insisted that the trouble with detective stories was that the writer cannot tell us until the last chapter many of the most interesting things about the most interesting characters. . . . Not until the last chapter, then, can the writer really get at the psychology, philosophy, and morals of the case. Since this was as much a part of Chesterton's raison d'etre as the execution of the crime itself, he liked it best when the first chapter of a mystery was also the last.
>
> So Chesterton liked his mysteries straight and simple. The Father Brown saga is noted for its lack of endless incidental clues that characteristically plagued detective literature around the turn of the century."
>
> —VINCENT PRICE

SELECTED BIBLIOGRAPHY

The Innocence of Father Brown (1911), *The Wisdom of Father Brown* (1914), *The Incredulity of Father Brown* (1926), *The Secret of Father Brown* (1927), *The Scandal of Father Brown* (1935).

Man of Many Literary Métiers:

AUTHOR
G. K. CHESTERTON

GILBERT KEITH CHESTERTON WAS AN ENGLISH NOVELIST, ESSAYIST, BIOGRAPHER, poet, historian, and journalist of luminous reputation in his time, but best remembered today for the 51 lighthearted short stories he wrote about the priest-detective called Father Brown. Born in 1874, he was the elder of two sons of London businessman Edward Chesterton, a father he always described as "Pickwickian." He briefly studied art, developing his natural talent as a caricaturist, a hobby he continued to pursue throughout his life. He began his professional literary career as a book reviewer and journalist for the liberal *Daily News.*

Many consider his long friendship with Hilaire Belloc to have been the most profound influence on his career, especially in matters of religion and politics. Chesterton was equally dissatisfied with capitalism and socialism and developed the theory of "Distribution," which advocated the widest possible ownership of property. With Belloc and his brother Cecil, he founded *The New Witness,* a weekly paper designed to attack political corruption. He converted to Catholicism in 1922, but had already created Father Brown, the most beloved Catholic literary character of the period, and published his first collection of Father Brown stories in 1911.

Chesterton's other notable works include his biographies of St. Thomas Aquinas (1933), Francis of Assisi (1923), Robert Browning (1903), and Charles Dickens (1906). An enormous man with a mustache and an overall Horace Rumpole look, Chesterton is widely believed to have been the model for Dr. Gideon Fell in the mystery novels of John Dickson Carr.

Chesterton died in 1936, a little more than a year after his most famous character first came to the screen in the English film *Father Brown, Detective.*

On Her Majesty's Secret Service

*They're the murky heroes of the Mystery! world—
twilight types who skulk and snoop, disguise and dissemble.
They do what they do for queen and country. They try to
enjoy it while they can—and avoid ending their service
in front of a foreign firing squad.*

- **Sidney Reilly**
  REILLY, ACE OF SPIES

- **Bernard Samson**
  GAME, SET, AND MATCH

SIDNEY REILLY

REILLY, ACE OF SPIES

Based on the book by
Robin Bruce Lockhart

ONLY ONCE IN THE ANNALS OF MYSTERY! HAS A SERIES BEEN BUILT
AROUND A HERO WHO REALLY LIVED—A MYSTERIOUS YOUNG RUSSIAN NAMED
SIGMUND ROSENBLUM, WHO WILL BE KNOWN FOREVERMORE BY THE ALIAS HE ADOPTED
AS A SECRET AGENT—SIDNEY REILLY, THE LEGENDARY "ACE OF SPIES."

But there's some debate about whether "hero" is the right word to describe the frequently ruthless Reilly, who's still regarded as a traitor by some of the nations he spied against, who generally discarded the women he loved—sometimes terminally—and who occasionally killed people in cold blood to achieve his ends. What is certain, though, is that Reilly was a brilliant, audacious agent who literally changed the course of history prior to World War I. He was an asset to the British government, having the ear of everyone right up to Churchill. But he was also an embarrassment—his flamboyance, his egomania, the fact that he was always working for himself, and later his self-avowed socialism having something to do with that.

Reilly, Ace of Spies was lavishly filmed on location in several European countries. It featured a large, extraordinarily rich cast that included several performers who would leave their mark on the Mystery! series: Leo McKern from *Rumpole of the Bailey,* David Suchet and Hugh Fraser of *Poirot,* and David Burke from *The Adventures of Sherlock Holmes.* Towering over them all, though, was the soft-spoken Sam Neill as the subtly romantic yet sinister man Vincent Price called "probably the greatest spy in history."

LIFE OF REILLY

The man who became Reilly was born in 1874 in southern Russia. In his teens he learned his mother, a Russian, had conceived him during an illicit affair with a physician from Vienna named Rosenblum. She kept the identity of his father a secret from everyone but her husband, who agreed to give the child his legal name, though he later took the name Rosenblum. When he was 21, Rosenblum ran away to South America and joined a jungle expedition. He wound up saving the life of a man named Major Fothergill who was so impressed by the young man's bravery, resourcefulness, and skill with languages that he offered him a job with British Intelligence.

The series begins in 1901 in the foothills of the Caucasus mountains. On a spy mission for the British, Rosenblum has been traveling through Persia observing Russian efforts to find oil. He's begun romancing Margaret (Jeananne Crowley), the wife of Reverend Thomas (Sebastian Shaw), and needs time to outwit the wily head of the border police, Tanyatos (John Rhys-Davies). Tanyatos suspects Reilly and warns him there's no way for any of the rail passengers to escape his surveillance.

PRODUCTION COMPANY
Thames Television

YEAR
1984

MAIN CAST
Sidney Reilly
SAM NEILL

Sir Robert Bruce Lockhart
IAN CHARLESON

Count Orlove
MICHAEL ALDRIDGE

Joseph Stalin
DAVID BURKE

Margaret
JEANANNE CROWLEY

Basil Zaharov
LEO MCKERN

But Reilly does get away by convincing Margaret to pretend she's having an affair with him. He leaves her and her sickly husband to face a prison term for their role in his escape—and a scandal over the "love affair" when they eventually are freed and return to England. When Reilly finally sees Margaret again in London, she has been disgraced through her association with him. He asks about her ailing husband, and she reports she's still married to him. "I should hope so," says Reilly. "He's a wealthy man halfway to the grave."

Reilly is a daring and efficient spy who's able to use anything—or anyone—to avoid capture by the enemy, a man seemingly without ethics or morals. In one episode, he poses as a shipping agent in the Manchurian city of Port Arthur, headquarters of the Russian Pacific Fleet, and supplies the Imperial Japanese Navy with information that permits the surprise attack that sinks the entire Russian fleet. In others he infiltrates a German shipyard and steals the plans for a new naval gun; convinces Australian oil explorer William Knox D'Arcy to sell his discoveries to England, setting up what later becomes British Petroleum; joins a conspiracy within the Soviet Union to topple the Lenin government; helps the FBI weed out Russian spies in America; and slips back into Russia to foment revolution, where Stalin puts a price on his head.

Along the way, Reilly makes and loses several fortunes, marries several different women—most of them bigamously—and romances many more. Neill plays him as an extremely intelligent man with charm he can turn on or off at will, an instinctive gambler who bets his life against long odds.

In bringing the story of Sidney Reilly to television, screenwriter Troy Kennedy Martin used as his primary source the book *Reilly, Ace of Spies* by Robin Bruce Lockhart, the son of Sir Robert Bruce Lockhart, who was a British diplomat assigned to the Bolshevik government. Lockhart, who knew Reilly well and was deeply involved with him in his espionage missions, naturally became a key character in the story (he was played by Ian Charleson).

FOREIGN RIGHTS

For authenticity, the series traveled to many different countries, but there was one country they couldn't film in: the Soviet Union, which considered Reilly a traitor. So other locales had to be arranged for the episodes that took place largely in Russia. As for how to deal with the many languages Reilly spoke (seven), the producers decided to have everyone speak English rather than create a 12-hour marathon of subtitles.

The treatment of Reilly's story in the series prompted the Soviet government to condemn *Reilly, Ace of Spies* through the government newspaper *Izvestia*, claiming it glorified a "founding father of international terrorism" who, aided by British Intelligence, tried to topple the Soviet government through a series of conspiracies that even involved assassination attempts on Soviet officials. Ironically, the report stated that Reilly had been arrested by the Soviet government, sentenced to death for treason, and executed by firing squad in 1925. It was the first official admission by the Soviets that Reilly had been executed. Yet rumors continue to circulate, insisting Reilly really didn't die in front of that Soviet firing squad after all, but escaped death by agreeing to become an informer for the Soviets. Futilely, author Lockhart fought against the series' conclusion that showed Reilly's execution, and, in 1987, with the publication of his second book, *Reilly, The First Man,* unearthed evidence that Reilly was still alive in the Soviet Union during World War II.

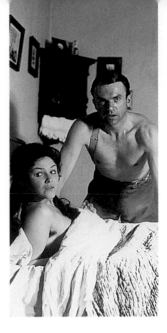

"Many women viewers have written in to say that although they find Reilly's treatment of the women in his life thoroughly reprehensible, they have to admit they also find him irresistible!"

—VINCENT PRICE

Ace of Hearts

Biographer Robin Bruce Lockhart wrote in his preface to *Reilly, Ace of Spies,* that Reilly was "said to possess 11 passports and a wife to go with each." The first of Reilly's television romances is Margaret Thomas, a minister's wife. Like most of Reilly's loves, Margaret is ill-used, even though he marries her after her husband dies suddenly. His philandering eventually drives her to alcoholism. One of Reilly's girlfriends, a prostitute named Rose (Michele Copsey), is murdered because of him. He lures lovely Nadia (Celia Gregory) away from her husband, Count Massino, and makes her his second wife, though he really isn't legally divorced from Margaret yet. Eventually, Nadine tires of his inattention and leaves him to marry philanthropist Alfred Nobel (only one reason why Reilly never got the Nobel Peace Prize). Reilly finds comely actor Pepita Bobadilla (Laura Davenport) hard to resist after he comes across her splashing around in his hotel bathtub, so he finally marries her, too. Among his other notable loves: Eugenie (Eleanor David), his secretary, whom he shoots and dumps in a lake because he thinks she's plotting against him, and art student Caryll Houselander (Joanne Pearce), a clairvoyant who's dumped by Reilly, but somehow doesn't see it coming. Many more women claimed to be wives of Reilly, and according to Vincent Price some 90 women were rumored to have been his mistresses. Too bad he didn't leave his little black book to Inspector Morse.

"Always the loner, always brewing more than one scheme at a time, always indulging his expensive tastes and his love of women, Reilly invariably found a way to dovetail the accomplishment of his professional objectives with the means to satisfy the hefty demands he made on his pocketbook."

—VINCENT PRICE

Heroes, Anti-Heroes, Non-Heroes:

ACTOR

SAM NEILL

JUICY PARTS LIKE SIDNEY REILLY, A ROMANTIC ADVENTURER WITH AN OMINOUS
air of danger about him, can make people see an actor in a whole new light, as *Reilly, Ace
of Spies* did for Sam Neill. Before Reilly, Neill was a respected young actor whose screen
characters were mostly troubled, dark, moody men—without the carnal charm
Reilly could turn on virtually at will. The Mystery! series showed his range and
opened up his leading-man potential, which ultimately took him to his most widely-
seen role to date—the heroic paleontologist in Steven Spielberg's tremendous
box-office hit *Jurassic Park.*

Born in Northern Ireland in 1947, Neill grew up in New Zealand, where
he began his acting career on the stage, then migrated to Australia to work in television shows, including the hit series *The Sullivans.* His first major starring role
in a movie was in the 1977 thriller *Sleeping Dogs,* the first film from New Zealand
to be released in the U.S. But it was Gillian Armstrong's critically acclaimed
1979 Australian film, *My Brilliant Career,* that finally made Neill's name known
internationally.

After the worldwide success of Reilly, Neill began to land more sympathetic
roles: the charismatic tycoon William Lowell Kane in *Kane & Abel* (1985), the loyal
husband of accused child-killer Meryl Streep in *A Cry in the Dark* (1988), Nicole
Kidman's valiant husband in *Dead Calm* (1988), and others. His roles now range
from colorful (the scandalous libertine artist in *Sirens,* 1994) to serious (Holly
Hunter's loveless husband in *The Piano,* 1993). In 1996 Neill returned to the realm of
mystery, playing the police detective who tracks down the killers of a Kansas family in a
CBS television remake of Truman Capote's classic *In Cold Blood.*

He Who Must Be Obeyed:

RUTHLESS VILLAIN
BASIL ZAHAROV
(LEO MCKERN)

It must have been shocking for loyal viewers of Mystery! tuning in to *Reilly, Ace of Spies* to see Reilly being held at gunpoint by their old friend, Horace Rumpole! Only in a manner of speaking, of course. In a brilliant casting move, the producers decided to fill the role of ruthless international arms dealer Basil Zaharov with Leo McKern, the rumpled, beloved actor best known for playing the easy-going, poetry-quoting barrister. Sporting a recklessly confident bearing only an exceedingly rich and powerful villain can afford and exuding a full measure of malevolent menace, McKern proved how versatile an actor he is.

A wealthy dealer in guns, chemicals, and even submarines, Zaharov was based in England, but sold to all nations, including Britain's enemies. He was so deeply entrenched in the heart of the government that he had access to secrets reserved only for British Intelligence and the king. Vincent Price referred to Zaharov as "the most powerful and ruthless weapons dealer of all time," suggesting he had more than earned his nickname as "the merchant of death" before he met up with Reilly.

In their first encounter, Zaharov definitely has the upper hand. "What a convenient sort of chap you are," Zaharov says, holding Reilly at gunpoint. "Officially, you don't exist."

Reilly is still grieving over the murder of his prostitute girlfriend by a brutish hoodlum hired by Zaharov. That same hoodlum is digging a grave in the basement behind Reilly—apparently for him. But Zaharov surprises Reilly this time, shooting the hoodlum instead, and shocks Reilly even further by offering him the chance to join his spy ring. Reilly refuses, setting up the later confrontations with Zaharov on the espionage front lines.

McKern played Zaharov with great relish as a man who is very accustomed to being in charge. Perhaps he was grateful to play "He Who Must Be Obeyed" for a change after so many years as the sorry Rumpole, whose own domineering wife he calls "She Who Must Be Obeyed."

BERNARD SAMSON

GAME, SET AND MATCH

*Based on the novels Berlin Game, Mexico Set,
and London Match by Len Deighton*

BERNARD SAMSON SEEMS AN UNLIKELY HERO FOR AN EPIC THRILLER.
BURNED-OUT AND WEARY, HE'S A MIDDLE-AGED MAN WHOSE WIFE HAS PASSED HIM
BY ON THE LADDER OF SUCCESS. HE LOOKS IN A MIRROR AND SEES A CASUALTY
OF WHAT HE CALLS "AN ACCUMULATION OF STRESS," A FAMILIAR
MALADY FOR THOSE WHO SPY FOR A LIVING.

Worse, he fears he may have lost his nerve. But viewers of *Game, Set and Match* were to learn Samson hadn't lost nearly as much nerve as he thought. The 13-hour series was faithfully adapted by John Howlett from author Len Deighton's trilogy of best-selling novels, *Berlin Game, Mexico Set,* and *London Match.* It took more than a year to film on locations reaching from the Berlin Wall to the jungles of Mexico and requiring 42,000 miles of travel for the huge international cast, which included some 3,000 extras. With production costs of $8.5 million—a huge sum for a British television serial—*Game, Set and Match* remains the longest, most ambitious single mystery ever investigated on the PBS series.

MYSTERY FOR THE MODERN AGE

For those who cringe at hearing Deighton's spy thriller described as a mystery and refuse to think of Samson as a detective, the truth is *Game, Set and Match* has a profound mystery at its center—Who is the double agent inside Britain's spy agency?—and Bernard Samson is the sleuth who finally solves it, often with traditional methods of detection. It was, in fact, a new kind of mystery, designed especially for the modern age of Cold War paranoia. Rather than figuring out who left the body on the library floor, Samson's job is to unravel hundreds of criss-crossed threads in a crazy quilt of espionage that routinely leaves lots of bodies strewn on all kinds of floors. In the process, viewers gain insight into the sort of modern espionage agency that makes the capacity to betray one's friends and family a required condition of employment, and the incentive to betray one's colleagues sometimes too compelling.

Samson (Ian Holm) is a disgraced specialist in German affairs who's working for MI6, the British service that parallels the American CIA. Raised in the post-war ruins of Berlin, Samson speaks fluent German and is an old hand at playing dangerous cat-and-mouse games with his agency's primary enemy—the Soviet KGB. Benched five years earlier after being blamed for a bungled attempt to lure a Polish military officer into defecting to the West, Samson has been "picking at the wound of failure" ever since, working in anonymity on MI6's "Berlin desk" while his wife, Fiona (Mel Martin), rises in the ranks to senior security officer at MI6.

PRODUCTION
COMPANY
Granada Television

YEAR
1989

MAIN CAST
Bernard Samson
IAN HOLM

Fiona Samson
MEL MARTIN

Bret Rensselaer
ANTHONY BATE

Dicky Cruyer
MICHAEL CULVER

Werner Volkmann
MICHAEL DEGEN

Gloria Kent
AMANDA DONOHOE

Giles Trent
HUGH FRASER

Erich Stinnes
GOTTFRIED JOHN

Frank Harrington
FREDERICK TREVES

While Samson broods on his own failure, his contempt for the even more inept people around him grows. He thinks of his boss, spy controller Bret Rensselaer (Anthony Bate), as a man who "has spent his life in a swivel chair, arguing with dictating machines and smiling at committees." The supervisors who surround him have "never seen a Russian close to, except over cucumber sandwiches at an Embassy party."

The blood starts to flow again in Samson's tired veins when he's called back to do one more dangerous job for MI6. He's told a leak has developed in the deep cover "Brahms" spy network he had set up years ago in East Berlin, and he's the only one who might be able to plug it. When he returns to the dark side of Germany, though, he begins to realize the leak may not be in his spy network after all, but rather in the London head-quarters of MI6.

SEARCHING FOR THE MOLE—AND REDEMPTION

Deighton's long, complex story is not just the saga of an obscure British agent searching for spies inside and outside his own agency. It's also the story of a disillusioned modern man searching for his path to personal redemption after years of soul-destroying spy activity. "A tragic hero for victims of bureaucracy everywhere," is how one critic defined Samson.

A sign of Samson's disillusionment is the fact that now there is virtually no one he trusts. In one sequence, Samson's old friend Werner Volkmann (Michael Degen) tells him a Russian major they're trying to lure into defecting is a wife-beater and that may be a motive for the man's willingness to discuss defection. The suspicious Samson warns that the Russians may have planted the wife-beating story just to give the man credibility. "Giving her a black eye on the off chance I might happen by?" Werner asks.

MODERN PARABLE

Samson's long journey to rehabilitation is a parable with modern parallels to the biblical Samson: Deighton's Cold War Samson has his locks shorn by his own Delilah, the beautiful Fiona, who turns out to be a traitor—and a Soviet mole.

Such allusions are one reason why so many considered *Game, Set and Match* to be an intellectual thriller with several levels of meaning for alert viewers. However, it also had many moments of bristling action that didn't take much thought to enjoy. In one scene, Samson walks into a trap in a Mexico City money-changer's office and has to shoot his way out. Samson and Rensselaer are attacked by shotgun-wielding thugs in a London laundromat scene and, in Berlin, Samson is kidnapped by KGB agents and taken to headquarters, where he expects to see them torture his young son.

Requiring both patience, because of its great length (one critic called it "the *Waiting for Godot* of spy stories"), and a good memory just to keep all the characters sorted out, *Game, Set and Match* was genuine adult television at its finest and was gener-ally acclaimed by those critics who took the time to penetrate its immense bulk. Despite the widespread critical praise for *Game, Set and Match*, it was a ratings disaster for Mystery! with the audience steadily declining during the 12-week run. Like commercial network executives, who stopped making long miniseries projects for the same reason, Executive Producer Rebecca Eaton vowed there would be no more such epics on Mystery!.

Artist of Espionage:

AUTHOR

LEN DEIGHTON

LEN DEIGHTON HAS OWNED A PERMANENT SEAT IN THE THRONE ROOM of great English espionage writers ever since the early 1960s, when he created a wisecracking working-class spy with no name who revolutionized spy fiction in a series of bestsellers beginning with *The Ipcress File.* His nameless, anarchic spy— given the name Harry Palmer in a series of hit movies starring Michael Caine—was the antidote to Ian Fleming's fanciful James Bond, who had started the spy craze in the early 1950s when the Cold War was in full swing.

Like John le Carré, Deighton set out to paint a faithfully realistic picture of the espionage scene. As he grew more accomplished as a writer and developed a wide network of insider contacts around the world, Deighton finally was able to create another memorable character, Bernard Samson, who occupied more than a decade of the author's literary output and was the subject of his enormously popular trilogy *Berlin Game, Mexico Set,* and *London Match.* The background of the Samson family emerged in the novel *Winter* and the story then continued in another trilogy—*Spy Hook, Spy Line,* and *Spy Sinker.* By the time of the publication of the final volume in the series, *Spy Sinker,* in 1990, a painfully-real portrait of a spy who ranks with le Carré's George Smiley had been comprehensively developed. In 1994, Deighton began publishing his third Bernard Samson trilogy—*Faith, Hope,* and *Charity.*

STEWARD TO BAKER TO SPY-MAKER

Deighton, who has been called "the poet of the spy story," was born in 1929. Before hitting the big-time with *The Ipcress File* in 1962, he had worked at a slew of temporary jobs from railway employee and pastry cook to airline steward and advertising

"The internal politics of the spy game is depicted as no more noble, and no less annoying, than that of any other large corporation. Samson and all his friends and enemies swiftly turn into real people, and the viewer soon cares about them—including the office buffoons and the enemy agents."

—DAVID BIANCULLI,
New York Post

illustrator. During his military service with the Royal Air Force, he was attached to the Special Investigation Branch, where he was trained as a photographer whose photos were published in most of the big national papers in England. Following his military service, Deighton enrolled at the Royal College of Art and became a successful illustrator. But during a vacation in France in 1960, Deighton fulfilled a lifelong dream by starting his first novel, which eventually became *The Ipcress File*.

Since becoming a best-selling author, Deighton has worked in movie production—he wrote the screenplay for *Oh, What a Lovely War!* and adapted his own *Only When I Larf*—and has divided his focus between spy novels, war novels, and non-fiction books, including several French cookbooks. Many of his novels have been filmed, including *Funeral in Berlin* and *Billion Dollar Brain*.

> *"This is Deighton's typically gray, overcast, unglamorous milieu, where there are no superheroes, only characters who are flawed, vulnerable and not necessarily noble. In novel after novel, Deighton peels back layers of deception, betrayal, and ambiguity to expose the cold pragmatism of espionage. On both sides of the wall, this is a pretty crummy bunch."*
>
> —HOWARD ROSENBERG,
> *Los Angeles Times*

SELECTED BIBLIOGRAPHY

The Samson Chronicles: *Berlin Game,* 1984; *Mexico Set,* 1985; *London Match,* 1986; *Winter,* 1987; *Spy Hook,* 1988; *Spy Line,* 1989; *Spy Sinker,* 1990; *Faith,* 1994; *Hope,* 1995; *Charity,* 1996.

At Holm with Samson:

ACTOR
IAN HOLM

Ian Holm, who was a foot shorter and 16 years older than Deighton's Samson, nevertheless made viewers believe Deighton's character was living inside his skin. Of course, he got more than enough practice: He was in all but four of the series' 664 scenes. He says that Bernard Samson "is the closest thing to me I've done in all these 35 years."

After training at the Royal Academy of Dramatic Art, Holm joined the Royal Shakespeare Company. He has appeared in the films *Chariots of Fire, Alien, Time Bandits,* and *Brazil,* among others. He played Paul Presset in Mystery!'s *We, the Accused,* and Poirot in *Murder by the Book.*

IN A CLASS BY THEMSELVES

They're not exactly detectives, but they do get to the bottom of lots of mysteries: a rumpled old defense lawyer, a professional "wish-fulfiller," a retired college professor, a female ex-cop, and all the other unique souls with a knack for sleuthing.

- **HORACE RUMPOLE**
  RUMPOLE OF THE BAILEY

- **PARKER PYNE, ET ALIA**
  AGATHA CHRISTIE STORIES

- **OLIVER AND DIANE PRIEST**
  OLIVER'S TRAVELS

HORACE RUMPOLE

RUMPOLE OF THE BAILEY
RUMPOLE'S RETURN
Written by John Mortimer

LIKE THE LEGAL SYSTEM HE SERVES, HORACE RUMPOLE IS FAR FROM
PERFECT—AND KNOWS IT. HE'S GROSSLY OVERWEIGHT, TIPPLES A BIT TOO MUCH
AT POMMEROY'S WINE BAR, AND IS CRUSTY AND CURMUDGEONLY.

He freely describes himself as "an Old Bailey hack" whose mind is stuffed with lots of stray bits and pieces of knowledge from a long career as a barrister, along with "memorable fragments" of the *Oxford Book of English Verse*, which he quotes *ad nauseam* at the most inopportune times.

That doesn't mean he isn't still an awfully appealing old bounder who's remarkably effective in both the courtroom and in the chambers of judges (who might toss him out on his ear, if they had their druthers). He's also extraordinarily popular on American television: *Rumpole of the Bailey*'s 16-year record makes it the longest-running series ever on Mystery!.

PERPLEXINGLY APPEALING

At first, Rumpole's appeal to an American audience seems bewildering. England's legal system may have inspired the traditions of American law, but, in modern practice, there are so many differences that much of what goes on in London's Central Criminal Court, commonly known as the Old Bailey, is hopelessly confusing to the many Americans who think a solicitor is some kind of door-to-door salesman and who don't know a barrister from a banister. In order to keep viewers clear about what they're about to see, *Rumpole of the Bailey* has taxed the interpretive services of the Mystery! hosts more heavily than any other series.

If the series was so obtuse to so many, why did it become so popular in the U.S.? Leo McKern, the only actor to ever play Rumpole on screen, always had a simple answer: "I think Americans are fascinated by all those funny people with those funny wigs on their heads." Certainly, the funny people had a lot to do with it, especially Rumpole himself. Rumpole's sense of humor clearly was a major reason for his success in a country that loves to laugh. Yet the more Rumpole episodes one watches, the more obvious the real source of his appeal becomes: Horace Rumpole is a very amiable underdog, whether he's at the Old Bailey or at home with his imposing wife, Hilda, and Americans love underdogs who somehow get the upper hand.

And of course we love his often nasty voice-overs, revealing what he's *really* thinking ("He must have been handsome when he was alive," about some pompous lawyer he's been negotiating with). It also helps to realize that, for all his imperfections, Rumpole's heart is in the right place. He may not be very ambitious, but he's having a

PRODUCTION COMPANY
Thames Television

YEARS
1980–1995

MAIN CAST

Horace Rumpole
LEO MCKERN

Hilda Rumpole
PEGGY THORPE BATES/ MARION MATHIE

Liz Probert
SAMANTHA BOND/ ABIGAIL MCKERN

Claude Erskine-Brown
JULIAN CURRY

Phyllida Trant Erskine-Brown
PATRICIA HODGE

Samuel Ballard, QC
PETER BLYTHE

Mr. Justice Featherstone
PETER BOWLES

Lady Marigold Featherstone
JOANNA VAN GYSEGHEM

Judge Bullingham
BILL FRASER

Henry
JONATHAN COY

Mr. Bernard
DENIS LILL

Fiona Allways
ROSALYN LANDOR

Uncle Tom
RICHARD MURDOCH

Dot Clapton
CAMILLE CODURI

ball knocking the starch out of a very stiff and hidebound legal system, trying to get it to dispense a little more justice for the rest of the common, ordinary underdogs out there.

As for Rumpole's suitability on the roster of a program devoted to mysteries, let's just say he got there on a legal technicality. Though Rumpole's overall case-load is light on genuine mysteries, he has solved more than a few in his day, including those two cases from his youth he's perennially boasting of: The Penge Bungalow Murder and the Great Brighton Benefit Club Forgery. What his cases reveal is an acute understanding of Britain's legal system, which is no surprise at all: Author/playwright John Mortimer was one of England's most famous defense attorneys for more than 40 years.

"Rumpole is the law in its context. It's like seeing the animals in their natural habitat at the zoo."

—MARVIN KITMAN,
Newsday

"Rumpole has very little patience with the judges who seem to him something less than the paragons of justice, and he often makes his sentiments known— both in court and elsewhere. Now, judges in England are selected by the Lord Chancellor from among a relatively small group of barristers. . . . Judges of the high court are invariably knighted on their appointment to the Bench, and that's why they're referred to during trials as 'my lord.' Imagine how galling it must be for 'our learned friend' Rumpole to refer to his nemesis, the pig-headed Judge Bullingham, as 'my lord.'"

—VINCENT PRICE

CASES AND CAUSES

Early on, Mortimer recognized that Rumpole's cases would also allow him to raise serious social issues, exposing millions of viewers to meaningful ideas, but without preaching or becoming too serious. "If I said [some of the things Rumpole does], I would put people's backs up," Mortimer says. "I'd sound left-wing and trendy. But I can have Rumpole be against authority, prisons, the death penalty, and the upper classes, and a big audience accepts these attitudes as . . . rather cozy." In *Rumpole's Return,* for instance, Rumpole defends the operator of an adult book shop against pornography charges and makes a strong case for free speech. (Mortimer, in real life, has done that on more than one occasion, most notably in the censorship case against the novel *Last Exit to Brooklyn.*) The mood in *Rumpole's Return* stays light, though, because Hilda—the formidable "She-Who-Must-Be-Obeyed"—finds some of the porno evidence Rumpole had been reviewing at home and mistakenly thinks he's become sex-obsessed.

In *Rumpole and the Fascist Beast,* he defends a right-wing candidate for Parliament who's determined to deport England's non-white immigrants, demonstrating, as Rumpole so often does, that everyone deserves a first-class defense, even scoundrels. In *Rumpole and the Female of the Species,* the old codger resorts to a rather naughty scam to help Fiona Allways (Rosalyn Landor) become a permanent member of chambers. It's all quite silly and lots of fun, but it also underscores the issue of anti-female bias in chambers.

Rumpole and the Bubble Reputation is one of the best examples of a serious legal issue—freedom of the press—being treated with great wit. Rumpole is hired to defend Machin (Norman Rodway), the editor of a scandal sheet, against a libel action brought by moralistic romance novelist Amelia Nettleship (Jennifer Daniel) after the *Daily Beacon* reports she's having an affair with a married man. Though Rumpole has no libel experience, he tells the editor libel cases are like "mother's milk to me," because he covets the enormous daily fees he'll be paid and the chance to show up the hypocritical author, who happens to be one of Hilda's favorites. For the record, though, he says he's standing up for the tabloid rag because the right to print the truth must be defended. Rumpole starts to feel a little uneasy about the *Daily Beacon*'s "fearless exposure" of the truth, though, when the editor's assistant (Caroline Mortimer) explains they mostly expose "who's bonking who." Later, he really questions his own ethics when the paper runs a photo of his colleague, Claude Erskine-Brown (Julian Curry), at a topless bar in an article on "London's Square Mile of Sin" and trashes his reputation, even though Rumpole knows Erskine-Brown was there on legitimate legal business.

For all his rough, often uncouth edges, Rumpole is a brilliant jurist. Though he frequently relies on trickery to get what he wants in the courtroom, he usually labors his way to the high moral ground before the episode is over.

In addition to the courtroom, chambers, and barrooms, Rumpole's kitchen is the site of important scenes in many episodes. There his wife, Hilda, proffers food and (usually) unsolicited advice. Many critics have observed that Rumpole's sarcastic thoughts about his wife don't exactly paint a rosy picture of his married life. Mortimer

"I think Hilda's most endearing quality is her outrageous jealousy of any woman who crosses Rumpole's path. From Hilda you realize that her rumpled, rotund renegade of a husband—who physically is well into his 'sunset years'—still has enormous sexual appeal! And isn't that a refreshing thing to see on television!"

—VINCENT PRICE

"I haven't tired of the old barrister, and I think this is because you can take today's events—social workers snatching children for suspected devil worship, the Court of Appeal having to eat the words of previous judges, the suggested reforms of the legal profession or the slender difference between actors and barristers—and write a Rumpole story about them. Any matrimonial dispute fits easily in the Rumpole marriage."

—JOHN MORTIMER,
in his memoirs *Murderers and Other Friends: Another Part of Life*

says he created Hilda to give Rumpole someone to talk with when he came home from the Old Bailey, but he doesn't hold to the theory that it's a bad marriage. "I really don't think they could live without each other," he says.

After the seventh series of Rumpole episodes, actor McKern "retired" from the role, which he had done almost annually from the second series on, but this time he seems to mean it. Though Mortimer has written another series of Rumpole stories since the show ended, Thames Television has announced no plans for a new series.

Still, it may be wise to remember that Horace Rumpole retired from his law practice after the first series and went to live near his son and daughter-in-law in Miami. As it turned out, retirement wasn't what it was cracked up to be, so Mystery! soon brought us *Rumpole's Return* and all the episodes that came after it. Maybe retirement still isn't what it's cracked up to be, and Rumpole will slap on his wig once again for old times' sake.

"Being a lawyer has almost nothing to do with knowing the law."

—HORACE RUMPOLE

"I think humor is very important in the law. The prosecution is always very severe, and if you're defending, it's vital to counteract that with humor."

—JOHN MORTIMER,
WETA Magazine

Queen's Counsel:

AUTHOR
JOHN MORTIMER

AUTHOR/PLAYWRIGHT JOHN MORTIMER CREATED RUMPOLE IN THE MID-1970s because he wanted to come up with a running character who would sustain him with lots of royalties and residuals in his old age. Already one of England's most famous barristers, Mortimer thought it might be fun to make his new character a barrister specializing in criminal defense so he could cobble his character's persona together from all the people he'd known over nearly 40 years as a renowned defense lawyer.

Rumpole's general look and his propensity for quoting Shakespeare, Wordsworth, Keats, and other poets, for example, came directly from Mortimer's own father, Clifford, a distinguished barrister in his own day, while his habit of calling difficult judges "old darling" came from Mortimer's colleague Jeremy Hutchinson. Pommeroy's Wine Bar, where Rumpole drinks glass after glass of "Château Fleet Street" or "Château Thames Embankment" is really El Vino on Fleet Street. And Mortimer's real-life wife, Penny, has accused him of taking notes during their arguments, so he can give her lines to Hilda.

CONFUSING ART WITH LIFE

Once when author Mortimer failed to win the case of a client accused of attempted murder, the condemned snapped at him, "Your Mr. Rumpole could have got me out of this!"

Mortimer never expected Rumpole to become a phenomenon who would bring him lasting international fame with a long series of books and television shows. And he certainly never anticipated such popularity on the other side of the Atlantic. By 1995, when all the first-run episodes of the series had been played on Mystery!, Horace Rumpole already was nearly as well known in America as he was in Mortimer's native England.

Mortimer was born in 1923, and grew up in the lap of the law. His father had a flourishing practice and lived and breathed legal principles. Mortimer's mother had been an art teacher. Both his parents inspired his interest in the arts, so by the time Mortimer was ready to start his university education at Oxford in 1940, he was more interested in a career as a writer than the one in law that his father had mapped out for him.

His education was interrupted by the war years, but Mortimer acquired valuable experience working on propaganda films for the Ministry of Information. After the war,

he returned to Oxford, earned his degree in 1947, and began practicing law in 1948. Still, he hadn't abandoned his goal of becoming a successful writer. His first novel, *Charade*, was published the year he earned his degree, and he completed two more the following year while also writing short fiction for women's magazines. He began writing plays for radio and finally made his great breakthrough in 1957 when the BBC produced his radio drama about a lawyer, *The Dock Brief*, which later was dramatized for television and, in 1962, became a feature film starring Peter Sellers and Richard Attenborough.

"I had the unoriginal thought that British law might, together with Shakespeare, Wordsworth, Lord Byron, and the herbaceous border, be one of our great contributions to the world."

—JOHN MORTIMER,
Clinging to the Wreck

"I write a kind of heightened realism to achieve a comic and slightly theatrical effect. People have compared my writing to G. K. Chesterton. If you read Chesterton, it all seems to be lit with slightly theatrical lighting. My writing, too, is based on reality, but up there, two feet off the ground."

—JOHN MORTIMER,
New York Times

QUEEN'S COUNSEL FOR HUMAN RIGHTS

In the meantime, Mortimer's legal career had expanded greatly from his humble beginnings as a divorce lawyer and volunteer for legal aid cases in the working-class East End of London. By 1966, he was named a Queen's Counsel or "QC," a special class of barrister who takes only major court cases, and began to specialize in human rights issues. For Amnesty International, he successfully helped defend African playwright Wole Soyinko against criminal charges in Nigeria. He soon was known as England's leading spokesman on free speech issues following his spirited defense of clients, including the publishers of American author Hubert Selby Jr.'s *Last Exit to Brooklyn*, accused under Britain's obscenity laws.

By the late 1970s, Mortimer's reputation as a dramatist had grown. He worked on a number of screenplays (for *The Innocents, The Running Man, Bunny Lake Is Missing, A Flea in Her Ear*, and *John and Mary*). His greatest critical and popular success came in 1981 when he adapted Evelyn Waugh's *Brideshead Revisited* for the landmark television miniseries that became a worldwide sensation. His teleplay *Paradise Postponed* was presented on Masterpiece Theatre. Among his original works, though, there is nothing to compare with the ongoing success of the Rumpole books and television plays.

Mortimer says his original mission with Rumpole was to use the character to make some serious points, but in an amusing way that would reach a wider audience. Rumpole has so many eccentricities that he sometimes borders on being a buffoon, but Mortimer makes sure we never lose sight of the fact that he has a razor-sharp legal mind, a big heart, and an unflagging commitment to the notion that everyone from scoundrels to downtrodden innocents deserves a first-class defense.

Mortimer had no actor in mind for Rumpole when he wrote *Rumpole of the Bailey* but began to think about it once he had finished. "I thought Alistair Sim could do Rumpole," Mortimer recalls, "but then I found out he was dead. So the producer, the director, and I sat down together and came up with a list of names."

One of those names was Leo McKern, who Mortimer says "was well-known, but not enormously famous." The minute he stepped into the role, Mortimer knew there would never be a better Horace Rumpole. Other actors have played Rumpole on the radio, but Mortimer can't conceive of anyone else playing the part for television. Mortimer now doubts McKern would be cast as Rumpole if the whole series were starting up today. He thinks British television is now too bottom-line oriented and dictated by ratings. "What would happen now is you'd have to go to a central scheduler, who would demand a big star—someone like John Thaw that everybody already has seen on television," he says. "It's really sad."

FULL CREATIVE CONTROL

From the beginning of *Rumpole,* Mortimer was able to create exactly the series he wanted. He believes he was given a level of creative control rare for a television writer because he came to television very early, when most dramas were broadcast live, and because he had a huge reputation that preceded him. Mortimer also has always written the *Rumpole* television scripts first, then "adapted" them for the printed page, reversing the usual process. The only stories he didn't do that way are the ones he wrote after *Rumpole* went out of production.

Though nothing is currently in the works, Mortimer is not against the idea of doing another Rumpole series, if McKern is willing. He thinks it may be harder to get another series authorized, though, because of economic changes in British television. "I used to just say I wanted to do another Rumpole series and they'd give me the money," he says. "I never wrote the scripts before they commissioned the show. Now you can wind up writing 12 scripts that never get made. I had the best of it. It would be terrible to be starting out in television today."

"I'm terribly proud that they quoted Rumpole twice during the O. J. Simpson trial. One of the defense lawyers told Judge Ito he thought they were getting 'a case of premature adjudication,' which is something Rumpole always says. Then one of the prosecution lawyers said, 'As Rumpole would say, it all comes down to the blood.'"

—JOHN MORTIMER

"Mortimer's script, with its cast of rotters, bounders, and grande dames, is often indistinguishable from a Fifties drawing-room comedy. But its civilized ethos breathes fresh air into television schedules filled with violence, bad language, and nudity."

—COMPTON MILLER,
Daily Express

SELECTED BIBLIOGRAPHY

Rumpole of the Bailey, 1978; *The Trials of Rumpole,* 1979; *Rumpole's Return,* 1980; *Rumpole for the Defence,* 1982; *Rumpole and the Golden Thread,* 1983; *Rumpole's Last Case,* 1987; *Rumpole and the Age of Miracles,* 1988; *Rumpole ala Carte,* 1990; *Rumpole on Trial,* 1992; *Rumpole and the Angel of Death,* 1996.

Not to Be Confused with Horace Rumpole:

ACTOR

LEO MCKERN

MILLIONS OF DIEHARD RUMPOLE FANS MUST BE EXCUSED IF THEY ASSUME
actor Leo McKern has been hanging about Pommeroy's bar since his youth,
quaffing *vin ordinaire* and pontificating on the sorry state of English jurisprudence
after a hard day at the Old Bailey. That's just the power of a great acting performance, given over a very long period of time by a very persuasive actor. As he has told us
so often, Leo McKern is *not* to be confused with Horace Rumpole, even if they do look
and act remarkably alike. "We're as different as chalk and cheese," McKern once said when
asked a disagreeable question about his similarities to Rumpole.

That seems to be the truth, from all available evidence. Rumpole is a staunch
liberal, like his creator John Mortimer, while McKern is an equally ardent conservative.
McKern wasn't even in England in his youth—he's a native of Australia—and the only
time he has ever actually set foot in the Old Bailey was as a spectator—an experience, by
the way, that he describes as "bloody boring."

Having acted with the Old Vic and the Royal Shakespeare Company, McKern
was known as a major character actor who could play anything from the classics to
modern comedy. Some of his memorable film and television characters include:
Oliver Cromwell in the Academy award-winning *A Man for All Seasons* (1966); the
comedy foil of The Beatles in *Help!* (1965); Sarah Miles' father, Ryan, in David
Lean's *Ryan's Daughter* (1970); villainous munitions czar Basil Zaharov, nemesis of
Reilly, Ace of Spies (1983); Gloucester in Laurence Olivier's *King Lear* (1983), and
many more.

Still, the public's undisputed favorite remains Rumpole, even if McKern
finally has finished with him after 39 episodes over 15 years. "What I don't like is
the public's tendency to forget everything else you've ever done," McKern said at the time
of his retirement from the part. "I'm like a little dogie struggling to its feet after having
the branding iron put on me."

The idea that an Australian actor would find immortal fame playing a very British barrister never ceases to amaze McKern, who remembers that he couldn't even get an acting job when he first came to England in 1946 because his Aussie accent was so thick. If it had been up to him, he probably would have stayed in Sydney, but McKern had fallen in love with actor Jane Holland, whom he followed when she left to seek her fame in London's West End.

McKern couldn't get any acting jobs there, but his accent wasn't his only handicap: He had lost his left eye in an industrial accident when he was 15 and had to wear a glass eye. Agents didn't see a lot of potential in a short and not particularly dashing one-eyed Australian immigrant. But McKern persevered and gradually got parts on stage and in movies, including the classic science fiction films *X the Unknown* (1956) and *The Day the Earth Caught Fire* (1961), and the international comedy hit *The Mouse That Roared* (1959). His wife Jane eventually retired from acting to raise their two daughters, Harriet and Abigail (who grew up to co-star with her dad on *Rumpole of the Bailey*).

McKern once described his chosen profession as "a passionate indulgence that one hopes will be noticed." Thanks to Rumpole, he's certainly noticed with great affection wherever he goes.

PARKER PYNE
ET ALIA

➤

AGATHA CHRISTIE STORIES

Based on the stories by
Agatha Christie

AGATHA CHRISTIE'S BEST-KNOWN SLEUTHS—HERCULE POIROT, JANE MARPLE, AND TUPPENCE AND TOMMY BERESFORD—ARE PILLARS OF THE MYSTERY! COMMUNITY, BUT MYSTERY! HAS ALSO PRESENTED TEN OTHER LESSER-KNOWN CHRISTIE HEROES AND HEROINES WHO REMAIN IN A CLASS BY THEMSELVES.

Most notable is the strange Parker Pyne, a colorful character who takes special pains to remind us he's not a detective at all, but rather "a specialist in every kind of human trouble," a sort of "fixer" who seldom leaves his office.

Played by veteran British character actor Maurice Denham, Parker Pyne is a retired bureaucrat who spent 35 years buried in statistical research, but who now operates a peculiar private agency that handles cases solicited through his advertisement in the personal "agony" columns. His ad asks: "Are you happy? If not, consult Mr. Parker Pyne."

Pyne is a witty, middle-aged man who may not cut a romantic figure, but he's enormously self-confident. He cheerfully tells his clients he has learned to file all manner of human unhappiness into five simple categories, and "once you know the cause of a malady, the remedy should not be impossible."

PYNE'S REMEDIES FOR UNHAPPINESS

Pyne appeared in the final two of ten *Agatha Christie Stories* presented in the fourth and fifth seasons of Mystery!. In *The Case of the Middle-Aged Wife*, Maria Packington (Gwen Watford) comes to Pyne upset over her inability to attract her straying husband, George (Peter Jones). Pyne's solution is to bring in his trusty operative Claude Luttrell (Rupert Frazer), a handsome young playboy, who takes up with Maria. She becomes so rejuvenated by his youthful attention that her husband becomes jealous and realizes what he's missing at home. In *The Case of the Discontented Soldier*, retired Major Wilbraham (William Gaunt) comes to Pyne unhappy over the boredom of his life on inactive duty. Pyne decides to involve him with an exotic female beauty, then plunge him into some kind of manufactured adventure. But the major doesn't respond well to Pyne's usually reliable staff vamp, Madeleine de Sara (Veronica Strong), so off the bench comes a pinch hitter, Freda Clegg (Patricia Garwood), who soon gets the major mixed up in a romantic caper that calls upon all the experience of his many years in the military. (Avid Agatha Christie fans no doubt recognized the chillingly efficient Miss Felicity Lemon in this story as the same individual who later worked as a secretary for Hercule Poirot.)

PRODUCTION COMPANY
Thames Television

YEARS
1983–1985

MAIN CAST
Parker Pyne
MAURICE DENHAM

"People think that writing must be easy for me. It's not. It's murder."
—AGATHA CHRISTIE

"All the stories exude the familiar well-loved Christie atmosphere of the 1920s and 1930s—sumptuously gowned women mingling with retired colonels and dancing the night away with clean-cut young men who are not always what they seem—despite their frequent appearances in the smartest nightclubs."

—VINCENT PRICE

THE ROMANTIC SIDE OF CHRISTIE

None of the other stories featured a recurring hero, and some weren't even mysteries by any stretch of the imagination. Still, these stories may have widened public appreciation of the great mystery writer because they revealed a more playful, romantic side of her nature. *The Manhood of Edward Robinson* is a madcap adventure reminiscent of *Young and Innocent,* Alfred Hitchcock's giddy British film from the 1930s. The hero is shy young Edward (Nicholas Farrell), who helps a sexy young woman (Cherie Lunghi) elude some villains. In one delightfully Hitchcockian scene, Robinson and the woman try to hide from her pursuers by joining a throng of tango dancers on a crowded dance floor. The trouble is they dance so well together that the crowd begins to part, so everybody watches them, including the bad guys.

The Magnolia Blossom is a bittersweet romance. Ciaran Madden plays a handsome matron who falls for a South African orange grower (Ralph Bates), who works for her husband (Jeremy Clyde), a ferret-faced lout you really don't want to root for, even when he becomes the victim of a financial scandal and she begins to get cold feet about leaving him.

In *The Red Signal,* a man falls in love with his best friend's wife (Joanna David), but begins to suspect that she's got a few screws loose. Little wonder, since she often wanders around with a dagger in her hand and a dazed look in her eyes. There's a seance, a death warning, and enough red herrings to choke all the seagulls in the North Sea. The hero is played by Richard Morant, later to play Bunter, the loyal sidekick to Lord Peter Wimsey.

CAPER-ON-THE-RAILS

The Girl in the Train is a typical Christie caper-on-the-rails. The hero is a young man (Osmond Bullock) taking a train journey to "clear his head" after being fired by his stockbroker uncle for being lazy. He meets a beautiful young woman (Sarah Berger), who may be a European duchess, and gets embroiled with foreign agents and the kind of intrigue that transforms idle boys into stalwart young men.

Elizabeth Garvie stars in *Jane in Search of a Job* as a penniless young woman who answers a newspaper ad—always an invitation to adventure in any Christie story—and finds herself in the middle of a plot involving pearls, the police, and mysterious grand duchesses.

The Mystery of the Blue Jar features Robin Kermode as a breezy young man who hears someone crying for help on the golf links one day and follows a murky trail of clues to the heart of a mystery.

The Fourth Man delves into the issue of multiple personalities as three learned men debate the curious case of a French girl (Fiona Mathieson) and try to figure out how she possibly could have strangled herself.

In a Glass Darkly is a tale deeply imbued with the supernatural. Matthew (Nicholas Clay) falls in love with Sylvia (Emma Piper), but is haunted by a vision he sees in a mirror the very day he meets her: Sylvia being strangled by a man with a scar on the back of his neck. Was it a hallucination—or a harbinger of a dreadful future?

"One never thinks of Christie in terms of sex. There are no sex scenes in her books. People don't seem to get physically close at all; steamy romance is not what she's famous for. In fact, she's rather famous for not having those things. She's considered to be prim and Victorian and stereotyped. But when you look at why people do things in her novels, the interesting thing is how often sexual passion is the essential motivator."

—GILLIAN GILL,
author of *Agatha Christie:
The Woman and Her Mysteries*

"The widespread popularity of Agatha Christie's work is nothing short of phenomenal itself. . . . Her only close competitors are Shakespeare, the Bible, and Sherlock Holmes. . . . One West African fan wrote to Christie to say that he was arriving in England shortly and asking if she would be his mother. A native cult in New Guinea used the front cover of one paperback edition of Evil Under the Sun as an object of worship. Even Anna Freud reported to one of her famous father's biographers that the pioneer of psychoanalysis liked to read murder mysteries and his particular favorites were Agatha Christie's."

—VINCENT PRICE

OLIVER
AND
DIANE PRIEST

OLIVER'S TRAVELS

Written by Alan Plater

IN *OLIVER'S TRAVELS*, ALAN BATES AND SINEAD CUSACK APPEAR
AS A NEW ROMANTIC TEAM OF SLEUTHS—THE FIRST FOR MYSTERY! SINCE THE
DEBUT OF AGATHA CHRISTIE'S TUPPENCE AND TOMMY BERESFORD MORE
THAN A DECADE EARLIER.

The four-part serial is a peculiar hybrid of several genres—part mystery, part old-fashioned romance, and part travelogue. Even the nature of the main characters' partnership is a hybridization: He's an amateur named Oliver who relishes puzzles (an unresolved one being whether that's his first or last name), while she's Diane Priest, a local woman police constable (WPC). That job title sort of makes her a professional, even though she's never done much real sleuthing for the police. Oliver and Diane are not really interested in detecting for a living—they'd much rather engage in witty badinage before, during, and after retiring to the bedroom—but they solve a few mysteries anyway, given a little help from their friends.

ARISTOTELIAN ILLOGIC

Oliver is a veteran professor of comparative religion, whose wit is as dry as a vermouth-free martini. He's a jazz enthusiast who also holds any number of oddball opinions, including the notion that the world started to go wrong about the time Bill Haley and the Comets turned up. He's appreciated by his students at Rhondda Valley University in Wales, but that's not the case with the vice chancellor, who informs Oliver one day that his course is being dropped because nobody's interested in comparative religion anymore.

Oliver takes being sacked rather calmly, but then he's a man with few responsibilities. He's single, has a comfortable pension, and will now be able to spend more time on his favorite pursuits: collecting lame jokes, listening to jazz, working crossword puzzles, and spotting meaningful anagrams (he notices Vice Chancellor T. H. Moody's name is an anagram for "Thy Doom"). Realizing his time is now his own, Oliver decides to do something he's always wanted to do: Meet "Aristotle," the best compiler of crosswords in all of England.

But when Oliver learns that Aristotle is missing—his rural cottage burned to the ground—he goes to the police to report it. "Sounds like a job for Princess Di," the desk sergeant tells Oliver at the local police station.

PRODUCTION COMPANY
BBC

YEAR
1996

MAIN CAST
Oliver
ALAN BATES

Diane
SINEAD CUSACK

Baron Farquhar/Kite
MILES ANDERSON

Cathy
CHARLOTTE COLEMAN

Michael
MORGAN JONES

Baxter
BILL PATTERSON

Mrs. Robson
MOLLIE SUGDEN

It turns out that's their nickname for WPC Diane Priest. It's also clear she gets stuck with all the weird people who walk in off the street. Oliver and Diane hit it off reasonably well. He's sort of rumpled and gray and not very tall, but is also, as he puts it, "world weary, yet curiously beguiling, wouldn't you say?" She admits she's attracted by his peculiar blend of erudition and charm. Oliver doesn't need to ponder his feelings for Diane: He likes her right away. She's pretty, has a carefree personality, and an absolutely infectious laugh. When she comes to his hotel later that day to tell him she's traced Aristotle to the Orkney Islands, he's also quite impressed with her detective skills. He vows to pursue his quarry there, but first offers to help her with any unsolved mysteries she'd like to clear up, just to show his gratitude.

As it happens, there is this baffling case involving the body of a farmer named Griffiths found floating in the river one day. Oliver promises to look into it, and she promptly forgets about him until he returns to the station the following day. It seems some evidence has been uncovered that incriminates a high-ranking police administrator, Superintendent Butler, in a land fraud scheme involving the murdered farmer's property. As Oliver puts it, "The Butler did it."

"There is no satisfactory anagram of my name in the English language. However, in French, we have the verb voiler *meaning to veil, cloak, or conceal. You could say I am a veiled, cloaked, and concealed man."*

—OLIVER

WITHOUT DAY JOBS

When Diane informs her superiors, they think she's gone bonkers and suspend her indefinitely from duty. That gives her a good reason to accept Oliver's invitation to join him on his search for Aristotle, which leads them on a long, colorful motor tour through some of the most scenic countryside in Great Britain, including the rolling valleys of Wales, historic Shrewsbury—where Brother Cadfael did his own sleuthing nine centuries earlier—a 12th-century castle in Gloucestershire, the spectacular Eilean Donan Castle at the Kyle of Lochalsh, and, ultimately, the remote Orkney Islands.

Oliver and Diane are surely the oddest pair in the files of Mystery!. Oliver's wife left him in 1979, and Diane is divorced with a giant lump of a son named Michael (Morgan Jones), whose degree in geology was not of much use in his most recent job as a hot dog vendor. Oliver is more committed to their "relationship" at first because an anagram of her name spells out "predestination." Diane's feet are more firmly planted on the ground.

Yet they do enjoy flirting with each other, and he keeps promising to tell her "that very funny thing I know about sex." But she keeps asking for separate rooms on their journey, while he holds out for at least connecting doors. Eventually, though, the connecting doors open, he tells her the funny thing he knows about sex, and they're seriously involved with each other, long before they reach journey's end. Ultimately, Oliver and Diane put all the plot pieces together in one of the most bizarre landscapes in the Orkneys—the fabled Stone Circle of Brodgar, a Stonehenge-like field of stone monuments—and realize they've solved their first murder case together while falling hopelessly in love.

Oliver's Travels is the most lightweight and meandering of all the Mystery! series. It was written by the veteran Alan Plater, whose credits include Miss Marple's *A Murder Is Announced* for Mystery! and *Barchester Chronicles, Fortunes of War,* and *A Very British Coup* for Masterpiece Theatre. The amiable lovers are played with great insouciance by Bates, (star of *Zorba the Greek, King of Hearts, An Unmarried Woman, The Fixer,* and *Women in Love*), and the charming stage star Cusack (daughter of theater immortal Cyril Cusack and real-life wife of Jeremy Irons). Oliver and Diane seem headed for wedlock at the close of *Oliver's Travels,* and screenwriter Plater leaves the door open for further travels, so there's no telling what may happen with this offbeat detective team in future days.

The Detection Club:

THE CRIME WRITERS' CONSPIRACY

IT SOUNDS LIKE A MYSTERY PLOT BY AGATHA CHRISTIE OR DOROTHY L. SAYERS: TWENTY-SIX RESPECTED CITIZENS ALL MEET IN A SINGLE ROOM IN LONDON TO INITIATE A NEW MEMBER INTO AN EXCLUSIVE CLUB DEVOTED TO MURDER AND MAYHEM.

Of course, if Christie and Sayers had free rein, the lights would probably go out during the ceremony and a body be found when they came on again. Naturally, someone would then rush to the phone and summon either Hercule Poirot or Lord Peter Wimsey. As far as we know, nothing of the sort has ever happened at any meeting of the legendary Detection Club, the oldest functioning organization for mystery writers in the world.

According to mystery writer and Detection Club founder Anthony Berkeley, members first began meeting in 1928 in the upstairs rooms of a rather down-at-heels bar. However, as no early records were kept, it's impossible to verify the date. In any case, by 1930, the club had 26 members, among them Christie and Sayers, who both later served as club president. Sayers served as club president from 1949 to 1958; Christie followed and presided until her death in 1976 but was so shy that she often had to have someone else make her speeches or propose toasts for her.

Originally limited just to writers of detective fiction, the club now includes authors of suspense stories, thrillers, spy tales, and the larger category of crime writing. A few American authors have been invited into the ranks, among them Patricia Highsmith and John Dickson Carr. Most of the authors represented in the Mystery! series either were or still are members, including Berkeley (who wrote *Malice Aforethought* under his pseudonym Francis Iles); Christie, Sayers, G. K. Chesterton, Dick Francis, Len Deighton, P. D. James, and Ruth Rendell (who wrote *A Dark-Adapted Eye* and *Gallowglass* as Barbara Vine).

MURDEROUS COLLABORATIONS

In the 1930s, when the club needed funds to maintain its own quarters in London, the members agreed upon a unique fund-raising scheme: They would collaborate on mystery yarns, which they would then sell for radio broadcast or publication in print. The first was a radio play called *Behind the Screen*, broadcast in 1930 from a script written by Christie, Sayers, Berkeley, E. C. Bentley, Hugh Walpole, and Ronald Knox. The first four later joined with Freeman Wills Crofts and Clemence Dane on *The Scoop*. Both scripts are now available in paperback editions. Other collaborative club mysteries include *The Floating Admiral, Ask a Policeman,* and *Verdict of Thirteen*.

Normally, club members just meet for dinner—at the Garrick Club or the Café Royale—and the opportunity to swap stories, which usually have something to do with murder and mayhem, of course. Once a year, they initiate new members. Once initiated, club members uphold the original rules established in the late 1920s, which include injunctions against eating peas off a knife, putting one's feet on the dinner table, and using poisons unknown to science or secret passages to assist the solution of a mystery. Club members also agree to write in the Queen's English and to put all their clues out in the open so that readers can't accuse the detectives of having an unfair advantage in solving the mystery. The initiation ceremony is a rather ornate affair devised by Chesterton and Sayers that involves the pledges swearing to various things while placing their hand on a skull named Eric. We'd like to tell you more, but members are sworn to secrecy about exactly what goes on during those ceremonies. So far, though, the ceremonies haven't resulted in any coroner's inquests.

CASES
FOR
INVESTIGATION

DENIZENS OF THE DARK SIDE

THE BIZARRE, INEXPLICABLE, AND SOMETIMES FRIGHTENING THINGS THAT TAKE place among the shadows on the dark side of human nature have fascinated mystery writers and readers for generations. By tagging along with investigators like Sherlock Holmes, Hercule Poirot, and Inspector Morse, mystery fans have experienced nearly every kind of menace, from devil worshippers and manifestations of the supernatural to vengeful murderers and serial killers. But in real life, there isn't always a heroic detective around to hold our hand, and that's why many Mystery! tales don't involve detectives at all, focusing instead on the villains and victims who keep detectives in business.

The truth is we often remember dark and dastardly characters more vividly than we do the heroes and heroines. Whom do we remember from Wilkie Collins' *The Woman in White,* the novel many consider the first mystery? Certainly not stalwart Walter Hartright, but devious Count Fosco and his cohort, the insufferable Frederick Fairlie. What about *Mother Love,* which has no real hero but whose poisonous Helena Vesey will be forever etched on our fearful psyches? The classic villain-driven mysteries like *Mother Love* or *The Dark Angel* don't need complex heroes like Tennison or Dalgliesh. They work better with ordinary people around them, victims a lot like us. When they shudder, we feel the chill; their screams sound very much like our own.

OLD FIENDS

Many mystery writers from the very beginning of the genre have veered away from the straight and narrow to create unforgettable fiends like Bram Stoker's Count Dracula or Sax Rohmer's Dr. Fu Manchu. These villains became the stars of the stories in which they appeared, while the traditional heroes who actually outwitted them were mere spear-carriers in the supporting cast.

DEEPLY DISTURBED TO THE PARANORMAL

Mystery! has given us a host of villain-heavy mysteries and psychological suspense stories, any one a suitable case for investigation. We've divided these "cases" into several thematic categories. First are the stories that involve disturbed individuals who commit heinous crimes. Some of them are identifiable sociopaths like the sadistic Sandor of *Gallowglass,* while others, such as Vera Hillyard of *A Dark-Adapted Eye,* are driven to kill by long-hidden psychological wounds. Perhaps the most interesting of all is the strange case of Dr. Jekyll and Mr. Hyde, which suggests we're all potential villains because we all have a dark side, an idea still very relevant today.

Then there are the stories about society's predators: serial killer Sweeney Todd, the demon barber of Fleet Street; the greedy conspirators of *The Dark Angel* and *The Woman in White,* who prey upon the innocent; and the political terrorists of *Die Kinder.*

There also are the villains who may not be villains at all, but rather victims of suspicion and wrongful prosecution—Max de Winter of *Rebecca,* Rachel of *My Cousin Rachel,* or William Wallace of *The Man from the Pru.* Then there's Alma Rattenbury of *Cause Célèbre,* who perhaps took the rap for her young lover, and Guy Foster of *Melissa* and Mark Omney of *The Limbo Connection,* who may have been framed for the murders of their wives. Finally there are the mysteries that defy rational solution, cases of the paranormal that include the tales from the *Shades of Darkness* series and the bewildering story of *Miss Morison's Ghosts.* While there is definite satisfaction in the successful resolution of a case by a clever detective, mystery fans seem to equally savor these spine-chilling tales of villainy and hair-raising accounts of the supernatural.

THE DEEPLY DISTURBED

A mother who bakes poisoned cookies, a doctor
who lets his dark side out, a woman who kills her sister,
a mental patient who idolizes a sadist, and a paranoiac
whose paranoia may be well-founded—they all have
one thing in common: They're deeply disturbed.

- *MOTHER LOVE*
- *DR. JEKYLL AND MR. HYDE*
- *A DARK-ADAPTED EYE, GALLOWGLASS*
- *DYING DAY*

PRODUCTION COMPANY
BBC

YEAR
1990

MAIN CAST
Helena Vesey
DIANA RIGG

Kit Vesey
JAMES WILBY

Angela Turner Vesey
FIONA GILLIES

Alex Vesey
DAVID MCCALLUM

George Batt
JAMES GROUT

Ruth Vesey
ISLA BLAIR

AWARDS
BAFTA Award,
Diana Rigg

*"Smiling grimly and speaking
in a cheery but firm tone, she comes
to resemble a satanic version
of Julie Andrews."*

ENTERTAINMENT WEEKLY

MOTHER LOVE

*Based on the novel by
Domini Taylor*

WHEN NOBODY'S WATCHING, HELENA VESEY OFTEN LEAFS THROUGH
HER PHOTO ALBUM, A RAPT EXPRESSION ON HER FACE, FINGERS IDLY STRAYING
OVER THE PICTURES THAT CHRONICLE HER LONG, LOVING RELATIONSHIP WITH
HER ONLY SON, CHRISTOPHER. "KITTEN," SHE MURMURS IN AN ALMOST
WORSHIPFUL TONE, "OH, MY KITTEN!"

Though Christopher is now a grown man, starting his career as a barrister and about to
marry, Helena still sees him as her darling boy. In her twisted mind, her "Kit" is her
reward for enduring years of betrayal and suffering as the victim of the heartless man who
fathered him—he's the life-preserver who keeps her afloat in a sea of despair. This self-
absorbed and dangerously unbalanced woman is the terrifying centerpiece of Domini
Taylor's novel *Mother Love* and one of the most memorable villains in television history.

SOCIOPATHIC DELUSION

Played with nerve-plucking conviction by Diana Rigg, Helena slowly degenerates
before our eyes, losing more control with each sign of Kit's independence—until
she finally slips over the edge into a state of frightening sociopathic delusion.
"She's hooked him . . . in the usual way they do it these days," Helena bitterly tells
her confidante, her inept, dim-witted cousin, George Batt (James Grout), upon
learning that Kit (James Wilby) has fallen in love with beautiful Angela Turner
(Fiona Gillies). "No beauty, no poetry. She simply opened her legs in a borrowed bed the
way that tart with a camera took my husband." The "tart" in question is Ruth Vesey (Isla
Blair), the acclaimed photographer/artist. She became the second wife of Helena's ex-
husband, famed orchestra conductor Alex Vesey (David McCallum), after he ended his
two-year mockery of a marriage with the warped, vindictive Helena.

Rigg's Helena is her masterpiece, an emotion-choked rendering that *Newsday*'s Marvin Kitman called "the bravura performance of the century," and which won her a BAFTA award. Rigg's constantly pained expressions reflect the struggle for control within this paranoid personality. As Helena's hatred builds, her face tightens into a grim mask, and her eyes glow like lumps of smoldering coal in shadowy sockets. "Disloyalty . . . is the worst of crimes and deserves the severest punishment," she mutters.

TAKING PUNISHMENT IN HER OWN HANDS

Murderously jealous even as a child—in flashbacks, we see her kill her ten-year-old best friend with a poisoned jam tart because the girl wasn't loyal enough—the adult Helena goes way beyond the obsessive smother-mother traumatized by the empty-nest syndrome while facing her own mid-life changes. "She sucks his blood to stay alive," Ruth explains to Angela about Helena's hold on her "Kitten."

Though Helena likes to say, "What can't be cured must be endured," she really has cures in mind for everyone with the temerity to betray her. When she gets out her well-thumbed copy of *The History of Criminal Toxicology*, it's clearly a bad omen for anyone who has crossed her lately. For Ruth and Cousin George, who falls from her favor rather quickly, Helena works out a two-for-one payback. Calling George, Helena pretends to be Ruth and asks him to run over to the Vesey estate to lock the door and rooftop vents of her windowless cement block photo studio. George, of course, has no idea the real Ruth is inside the studio. When she suffocates, all evidence points to him, and he winds up in prison for life.

When Alex marries a beautiful American movie star and starts a third family, Helena's hatred knows no bounds. Her plan for revenge is only slightly delayed when Kit is diagnosed with a brain tumor that leaves him paralyzed and comatose.

PULLING OUT ALL STOPS

As he lies unconscious, hooked by tubes to a respirator, Helena brings her helpless son up to date on her detailed master plan for vengeance, which includes poisoning Vesey's two youngest children with home-baked animal cookies, covered with deadly marzipan. When Helena accidentally learns her beloved Kit had been deceiving her all along by secretly visiting his father, she knows she's truly "an outcast from life's feast" and angrily starts pulling out his tubes.

Her ultimate vengeance thwarted, Helena ends her days in a pathetic, sad-eyed trance in a lunatic asylum. The final image of Rigg's tortured eyes gazing out at the viewer from her padded cell is haunting—and definitely not to be watched anywhere near Mother's Day.

"The fact that she insists on calling the squirming lad Kitten tells you practically everything you need to know, including the reminder that cats and people are the only British species to kill for pleasure."

GUARDIAN

"I had never conducted, but I spent so much time with my father [he was first violinist with the Royal Philharmonic Orchestra and Sir Thomas Beecham's concertmaster] and a whole selection of conductors . . . But I'm certain the musicians [of the BBC Symphony Orchestra] were grumbling, 'Who is this actor who's going to put us through this boring hour?' But in the end they began to get interested, and once we began rehearsing a piece by Mozart, we were really having a good time together."

—DAVID MCCALLUM

> "Insofar as Mother Love *has a subtext,
> it proposes a fatal opposition between
> possessive greed and life-giving
> generosity, between sexual sublimation
> or displacement and performance art."*
>
> —JOHN LEONARD
> *New York*

> *"Literature is filled with stories of
> women who nobly sacrifice their lives
> for the sake of their sons and daughters.
> But it's the vengeful mothers like Medea
> who stay in our minds, because women
> who murder their children violate
> one of the primal bonds of nature,
> committing perhaps the ultimate act
> of evil. What impulse could twist the
> pure, unselfish love of mother for child
> into the desire to kill? The question has
> no easy answer. And if it did, would
> we want to know it?"*
>
> —DIANA RIGG

A Chilling Helena Vesey:

ACTOR
DIANA RIGG

DIANA RIGG KNEW THE MOMENT SHE FINISHED READING ANDREW DAVIES' SCRIPT of *Mother Love* that Helena Vesey was the role of a lifetime—one she absolutely had to play. "I think it's probably the best thing I've ever done for television," she says. She relished the idea that she would be physically transformed for the role and especially liked the severely pulled-back hairdo symbolizing the tightly-wound personality of a mother who can't let go of her grown son—even if it means killing to keep him in her grasp.

Rigg is not the kind of actor who psychoanalyzes her characters, nor does she make up years of "back story" to fill in the periods before the story begins. Yet, while preparing to play Helena, Rigg reached a number of conclusions about why the psychopath turned out the way she did. Glimpses of her childhood, for instance, show that Helena's mental problems weren't just the result of empty-nest syndrome or hormones gone haywire, but instead were rooted deep in her youth. In flashback scenes, she poisons a childhood friend who offends her and keeps that secret all her life, a harbinger of things to come. "She was a little bit mad even then," says Rigg. "I hate to say this, but I think some children are born with a mental disorder."

Rigg says Helena was an extremely difficult character to play because of the need to constantly show her twisted emotional condition and keep that mood consistent. She also needed to place her faith in director Simon Langton, who reined her in whenever necessary and earned her respect for helping her hold the long, sustained performance on an even keel.

PSYCHOSEXUAL CONNECTION

Rigg felt there was a distinct psychosexual element in the relationship between Helena and her son, Kit, that had to be considered. She sees a near-Oedipal aspect of their love, but believes Helena ultimately considered Kit to be an essential part of her own personality, as if they were somehow permanently melded into one soul. In the final scenes, when Helena begins to realize Kit, too, has betrayed her, her fury erupts. Rigg remembers her original unhappiness with these scenes because Davies' script had Helena making growling noises like an enraged animal. She balked at playing her that way, protesting so much that the producers consulted psychiatrists for their opinions on the credibility of such behavior. "I thought it was going way over the top," says Rigg.

The professional opinions supported Rigg, and the animal noises came out. The psychiatrists felt it was more likely Helena would become catatonic than go berserk. And that's the way *Mother Love* ended—with Helena blankly looking out at the viewer from her padded cell. "I'm sure she's still sitting there," says Rigg, "as mad as ever."

A Man of Many Names:

AUTHOR
DOMINI TAYLOR
(ROGER LONGRIGG)

The 1983 novel *Mother Love* was Domini Taylor's first, although the author had been publishing for thirty years—but under one of the several other names he uses! The real author behind the pseudonym Domini Taylor is Edinburgh-born Roger Longrigg, a British Army veteran and something of a Renaissance man with an Oxford degree in modern history and a resume that includes time spent as a journalist, nightclub entertainer, yacht skipper, advertising man, racehorse owner, bodyguard, film producer, critic, and pest exterminator. As a writer, he was previously best known under another pen name, Ivor Drummond. Under that name, Longrigg wrote a series of popular spy thrillers, including *The Frog in the Moonflower* and *The Tank of Sacred Eels,* that have earned him the title of "the true heir to James Bond." In addition to novels, Longrigg has also written for radio, film, and television.

"[Helena] is wildly repressed, and this comes out in her brittle, prissy behavior. I found the mad bits rather hard going. . . . but there is a bit of madness in all of us, and you have to call upon it in order to play it. I had to unscrew my personal lid in order to play this mad woman."

—DIANA RIGG

"The overall effect is theatrical but impressive, as if Gertrude Lawrence were screen-testing for the role of Mrs. Danvers in Rebecca. . . . *an alternative title for this series might be* Foetal Attraction.*"*

—CHRISTOPHER TOOKEY,
Daily Telegraph

DR. JEKYLL AND MR. HYDE

Based on the novel by
Robert Louis Stevenson

PRODUCTION COMPANY
BBC and Time/
Life Films

YEAR
1981

MAIN CAST
Dr. Jekyll/Mr. Hyde
DAVID HEMMINGS

Ann Coggeshall
LISA HARROW

Utterson
IAN BANNEN

Lanyon
CLIVE SWIFT

Kate Winterton
DIANA DORS

"The Dr. Jekyll of Stevenson's story existed in an introspective world of personal contrasts within the individual. We kept the character intact, but wanted to bring him out of his laboratory and place him well within the historical context of turn-of-the-century London."

—PRODUCER JONATHAN POWELL

DR. HENRY JEKYLL IS A CHARACTER USUALLY SERVED UP WITH ROMANTIC INTERPRETATIONS. HE'S NEARLY ALWAYS YOUNG AND HANDSOME, EARNEST AND ENERGETIC, DEDICATED AND INTELLIGENT, POSITIVELY SHIMMERING WITH THE EXCITEMENT OF HIS NEW DISCOVERY: A CHEMICAL FORMULA THAT CAN SEPARATE THE GOOD AND EVIL ELEMENTS OF A SINGLE PERSONALITY.

Perhaps that's why the first half of the standard Jekyll-Hyde movie is so often an endurance test. Jekyll is dull, dull, dull. We're waiting for the fun to begin with that first gulp of elixir and the arrival of Mr. Hyde.

That's also why David Hemmings' Jekyll was such a relief in the BBC's two-hour *Dr. Jekyll and Mr. Hyde.* His Jekyll is so bent that Mr. Hyde hardly needs to show up. With his unkempt mutton-chop whiskers and the makings of a pretty fair beer gut, he more resembles a middle-aged tosspot than a young scientific genius on the verge of a great discovery. His Jekyll is so physically unappetizing that he can't ever seem to come up with a date and is not satisfied with sitting home alone thumbing through corset ads in the latest illustrated weeklies. So he usually winds up satisfying his need for female companionship in one of the town's gamier sex parlors, run by Kate Winterton (Diana Dors, the former English screen siren).

UNLEASHING MAYHEM WITH FORMULA 33

Troubled by this dark side in his own personality, Jekyll is anxious to get on with his experiment and separate out the bad parts. Yet as soon as he quaffs some of his Formula 33—a combination of mescal, opium derivatives, and Lord-knows-what-else—his dark side rears up as a younger, randier, and decidedly more robust rakehell who calls himself Edward Hyde. All at once, Hyde is dominant, spending Dr. Jekyll's money extravagantly and having his kinky way with lower-class women simply by flaunting his "association" with the eminent Dr. Jekyll.

What adapter Gerald Savory and producer Jonathan Powell obviously set out to do was to place Robert Louis Stevenson's troubled hero smack in the middle of the morally ambiguous environment that actually existed in late 19th-century London, having Dr. Jekyll prowl the same tawdry dens frequented by both Frank Harris in his erotic memoir *My Life and Loves* and the anonymous Victorian hellraiser who wrote that underground erotic classic, *My Secret Life*. In a city sharply divided by class distinctions, the notorious Hyde barely causes a stir—until, of course, he lets his tastes run to violence and mayhem.

Hemmings dives into Mr. Hyde with obvious relish, displaying a tangy quality of profligacy that falls just a beat short of vintage Peter O'Toole at his eye-rolling best. In one scene, his Hyde accosts a 14-year-old flower girl in a manner that would make Humbert Humbert blush and lures her up to his room. "What's your specialty?" he asks. When she seems bewildered by his question, he grows even more assertive, telling her, "Take off your clothes, Mary, and I'll tell you what I'm going to do to you." Just to make sure we're clear on what Hyde has in mind, director Alastair Reid cuts to a close-up of a spurting hypodermic needle, one of the many sexual symbols in this most decadent version of Stevenson's 1885 mystery classic.

"Ann Coggeshall [the wealthy young widow introduced in the television version] is a social reformer who brings Jekyll into contact with what Disraeli called 'the two nations'—the mutually exclusive realms of the very rich and the extremely poor. And, since she is at once attracted to Hyde as well as to Jekyll, the repressiveness of Victorian morality comes to the fore. It was a time when a gentleman's visits to a brothel were socially acceptable, while kissing the lady he loved would be a shocking display of disrespect. [The tale is sharpened by] placing the characters within the context of a society that was itself schizophrenic in many respects."

—PRODUCER JONATHAN POWELL

A FRIGHTENING MULTITUDE OF JEKYLLS AND HYDES

Dr. Jekyll and Mr. Hyde is surely the most familiar of all the stories told in the history of Mystery!. By the 1990s, the film and television versions of the story numbered in the dozens. Of the many silent movie versions, the earliest known is a short 1908 American film. A Danish version made the following year suggested Mr. Hyde was simply a figure from a bad dream that Dr. Jekyll had one night. Most famous was Paramount's 1921 film starring John Barrymore, who did his transformations on camera with a minimum of makeup, mostly by messing up his lanky hair and twisting his features into a rodent-like expression.

The first great sound version was director Rouben Mamoulian's 1931 *Dr. Jekyll and Mr. Hyde* with handsome Fredric March, who won the best actor Academy Award for it. Spencer Tracy had a go at the role in *Dr. Jekyll and Mr. Hyde* (1941). His Hyde, like Barrymore's, looked less like a monster and more like a mentally-warped party animal using the Marquis de Sade style book.

Over the years, the movies have given Dr. Jekyll a son (Louis Hayward, 1951), a daughter (Gloria Talbott, 1957), and a sex change operation (*Dr. Jekyll & Sister Hyde*, 1971). Jekyll and Hyde have met Abbott and Costello (1954), Stan Laurel (*Dr. Pyckle & Mr. Pride*, 1925), Sylvester the Cat (*Dr. Jekyll's Hyde*, 1958), Mighty Mouse (*Mighty Mouse Meets Jekyll & Hyde Cat*, 1944), and Jerry Lewis (*The Nutty Professor*, 1963).

The closest in spirit to the Mystery! version may be *The Two Faces of Dr. Jekyll* (1960), in which actor Paul Massie's Dr. Jekyll is an ineffectual loser, but his Mr. Hyde is handsome, self-confident, and cool.

PSYCHOLOGICALLY PHANTASMAGORIC

The transformation scenes in any version of *Dr. Jekyll and Mr. Hyde* are always dramatic highlights—and in Mystery!'s, Hemmings doesn't let us down. In one scene, a swinging kerosene lamp alternately leaves Jekyll in light and shadow until he's finally revealed as Mr. Hyde with stunning impact. In another, Jekyll's bride-to-be, Ann Coggeshall (Lisa Harrow), wakes up in bed with him in the "hairy phase" of transformation, which gives her a world-class shock.

In one of his best-ever film performances, Hemmings plays Jekyll very much as a hypocritical Victorian whose subliminal drives to indulge his perversities might well have overwhelmed him sooner or later, even without the aid of Formula 33. Though this *Dr. Jekyll and Mr. Hyde* has its modern touches, including psychedelic visions and electronic music, it definitely evokes the repressive Victorian age and reminds us how much easier it is today to let loose our Mr. Hydes.

DOUBLE DUTY IN THE MAKEUP CHAIR

The physical separation of Jekyll into Hyde posed a challenge for the production's makeup team, which labored 4 1/2 to 5 hours at a stretch to transform the actor into Dr. Jekyll, then an additional 45 minutes for each of the 24 some further stages Jekyll passes through, which elapse in moments on screen. Makeup artist Sylvia Thornton compiled a manual of sketches and instructions that was as thick as the production script itself.

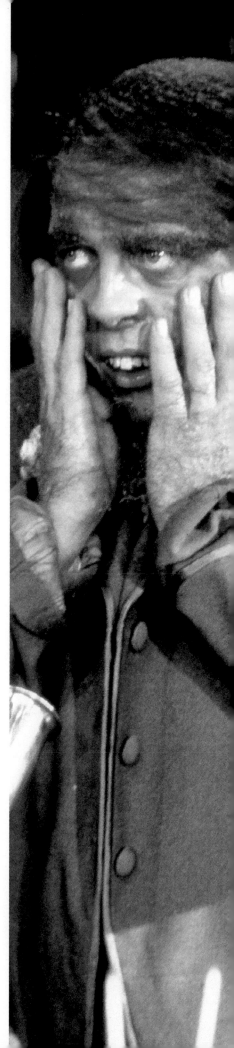

Struggling with Two Sides:

AUTHOR
ROBERT LOUIS STEVENSON

Born in Edinburgh, Scotland, in 1850, Robert Louis Stevenson, not unlike his famous dual personality Jekyll and Hyde, was pulled in two opposite directions—between the moral rigidity of his Calvinist heritage and the wild romanticism of his bohemian inclinations. He struggled, too, with long, debilitating bouts of tuberculosis in between adventurous travels across Europe, America, and the South Seas, locales which often turned up later in his tales like *Treasure Island.* Like Rudyard Kipling and Nathaniel Hawthorne, he was fascinated by dreams and was awakened one night by his wife as he thrashed around in the throes of one. "You should'nt have woken me," he said. "I was dreaming a fine bogey tale." He pieced together what he could remember, and three days later that tale became one that has haunted people all over the world since it was published—*The Strange Case of Dr. Jekyll and Mr. Hyde* (1885).

It was an enormous success in both America and Britain, where it was published as a so-called 'shilling shocker.' Stevenson's cousin and first biographer Graham Balfour wrote, "Its success was probably due rather to the moral instincts of the public than to any conscious perception of the merits of its art. It was read by those who never read fiction, it was quoted in pulpits and made the subject of leading articles in religious newspapers."

Though trained as a lawyer, Stevenson never practiced, finding writing poems, essays, and novels much better suited to his nature. He is best known for *Treasure Island, Kidnapped,* and *A Child's Garden of Verses.* He died at age 44 in Samoa, where he and his American wife had gone and where he worked with the Samoans to combat the injustices of the British governors.

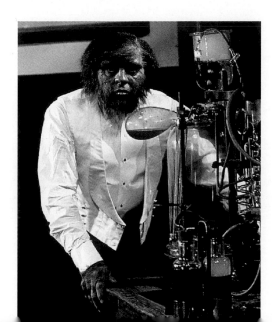

A DARK-ADAPTED EYE

GALLOWGLASS

*Based on the novels by Ruth Rendell
(writing as Barbara Vine)*

A DARK-ADAPTED EYE

PRODUCTION COMPANY
BBC

YEAR
1995

MAIN CAST
Faith
HELENA BONHAM CARTER

Vera
CELIA IMRIE

Eden
SOPHIE WARD

Helen
POLLY ADAMS

John
ROBIN ELLIS

Francis
STEVEN MACKINTOSH

GALLOWGLASS

PRODUCTION COMPANY
BBC

YEAR
1995

MAIN CAST
Sandor
PAUL RHYS

Joe Herbert
MICHAEL SHEEN

Nina Abbott
ARKIE WHITELEY

Paul Garnet
JOHN MCARDLE

MYSTERY! TURNED AN UNSETTLING NEW CORNER IN 1995 WHEN IT VEERED WILDLY FROM THE PATH OF CONVENTIONAL DETECTIVE DRAMA AND PLUNGED DOWN THE DARK AND DISTURBING ROADS TAKEN BY ENGLAND'S ACCLAIMED MYSTERY WRITER BARBARA VINE, *NOM DE PLUME* OF RUTH RENDELL.

Nobody explores the twisted criminal mind more compellingly than Vine, which is what distinguished the television versions of her bestsellers *A Dark-Adapted Eye* and *Gallowglass* from anything ever seen before on Mystery!. Faithfully adapted from her books, the two programs set a new standard for the serious examination of psychosexual personalities through television drama. Both are complex, intellectually demanding stories that their mutual director, Tim Fywell, often chose to tell in a challenging, non-linear style, resulting in dramas of great artistry that cheered the multitudes of Vine-aholics, but may have left fans of Lord Peter Wimsey, Hercule Poirot, and Rumpole of the Bailey cold and confused.

CONVOLUTED CASES

Though there is certainly detective work to be done in these convoluted stories, detectives never actually appear in either one. Instead, both programs take us to the headwaters of the psychological currents flowing through them, showing us what propels the tragic events that follow. Our tour guide in *A Dark-Adapted Eye* is Faith Severn (Helena Bonham Carter), the young niece of both Vera Hillyard (Celia Imrie) and her much younger sister, Eden (Sophie Ward). During the German bombing raids of World War II, Faith is sent to live with her aunts and forms lasting impressions of them both. Those impressions don't really change until a generation later when a scandal-probing journalist forces Faith to finally penetrate the darkness that has surrounded the truth about her aunts.

At first, Vera seems a stern, rather severe woman. Though married, she seems unloving and unloved. Her passion is distilled into a sort of fanatic devotion to her sister, Eden, a stunning beauty she's grooming to be everything she's not and to have everything she never had.

All this changes, though, when Eden leaves her hometown boyfriend behind and goes off to the women's military service. Vera sees more and more of Eden's beau, and though her husband hasn't been home in ten months, she suddenly turns up with Jamie, a baby boy presumably fathered by Eden's boyfriend. Surprisingly, Vera becomes the most doting mother Faith has ever seen. After the war, when Eden has married into the British aristocracy, she suffers a miscarriage and learns she'll never be able to have another child. That's when she begins to look with envy on Vera's happy and contented son, Jamie, and finally decides he would be better off living with her. A bizarre tug of war develops between the formerly inseparable sisters, who once had an almost mother-daughter relationship, and leads them to the final act of their family tragedy. It's a beautifully performed drama with the fine edge of reality.

There's a familiar, fundamental truth about the light Faith finally turns on her family. To a certain degree, we all grow up with clouded visions of our own families because we're part of them and have no real perspective. Only much later, when we start our own families, do we sometimes see the relatives we grew up with as they really were.

"*But it is not just the handling of the plot* [*in* A Dark-Adapted Eye] *that one admires, but the exactness of detail about wartime life and manners, the emotional emphasis gained through the shifts in time, the brilliance with which minor characters are seen at crucial moments which illuminate their characters. T. S. Eliot defended Wilkie Collins against Victorian critics who called him a mere writer of sensational melodrama by saying that in Collins' time 'the best novels were thrilling.' Barbara Vine's book is thrilling in this sense, a modern novel with the Victorian virtues of a carefully devised plot unfolded for the reader with the most cunning art. Wilkie Collins would have admired it, and so would Dickens.*"

—JULIAN SYMONS,
Sunday Times

THROUGH A GALLOWGLASS DARKLY

In *Gallowglass*, Vine's great affinity for offbeat characters is in full flower—and the
Mystery! production has rounded up a letter-perfect cast to bring them to life, starting
with weak-chinned Michael Sheen as Joe, an unloved orphan whose foster parents
reject him after he is dumped on the street due to financial cutbacks at the mental
hospital where he had been a patient. Joe has never experienced love, so he knows
precious little about the rules. When he's about to throw himself in the path of a
speeding train, it's only natural that he fall in love with the handsome young man
who saves his life by pulling him away. "I saved your life, so your life belongs to me
now," says the commanding "Sandor" (Paul Rhys), an erudite, but spoiled young
aristocrat, whose real name is Alexander.

SLAVE AND STOOGE

That's all right with Joe, who willingly becomes Sandor's "gallowglass," an ancient
Gaelic word for the servants of mercenary chieftains. He graciously endures
Sandor's verbal abuse—Sandor tells him he looks like "a skinned weasel"—and even his
cruel acts of sadism, like the razor slashes Sandor dispenses whenever Joe displeases him
because he wants to believe Sandor really cares for him. Joe doesn't realize that Sandor
needs a willing stooge to help him kidnap Nina Abbott (Arkie Whiteley), a one-time
supermodel who's been a recluse ever since a gang of Italian kidnappers held her for ransom nearly a decade ago. Sandor had belonged to that gang and was Nina's watchman. He
has been obsessed with her ever since and is more interested in renewing their "relationship" than he is in collecting the millions they intend to demand from her security-
conscious new husband.

Gallowglass is driven by the heavy tides of misdirected love. Sandor loves Nina. Joe
loves Sandor. Nina loves Paul (John McArdle), her class-conscious bodyguard, and Paul
loves her, too, but has to choose between her and his adolescent daughter, Jessica
(Harriet Owen), who becomes the pawn in the kidnapper's scheme. Stirring it all up
is Tilly (Claire Hackett), Joe's foster sister, who comes between Joe and Sandor while
nudging her way into the kidnap plan. Full of unexpected twists and turns and curious
sexual alignments, *Gallowglass* may be the kinkiest of all Mystery! programs—a masterpiece of character study, illuminated by two glowing performances from Rhys as the
seductive Sandor and Sheen as his lovably geeky gallowglass. Though Rendell's Inspector
Wexford detective stories also have come to television, they're seriously overshadowed by
the memory of this pair of Barbara Vine psychodramas, which displayed the author in all
her wicked majesty.

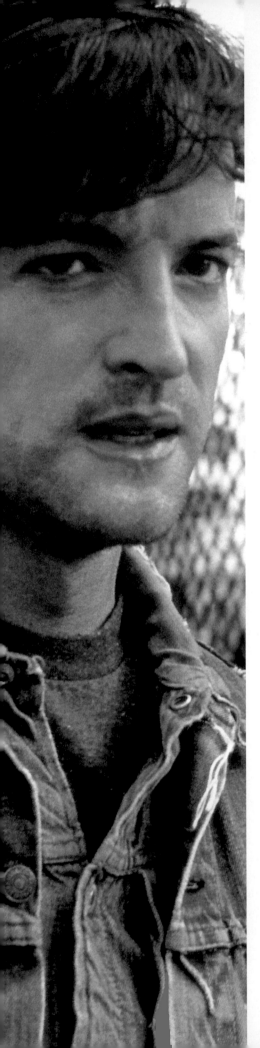

A Man Like a Razor:

TWISTED VILLAIN
SANDOR

(PAUL RHYS)

The best word to describe Sandor is "twisted." Raised in a well-to-do British household and sent to the best schools, he prefers to hang out with low-lifes. He rejects the love of his mother but continues to abuse her hospitality by charging all his excesses to her credit card account. That might be considered a reasonably common degree of "twist" in a spoiled brat, but Sandor is twisted several notches beyond all that. While attending school in Italy he helped a Calabrian gang kidnap the young wife of an Italian millionaire. As her personal "keeper" he kept her on a chain and had sex with her repeatedly. Later, after her husband had paid up, Sandor gave back his share of the loot in hopes of arranging a rendezvous with the woman. To nobody's surprise but his, she ignored his letters.

That left Sandor's warped ego twisted even more, and he descended to more routine crimes. After robbing a storekeeper, he slashed the man with a razor, was caught, and sent to prison. That razor is an essential extension of Sandor's malicious personality. Once, out of sheer meanness, Sandor slashes the lip of his gallowglass Joe while giving him a shave. Another time, he leans over and slices the back of Joe's hand.

With his smoldering eyes, brooding good looks, and European elegance, Sandor has a certain captivating appeal. But only to those who fail to be warned by his oily smarminess, which quickly turns to malicious manipulativeness and sadistic destructiveness.

So convincingly creepy is Rhys that one might find it a bit difficult to accept him in say, a good-guy role. But he has played all kinds of men, from Sydney Chaplin in Richard Attenborough's *Chaplin* to Vincent van Gogh's brother in Robert Altman's *Vincent and Theo*.

The Dark Side of Ruth Rendell:

AUTHOR
BARBARA VINE

IN 1986, SOMETHING TRULY PHENOMENAL HAPPENED IN THE WORLD OF mystery: Ruth Rendell split herself in two and created her alter ego, Barbara Vine. More than a pen name, like George Eliot was for Mary Ann Evans, or a literary alias, like Richard Bachman was for Stephen King, Barbara Vine really is a sort of second personality for Rendell, who has written that she recognizes "two aspects of personality" in herself. Barbara is the side of her who had no literary voice until 1986 when her first novel, *A Dark-Adapted Eye,* was published.

Rendell was born in 1930 to parents who both were schoolteachers. Though her legal name was Ruth, her mother's Scandinavian parents couldn't pronounce it comfortably, so they started calling her Barbara, as did her mother, while her father called her Ruth. As she grew up, Vine began to see two distinct personalities building around the two names: Ruth was the "tougher, colder, more analytical" side of her while Barbara was her softer, more feminine side. The more aggressive Ruth was the one who created Inspector Wexford, her popular detective hero, and a long string of best-selling novels of mystery and suspense. But Rendell finally decided it was time to let readers hear from the other side of her persona, writing more intuitive, personal, and often intensely dark psychological novels, invariably in the first person. Since the widely-acclaimed publication of *A Dark-Adapted Eye* and the other Barbara Vine novels, the literary world has reappraised Rendell many times, generally proclaiming her to have surpassed the limits of the mystery genre and become one of England's foremost writers of serious fiction.

COMPULSIVE WRITER

Rendell grew up in East London and left school at 18 to become a newspaper reporter. She married Don Rendell, a fellow journalist, at 20 and gave birth to their son three years later. The Rendells were divorced in 1975 but got back together two years later and were remarried. They own a 16th-century farmhouse in Suffolk, the setting for her Wexford novels.

> *"In the realm of science, there is a phenomenon called 'dark adaptation.' It's a condition of vision caused by remaining in darkness so long that the retina becomes extremely sensitive. A person whose vision has been affected in this way is said to possess a dark-adapted eye."*
> —DIANA RIGG

SELECTED BIBLIOGRAPHY
(As Barbara Vine)

A Dark-Adapted Eye, 1986; *A Fatal Inversion,* 1987; *The House of Stairs,* 1989; *Gallowglass,* 1990; *King Solomon's Carpet,* 1992; *Anna's Book,* 1993; *No Night Is Too Long,* 1995; *The Brimstone Wedding,* 1996.

At 33, Rendell published her first novel and has since published more than 45 books. A compulsive writer, she says she starts another novel as soon as she's finished one and equates her approach to writing to chain-smoking. Rendell and her alter ego have won a combined total of three Edgar awards and four Gold Dagger awards for their mysteries.

The two Barbara Vine novels adapted for Mystery! represent just a small percentage of the Rendell-Vine stories brought to the screen so far. There has been a British Inspector Wexford series starring George Baker and a number of shows adapted from her books, including *Wolf to the Slaughter* (1987), *A Guilty Thing Surprised* (1988), *A Fatal Inversion* (1992), *Master of the Moor* (1994), and *Vanity Dies Hard* (1995).

Driven by Psychological Dramas:

DIRECTOR
TIM FYWELL

Tim Fywell, the man who directed Barbara Vine's *A Dark-Adapted Eye* and *Gallowglass* for Mystery!, was a stage director who had made neither films nor television programs when he read his first Vine book, *A Fatal Inversion.* Though Rendell's Inspector Wexford mysteries had long been television staples, the Vine novels were considered unlikely material for the screen because they tended to have disturbed people in the foreground and were thought to be too complex for the mass audience. But that was the sort of material that most interested Fywell.

After shopping his idea around, he finally found an interested producer—Phillippa Giles. *A Fatal Inversion* was an enormous hit in England, so the BBC asked for more, and they did *Gallowglass* and *A Dark-Adapted Eye.*

Fywell was the ideal man for the director's job. He's deeply interested in probing the psychology of characters, especially of normal people who are driven to commit criminal acts, even murder. Much of his subsequent work has been in that vein, including two episodes of the acclaimed *Cracker* psychological mystery series, and HBO's Emmy-nominated psychosexual movie *Norma Jean and Marilyn* (1996). "That's sort of what appeals to me about the Barbara Vine stories," he says. "She wants to know what motivates people to do these crimes. You know who the perpetrators are. She's sort of saying that even though these people are doing very dark deeds, they're being driven to that point. You can see them and say, 'There but for the grace of God . . .'"

DYING DAY

Written by John Bowen

PARANOIA, THE MOST PERVASIVE NEW ELEMENT OF THE MYSTERY GENRE
IN THE LAST HALF OF THE 20TH CENTURY, WAS CERTAINLY THE KEY INGREDIENT
OF *DYING DAY,* A TWO-PART ORIGINAL THRILLER BY JOHN BOWEN.

Psychiatrists define paranoia as a systematic form of delusion that most often convinces sufferers they're being persecuted. But what if your fears are not a delusion and you're really being persecuted? That's the question for Anthony Skipling (Ian McKellan), who meets a curious fellow on a London commuter train one day and suddenly finds himself in the grip of genuine fear. The man explains he's a naturalist who records the sounds of various species in their natural habitats. He has even recorded men chatting in their favorite pubs. The man is so lost in his own story that he nearly misses his train stop. When he bolts for the door, he leaves his tape behind. Unable to trace the man, Skipling plays the tape that night and is shocked to hear his own name mentioned in a conversation that's clearly audible in all the hubbub of saloon talk. When he listens closely, he discovers the men are indeed talking about him—and their plans to murder him on a day that's rapidly approaching!

ERASED TAPES AND DISAPPEARING BODIES

Taking the tape to the police, Skipling plays it for them—but the murder plot discussion is no longer there. Skipling tells them someone must have erased that part of the tape while he wasn't looking, but he gets only funny looks in return. The police advise him to consult a good doctor for treatment of his paranoia. Actually, it's not all that unreasonable to assume Skipling has a few screws loose. He's a fussy little man, obsessively methodical in his habits, who has grown even more insular since his wife, Doris (Gwyneth Powell),

PRODUCTION COMPANY
Thames Television

YEAR
1982

MAIN CAST
Anthony Skipling
IAN MCKELLAN
Doris Skipling
GWYNETH POWELL
Mountjoy
CYRIL SHAPS

left him. Now he's become obsessed with proving he's not paranoid.

The following night while on the train Skipling sees the same man again, but this time his face is bloody, his glasses are smashed, and he's apparently dead. Skipling goes to the police again, but they find no body. Once again, they assume he's a nut and vow not to take him seriously again. That doesn't stop Skipling, who methodically investigates his own "case." Inevitably, he concludes he's being framed in a plot that somehow involves Doris and her aged, wealthy, and eccentric lover Mountjoy (Cyril Shaps). He finally comes face to face with Mountjoy at the train station on the very day the conspirators on the tape had said they were going to murder him.

Author Bowen's climax is profoundly ironic and in perfect keeping with the overall atmosphere of paranoia that made *Dying Day* a most relevant and contemporary addition to Mystery!.

> *"Although classic mysteries feature a multitude of relatives and chance acquaintances—everyone's always related, if not by birth, then by happenstance—these are mere teacup coincidences compared to the personal involvements and shared histories that exist in a psychological thriller."*
>
> —Vincent Price

THE PREDATORS

A barber who picks your pocket and slits your throat, an uncle who's after your inheritance, an exact double who takes your place, a doctor who gives you poison, and terrorists who kidnap your kids. They're predators and they're out there, so watch out !

- *SWEENEY TODD*
- *PRAYING MANTIS*
- *THE DARK ANGEL*
- *THE WOMAN IN WHITE*
- *BRAT FARRAR*
- *DIE KINDER*
- *MALICE AFORETHOUGHT*

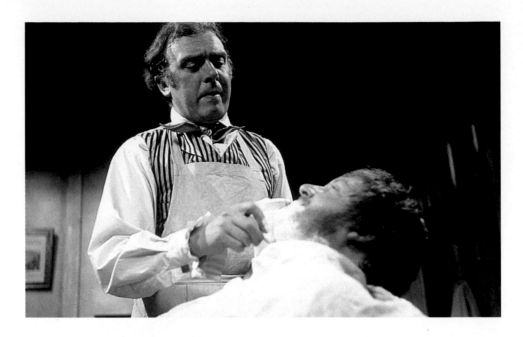

SWEENEY TODD

Based on the play by
George Dibdin Pitt

WHEN WE GNASH OUR TEETH OVER THE FACT THAT TODAY'S KIDS CAN BUY
TRADING CARDS BEARING THE LIKENESSES AND "ACCOMPLISHMENTS"
OF SERIAL KILLERS, IT MIGHT BE WELL TO REMEMBER THAT SEVERAL GENERATIONS
OF GROWN-UPS ALREADY HAVE TURNED ANOTHER PREDATORY SERIAL KILLER—
SWEENEY TODD—INTO A SORT OF CULTURAL FOLK HERO.

PRODUCTION COMPANY
Thames Television

YEAR
1982

MAIN CAST
Sweeney Todd
FREDDIE JONES

Mrs. Lovett/Molly
HEATHER CANNING

Crumbles/Dr. Fogg/
Dr. Makepeace
RUSSELL HUNTER

Charley/Charlotte
MEL MARTIN

Brogden/Mundel/
Hopkins
PETER SALLIS

And until they do *Ted Bundy—The Musical,* or something worse, Sweeney Todd is likely to remain the only serial killer ever to be honored as the title character in a Broadway musical. He supposedly really existed at one time, though records are scarce and he may have used a different name. In a book exploring the origins of the mad barber, British journalist Peter Haining uncovered a few possibilities: a 1785 story about a barber who murdered a man on London's Fleet Street, a Victorian ballad about bodies found in a butcher shop, and a 14th-century French ballad about a barber who slit his clients' throats then stashed the bodies in a pie shop.

The latter is probably the one on which Thomas Peckett Prest based his 1846 story *The String of Pearls: A Romance.* In it, Mr. Todd dumps the bodies of his murdered clients into his basement, then chops them up for a neighboring shop owner to use as the filling for her tasty meat pies. As London police searched for the missing men, the story goes, hungry Londoners were devouring the evidence with relish.

Prest's gory tale was published as an 18-part serial in the "penny dreadfuls," Victorian versions of tabloid newspapers, where it might have appeared alongside a story by Dickens or Poe. It had all the elements of a Victorian potboiler—bodies, purloined pearls, and villains who get their comeuppance.

Sweeney Todd remains the only production of its kind in the long run of Mystery!—a thriller performed live like a play and filmed over 16 hours in one rather arduous day. The demon barber was played by Freddie Jones, a British Vincent Price (a stage and screen actor, he made a specialty out of appearing in British horror films). Heather Canning played Mistress Lovett, who runs the meat pie shop next door to Todd's tonsorial parlor. Featured as the woman who poses as a boy to catch Todd at his dirty work was lovely Mel Martin, best known as the star of *Love for Lydia* on Masterpiece Theatre.

The story of Sweeney Todd has been recycled countless times: There were at least two silent film versions, a popular 1936 British movie thriller starring the aptly-named Tod Slaughter, and a 1973 London stage revival that inspired Stephen Sondheim's musical, which in turn inspired the Mystery! production, which became one of the all-time ratings hits for the series.

Vincent Price, by the way, told viewers in his introduction that Sweeney Todd has evolved into the British version of the bogeyman. He quoted one of his English friends as saying he kept his children quiet at night by telling them, "Sweeney Todd is coming to make you into pies!"

"Melodrama provided Victorian audiences with all forms of violence and disaster; one could always be assured of a hero, a heroine, a diehard villain, and one inevitable outcome: Good triumphs over evil. Sweeney was a natural for this dramatic form, and the character became so popular he soon began to appear in other dramas as a walk-on villain."

—VINCENT PRICE

"As a result of the Sweeney Todd legend, in Victorian times the word 'barber' was considered vulgar in polite society. You could say 'hairdresser,' or 'coiffeur,' or even 'tonsorial artiste'— but never 'barber.'"

—VINCENT PRICE

PRAYING MANTIS

*Based on the novel Les Mantes Religieuses
by Hubert Monteilhet*

**PRODUCTION
COMPANY**
Portman Productions

YEAR
1985

MAIN CAST
Christian Magny
JONATHAN PRYCE

Beatrice Manceau
CHERIE LUNGHI

Vera Canova
CARMEN DU SAUTOY

Paul Canova
PINKAS BRAUN

Gertrude
ANNA CROPPER

IN *PRAYING MANTIS,* FANS OF MYSTERY! WERE INTRODUCED TO A PAIR
OF THE MOST DIABOLICALLY MURDEROUS AND COLD-HEARTED FEMALE PREDATORS
IN THE HISTORY OF THE SERIES: VERA CANOVA (CARMEN DU SAUTOY) AND
BEATRICE MANCEAU (CHERIE LUNGHI), TWO ALLURING WOMEN WHOSE HEARTS
COULDN'T HAVE BEEN ANY COLDER IF THEY CAME PACKED IN DRY ICE.

Vera, a bored French housewife, can't wait to get her hands on the big insurance payoff
she's due upon the death of her husband, Paul (Pinkas Braun), a plodding academic. She
dreams of living a grand new life with her younger lover, Christian (Jonathan Pryce).
She's so venal and unsentimental that she's even willing to consider murder to get what
she wants—but she'd much rather have Christian do the dirty work for her.

PERILOUS SPOUSE-SWAPPING

That makes a certain amount of logistical sense because Christian happens to be Paul's
assistant and he certainly knows the old boy's routine, even his occasional "secret" trysts
with Christian's lovely wife, Beatrice. Their plan calls for Christian to surprise Paul in the
act of adultery with Beatrice, giving him a legal reason to kill them both in anger—since
French law considers a so-called *crime passionnel* a justifiable form of homicide. Christian
agrees to go along with Vera's diabolical plot, though he really has no stomach for it.

What they don't count on, though, is the suspicious nature of Beatrice, who thinks
Christian is cheating on her and arranges to have their bedroom bugged. When she plays
back the tapes, she discovers Christian has been two-timing her with Vera, and they are
plotting to kill her and Paul. Armed with the tapes, the angry Beatrice plans to turn the
tables on the conspirators, forcing them to go through with their plan to kill Paul, but
blackmailing them into cutting her in on the insurance payoff.

Beatrice torments Vera further by driving Christian to suicide. Then, when she publishes her own fake obituary notice, Vera is pushed to the verge of a nervous breakdown, knowing the police will get the tapes and come calling for her soon. It's really just Beatrice's cruel joke, though, before turning the tapes over to Vera and finally letting her off the hook. But fate intervenes and Beatrice is run over by a truck virtually at Vera's doorstep, which seems to guarantee that the police will get the tapes after all.

It's easy to understand why French novelist Hubert Monteilhet decided to name his story after the insect known as the praying mantis. The female mantis is the deadlier insect, frequently devouring the male during the act of mating. Monteilhet thought that symbolized what happened in the real-life French murder case upon which he based his novel.

Lunghi, a Masterpiece Theatre stalwart (*The Buccaneers*, *Kean*, *Edward and Mrs. Simpson*, and *Strangers and Brothers*), plays Beatrice as a crafty and sadistic woman who pays Vera back double for stealing Christian from her. Equally wicked is Du Sautoy, who plays Vera with what one critic called "snaky chic." There are hints that she is no stranger to murder and may have helped Paul's first wife to an early grave back in the days when she was the first Mrs. Canova's nurse. Together these two treacherously predatory women seem frighteningly like French naturalist Jean-Henri Fabre's description of the praying mantis: "an ogre in ambush that demands a tribute of human flesh."

"Lean and hungry, the stick-like insect with its upright-stance and its forelegs raised in apparent prayer has always been a source of fascination for man. Some ancient cultures believed that the insect was created to demonstrate to human beings the correct attitude for prayer. Even the Greeks named the insect mantis, *meaning soothsayer, prophet, diviner. But it is the darker side of this carnivorous insect which concerns us here. You see, the praying mantis eats nothing but living food."*

—VINCENT PRICE

"In a world where human nerves are under constant strain, nothing is more likely to soothe our cares than the innocent enjoyment of other people's suffering. The morbid secretions of certain souls have the capacity to amuse decent men—an irreplaceable therapeutic value."

—HUBERT MONTEILHET, in an introductory note to *Praying Mantis*

THE DARK ANGEL

Based on the novel Uncle Silas
by Sheridan le Fanu

THANKS TO THE INSPIRED NASTINESS OF TWO GREAT ACTORS—PETER O'TOOLE
AND JANE LAPOTAIRE—PLAYING TWO CLASSIC VILLAINS, PITY STARTS
PILING UP IN GREAT HEAPS FOR 17-YEAR-OLD MAUD RUTHYN (BEATIE EDNEY)
FROM THE OPENING MINUTES OF *THE DARK ANGEL*.

**PRODUCTION
COMPANY**
BBC

YEAR
1991

MAIN CAST
Uncle Silas
PETER O'TOOLE

Maud Ruthyn
BEATIE EDNEY

Madame de la Rougierre
JANE LAPOTAIRE

Austin Ruthyn
ALAN MACNAUGHTAN

Dudley Ruthyn
TIM WOODWARD

Maud is heir to the fortune of her ailing father (Alan MacNaughtan), a man whose honorable intentions are to make sure his virginal daughter will turn out well. But honorable intentions are no guarantee of happiness in Gothic thrillers, where there always seem to be plenty of villainous characters just itching to get their scabrous fingers on virginal daughters and their fortunes.

Take, for instance, Madame de la Rougierre (Lapotaire), the French governess Maud's dad hires for her. She's a black-robed, black-wigged, booze-guzzling old bat who may have trained for the job by cutting tails off puppy dogs. If Maud strikes a false note during her piano lesson, for instance, the governess punishes her by whacking her fingers with a baton, then cruelly bending them backward to nearly the snapping point. To make up for it, she plunges the aching fingers into her gooey mouth and nurses them greedily, promising to take away the pain.

SINISTER UNCLE SILAS

Worse is in store for Maud when her father dies and she learns she's being sent to stay with her Uncle Silas (O'Toole), who will take over as her guardian until she's 21. Silas has been the black sheep of the Ruthyn family ever since the mysterious death of a fellow gambler, whose body was found "not in a pool, but in a perfect pond of blood." Although Silas was the prime suspect in that case, he never was arrested. He claims to be reformed of his decadent ways and promises to protect Maud from unsavory influences. "As a former sinner," he tells her, "I can smell the sin of others."

This is not as comforting to Maud as she would like, especially when Uncle Silas gives her another of his special sloppy kisses on the mouth after snarfing down a pint or two of laudanum, a concoction of opium and alcohol that's his favorite after-dinner refreshment. She also gets a bit downhearted when she discovers that all her inheritance will go to Silas if she should happen to die before she turns 21.

Maud begins to suspect her chances of having a 21st birthday party are growing slim when she wanders about her uncle's drafty manor one night and finds an unwelcome guest living there: the sinister Madame de la Rougierre. Her spirits sink even further when Silas starts pushing her toward marriage to her Cousin Dudley (Tim Woodward), a lustful lout who looks as if he'd like to ravish her or hack her to pieces, but can't make up his mind which comes first.

Joseph Sheridan le Fanu's 1864 novel *Uncle Silas* was filmed in 1947 as *The Inheritance* with Jean Simmons playing Maud. The archly scripted Mystery! version was much darker and considerably nastier because it let the two central villains really let their hair down.

O'Toole, star of *Lawrence of Arabia,* has seldom been naughtier, giving a frightfully wicked performance revealing what one critic called "the very worm-eaten soul of decadence." Lapotaire, best known to television viewers for playing French chanteuse Edith Piaf in a television biography, was his match throughout, making up in sheer energy what she may have lacked in subtlety. With a sweet young thing like Beatie Edney *(Highlander, Northanger Abbey)* to paw over, they literally romped their way through the atmospheric proceedings. Director Peter Hammond and his inspired cast made *The Dark Angel* a thrilling haunted house ride through one of the kinkier suburbs of Mystery!.

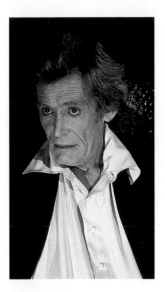

"I don't often get nice, big gory villains—[Uncle Silas] is a lovely villain. He's charming, disconcerting, but whatever he does is hypocrisy because all he's really interested in is evil."

—PETER O'TOOLE

Like Characters in His Novels:

AUTHOR
SHERIDAN LE FANU

Le Fanu might easily have been a character in one of his gloomy, melodramatic stories. He might even have been a stand-in for Maud Ruthyn's father, bearing somewhat of a resemblance to him.

Le Fanu was born in 1814 to a middle-class Dublin family. As owner and editor of a number of newspapers, he published many of his first stories, rising to prominence in Irish society. But when his wife died tragically in 1858, he retreated to his bed, where, obsessed by the fear of death, he wrote ghost stories until he fell asleep. Upon awakening, he continued writing, weaving into his tales the dreams he had just had.

He had a recurring nightmare of a menacing gothic mansion about to fall on him as he stood before it. When he died of a heart attack in bed, at age 59, his doctor said, "I feared this; that house fell at last." Perhaps that house was the basis for the one in *The Dark Angel*.

THE WOMAN IN WHITE

Based on the novel by
Wilkie Collins

A PERFECTLY SANE WOMAN IS DRUGGED AND PLACED IN A LUNATIC
ASYLUM BY A PREDATORY VILLAIN WHO WANTS TO GET HIS HANDS ON HER ESTATE.
THAT'S THE FAMILIAR PREMISE OF WILKIE COLLINS' *THE WOMAN IN WHITE,* ONE
OF THE EARLIEST AND MOST ENDURING TALES IN THE ANNALS OF MYSTERY FICTION.

**PRODUCTION
COMPANY**
BBC

YEAR
1985

MAIN CAST
Walter Hartright
DANIEL GERROLL

Laura Fairlie
JENNY SEAGROVE

Anne Catherick
DEIRDRA MORRIS

Count Fosco
ALAN BADEL

Marian Halcombe
DIANA QUICK

Frederick Fairlie
IAN RICHARDSON

Sir Percival Glyde
JOHN SHRAPNEL

Collins' hobby was collecting police accounts from the new field of criminal detection. He found a fascinating account of an unfortunate woman while combing through the files of the French police during a vacation in France midway through the 19th century with his friend Charles Dickens, a relative by marriage. He couldn't get the nightmarish story out of his mind.

TRUTH STRANGER THAN FICTION

Then, after Collins returned to London, he was taking an evening stroll with his brother and the painter John Millais when a woman dressed entirely in white robes rushed past them and up the street. Collins ran to her aid and discovered she was a well-bred young woman named Caroline Graves, who was fleeing from a man who had kept her locked up in his house for months. That chance encounter turned out to be the catalyst Collins needed to finally make creative use of the story idea that had been germinating in his mind since reading that French police case. He put the two ideas together and came up with *The Woman in White.*

It became a literary sensation in Victorian England when it was serialized in Dickens' literary magazine, *All the Year Round,* in 1860, eclipsing even the clamor over Dickens' own *A Tale of Two Cities,* which had been serialized the month before. *The Woman in White* also fostered a fad in women's fashions—white cloaks and bonnets were suddenly

THE REAL WOMAN IN WHITE

*The story of Caroline Graves, the real
"woman in white," is almost as intriguing
as Collins' tale. After helping Graves the
night he encountered her, Wilkie Collins
began a romantic relationship with her
that lasted the rest of his life. They lived
together for 11 years, split up, then came
back together after various marital relationships with others. Graves was at his
bedside when he died in 1889 and was
buried in his grave when she died six
years later.*

the rage. A popular song called *The Woman in White* sold sheet music by the bale.

That immense popularity was easy to understand. Collins had fashioned a page-turner out of that kernel of a plot. In his story, Caroline Graves becomes Anne Catherick (Deirdra Morris), a sane woman locked up in an asylum by Sir Percival Glyde (John Shrapnel), a fraudulent English aristocrat who fears Anne knows about his illegitimate birth and might someday expose him.

Collins then has Anne escape from the asylum in a white gown and run into the youthful hero, artist Walter Hartright (Daniel Gerroll), one night on foggy Hampstead Heath. Hartright is haunted by his brief meeting with this "woman in white" and is soon plunged into the heart of the tangled affairs that surround her tragic story.

The central focus is an evil conspiracy by the now debt-ridden Sir Percival, aided by his scheming henchman Count Fosco (Alan Badel), to marry beautiful young heiress Laura Fairlie (Jenny Seagrove) and take over her estate by faking her death, burying Anne in the family crypt, and putting Laura in the asylum under Anne's name.

SEEDS OF A CONTEMPORARY PSYCHOLOGICAL THRILLER

Take away certain melodramatic trappings of the Victorian novel, like the odd coincidence that makes Hartright the art teacher for Laura Fairlie, and you have a psychological thriller about treachery, insanity, and greed that today might spring from the pen of a Barbara Vine or Domini Taylor. Laura's homely half-sister, Marian Halcombe (Diana Quick), for instance, seems to be a classic case of sublimated desires. Then there's the bizarre, androgynous Frederick Fairlie (Ian Richardson), the effete and intolerably delicate guardian of both Laura and Marian. He's as puzzling as the shadowy cousin in Truman Capote's *Other Voices, Other Rooms*. And, most especially, there's Count Fosco, one of literature's classic villains. As special adviser to the corrupt Sir Percival, Fosco is the one who dreams up the whole sinister scenario for safeguarding Sir Percival's secret. Fosco is also a physically repellent tub of lard who loves to let his pet mice crawl all over him and nest under his shirt collar.

VICTORIAN GHOSTLINESS

When the BBC decided to film *The Woman in White,* the idea was to retain the moody Victorian atmosphere while enhancing the colorful aspects of Collins' characters. Producer Powell had made another Victorian classic for Mystery!—Robert Louis Stevenson's *Dr. Jekyll and Mr. Hyde*—and knew exactly how to recreate the period. Filmed on location in Cumberland and East Anglia, *The Woman in White* often evoked the look of restored Victorian art works in its effort to recapture the atmosphere of a bygone era. The eerie harp music, noted one critic, lent an "air of Victorian ghostliness."

The book was faithfully adapted by Ray Jenkins and brought to life by an exceptional cast with truly unforgettable moments supplied by actors Badel and Richardson. Producer Powell gambled on the offbeat casting of Shakespearean actor Badel, who was neither Napoleonic nor fat—as Collins had described Count Fosco—and Badel responded by turning the part into a tour-de-force, his last great performance before his untimely death in 1981. His Fosco is Machiavelli-smooth—some might even say slimy—and deceptively disarming as he dotes over his tiny pets, his mercenary heart revealing itself in so many devious ways that the cockatoo on his shoulder might as well be a vulture.

Ian Richardson was another brilliant bit of casting but not at all a predictable choice for the ludicrous Frederick Fairlie, whom Collins described as having a "frail, languidly fretful, over-refined look." "He's an aberration of nature," says Richardson, admitting he instantly recognized Fairlie as a great character of Dickensian stature. Transformed by makeup into the pale shadow of a normal man, Richardson played Fairlie as a creature almost totally exhausted by the effort of living. "She creaks! Her shoes, her bones!" he complains when a maid innocently walks into his room. When he lifts a lacy handkerchief to shield his eyes from a vagabond ray of sunlight, he makes it seem as if the hanky is lined with lead.

The many scenes brilliantly played by Badel and Richardson helped make *The Woman in White* a showcase for memorable acting, and the creepy atmosphere effectively captured the mood of the Collins classic.

"Collins also made a deliberate choice when he decided that the villain [Count Fosco] would be Italian. Twenty years after the novel first appeared, he confessed tht he made Fosco a foreigner 'because his crime was too ingenious for an English villain.'"

—VINCENT PRICE

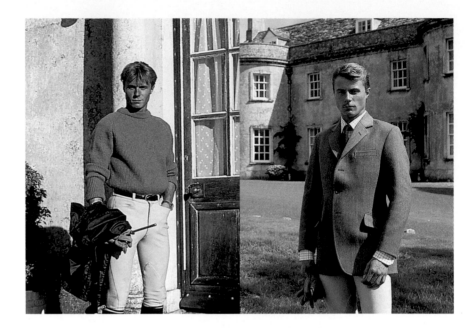

BRAT FARRAR

*Based on the novel
by Josephine Tey*

WHEN BRAT FARRAR LEARNS HE'S A DEAD RINGER FOR THE MISSING HEIR
TO A FORTUNE, HE BOLDLY ATTEMPTS TO PASS HIMSELF OFF AS THE
LONG-LOST MAN. HE'S A FAMILIAR SORT OF PREDATOR IN THE MYSTERY GENRE,
THOUGH. THE UNIQUE ASPECT OF JOSEPHINE TEY'S CLASSIC STORY
IS THAT WE WIND UP ROOTING FOR HIM.

**PRODUCTION
COMPANY**
BBC

YEAR
1986

MAIN CAST
Brat Farrar/Simon Ashby
MARK GREENSTREET

Eleanor Ashby
DOMINIQUE BARNES

Beatrice Ashby
ANGELA BROWNE

Mr. Sandal
COLIN JEAVONS

Alec Loding
FRANCIS MATTHEWS

George Ledingham
FREDERICK TREVES

The Mystery! version of Tey's 1949 bestseller stands out from the pack of gimmicky films about evil twins or doppelgangers because the author reversed the usual theme: Instead of making Brat a greedy conniver, she made him a conscience-driven double who surfaces just in time to uncover a terrible secret long buried by the missing heir's crafty twin brother everybody respects.

Tey's hero is a foundling who ran away from an orphanage in England at age 15 to become a wanderer, eventually making his way through Mexico to the United States, where he found employment as a ranch cowhand, becoming an expert horseman and experienced blacksmith. He returns to England eight years later and runs into an unemployed actor named Alec Loding, who mistakes him for his former neighbor in Dorset, Simon Ashby, who is about to inherit a large estate.

A BRAZEN PLAN

Once Loding discovers his mistake, he begins to develop a bold and imaginative plan: What if Brat were to pretend to be Patrick Ashby, Simon's twin brother, who disappeared when he was just a teenage boy after their parents were killed in a plane crash? Could he share in the inheritance? Patrick had left a farewell note on a cliff overlooking the sea and has been presumed dead, even though the note didn't say he was going to kill himself. Could Alec and Brat convince the Ashby family that Patrick had just run away from home?

Though Brat is hard up, it isn't the promise of wealth that finally makes him buy into Loding's scheme, but rather the fact that the Ashby estate includes a stud farm, a riding stable, and some of the finest horses in Dorset. For the horse-loving Brat, that's a temptation that can't be resisted.

Tey's story gains depth and texture when Brat begins his impersonation and discovers he deeply craves the warm family relationships Simon takes for granted, but that Brat has never experienced in his sad, vagabond life. The more warmly Brat is embraced by his new family, the more intense his feelings of guilt become. Worse yet, he begins to fall in love with lovely Eleanor Ashby. How could she ever love him, believing him to be her long-lost brother? Even if Brat reveals his deception, how could she love such a scoundrel?

Simon, though, holds out against accepting Brat as the missing Patrick. Does that mean Simon knows what really happened to his missing brother? Ultimately, Brat decides the real Patrick may have been murdered and sets out to prove it. Tey's story moves to a startling conclusion with a series of abrupt twists—and the long-awaited showdown between Brat and Simon.

SPLIT-SCREEN WIZARDRY

The double exposure technique of splitting the screen image meant that the same actor—little known Mark Greenstreet, a distant cousin of the beloved American character actor Sydney Greenstreet—could play both Brat and Simon. As Brat, the handsome, blond Greenstreet was clean-shaven, sported a light tan, had tousled hair, and spoke with a slight American accent. As Simon, he lost the tan, put on a mustache, parted his hair neatly, and let his natural British accent come out. Still, a great deal of camera wizardry was necessary to bring off the illusion, which at times finds Greenstreet in the same picture with himself—at one time even fighting his exact double. In one scene Simon puts his hand on Brat's shoulder, in another he casts a shadow while walking in front of him.

The clever special effects, coupled with the equestrian ambiance of the setting gave *Brat Farrar* an offbeat feel that freshened up Tey's hoary plot, making it a deft psychological thriller. But the enduring appeal of *Brat Farrar* is watching a lonely young man with a damaged soul be transformed into a courageously honest man of honor by loving and being loved in return by the people who otherwise might have been his victims.

"Although Tey has come to be known as the mystery writer for people who don't ordinarily read mysteries, she did count as one of her biggest fans the master of suspense, Alfred Hitchcock. He based one of his own favorite films, Young and Innocent, *on Tey's early novel* A Shilling for Candles."

—VINCENT PRICE

Doppelganger in Her Own Write:

A U T H O R
JOSEPHINE TEY

Like her literary hero Brat Farrar, Josephine Tey had a dual identity. What's more, her doppelganger also had a double. Tey was born Elizabeth Mackintosh in Inverness, Scotland, in 1896. Unlike many of the other mystery writers we've encountered, she kept the violence to a minimum and placed her characters in a real world that readers could accept. When she died in 1952, she left behind some of the bestselling mystery novels in history, including *Miss Pym Disposes* and *The Daughter of Time*.

A shy, extremely private person, Mackintosh followed the hallowed tradition of many female authors from George Eliot to Isak Dinesen of adopting a male pen name—Gordon Daviot—and wrote several successful works under that name, including the play *Queen of Scots*. A devoted historian, she also wrote the play *Richard of Bordeaux* in 1933, in which actor Sir John Gielgud had his first major commercial success.

When she later "took to crime" (her words) Mackintosh wrote as Josephine Tey, which was her grandmother's maiden name, and became one of the world's most popular mystery writers. She created the Scotland Yard detective Alan Grant, who appeared in all but a handful of her mysteries.

DIE KINDER

Written by Paula Milne

PAULA MILNE'S CONTEMPORARY THRILLER BEGINS
WITH THE ABDUCTION OF TWO CHILDREN IN ENGLAND BY THEIR FATHER,
WHO TAKES THEM TO HIS NATIVE GERMANY.

PRODUCTION COMPANY
BBC

CAST
1991

MAIN CAST
Sidonie Reiger
MIRANDA RICHARDSON

Lomax
FREDERIC FORREST

Stefan Reiger
HANS KREMER

Alan Mitchell
SAM COX

Karin Muller
TINA ENGEL

Crombie
DEREK FOWLDS

But the story really begins some 20 years earlier, when a group called the Red Liberation Front (RLF)—loosely based on the Baader-Meinhof gang—bombs a Hamburg department store, setting off the repercussions that drive this tense drama.

When she discovers that her children have been snatched from their school, Sidonie Reiger (Miranda Richardson), an Englishwoman, seeks help from both Scotland Yard and the German police but finds they're more interested in her ex-husband, Stefan (Hans Kremer). Frustrated and desperate, she hires an American expatriate private eye named Lomax (Frederic Forrest) to help her. He's an embittered Vietnam War vet now living in Germany, who has become a specialist in tracking down missing persons. But he's for sale to the highest bidder, and Sidonie's bid isn't always the highest. Nevertheless, she eventually learns that Stefan had been "closely associated" with Karin Muller (Tina Engel), the former leader of the RLF, who's been in hiding ever since the bombing—that's why the police are so interested in him. The RLF is also after Karin, so they kidnap the children to force Stefan to find her.

EXPLORING THE PAST

But *Die Kinder* is much more than a tale of suspense and intrigue. Dramatist Milne tackles head on some pretty meaty and sometimes uncomfortable issues. In addition to "the human story of marital kidnap," she says she wanted to explore the legacy of the political protests in Germany in the 1960s. "It wasn't Vietnam they were raising their voices against," she discovered after a spending a year in Germany. "It was their past, 'the veil of silence in the family.'" It was also against the materialism of their parents, who used financial success as a way to regain their "national pride." And the legacy, Milne found, was the idealism of the emerging Green Party, on one hand, and the "dark nihilism" of the Baader-Meinhof gang on the other. She used the kidnapping to set in motion a journey through the "political underbelly of contemporary Germany," where different factions were trying to destroy—and uphold—both legacies.

Ultimately, *Die Kinder* is about confronting one's past, whether to bury it, as the older generation seems to do, relive it, as the RLF wants to do, run from it, as Stefan needs to do, or learn from it, as Sidonie and Lomax try to do. Sidonie, who was involved with Stefan in his radical days, now finds she has different priorities, and the burnt-out Lomax faces what may well be his last chance for redemption. As for *die kinder* (which means the children in German), Sidonie's were merely the pawns. The title refers even more pointedly to the radicals of the past—listed in police computer files under *Die Kinder*—who have perhaps grown—or not—in the past 20 years.

TOO HOT TO HANDLE

Co-financed by the BBC and WGBH, Die Kinder *was also offered to several German networks and production entities for investment, but the sensitivity of some of the issues addressed in the series made them wary, and none participated. Dramatist Paula Milne says residual anti-German feeling in England, stemming from the blitz bombings of World War II, made the series controversial. "But it was quite successful in America," she says. "There's a much more cosmopolitan attitude [there]."*

Mostly a Villain:

ACTOR
FREDERIC FORREST

Frederic Forrest says he felt comfortable playing the part of Lomax because he fashioned it after a character he knows well: Sam Spade, the private eye of *The Maltese Falcon* and other mysteries by author Dashiell Hammett (Forrest had played the hardboiled author in *Hammett*, a film made in 1983 by German director Wim Wenders).

Although he played Lomax "like a classic mercenary," Forrest says that he and director Rob Walker also humanized the character a little because they thought the original script made him look too much like a "really bad guy." "He was devised as a character who would parody the genre figure of the dissolute detective," says Milne. "He's a man who discovers morality in himself, yet lives on the edge of the law—like Shane."

Most of Forrest's roles have been heels or villains. Though Lomax shows a noble character in the climax of *Die Kinder*, he's pretty unsavory most of the way. Forrest says he's "played some really terrible people who have done really despicable things," (he's played Lee Harvey Oswald, the cruel Blue Duck in *Lonesome Dove*, and the self-destructive rock musician opposite Bette Midler in *The Rose*, for which he was nominated for an Oscar). "You just have to pray for those people—and know that somebody has to play them," he says. Still he'd like to have the occasional hero role—and Lomax came close to being one.

PRESENT MEETS THE PAST AND FUTURE

Director Rob Walker brought a stark sense of reality to *Die Kinder*. It helped that
he had lived in Germany during the 1960s, even participating in the student movement. It also helped that he used a number of German actors who brought a
dimension to the script that Milne, an "outsider," says she would never even have
imagined. Then, too, there were the authentic locales, Hamburg and Berlin, which
at the time of filming just happened to have thousands of people demonstrating in
the streets yet again—this time tearing down the Berlin Wall and celebrating the
reunification of Germany. "It was a fantastic time to be filming there," says Milne.
"I wanted to show that the American investment in the colonization of Europe was
coming to an end."

Acknowledging that initially she saw a problem in getting a British audience
interested in a story about German politics, she says, "During the three years it
took to write the scripts, we saw the frail emergence of our own Green Party. Our
relationship to Europe was changing. We were not looking over our shoulders at
our past activities anymore, but starting to look across the Channel to the future—
to Europe."

HOLE IN THE WALL

Important scenes that called for filming
around the historic Berlin Wall were problematical because the wall was being torn
down—in sometimes dramatic fashion—as
the Cold War came to an end with the
reunification of East and West Germany.
One day the film company showed up at a
location alongside the wall that had been
scouted out in advance, only to find that
particular section of wall gone. Stringing
out in procession, the filmmakers had to
walk on for blocks to find a section of
wall still standing.

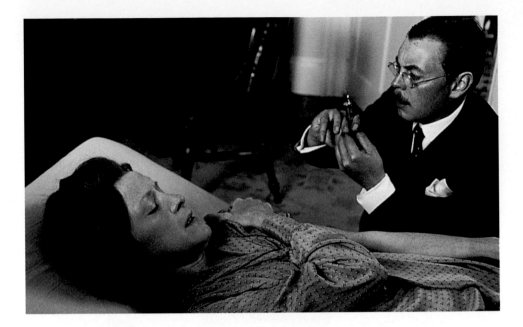

MALICE AFORETHOUGHT

Based on the novel by
Francis Iles

**PRODUCTION
COMPANY**
BBC and
Time/Life Films

YEAR
1981

MAIN CAST
Dr. Bickleigh
HYWEL BENNETT

Julia Bickleigh
JUDY PARFITT

Madeleine Cranmere
CHERYL CAMPBELL

Denny Bourne
CHRISTOPHER GUARD

Sir Francis Lee-Bannerton
THORLEY WALTERS

AWARDS
BAFTA Award,
Cheryl Campbell

DR. EDMUND BICKLEIGH IS A LONG-SUFFERING HUSBAND WHOSE SNOBBISH WIFE, JULIA, HAS TORMENTED HIM FOR YEARS. WHILE INDULGING IN FANTASIES ABOUT AND EVEN FLIRTATIONS WITH OTHER WOMEN, BICKLEIGH IS SMITTEN BY ONE—THE BEAUTIFUL HEIRESS MADELEINE CRANMERE—AND BEGINS AN AFFAIR WITH HER.

Though Bickleigh has hopes of obtaining a divorce from his shrewish wife, Madeleine says she could never marry a divorced man. In Bickleigh's twisted mind, that leaves him with only one possible course of action, if he still wants Madeleine: He must murder his wife to avoid a divorce.

That's the basic premise of *Malice Aforethought,* the famous 1931 novel of psychological suspense by Francis Iles, a pseudonym for mystery writer Anthony Berkeley. The book, hailed as "the best shocker ever written," created a sensation when it revolutionized the mystery genre by revealing the identity of the killer from the start, then generating suspense by making readers wonder if he would get away with his clever crime. It's now a familiar formula, best delineated in Peter Falk's long-running series *Columbo.* Iles used the same gimmick in his subsequent novel, *Before the Fact,* but when Alfred Hitchcock turned it into the classic thriller *Suspicion* in 1941, he insisted on having the poisoner husband, played by Cary Grant, turn out to be innocent of plotting the death of his wife (Joan Fontaine).

Malice Aforethought came to Mystery! in 1981 as a four-part serial starring Hywel Bennett as Bickleigh, Judy Parfitt as Julia, and Cheryl Campbell as Madeleine, and produced by Richard Beynon who produced *Rebecca* and *Lord Peter Wimsey* for Masterpiece Theatre.

SYMPATHY FOR THE DOCTOR

Though Dr. Bickleigh is a predator-killer, he's one who gains the viewer's understanding, if not outright pity. He's a classic example of a "little man" locked into a loveless marriage with a strong-willed, verbally abusive older woman who seems determined to make him pay for all the shortcomings of the male sex. We may detest him for his crime, but we understand he's driven to commit murder out of a yearning for something we all crave—happiness with someone we can love wholeheartedly and who will love us in return.

Still, he's remarkably well-equipped to be a predator. As a medical doctor, Bickleigh has access to drugs and chemicals not readily available to the average harassed husband. He's already treating Julia for severe headaches with morphia, so when he decides to murder her, he simply drops onto her daily grapefruit a drug that increases headaches, then "cures" them with ever larger injections of morphia until the final lethal dose. The villagers, whose lives are centered around gossip juicily dished over teacups and cakes, assume Julia has overdosed herself in a desperate bid to relieve her pain.

FOOD POISONING FOR THOUGHT

But as soon as Bickleigh removes the obstacle of his wife, he discovers Madeleine has fallen in love with someone else—Denny Bourne (Christopher Guard). He's devastated. He's even more dismayed when he learns that not only Madeleine but Chatford, the husband of another former mistress, suspect him of having murdered his wife. So he does the only sensible thing—he mixes botulism-causing bacteria into potted meat sandwiches he serves them for tea. Alas, they don't die but only become ever so ill.

Though Bickleigh gets away with the diabolical murder of his wife, Iles' irony-laced story ultimately finds him facing execution for another death the authorities mistakenly think was murder. We know Bickleigh didn't commit this "murder," but the authorities don't. Fate has marked him for punishment, even if it comes to him in a rather roundabout way.

THE DOCTOR IS IN

Virtually every scene of **Malice Afore-thought** *was filmed on location in the cozy village of Hampshire near Winchester. Producer Beynon hoped to find a few suitable old houses with the proper 1930s period look to stand in for Bickleigh's place, which has tennis courts, an attic, and a medical office with a separate side entrance. Location scouts actually turned up a single house that had everything they needed. What's more, it was even owned by a doctor, who not only agreed to rent it for the film, but also to serve as medical consultant, coaching Bennett in the use of authentic 1930s hypodermics and occasionally filling in for the actor when a close-up of his hands was needed for a medical procedure.*

A Mysterious Life:

AUTHOR
FRANCIS ILES
(ANTHONY BERKELEY COX)

Mystery writer Anthony Berkeley created a new author—Frances Iles—for his 1931 novel *Malice Aforethought*. The book became such a phenomenal bestseller that the make-believe Iles became a popular author in his own right with another bestseller the following year, *Before the Fact*, and book reviews in the *London Daily Telegraph*. Actually, both names were pseudonyms for the mysterious Anthony Berkeley Cox, a British journalist who began his career writing humorous sketches for *Punch* magazine.

Cox first delved into mystery fiction in 1925 with *The Layton Court Mystery*, which was published anonymously. He started calling himself Anthony Berkeley with his next novel and quickly became one of England's most popular mystery writers. In 1928, he founded the legendary Detection Club with such famed mystery writers as Dorothy L. Sayers and Agatha Christie, then lampooned it in his novel *The Poisoned Chocolate Case*. It was a tribute to his authorial acumen that in one of the club's collaborative efforts, *The Floating Admiral*, he was assigned the final chapter—"Cleaning up the Mess."

Among the many mysteries of Cox's life: He ran a company called A. B. Cox, Ltd., but never disclosed what kind of business it was. And, in 1939, he retired both Anthony Berkeley and Francis Iles as mystery writers, but without any explanation. He died in 1970.

RAISING REASONABLE DOUBTS

*Did she drown by accident or was it murder?
Was he poisoned or did he die of natural causes? Did
he bludgeon his wife or was it an unknown intruder? Was
his wife's death justifiable homicide? Did they kill their
wives or were they framed? These are the mysterious
deaths that raise reasonable doubts.*

- *REBECCA, MY COUSIN RACHEL*
- *THE MAN FROM THE PRU*
- *CAUSE CÉLÈBRE*
- *WE, THE ACCUSED*
- *THE LIMBO CONNECTION*
- *MELISSA*

REBECCA

**PRODUCTION
COMPANY**
BBC

YEAR
1980

MAIN CAST
Maxim de Winter
JEREMY BRETT

Mrs. de Winter
JOANNA DAVID

Mrs. Danvers
ANNA MASSEY

Colonel Julyan
ROBERT FLEMYNG

Jack Favell
JULIAN HOLLOWAY

Beatrice
VIVIAN PICKLES

*MY COUSIN
RACHEL*

**PRODUCTION
COMPANY**
BBC

YEAR
1985

MAIN CAST
Rachel Sangalletti
GERALDINE CHAPLIN

Philip Ashley
CHRISTOPHER GUARD

Ambrose Ashley
JOHN SHRAPNEL

Rainaldi
CHARLES KAY

Louise Kendall
AMANDA KIRBY

Nick Kendall
JOHN STRATTON

REBECCA

MY COUSIN RACHEL

*Based on the novels by
Daphne du Maurier*

WIDOWER MAX DE WINTER, THE MOODY HERO OF *REBECCA*,

IS HAUNTED BY THE MEMORY OF HIS BEAUTIFUL DEAD WIFE. BUT IS IT

BECAUSE HE MURDERED HER?

Youthful Philip Ashley, the equally troubled hero of *My Cousin Rachel,* is also a haunted man. He let his cousin Rachel fall to her death because he believed she was poisoning him. But now he wonders, Was she really innocent? The best romantic mysteries of the late Daphne du Maurier, *Rebecca* and *My Cousin Rachel* are a pair of "haunted" love stories so psychologically complex and with such enigmatic characters that they leave us with troubling notions about the possible guilt or innocence of their leading characters.

Hugh Whitemore's literate adaptations preserve the tantalizing ambiguity of du Maurier's originals, and the faithful dramatizations remain among the most memorable of all Mystery! series.

REBECCA OF THE CORNISH COAST

Rebecca is the story of an introverted and unsophisticated 19-year-old (Joanna David) who's employed as a traveling companion to an elderly American woman. While stopping in Monte Carlo, they meet wealthy English widower Max de Winter (Jeremy Brett), who's attracted to the honest, uncomplicated young woman, whose name we never learn. After a whirlwind courtship, Max proposes marriage. She accepts and returns with him to the de Winter family home, Manderley, a brooding mansion on the Cornish coast.

Almost immediately, the young bride realizes she'll be living in the long shadow of

Rebecca de Winter, Max's first wife, a great beauty and renowned hostess who died in a tragic boating accident the year before. The new Mrs. de Winter is constantly reminded of her own inadequacies by Mrs. Danvers (Anna Massey), the embittered housekeeper who was devoted to Rebecca and resents the woman who dares take her place. As the weeks go by, the new Mrs. de Winter begins to learn startling things about her husband's first wife and the nature of their marital relationship, then discovers a number of suspicious circumstances that suggest Rebecca's death may not have been an accident.

JEALOUSY AT THE ROOT

Rebecca is an atmospheric story that's first and foremost about jealousy. For the naive young heroine, it's natural to covet the passionate affection she mistakenly believes her husband still has for the spellbinding Rebecca and also to be affected by the constant praise heaped on Rebecca by Mrs. Danvers, even though she knows it's irrational to be jealous of a ghost.

Jealousy also is a critical motivation for the darkly unbalanced Mrs. Danvers. Massey plays her as a frustrated woman with a sexual attraction to her former mistress, suggesting she has harbored feelings of jealousy toward Max for years because he had the good fortune to be Rebecca's lover instead of her. Massey's lesbian take on Danvers is now the accepted interpretation. It was acknowledged in the Oscar-nominated 1996 documentary *The Celluloid Closet,* and Dame Diana Rigg, who plays Danvers in the 1997 Masterpiece Theatre remake of *Rebecca,* says, "There is a touch of lesbianism in this one, too." For all its psychological twists and turns, *Rebecca* is a great romantic story about a young woman finally winning the heart and soul of the tragically haunted man she married in the heat of infatuation.

"You know, we're set up to hiss Mistress Rebecca, retroactively. Maybe she was a cad, all bad. But let's take Rebecca's side. Was she an oppressed appendage of the aristocracy? A bright woman expected to do nothing but plan fancy dress balls and send scented letters? As for the truth about her relationship with Mrs. Danvers, we'll never know. And so the drama of Rebecca *ends with just a single nagging question dangling: Why didn't Maxim de Winter divorce Rebecca?"*

—GENE SHALIT

HURDLING PAST HITCHCOCK

Naturally, the biggest hurdle the television version of *Rebecca* had to get over was the inevitable comparison to Alfred Hitchcock's famous movie adaptation, released in 1940, just two years after du Maurier's book zoomed to the top of bestseller lists. Though no one seriously believes the Mystery! version of *Rebecca* is superior to the Hitchcock film,

it was distinctive enough to trigger widespread praise, including a firm endorsement from Daphne du Maurier, who wrote to producer Beynon, saying, "I do not think the present script could be improved in any way at all." The Mystery! version had one major asset the Hitchcock film lacked: length. Hitchcock had to tell the story in 130 minutes while the BBC's director, Simon Langton, had nearly four hours. The Hitchcock script also altered the original story in one major respect: Rebecca's death becomes an accident rather than murder. Whitemore's television script scrupulously followed the original, with only one minor change: He added a scene showing Max and his new wife in bed during their honeymoon.

The Mystery! version starred Jeremy Brett at the peak of his romantic leading-man period, before he became Sherlock Holmes in the long-running Mystery! series. Brett saw Max as a self-centered man who was thinking only of himself when he married such a young, inexperienced bride. But Brett loved the "dark, sad, and angry" character and felt he became quite sympathetic as he finally began to cope with his past. Initially, Brett rebelled when told he'd have to grow a mustache for the part. He felt that would make viewers immediately think of Olivier, who wore a mustache in *Rebecca*. He finally relented and wore the lip whiskers. Joanna David, who went on to work in several subsequent Mystery! series, prepared for her role by reading and re-reading the novel—which is narrated by her character—to gain insight into what the new Mrs. de Winter is thinking in every scene. Seventeen years later, Joanna David's actor-daughter, Emilia Fox, played the same role in the 1997 remake of *Rebecca*.

Of the three central performances in *Rebecca*, probably the most praise was lavished on Anna Massey, whose Mrs. Danvers was more recognizably human than Judith Anderson's in the Hitchcock version. Anderson had played Danvers with wild-eyed energy, almost like one of the mythical Greek furies. Massey saw Mrs. Danvers as "a sort of imaginary sorceress," but "with totally human qualities."

DOUBLE JEOPARDY JEALOUSY

Anna Massey might have found other reasons for being jealous of the relationship between Max de Winter and both his brides: She was in fact the real-life wife of the actor who played Max, Jeremy Brett.

MENTOR MAX

Ironically, the first Max de Winter, Sir Laurence Olivier, had served as a mentor to the second one, Jeremy Brett, in the theater, and Brett was the godfather to Olivier's daughter, Julie. They had worked together in plays at the National Theatre, and Brett had been directed by Olivier on stage. When Olivier heard his friend had been cast in one of his most famous roles, he called Brett and kidded him, saying, "You might have waited until I was dead!"

WHAT ABOUT MR. DANVERS?

Many fans of Rebecca *have wondered why we never heard anything about Mr. Danvers. The reason may be that there never was a Mr. Danvers. Dame Diana Rigg, who plays Mrs. Danvers in the 1997 remake, says it was common for English housekeepers of the period to call them-selves "Mrs." even if they had no husbands. "I think it just made their progress through the house easier," says Rigg. "In other words, hands off! Not that anybody would want to put their hands on Mrs. Danvers, you understand."*

Wicked Witch of the West Country:

VILLAIN
MRS. DANVERS
(ANNA MASSEY)

Du Maurier described Mrs. Danvers as "someone tall and gaunt, dressed in deep black, whose prominent cheekbones and great, hollow eyes gave her a skull's face, parch-ment white, set on a skeleton's frame." That described, with uncanny precision, Anna Massey's image as Mrs. Danvers. Massey plays her as a woman so intensely devoted to the memory of her dead mistress that she treats the new Mrs. de Winter as an interloper.

"Do you think the dead come back?" she asks her mistress at one point, looking beyond her into the dusk that's enveloping Manderley. "Sometimes I think Rebecca comes back to Manderley and watches you and Mr. de Winter together." Already self-conscious about her lack of breeding and inexperience at running a household, the young bride is made to feel a sense of guilt about taking the place of the woman Mrs. Danvers so adored. Danvers even goes so far as to press her mistress to jump to her death from a window in order to end all the humiliation she's causing Maxim.

Though there's only a hint of it in the book, Massey's performance is built around her belief that Mrs. Danvers was a victim of her own subconscious longing for Rebecca, a stifled passion that left her a lonely, dispirited woman, eternally resentful of the woman who would replace her beloved mistress. As Massey told interviewer Tim Heald in 1980, "I think she was profoundly homosexual."

Before her fiery death in the blaze that ultimately consumes Manderley, it becomes clear Mrs. Danvers is the symbolic representation of the evil that pervades the once-grand estate.

"It's clear [Mrs. Danvers] is not a member of the Cornish branch of Welcome Wagon."

—GENE SHALIT

RACHEL, RACHEL

Curiously, there's a "victim of passion" in du Maurier's *My Cousin Rachel,* too, but it's hard to decide who it is—the young narrator Philip Ashley (Christopher Guard) or the object of his obsessive passion, his widowed cousin Rachel (Geraldine Chaplin). *My Cousin Rachel* is an even darker work than *Rebecca* as it exposes the psychological roots of jealousy and obsessive love.

KEEPING THEM GUESSING

When Geraldine Chaplin agreed to play Rachel, she wanted to know if director Brian Farnham wanted her to suggest guilt or innocence. He told her he didn't care, as long as she didn't let him in on what she'd decided. Chaplin made up her mind to play some scenes as though Rachel is guilty, others as if she's innocent.

Young Philip is an orphaned member of the wealthy Ashley family, raised by his bachelor cousin Ambrose (John Shrapnel) in Ambrose's sprawling estate in 19th-century Cornwall. Because Ambrose has never married, Philip is his designated heir, and their relationship is like father and son. For his health, Ambrose winters in Italy while Philip helps run the estate in his absence. But one year Ambrose fails to return, finally writing to say he has met a distant cousin, the Contessa Rachel Sangalletti, a young widow. He has fallen in love and impulsively married her. Shocked, Philip grows more concerned when he learns his cousin has fallen ill and can't return home. Philip decides to leave for Florence, but by the time he arrives, Ambrose is dead and his widow has left their villa with all her husband's belongings.

Already jealous of Rachel, Philip is furious when he finally receives letters Ambrose had written him before he died suggesting Rachel had become his "torment" and may be in league with her shifty adviser, Rainaldi (Charles Kay), to poison him and take over the Ashley estate. "She has done for me at last," Ambrose wrote.

Angrily vowing vengeance, Philip returns to Cornwall. When he learns Rachel is coming to visit, he prepares to challenge her. To his surprise, though, she turns out to be a small, sweet, gentle, and thoughtful person of almost irresistible charm. She quickly wins over the household staff, the gardener, and even Philip's favorite dog. Philip begins to wonder if perhaps Ambrose had been mistaken about Rachel because he was delirious with the hereditary brain fever that has afflicted generations of Ashley men. Just a few weeks after her arrival, Philips realizes he's falling in love with his cousin's widow.

Du Maurier fans have debated Rachel's guilt or innocence for years. Is she a decent person whose great flaw is her profligate spending of the Ashley funds, pushed on her by Philip as his passion for her becomes obsessive? Or is she a cunning manipulator who subtly seduces Philip because she needs his signature on the unsigned will that gives her the Ashley estate and free rein to bleed it dry? Du Maurier littered the Cornish landscape with clues, but left it up to us to draw our own conclusions right to the shocking finale when the vengeful Philip fails to warn Rachel of danger as she innocently strolls across an unsupported new bridge that he knows will collapse.

Chaplin's enigmatic portrayal results in one of her finest performances on film, a complex characterization that's all the more impressive because of the authentic Italian accent she adopted for Rachel. Christopher Guard's performance is more straightforward. His Philip is an impetuous, callow youth who's simply not in Rachel's league, guilt or innocence aside.

Both *Rebecca* and *My Cousin Rachel* leave viewers wondering what will become of the characters they've gotten to know so well. What kind of life will the second Mrs. de Winter have with her husband, so shattered by the destruction of Manderley and the nightmares associated with it? And what of Philip Ashley? Will he recover from the guilt he feels over the role he played in Rachel's death? Will he finally find the happiness Louise Kendall might bring him? Fortunately or unfortunately, we can't tune in for more.

". . . refreshingly old-fashioned, full of driving storms and blazing fires, sweating horses and steaming roasts, muddy boots and velvet gowns. And not a cocaine deal or linen jacket in sight."

—CLIFFORD TERRY,
Chicago Tribune

Winning Writer Since a Teen:

AUTHOR
DAPHNE DU MAURIER

REBECCA AND MY COUSIN RACHEL, ALONG WITH THE EARLIER JAMAICA INN, were the most evocative novels Dame Daphne du Maurier ever wrote about the landscape she knew best—the windswept, brooding Cornish coast with its treacherous rocks and dark mansions.

But she was born into a different world—cosmopolitan London of the Bloomsbury period—to a family of celebrities. When she was born in 1907, her father, Gerald du Maurier, already was England's leading stage actor, the Laurence Olivier of his time. Her grandfather was the acclaimed novelist and illustrator George du Maurier, known for the novel *Trilby*, which gave the world the immortal villain Svengali. Du Maurier's great-great grandmother was a Regency courtesan, protected by the Duke of York, and her mother, Muriel, was an actor.

Du Maurier began writing in childhood and at age 14 won a short story contest at her school. In her memoirs, she tells about the influence of fairy tales on her as a youngster, especially Snow White, which taught her that women can be even more evil than men. She held a special regard for the power of witches because, "They were sometimes beautiful, and then you could not tell until it was too late." Max de Winter surely could have said the same about his late wife, Rebecca, and Philip Ashley surely suspected it of his cousin Rachel.

Shortly after her first novel, *The Loving Spirit*, was published in 1931, du Maurier married Frederick Arthur Montague Browning, a military man who had been treasurer to the Duke of Edinburgh. Never completely happy in London, they moved to Land's End and remained mostly in that remote stretch of the Cornish coast. In 1943, du Maurier and her husband actually moved into Menabilly, the 70-room mansion she had used as the model for Manderley in *Rebecca*.

On those rare occasions when she talked about the creative process, du Maurier said she never based her characters on real-life people, but let the characters "find" her. When writing *Rebecca,* she told friends, she actually imagined herself as the second Mrs. de Winter and tried to feel the same emotions her character might have felt. She frequently began her novels with intensive research into the history and geographical features of the setting she had chosen for her story. By the time she finally began to write, she had everything well in mind and often completed a novel in just a few months. Du Maurier's great literary success began in the mid-1930s and literally skyrocketed her to fame in 1938 with the publication of *Rebecca,* which sold as well in America as it did in Britain. In addition to *Rebecca* and *My Cousin Rachel,* many of her novels and short stories were turned into popular films, including *Jamaica Inn, Frenchman's Creek, Hungry Hill, The Scapegoat, The Birds,* and *Don't Look Now. Rebecca* won the National Book Award in 1938, and in 1978, du Maurier was made a Grand Master by the Mystery Writers of America. In 1969, she was named Dame Commander Order of the British Empire. She died in 1989.

SELECTED BIBLIOGRAPHY

The Loving Spirit, 1931; *I'll Never Be Young Again,* 1932; *The Progress of Julius,* 1933; *Jamaica Inn,* 1936; *Rebecca,* 1938; *Come Wind, Come Weather,* 1940; *Frenchman's Creek,* 1942; *Hungry Hill,* 1943; *The King's General,* 1946; *The Parasites,* 1949; *My Cousin Rachel,* 1951; *The Apple Tree: A Short Novel and Some Stories,* 1952; *Mary Anne,* 1954; *The Scapegoat,* 1957; *Castle d'Or,* 1962; *The Glass Blowers,* 1963; *The Flight of the Falcon,* 1965; *The House on the Strand,* 1969; *Rule Britannia,* 1972.

PRODUCTION
COMPANY
BBC/Scotland and
Liverpool Films

YEAR
1991

MAIN CAST
William Wallace
JONATHAN PRYCE

Julia Wallace
ANNA MASSEY

Amy Wallace
SUSANNAH YORK

Detective
Superintendent Moore
TOM GEORGESON

Hemmerde K. C.
RICHARD PASCO

THE MAN FROM THE PRU

Written by Robert Smith

**DID MILD-MANNERED INSURANCE SALESMAN WILLIAM WALLACE BEAT
HIS WIFE TO DEATH WITH AN IRON BAR IN THEIR LIVERPOOL HOME? THAT QUESTION
HAS FASCINATED EVERYONE FROM MYSTERY FANS TO READERS OF NEWSPAPER
ACCOUNTS OF JULIA WALLACE'S MURDER IN 1931. IN FACT, IT'S OFTEN REFERRED TO
AS THE MOST PUZZLING MURDER IN BRITISH HISTORY.**

Mixing flashbacks with courtroom scenes, *The Man From the Pru* portrays Wallace
(Jonathan Pryce) and his dour, plain wife Julia (Anna Massey) living a dreary life in
dreary Liverpool. He sold insurance for Prudential and she waited at home, occasionally
playing the piano rather badly to lift her spirits. They had no children and, from all
appearances, seldom went about the business that makes them.

Wearing a fussy little mustache, bowler hat, wire-rimmed spectacles, and an expression of constant boredom, Pryce played Wallace as a drone grown used to his particular
hive. Even under a microscope, you wouldn't find a frill on him. He and Julia seemed
the least likely pair to be involved in anything as out of the ordinary as a love
affair—or a murder. Yet a murder did occur, all right. The television drama suggests a few possible alternative scenarios to the official police version of the crime.

JUST THE FACTS, PLEASE

Julia was beaten to death in her parlor on a night when her husband had been
called out to meet a potential customer. Wallace told police he couldn't find the
customer's address and ultimately discovered it didn't exist. When he returned home, he
found his wife's body—and a burgled strongbox. Wallace believed he had been purposely
lured away so someone could break into the house. He concluded Julia had surprised the

> *"Everything that the accused (Wallace)
> said or did might be construed as the
> behavior either of an innocent man
> caught in a trap—or of a guilty man
> pretending to be caught in a trap."*
>
> —DOROTHY L. SAYERS

burglar and been killed by him. Police didn't believe the story, even though Wallace gave them the names of people he had asked directions from on the streetcar—investigators thought it sounded too much like a manufactured alibi. But what would be his motive for killing his wife? That's the problem that bothered many who studied the case, including mystery author Dorothy L. Sayers.

The Man from the Pru suggests two possible motives: Wallace was angry because he had discovered his wife was having an affair with Gordon Parry (Gary Mavers), a womanizing fellow Prudential salesman who already was in trouble for embezzling funds from the company. But no evidence ever was produced that Julia had ever played around with anyone, let alone Parry, an unlikely ladies' man. The program also suggests Wallace was enamored of his sister-in-law, Amy (Susannah York), who seemed to make him come to life whenever she spent any time with him. Again, there was no evidence Wallace ever had anything more than a chat with Amy, though he certainly had the opportunity.

"Whether Wallace was guilty or innocent, the story is of a sort that could only have been put together by the perverted ingenuity of a detective novelist."

—DOROTHY L. SAYERS
(who attended Wallace's trial)

*"Wallace couldn't have done it—
and neither could anybody else."*

—MYSTERY WRITER
RAYMOND CHANDLER
(who called it "the *non-pareil* of
all murder mysteries")

PRYCELESS PERFORMANCES

A veteran stage and screen actor, Jonathan Pryce had the controversial male lead in Broadway's **Miss Saigon** *and has appeared in a large number of critically acclaimed films like* **Carrington** *(1995), but he's still best known as the sophisticated fellow in those Infiniti automobile ads—despite the rave notices he earned for* **The Man From the Pru.**

AFFECTLESSNESS WALLACE'S UNDOING

During his murder trial Wallace was so lifeless and undemonstrative that many students of the case now believe that his listless behavior was more responsible for putting a noose around his neck than the evidence gathered by police. Even at the murder scene he was reported to have been emotionless, idly leaning over his wife's mutilated corpse to flick cigarette ashes into a bowl. Those reports may have influenced the jury, which failed to understand Wallace was a follower of Stoicism. "I have trained myself to be a stoic," he said. "For forty years I have drilled myself in iron control and prided myself on never displaying an emotion outwardly in public." At any rate, Wallace was convicted and sentenced to hang.

Still, doubts of Wallace's guilt continued to swirl through legal circles. Clearly, the police had bungled parts of the investigation, especially fixing the time of death. Some witnesses altered their stories, indicating Julia was still alive much later than originally believed. And no clear, convincing motive ever emerged. Wallace continued to maintain his innocence, claiming his wife's death had cost him his closest friend.

ANOTHER BLOODY GLOVE

Finally, an appeals court reversed the conviction, and Wallace was set free because the evidence was all circumstantial. Never a healthy man, he died two years later. In a diary found after his death, Wallace had written that he suspected Parry was the killer, saying he had been "friendly" with Julia. In 1981, 50 years after the murder, a garage mechanic who had serviced Parry's car went public with a startling bit of information: He had found a bloody glove in Parry's car right after the murder. He said he gave the information to police, who did nothing about it. The case is still officially listed as unsolved. Though the BBC drama suggests alternative solutions to the murder, it never nudges the viewer too far toward any firm conclusions about who really did it.

In Wallace, a man more complicated than his bloodless bearing might suggest (he had sought his fortune in Calcutta and Shanghai, dabbled in science, and was a follower of Stoicism), Pryce gave us an honest portrait of one of the most enigmatic characters in the annals of crime.

> *"[Julia Wallace was] starved for company and affection and rarely ventured out of their home. . . . She was regarded as something of an eccentric. We know she made her own underwear. I had to wear a flannel petticoat for the part. . . . Julia clearly enjoyed [Gordon Parry's] attention—she may have rejected Parry and he felt emasculated. . . . But when I'm on the set with Jonathan, I feel certain Wallace could have done it."*
>
> —ANNA MASSEY

> *"People seemed frightened of me [when we were filming on the streets of Liverpool]. Wallace was a well-known figure in the area, and people seemed to remember him immediately when they saw me. In a way, it was pleasing to know I got it right. . . . There was something odd about him and his wife, something anachronistic about their lifestyle. . . . Since the man gave away so little in his mannerisms, it's down to a certain look, a stillness, to convey his concentration, his internal life."*
>
> —JONATHAN PRYCE

CAUSE CÉLÈBRE

Based on the play by
Terence Rattigan

ALMA RATTENBURY WAS THE 38-YEAR-OLD WIFE OF BOURNEMOUTH
ARCHITECT FRANCIS RATTENBURY, WHO WAS BLUDGEONED TO DEATH IN 1935.
POLICE ACCUSED RATTENBURY'S 18-YEAR-OLD CHAUFFEUR OF THE MURDER,
BUT SUSPECTED ALMA HAD PUT HIM UP TO IT BECAUSE SHE WAS
HAVING AN AFFAIR WITH THE YOUNG MAN.

Their murder trial remains one of the most scandalous in English courtroom history. Not surprisingly, the 1988 television adaptation of *Cause Célèbre,* Terence Rattigan's stageplay about the famous murder case, has become one of the most acclaimed programs ever carried on Mystery!.

Most people who followed accounts of the Rattenbury murder trial in England's Old Bailey took a strong dislike to Alma and felt the strapping young chauffeur—he's called George Bowman in the program because the real person was still living when the show was filmed—was not only Alma's lovesick dupe but also the crime's second victim.

ALMA'S SCARLET A

Before playing DCI Jane Tennison in the *Prime Suspect* series, Helen Mirren tackled the distasteful role of Alma Rattenbury. Reporters were so sure Alma had corrupted Bowman (David Morrissey) and conspired with him to murder her husband that they vilified her in print before and during the trial. Branded an adulteress, she actually was threatened by a mob of outraged Londoners when she first showed up at the trial. In one scene, a juror even asks to be excused because of her intense hatred of Alma.

Mirren prepared to play Alma by reading as much background material on the woman as she could find. She even went to the actual Rattenbury house, where she visited

PRODUCTION
COMPANY
Anglia Television

YEAR
1988

MAIN CAST
Alma Rattenbury
HELEN MIRREN

Francis Rattenbury
HARRY ANDREWS

T. J. O'Conner
DAVID SUCHET

George Bowman
DAVID MORRISSEY

Irene Riggs
NORMA WEST

Alma's bedroom and stood in the living room where the murder was committed until she began to feel as Alma may have felt. Mirren finally decided to play her with a strong element of sympathy because she pictured Alma as a woman with 1980s attitudes, tragically condemned by the judgmental mores of 1930s England.

Certainly, puritanical Londoners of the 1930s were repulsed by the idea of a 38-year-old woman betraying her husband by seducing his 18-year-old chauffeur. But *Cause Célèbre* shows her husband, Francis (Harry Andrews), as a distant, hard-drinking, and miserly man who lacks passion and hasn't been intimate with his wife in years. Given this background, it's soon easy to understand why his much younger, hot-blooded wife might be attracted to the young hunk who seems to strike a pose every time she looks his way.

CONDEMNED BY CLASS

Cause Célèbre also suggests that another factor worked against Alma: the British class prejudice prevalent during the period. Alma wasn't just having an affair with a young man half her age, she was having one with a member of the servant class!

She also had the bad taste to be best friends with her maid, who stood by her throughout the trial.

Though *Cause Célèbre* shows Bowman beating Francis Rattenbury to death with a mallet, Alma actually confessed to the crime, saying, "I was playing cards with my husband when he dared me to kill him, as he wanted to die. I then hit him with the mallet. I would have shot him if I'd had a gun." Later, though, Alma's lawyer (played by David Suchet, the inimitable Hercule Poirot), discusses how he plans to make the jury see that his client is trying to shield the true killer. "I shan't hesitate to remind the jury that [she's] a poor, weak woman who couldn't drive a peg into peat in under 40 whacks."

As public attitudes about infidelity altered over time, Alma has gained sympathy simply because she was willing to sacrifice herself to save the life of her young lover.

Cause Célèbre portrays her not as a wicked conspirator, but as a neglected woman, famished for affection. She's even shown kissing the cheek of the policeman who arrests her. After both Alma and her lover tried to protect each other with conflicting confessions, the jury decided to acquit Alma, but convicted Bowman. He served only seven years for the murder and returned to live in Bournemouth. Alma, however, committed suicide a few days after the trial ended.

> "Alma's lawyers think it odd that her sworn testimony to the police made no mention of young George Bowman. He had, after all, been sharing her bed almost since the day he'd come to work for the Rattenburys as odd-job man. But then Alma's story changes almost daily. And while Bowman claims to have murdered under the influence of cocaine, he can't describe what the drug looks like."
>
> —VINCENT PRICE

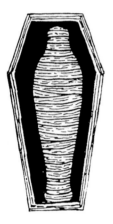

> "According to all my research for the role, Alma was very well loved by all who knew her and hated by everyone who didn't know her. She had the attitude of a 1980s woman in the 1930s, a kind of rebel of her time. She was trapped in the bourgeois life of suburban Bournemouth. . . . This was a story I felt more strongly about than anything I'd ever done on film or in television. . . . It wasn't as if she was in my body but as if she was next to me and was my friend—one I really loved and felt for and wanted justice for."
>
> —HELEN MIRREN

WE, THE ACCUSED

Based on the novel by
Ernest Raymond

MURDER IS SELDOM DEFENSIBLE WHEN IT'S PLOTTED IN ADVANCE, BUT
SOMETIMES THERE ARE CIRCUMSTANCES THAT AT LEAST MAKE US UNDERSTAND,
IF NOT ACTUALLY SYMPATHIZE, WITH KILLERS.

Such is the case with schoolmaster Paul Presset (Ian Holm) who is tormented by his sickly wife, Elinor (Elizabeth Spriggs) whose voice is an incessant whine. With her dreadful wig worn over her ratty hair, she is as appetizing as a round of Limburger cheese left out in the sun. They haven't slept together in years, so sex is but a dim memory to Paul (Elinor wants nothing to do with it). When a plain and equally lonely schoolteacher, Myra Bawne (Angela Down), begins to show interest in Paul, he imagines a new life with her, one that would give him the love and companionship he craves—if he can just get rid of his awful wife.

When his thoughts turn to murder, one might expect the audience to lose interest in him. But to the contrary, he remains a sympathetic character even as he plots Elinor's demise. This is not an unexpected outcome, either. In a number of television movies dealing with the "battered wife syndrome," for instance, audiences have sided emotionally with the abused women who killed their husbands, because viewers understood they had been horribly abused by their husbands. In *We, the Accused*, that Elinor, who vilifies and humiliates her husband, is the abuser and Paul the abused.

Paul uses arsenic from a tin of weed-killer to kill Elinor. Her sudden death arouses little suspicion because she's already suffering from heart disease. It's the sudden appearance of Presset and Myra Bawne as a loving couple that finally prompts suspicion, leads to an exhumation of Elinor's body, and brings about the murder charge that turns them both into fugitives. (Curiously enough, by following his wife's wishes to be buried rather than cremated, Presset supplies the police with the evidence they need.)

PRODUCTION COMPANY
BBC

YEAR
1983

MAIN CAST
Paul Presset
IAN HOLM

Myra Bawne
ANGELA DOWN

Elinor Presset
ELIZABETH SPRIGGS

Detective Inspector Boltro
IAIN CUTHBERTSON

"Within the ranks, the classic poison [arsenic] is often called 'inheritance powder'—because of the tendency of family members to use it on each other!"

—VINCENT PRICE

By the third of five episodes, Paul and Myra are on the run from the police. Paul finally tells Myra, who had no part in the murder, what he has done. She decides to stand by him, even if it makes her an accessory to murder. By watching him with the gentle Myra, we see what kind of husband Paul might have been if he'd never met the inhumane Elinor, and he retains our sympathy. When they're finally apprehended, Paul again displays his true character, showing concern only for the innocent Myra and not himself.

We, the Accused was extremely popular with English critics, who equated the story to the famous case of Dr. Crippen, who also murdered his wife, and to Dennis Potter's acclaimed drama about a similar situation, *Pennies from Heaven*. The sad story of Paul and Myra was adapted from a popular 1935 novel by Ernest Raymond that's often been compared to Theodore Dreiser's *An American Tragedy*.

One of the first realistic, character-driven crime novels, *We, the Accused* was praised for its accuracy and faithful depiction of courtroom, prison, and death-row scenes. The author, Ernest Raymond, had, in fact, accompanied a real police detective on several cases to give his writing an authentic feel and had even spent considerable time talking with a man who received a last-minute reprieve after months on death row. It is thought by some that Raymond's novel had certain influence on the movement for abolition of the death penalty in England.

Of Mysterious Parentage:

AUTHOR
ERNEST RAYMOND

Raymond was a former Anglican priest who gave up his holy orders to concentrate on books that frequently criticized middle-class values and concerned a search for faith. (For that reason, it may be significant that Presset disguises himself as a minister while running from the police.) Though *We, the Accused* is considered his best novel (when it was published in 1935, the *New York Times* called it "an example of a perfect novel"), Raymond came to prominence with his first novel, *Tell England* (1922), which was based on his experiences as a young army chaplain at Gallipoli, where thousands were slaughtered.

Raymond, who died in 1974 at age 86, was a fascinating character in his own right. He and his cousin, Dorothy, were raised in a strange household where everybody seemed related, but nobody had the same surname. When he investigated his family background, he learned he was illegitimate, Dorothy was his sister, not his cousin, that their real father was the general who ran their household, and that his real mother was a woman who lived nearby. That's why it's not surprising that many of Raymond's 50-plus novels deal with the evil that often lurks in otherwise respectable middle-class families.

THE LIMBO CONNECTION

Based on the novel
by Derry Quinn

NOTHING BRINGS ON ACUTE PARANOIA LIKE BEING SUSPECTED OF MURDER—AND NOT KNOWING FOR SURE THAT YOU'RE INNOCENT. THAT'S THE DILEMMA OF SCREENWRITER MARK OMNEY (JAMES BOLAM) IN *THE LIMBO CONNECTION*, A CRITICALLY-ACCLAIMED THREE-PART THRILLER.

His marriage and just about everything in his life is on the rocks—especially the liquor he swills down in growing quantities. He drinks to forget about the unrelenting case of writer's block that has brought his career—and his earning power—to a standstill. In the meantime, his wife, Clare (Suzanne Bertish), is raking in money as a popular London gossip columnist. Whenever she berates him for all this, he feels like she's running his aching head through a pencil sharpener. The result is usually a furious quarrel, sometimes in public places, with plenty of humiliation to go around.

LOST WEEKNIGHT

After one of these fiery arguments, Mark goes pub-crawling and manages to lose about 12 hours of his sorry life in a boozy blackout. All he remembers is picking up an old girl-friend, actor Annabelle Fraser (Rosalind Ayers), and hitting a few hot spots. When he finally sobers up, he learns Clare has been in an auto accident and has disappeared from the clinic where she was taken. When several days pass and Clare's still missing, the police begin to consider foul play—and guess who's their prime suspect?

Put yourself in Mark's shoes: He's reasonably sure he's not capable of murder, no matter how mad Clare sometimes made him, but how can he convince the coppers of that with his miserable record? His only hope seems to be in finding out what happened to Clare before they decide to arrest him for her murder. Tautly directed by Robert Tronson

PRODUCTION COMPANY
Thames Television

YEAR
1983

MAIN CAST
Mark Omney
JAMES BOLAM

Annabelle Fraser
ROSALIND AYERS

Clare Omney
SUZANNE BERTISH

Dr. Walcott Brown
MICHAEL CULVER

Blanche Terraine
BEATRIX LEHMANN

in the style of an old-fashioned thriller, *The Limbo Connection* is suffused with a mood of urban paranoia as Mark wonders whom to trust while retracing Clare's movements.

When he learns Clare drove her car off the road because she was suffering from severe food poisoning, Mark wonders if someone purposely poisoned her. Gossip columnists make lots of enemies. And what about Annabelle? Could jealousy have driven her to kill Clare? And then there's the mysterious Dr. Walcott Brown (Michael Culver), who runs the very private Meadowbrook Clinic where Clare was taken after her accident. Blanche (Beatrix Lehmann), an aging drunk who hangs out at a neighborhood pub, tells Mark the clinic is known for strange goings-on, which may include life-prolonging experiments with elderly female patients in the so-called "twilight wing." Could Clare have become a victim of these experiments?

But most of all Mark worries about what may lurk in the dark recesses of his own mind. If Clare represented all that was wrong with his life, could he have "erased" her from it during that long blackout? Ultimately, all Mark's questions are answered in suspenseful classic thriller fashion.

MELISSA

Written by Francis Durbridge

IF THE FRAME FITS, BY ALL MEANS *DON'T* BUY IT! THAT'S THE

OPERATING PRINCIPLE IN MOST MYSTERIES OF THE "I'VE BEEN FRAMED!" GENRE,

SO WHY AREN'T THE POLICE MORE UNDERSTANDING?

**PRODUCTION
COMPANY**
BBC

YEAR
1982

MAIN CAST
Guy Foster
PETER BARKWORTH

Melissa Foster
MOIRA REDMOND

Paula Hepburn
JOAN BENHAM

Felix Hepburn
RONALD FRASER

Don Page
RAY LONNEN

Detective Chief
Inspector Carter
PHILIP VOSS

Take the case of journalist Guy Foster (Peter Barkworth) in *Melissa*. When friends Felix and Paula Hepburn (Ronald Fraser, Joan Benham) arrive to take Guy and his wife, Melissa (Moira Redmond), to a party being given by famous race car driver Don Page (Ray Lonnen), he begs off. His newspaper has gone out of business, and he's struggling to finish the novel he hopes will mean a new career for him.

Later that evening, Melissa calls to tell him that one of the party guests, a wealthy investor, would like to meet him and discuss his plan to publish a magazine. She asks Guy to meet her at the man's home and he reluctantly agrees. Driving there, he is forced to slow down by emergency vehicles partially blocking the roadway. Then he sees the body of a woman being carried down an embankment. Looking closer, he sees it's Melissa. She has been strangled.

A TANGLED WEB

Almost immediately, Guy is suspected. It seems Melissa never reached the party because she had forgotten her handbag at home and went back to get it. When she didn't turn up, Felix called the Fosters, but nobody answered. What about the wealthy investor Melissa told Guy about on the phone? The party guests say no such person attended the affair. Most incriminating, though, is the fact that Guy and Melissa had not been getting along—and too many people know it.

The vise of suspicion tightens further when police trace a doctor's prescription found in Melissa's handbag. Guy tells them he has never heard of the doctor, but the

doctor, a neurologist, says Melissa had consulted him about her husband's temper tantrums, and Guy had become his patient. The receptionist confirms that Guy had visited the doctor's office. Police then learn that Melissa's friend Don Page had recommended she see the doctor because she was so frightened of her husband.

At times doubting his own sanity—and who can wonder—Guy has no choice but to try to get to the bottom of the mystery. But the deeper he probes into what appears more and more to be a frame-up, the more he's tangled in the web of suspicion, which ultimately includes yet another murder. Before Guy finally is cleared of charges and Melissa's real murderer is revealed, he uncovers a treacherous conspiracy of deceit, blackmail, and murder.

AUTHOR'S HOOK

Melissa was the creation of veteran dramatist Francis Durbridge, who was better known to mystery readers under his pen name Paul Temple, which he shared as a joint pseudonym with other writers. Besides his Paul Temple detective stories, Durbridge was the prolific author of radio and television serials for the BBC. Several of his stories became feature films, including *Postmark for Danger* (1955). Durbridge's specialty in his serialized dramas was the "hook"—a stunning development at the end of each episode that made sure his audience would be back for the next chapter. That device was certainly on display in *Melissa*.

THE PARANORMAL

*One of life's great mysteries is
whether or not there's another plane of
existence beyond our own. It's a subject so
perplexing that these unusual stories
had to be included on Mystery!.*

- *MISS MORISON'S GHOSTS*
- *SHADES OF DARKNESS*

MISS MORISON'S GHOSTS

*Based on the book The Adventure
by Elizabeth Morison and Frances Lamont*

**IN THE ANNALS OF UNEXPLAINED PHENOMENA, THE STORY OF WHAT
TWO DISTINGUISHED EDUCATORS—ANN MOBERLY AND ELEANOR JOURDAIN—
MAY OR MAY NOT HAVE EXPERIENCED DURING A TOUR OF VERSAILLES IN 1901
STILL STIRS SERIOUS DEBATE BETWEEN BELIEVERS AND NONBELIEVERS.**

**PRODUCTION
COMPANY**
Anglia Television

YEAR
1983

MAIN CAST
Miss Elizabeth Morison
DAME WENDY HILLER

Miss Frances Lamont
HANNAH GORDON

The Reverend Oliver Hodgson
BOSCO HOGAN

Dr. Hadley
VIVIAN PICKLES

Lord Kavanagh
NIALL TOIBIN

Yet there's little debate about the fact that once their story was adapted for television, it became the most offbeat and perplexing single program in the long history of Mystery!, a ghost story with feminist ramifications called *Miss Morison's Ghosts*.

It all began when Miss Moberly decided to retire as principal of St. Hugh's, an exclusive college for women that was hoping to be accepted as one of the colleges of all-male Oxford University. Her successor, Eleanor Jourdain, was hired on as vice-principal to learn the job under the retiring administrator. In order that they might get to know each other better, Miss Moberly proposed that they travel together on a holiday to France.

VISITATIONS AT VERSAILLES

But when the two women reached the enormous palace at Versailles, not far from Paris, they had an experience that not only forced them to know each other a lot better, but also bonded them for life: They took a stroll through the elaborate palace gardens and suddenly found themselves mingling with Marie Antoinette and her court! Moberly and Jourdain were both intelligent, well-grounded women who knew it just wasn't possible to mill about with people who had died more than 100 years earlier. Yet they both saw what they saw and felt what they felt. Though they confided what they'd been through to friends, they soon realized nobody was going to believe them. They spent ten years researching the subject and came up with such convincing evidence (which they published in a book called *The Adventure*) that many believed in the truth of much of their account. Others were won over by the fact that they were published by one of the most reputable English publishers. In their book, however, the women changed their names and the name of their school to avoid further ridicule. Miss Moberly became Elizabeth Morison, Miss Jourdain became Frances Lamont, and St. Hugh's became St. Gilbert's. Still, the news of what they claimed to have seen spread far enough to jeopardize their plan to have their school accepted into Oxford. Male opponents of the idea used their "ghost" story as an excuse to deride their suitability for inclusion at Oxford.

Ian Curteis' television adaptation of their story identified them with the pseudonyms they used in the early editions of their book. Both roles were played by outstanding British actors—Dame Wendy Hiller as Miss Morison and Hannah Gordon as Miss Lamont—who portrayed them as distraught, but sincere women struggling to find an explanation for what they'd seen that would satisfy the men then ruling Oxford.

RETROCOGNITION OR HALLUCINATION?

Both women were single and the daughters of clergymen. Both also had experienced psychic "episodes" in the past. They had never met until shortly before the Versailles incident and neither had been involved in any kind of prank or bizarre report before. Living with the aftermath of their experience plunged them into years of psychic research and a friendship that lasted the rest of their lives. Did they actually see the spirits of Marie Antoinette and members of her court? Some believe they may have experienced "retrocognition"—the supernormal awareness of past events—while others think they may have shared a "telepathic hallucination." Their ability to describe in great detail the dress, behavior, and speech of the "ghosts" continues to baffle critics. And the story of their curious adventure, with the bigotry against women it revealed at Oxford, remains an unforgettable episode of Mystery!.

"At the turn of the century, systematic investigation of psychical or paranormal events had been seriously researched for several previous decades. This included the study of telepathy, pre-vision, apparitions of the deceased, and the movement of objects in a manner unknown to the physical sciences. The impetus for launching modern psychical research came from a group of scholars at Cambridge University in England who felt it was scandalous that numerous reports from serious and trustworthy people regarding such experiences should receive no scientific investigation. In London, with the help of other leading scholars, they formed a strong and effective scientific group called the Society for Psychical Research. Within a few years, many outstanding British intellectuals were active members. The group developed a systematic program of investigation into problems varying as widely as experimental telepathy, hallucinations, and the observation of spiritist mediums—in or out of 'trance.'"

—VINCENT PRICE

SHADES OF DARKNESS

Based on stories by Edith Wharton, May Sinclair,
Walter de la Mare, C. H. B. Kitchin,
and L. P. Hartley

**PRODUCTION
COMPANY**
Granada Television

YEAR
1984

BEWITCHED
————

THE INTERCESSOR
————

SEATON'S AUNT
————

*THE LADY'S MAID'S
BELL*
————

AFTERWARD
————

THE MAZE
————

FEET FOREMOST

IN A RARE TIP OF THE HAT TO THE IMPORTANCE OF GHOSTS
AND OTHER UNEXPLAINED PHENOMENA TO THE MYSTERY GENRE, MYSTERY!
DEVOTED SEVEN CONSECUTIVE WEEKS OF ITS FOURTH SEASON TO NOTHING
BUT STORIES OF THE PARANORMAL, ALL BASED ON FAMOUS SHORT
STORIES BY WELL-KNOWN WRITERS.

For certain kinds of strictly rational mystery fans, ghosts belong in a different department of the literary world: the one where writers like Stephen King, Clive Barker, Peter Straub, and Dean Koontz milk a very productive cash cow. But the fact is many proper mysteries include a suggestion of the supernatural, and many rational characters in mysteries fall back on a belief in ghosts when they're frightened badly enough—just the way some atheists wind up praying in foxholes when the bombardment begins.

WHARTON'S PHANTOMS

Author Edith Wharton, not normally known for ghost stories, clearly seems to accept the probability of paranormal visitations in three stories that appeared on *Shades of Darkness.* In *Bewitched,* Eileen Atkins *(She Fell Among Thieves)* plays the wife of a once robust man who seems to be wasting away to nothing. She knows why: He's having a love affair with the restless ghost of another villager's dead daughter. The local minister takes her seriously, because he knows the villagers once burned a member of the same family for witchcraft.

Following Wharton's tale came *The Intercessor,* based on a story by British novelist May Sinclair, in which a young historian, played by John Duttine, seeks a quiet place in

the country where he can write in peace. His sole stipulation: He can't abide children because they're so noisy. So, naturally, he's kept awake nights by the eerie sound of a ghostly child crying.

The third story was *Seaton's Aunt* by Walter de la Mare, a distinguished essayist and author who not only believed in ghosts, but claimed to have seen three of them in his lifetime. In this story, a schoolboy is terrified of his aunt (Mary Morris), but is forced to live with her when his parents are killed. The young man believes his aunt actually draws vital energy from him in order to sustain her own life. He sets out to prove his fears are real by inviting a school friend to spend the night with him.

Following was another tale by Edith Wharton, *The Lady's Maid's Bell,* which was Wharton's first ghost story. Joanna David *(Rebecca)* starred as Hartley, the new maid to Mr. and Mrs. Brympton, whose household is believed to be haunted by the spirit of their last maid, Emma. Sure enough, the ghostly Emma soon turns up, drawing Hartley into the scandalous goings-on between Mrs. Brympton and her randy next-door neighbor, Mr. Ranford.

UNUSUAL CURE FOR TYPHOID

In **The Lady's Maid's Bell** *by Edith Wharton, the maid who consorts with ghosts had recently recovered from a bout with typhoid fever. In real life, Wharton, at age 9, suffered a relapse of a serious typhoid infection after reading a ghost story that terrified her. From then on, she was unable to sleep in the same room with any book containing a ghost story for fear of coming down with fever again. Wharton later confessed she didn't get over that fear until she was 28.*

"It is in the warm darkness of the prenatal fluid, far below our conscious reason, that the faculty dwells with which we apprehend the ghosts we may not be endowed with the gift of seeing."

—EDITH WHARTON

Another Wharton story—*Afterward*—came next. It was an unusual twist on the standard story of the young newlyweds who buy a beautiful old house only to find it's haunted. In this case, a young American husband and his wife come to England, purposely looking for a grand old haunted house. They get the house and are assured a ghost will make an appearance before too long. For once, the real estate agent didn't sell them a bill of goods. There is a ghost, all right, but it's one the husband hoped he'd never have to face.

Sixth in the series was *The Maze*, based on a story by detective writer C. H. B. Kitchin. Francesca Annis *(Partners in Crime)* plays Catherine, a woman who comes back to her ancestral home after many years. Her 8-year-old daughter, Daisy, is fascinated by the maze of hedges in the garden, but Catherine is deathly afraid of what might lurk there. One day Daisy takes the hand of a strange man and follows him into the maze.

The final story, L. P. Hartley's *Feet Foremost*, is the only one that takes place in modern times. It stars Jeremy Kemp as Anthony, a young man who kindly helps a disabled woman into the Ampleforth house, unaware of the legend of Lady Elinor, a ghost who waits to be carried across the threshold of this very same house and then wreaks vengeance on the bearer. When Anthony seems to be stricken with a sudden, debilitating disease, he seeks a way for the curse to be lifted.

After showing these seven pure ghost stories, Mystery! put the subject away on the back shelf and went back to more traditional mysteries. There hasn't been a genuine ghost story since.

GHOSTLY VISITS TO MYSTERY!

Daphne du Maurier's classic **Rebecca** *wouldn't be quite so haunting if Mrs. Danvers didn't keep reminding us that her dead mistress might be watching over Manderley. In Antonia Fraser's* **Quiet As a Nun,** *investigator Jemima Shore doesn't believe in ghosts, but she still trembles as she climbs the shaky ladder to the mysterious dark tower at Blessed Eleanor's Convent after hearing the schoolgirls' prattle about seeing the ghostly Black Nun. In Francis Durbridge's* **Melissa,** *hero Guy Foster wakes from a night of drinking to answer a persistently ringing telephone and the voice on the other end seems to be his wife, Melissa—even though he has personally seen her dead body. And what would Conan Doyle's* **The Hound of the Baskervilles** *be without the threat of that ghostly killer-dog?*

"[Edith Wharton] admitted that writing a ghost story was never easy. She thought that it was not enough just to believe in ghosts or even to have seen one—the only suggestion that Wharton made to the prospective ghost writer was that the teller of supernatural tales should be well frightened in the telling."

—VINCENT PRICE

"Writers whose work concerns the occult are not blind to the sexual connotations often associated with ghosts. One of the reasons Edith Wharton's ghost tales are so effective is that they often revolve on the working of emotional forces, often times erotic in nature, instead of being merely about bloodless apparitions."

—VINCENT PRICE

"[British novelist] L. P. Hartley follows the lead of his mentor, Henry James, whose ghosts in The Turn of the Screw are probably the most famous of all modern literature. James and Hartley were convinced that for one to truly feel the ghostly presence, the writer must develop the history of a character's normal relationship to it. But Hartley also knew that there must come a time—and it must strike the reader with a shock of surprise and horror, a tingling of the spine—when we realize that the ghost is not, after all, one of us."

—VINCENT PRICE

IV

CASE CLOSED

TRIVIA QUIZ

SCORING

90–100 CORRECT ANSWERS
YOU'VE ANSWERED WITH *ABSOLUTE CONVICTION*; OBVIOUSLY YOU'VE GOT *A TASTE FOR DEATH*.

80–89 CORRECT ANSWERS
YOU'LL UNDOUBTEDLY BE A MYSTERY FAN UNTIL YOUR *DYING DAY*.

70–79 CORRECT ANSWERS
A SCORE NOT QUITE GOOD ENOUGH TO BRING HOME TO *MOTHER, LOVE*; PERHAPS YOU'LL DO BETTER THE *SECOND TIME AROUND*.

UNDER 70 CORRECT ANSWERS
WE TELL YOU THIS WITH NO *MALICE AFORETHOUGHT*: THIS QUIZ HAS CLEARLY FOUND YOU *DRIVEN TO DISTRACTION*.

—1—

In which story does this cuddly canine appear?

—2—

Who is Melissa?

a. *the kidnapped daughter of a politician*
b. *an escaped serial murderess*
c. *an actress slain while performing on stage*
d. *the purportedly-dead wife of a journalist*

—3—

Three of this renowned American author's short stories are dramatized in *Shades of Darkness*. Who is she?

—4—

Helena Vesey's overbearing *Mother Love* is directed at her daughter Angela. True or False?

—5—

Which two *Inspector Morse* stories find Morse and Lewis leaving England?

BONUS QUESTION:
Where do they go?

—6—

Which sleuth solves the mystery of *The Black Tower*?

a. *Hercule Poirot*
b. *Adam Dalgliesh*
c. *Sergeant Cribb*
d. *Maigret*

BONUS QUESTION:
How?

—7—

At what point in the story do we meet the eponymous *Rebecca*?

—8—

Match the real names and *noms de plume* of these mystery authors:

a. *Anthony Berkeley Cox*
b. *Elizabeth Mackintosh*
c. *Roger Longrigg*
d. *Edith Pargeter*

1. *Ellis Peters*
2. *Domini Taylor*
3. *Frances Iles*
4. *Josephine Tey*

—9—

Who finds himself in a compromising situation in *Rumpole and the Miscarriage of Justice*?

a. *Horace Rumpole*
b. *Claude Erskine-Brown*
c. *Samuel Ballard*
d. *Mr. Justice Featherstone*

—10—

Who is Laura Fairlie's new husband in *The Woman in White*?

a. *Walter Hartright*
b. *Count Fosco*
c. *Sir Percival Glyde*
d. *Frederick Fairlie*

—11—

In which century do the *Cadfael* mysteries take place?

a. **10th**

b. **12th**

c. **14th**

d. **16th**

—12—

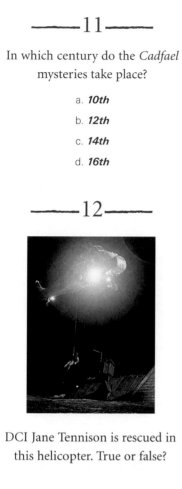

DCI Jane Tennison is rescued in this helicopter. True or false?

—13—

What connection does *Quiet As a Nun*'s Jemima Shore have with deceased nun Sister Miriam?

—14—

Who accompanies Miss Marple in her search for the truth in *Nemesis*?

a. **her friend Margery**

b. **her nephew Raymond**

c. **her assistant Grace**

d. **her godson Lionel**

BONUS QUESTION:
What is the name of the village where the mystery is unraveled?

—15—

Match the sleuths with their police contacts/official supervisors:

a. **Poirot**

b. **Morse**

c. **Jane Tennison**

d. **Tommy and Tuppence**

e. **Miss Marple**

1. **Chief Superintendant Strange**

2. **Chief Inspector Japp**

3. **Inspector Marriott**

4. **Chief Superintendant Mike Kernan**

5. **Detective Inspector Slack**

—16—

Who are the Baker Street Irregulars?

—17—

In *Inspector Morse* Kevin Whately portrays Morse's voluble sidekick Lewis; in which of the *Miss Marple* mysteries is he seen as the far-from-talkative Detective Sergeant Fletcher?

a. **A Murder Is Announced**

b. **Sleeping Murder**

c. **Murder at the Vicarage**

d. **Nemesis**

—18—

Where do Charters and Caldicott make their very first dramatic appearance?

—19—

Who is Inspector Alleyn's mother?

—20—

Who is Poirot's faithful secretary?

a. **Miss Peach**

b. **Miss Lemon**

c. **Miss Berry**

d. **Miss Appleton**

—21—

In *The Memoirs of Sherlock Holmes*, what is in *The Cardboard Box*?

—22—

Who witnesses the murder of the artists' model in *Artists in Crime*?

—23—

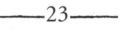

This shooting takes place in *Die Kinder*. True or false?

—24—

Why does steeplechase jockey Sid Halley give up the racing game?

—25—

What is a gallowglass?

a. *a feudal term for a servant*

b. *a scene of medieval execution*

c. *a cathedral window*

d. *a horror-film villain*

—26—

The first case solved by P. D. James' Inspector Dalgliesh on Mystery! involved the murder of his wife. True or False?

BONUS QUESTION:
What is Dalgliesh's hobby?

—27—

To whom does Dr. Jekyll (and Mr. Hyde) become engaged?

a. *Annabelle Fraser*

b. *Anna Massey*

c. *Ann Coggeshall*

d. *Anne Catherick*

—28—

In *The Memoirs of Sherlock Holmes*, what is *The Red Circle*?

a. *a valuable ruby*

b. *a plate of fine china*

c. *a brotherhood of killers*

d. *a bloodshot eye*

—29—

While holding court at Pommeroy's, what wine does Rumpole of the Bailey prefer?

—30—

What was Inspector Morse's nickname when he was a student at university?

BONUS QUESTION:
In which story is this revealed?

—31—

In *Maigret on the Defensive*, the Chief Inspector is falsely accused of attempting to intoxicate and seduce a young woman. Why?

—32—

Who is Mycroft Holmes to Sherlock Holmes?

a. *his evil twin*

b. *his long-lost father*

c. *his grandfather*

d. *his older brother*

—33—

Who finds himself on the other side of the law in *The Veiled Lady*?

a. *Inspector Morse*

b. *Poirot*

c. *Sherlock Holmes*

d. *Sergeant Cribb*

BONUS QUESTION
What crime does he commit?

—34—

What conclusions are reached about *Miss Morison's Ghosts*?

—35—

What sort of nefarious goings-on does Miss Marple discover *At Bertram's Hotel*?

a. *art fraud*

b. *white slavery*

c. *blackmail*

d. *drug trafficking*

—36—

Which Poirot mystery does *not* involve a murder?

a. *The Double Clue*

b. *Hickory, Dickory, Dock*

c. *The Cornish Mystery*

d. *The Dream*

—37—

In which series can this still life can be found?

—38—

What real-life ship plays a part in the fictional goings-on in *The Secret Adversary*?

—39—

The industry involved in the intrigue in *Devices and Desires* is:

a. **textile manufacturing**

b. **automobiles**

c. **pornography**

d. **nuclear power**

—40—

What is Sweeney Todd's nickname?

—41—

Who is the accused murderess in *A Dark-Adapted Eye*?

a. **Vera**

b. **Faith**

c. **Eden**

d. **Helen**

BONUS QUESTION:
Who is the victim?

—42—

What was Cadfael's profession before he became a monk?

—43—

In which story does Inspector Morse break the law?

a. **Service of All the Dead**

b. **Absolute Conviction**

c. **Fat Chance**

d. **Twilight of the Gods**

BONUS QUESTION:
How...and why?

—44—

What is the relationship between the two women who comprise *Chandler & Co.?*

a. **sisters**

b. **college roommates**

c. **former sisters-in-law**

d. **ex-wives of the same man**

—45—

Why do government officials pressure Adam Dalgliesh to halt his investigation at a psychiatric clinic in *A Mind to Murder*?

—46—

This hospital tableau is a clue for whom?

a. **Lord Peter Wimsey**

b. **Sergeant Cribb**

c. **Inspector Alleyn**

d. **Hercule Poirot**

—47—

Who is *The Dark Angel*?

BONUS QUESTION:
Name the actor who plays the role.

—48—

Who experiments with these sinister substances?

—49—

When she's not roaming the English countryside solving crimes, where does Miss Marple reside?

BONUS QUESTION:
Where is it located?

—50—

What is Poirot's quarry in *The Adventure of the Western Star*?

a. **a constellation**

b. **a film actor**

c. **a railroad car**

d. **a diamond**

—51—

In *The Day of the Devil*, who is the bad guy trying to get Inspector Morse's goat?

a. **John Peter Barrie**

b. **Charles Arthur Francis**

c. **Richard William Aaron**

d. **Edward Philip Stephen**

BONUS QUESTION:
What has this villain done?

—52—

Kenneth Colley, featured as Adam Dalgliesh's assistant in *Unnatural Causes*, portrays a less-than-honorable Chief Inspector in which *Inspector Morse* story?

—53—

In which story do we meet Campion's future wife?

BONUS QUESTION:
What is her name?

—54—

What is the "classic" name of the character played by Eileen Atkins in *She Fell Among Thieves?*

—55—

Who of the following is *not* a colleague of *Prime Suspect*'s Jane Tennison:

  a. ***Tony Muddyman***

  b. ***Bill Otley***

  c. ***Jane Penhaligon***

  d. ***Robert Oswalde***

—56—

Name the actors who have portrayed Maigret's wife.

BONUS QUESTION:
Which one has had a mystery series of her own, and what is its title?

—57—

Which is *not* based on a true story?

  a. ***Reilly, Ace of Spies***

  b. ***Cause Célèbre***

  c. ***Rebecca***

  d. ***The Man from the Pru***

—58—

Who helped solve this unseemly murder?

—59—

Match the *Partners in Crime* story with the detective whose methods are being parodied there:

  a. ***The Man in the Mist***

  b. ***The Case of the Missing Lady***

  c. ***The Clergyman's Daughter***

  d. ***The Sunningdale Mystery***

  e. ***The Affair of the Pink Pearl***

  1. ***Dr. John Thorndyke***

  2. ***Baroness Orczy's "The Old Man in the Corner"***

  3. ***Father Brown***

  4. ***Roger Sherringham***

  5. ***Sherlock Holmes***

—60—

In *Malice Aforethought*, Edmund Bickleigh contemplates murdering his wife because his mistress tells him she will not marry a divorced man. True or false?

—61—

The intrigue in *Gaudy Night* takes place at the wedding of Lord Peter Wimsey and Harriet Vane. True or false?

—62—

Which of the following is *not* an Agatha Christie character?

  a. ***Theodora Darrell***

  b. ***Colonel Kingston Bruce***

  c. ***Jack Favell***

  d. ***Lucy Eyelesbarrow***

  e. ***Alistair Blunt***

—63—

Who is this man and whom is he after?

—64—

Parker Pyne appears in which of the following *Agatha Christie Stories?*

a. *The Mystery of the Blue Jar* and *The Fourth Man*

b. *Magnolia Blossom* and *The Red Signal*

c. *The Case of the Middle-Aged Wife* and *The Case of the Discontented Soldier*

d. *In a Glass Darkly* and *The Girl in the Train*

—65—

Who is charged with murder in *We, the Accused?*

BONUS QUESTION:
Who is the victim?

—66—

The Woman in White is considered the first English detective story. True or false?

—67—

Put the nine Adam Dalgliesh stories in their proper *published* chronological order. (Hint: This is not the order in which they've been produced for television.)

BONUS QUESTION:
In what order have they been produced for television?

—68—

Whose identity does Brat Farrar claim?

a. *Patrick Ashby*

b. *Alec Loding*

c. *George Ledingham*

d. *Mark Greenstreet*

BONUS QUESTION:
What is the true relationship between the two men?

—69—

What is the real name of *My Cousin Rachel?*

—70—

Which sleuth is interested in these forensic exhibits?

—71—

Lord Peter Wimsey meets Harriet Vane for the first time when she is on trial for killing her lover. True or false?

—72—

In *The Million Dollar Bond Robbery,* exactly how does Poirot get to the United States?

—73—

Who is revealed as the traitor in *Game, Set, and Match?*

—74—

Other than co-starring in *Mother Love,* what else do Diana Rigg and David McCallum have in common?

—75—

The program title *Die Kinder* refers to a gentle way to commit murder. True or false?

—76—

What discovery leads to the investigation in *Prime Suspect 2?*

a. *a buried female skeleton*

b. *a burned-out tenement flat*

c. *a pocket diary with incriminating phone numbers*

d. *the body of a slain police officer*

—77—

The Mazarin Stone, dramatized in *The Memoirs of Sherlock Holmes,* is actually based on *two* Conan Doyle stories. What is the second one?

—78—

Which of the *Agatha Christie Stories* involves the death of Sir Alington West?

a. *Magnolia Blossom*

b. *The Manhood of Edward Robinson*

c. *The Fourth Man*

d. *The Red Signal*

BONUS QUESTION:
How does he die?

—79—

Who is/are fleeing from the helicopter?

a. *Elly Chandler and Dee Tate*

b. *Oliver and Diane Priest*

c. *Bernard Samson*

d. *Sandor*

—80—

In *The Affair at the Victory Ball*, as what literary figure does Poirot's colleague Captain Hastings attend a masquerade?

BONUS QUESTION:
What is Hastings' first name?

—81—

Who is the first murder victim in *A Taste for Death*?

a. *Domimic Swayne*

b. *Lady Ursula Berowne*

c. *Theresa Nolan*

d. *Sir Paul Berowne*

BONUS QUESTION:
How does he/she meet his/her demise?

—82—

In *Dying Day*, where does Anthony Skipling's paranoid nightmare begin?

—83—

Which of the following actors has *not* portrayed Dr. Jekyll and Mr. Hyde?

a. *David Hemmings*

b. *Fredric March*

c. *John Malkovich*

d. *Jerry Lewis*

e. *John Barrymore*

BONUS QUESTION:
Who won an Academy Award for the role?

—84—

Reilly, Ace of Spies is based on the real-life exploits of Sigmund Rosenblum. True or false?

—85—

Who is the object of Alan Bates' quest in *Oliver's Travels?*

BONUS QUESTION:
Does he succeed?

—86—

Game, Set, and Match is based on a Len Deighton novel of the same name. True or false?

—87—

Which *Father Brown* story takes place in Paris?

BONUS QUESTION:
What gruesome discovery is made there?

—88—

These co-stars of *Cause Célèbre* also star on their own in two popular mystery series. Who are they?

—89—

Name four (dramatized) Agatha Christie mysteries that are inspired by nursery rhymes.

—90—

Sergeant Cribb investigates suspicious goings-on at a music hall in *Swing, Swing Together*. True or false?

—91—

Who has a cameo appearance in the final episode of *Rumpole of the Bailey*?

—92—

Who among these mysterious ladies has *not* been named a Dame?

a. *Wendy Hiller*

b. *P. D. James*

c. *Diana Rigg*

d. *Agatha Christie*

e. *Ngaio Marsh*

—93—

In *The Limbo Connection*, whose disappearance is being investigated?

a. *Annabella Fraser*

b. *Clare Omney*

c. *Mark Omney*

d. *Blanche Terraine*

—94—

This body was found in which show?

—95—

How does a chunk of ice figure in Campion's *Case of the Late Pig*?

—96—

Agatha Christie's Miss Marple mysteries are set in the years immediately preceding World War II. True or false?

—97—

Who is Vera's lover in *Praying Mantis*?

—98—

How is the victim killed in *The Man from the Pru*?

a. *shot*

b. *stabbed*

c. *poisoned*

d. *beaten*

BONUS QUESTION:
Who is the murder victim?

—99—

Mel Martin plays Adam Dalgliesh's romantic interest in which *two* stories?

BONUS QUESTION:
Why does she leave him?

—100—

These actors are best known for their starring sleuth roles, but also appear in other mystery series. Match the performer with the show on which he/she guests:

a. *Roy Marsden*

b. *Francesca Annis*

c. *John Thaw*

d. *Leo McKern*

e. *Patrick Malahide*

1. *Shades of Darkness*

2. *Sherlock Holmes (The Last Vampyre)*

3. *Inspector Morse*

4. *Reilly, Ace of Spies*

5. *Sherlock Holmes (The Sign of Four)*

ANSWERS

1. *The Hound of the Baskervilles* (Sherlock Holmes)
2. d.
3. Edith Wharton.
4. False; Angela is the wife of Helena's son Kit, on whom her *Mother Love* is lavished.
5. *Death of the Self, Promised Land.*
   BONUS QUESTION: Italy, Australia.
6. b.
   BONUS QUESTION: He discovers contraband hidden in patients' wheelchairs (interestingly, a nearly identical device was used in the *Inspector Morse* story *Deceived by Flight*).
7. Never; she is already dead by the time the story begins.
8. a-3, b-4, c-2, d-1.
9. d.
10. c.
11. b.
12. False. Commander Adam Dalgliesh is rescued in it.
13. They were friends in convent school.
14. d.
    BONUS QUESTION: Abbey Ducis.
15. a-2, b-1, c-4, d-3, e-5.
16. A group of street urchins who occasionally help Sherlock Holmes.
17. a.
18. In Alfred Hitchcock's film *The Lady Vanishes.*
19. The Dowager Duchess of Devonshire.

20. b.
21. A pair of human ears.
22. All the artists in Agatha Troy's studio who were preparing to sketch her.
23. False. It takes place in *Game, Set, and Match.*
24. Halley is thrown from a horse and his hand is crushed, permanently disabling him.
25. a.
26. False; Dalgliesh's first case involves the murder of a teenage girl in Norfolk (his wife died in childbirth).
    BONUS QUESTION: Writing poetry.
27. c.
28. c.
29. Château Thames Embankment or Château Fleet Street.
30. Pagan.
    BONUS QUESTION: *Deceived by Flight.*
31. Dr. Francois Melan seeks to discredit Maigret because he (inaccurately) thinks the Chief Inspector is on to *his* perverse practice of murdering women; of course in the end Maigret does figure this out and is himself vindicated.
32. d.
33. b.
    BONUS QUESTION: Burglary; Poirot is arrested for breaking into the home of Mr. Lavington.
34. Perhaps the women do have the "gift" of awareness of past events, or maybe at Versailles they share a telepathic halluci-

nation . . . essentially, it remains a mystery.
35. c.
36. a.
37. *The Limbo Connection.*
38. The *Lusitania.*
39. d.
40. The Demon Barber of Fleet Street.
41. a.
    BONUS QUESTION: Eden.
42. He was a professional soldier in the Crusades.
43. a.
    BONUS QUESTION: He lies on the witness stand to protect accused accessory-to-murder Ruth Rawlinson, with whom he has become romantically involved.
44. c.
45. Burned-out agents are sometimes sent there, and the government doesn't want this revealed to the public.
46. c.
47. Uncle Silas Ruthyn.
    BONUS QUESTION: Peter O'Toole.
48. Dr. Jekyll.
49. St. Mary Mead.
    BONUS QUESTION: In the home county of Downshire, about 25 miles south of London.
50. d.
51. a.
    BONUS QUESTION: He is a murderous occultist who has escaped from an asylum.
52. *Second Time Around.*

53. *Sweet Danger.*
    BONUS QUESTION: Lady Amanda Fitton.

54. Vanity Fair.

55. c. (Jane Penhaligon is the female detective in Robbie Coltrane's *Cracker* series of mysteries).

56. Ciaran Madden, Barbara Flynn.
    BONUS QUESTION: Barbara Flynn, *Chandler & Co.*

57. c.

58. Miss Marple.

59. a-3, b-5, c-4, d-2, e-1.

60. True.

61. False; it takes place at Harriet's college reunion (however, at the end of the story she does agree to marry Wimsey).

62. c.

63. Mansel. He's after Vanity Fair in *She Fell Among Thieves.*

64. c.

65. London schoolmaster Paul Presset.
    BONUS QUESTION: His wife Elinor.

66. False; that distinction goes to another Wilkie Collins mystery, *The Moonstone.*

67. *Cover Her Face* (1962), *A Mind to Murder* (1963), *Unnatural Causes* (1967), *Shroud for a Nightingale* (1971), *The Black Tower* (1975), *Death of an Expert Witness* (1977), *A Taste for Death* (1986), *Devices and Desires* (1989), *Original Sin* (1994).
    BONUS QUESTION: *Death of an Expert Witness, Shroud for a Nightingale, Cover Her Face, The Black Tower, A Taste for Death, Devices and Desires, Unnatural Causes, A Mind to Murder, Original Sin.*

68. a.
    BONUS QUESTION: There is no blood relation—they are exact looka-likes.

69. Contessa Sangalletti.

70. Inspector Alleyn.

71. True; this occurs in the story *Strong Poison.*

72. On the inaugural voyage of the *Queen Mary.*

73. Fiona Samson.

74. Both portrayed supersleuths in 1960s-era television series, Rigg as Emma Peel in *The Avengers* and McCallum as Ilya Kuryakin in *The Man from U.N.C.L.E.*

75. False; it refers to the children kidnapped by the German ex-husband of Sidonie Reiger.

76. a.

77. *The Three Garridebs.*

78. d.
    BONUS QUESTION: He is shot.

79. b.

80. The Scarlet Pimpernel.
    BONUS QUESTION: Arthur.

81. d.
    BONUS QUESTION: His throat is cut.

82. On a London commuter train.

83. They all did; Jerry Lewis' *The Nutty Professor* (remade in 1996 with Eddie Murphy in the title role) is a comedic variation on the Stevenson theme.
    BONUS QUESTION: Fredric March.

84. True; Sidney Reilly is the name Rosenblum took as a spy.

85. Crossword compiler Aristotle.
    BONUS QUESTION: No; Aristotle has been dead for years.

86. False; the series is based on a trilogy of Deighton novels, *Berlin Game, Mexico Set,* and *London Match.*

87. *The Secret Garden.*
    BONUS QUESTION: A decapitated body in the garden.

88. Helen Mirren (*Prime Suspect*) and David Suchet (*Poirot*).

89. *A Pocketful of Rye; Hickory, Dickory, Dock; One, Two, Buckle My Shoe; How Does Your Garden Grow?*

90. False; *Abracadaver* is about a music hall murder (*Swing, Swing Together* involves intrigue at Elfrida College for young ladies).

91. Series creator-writer John Mortimer.

92. b; P. D. James' official name is *Baroness* James of Holland Park of Southwold in the County of Suffolk.

93. b.

94. *My Cousin Rachel.*

95. The killer placed the ice under a heavy stone urn and balanced the urn so that it would fall on the intended victim when the ice melted.

96. True *and* false; Christie's written stories begin circa 1930 and proceed into the 1950s, but the television adaptations place them all in the late 1940s and early 1950s.

97. Christian Magny.

98. d.
    BONUS QUESTION: Julia Wallace.

99. *Cover Her Face* and *Unnatural Causes.*
    BONUS QUESTION: She feels he has too little time for her.

100. a-2, b-1, c-5, d-4, e-3.

LIST OF PHOTOGRAPHS

EDWARD GOREY
Page 8 Edward Gorey and Derek Lamb

SHE FELL AMONG THIEVES
Page 16 Robert Chandos (Malcolm McDowell), left, Vanity Fair (Eileen Atkins), center, Jenny (Karen Dotrice), right

SHERLOCK HOLMES
Page 27 Top: with Irene Adler (Gayle Hunnicutt) in *A Scandal in Bohemia;* bottom: with Dr. Watson (Edward Hardwicke)
Page 28 Top right: with Dr. Watson (David Burke); bottom: the Baker Street Irregulars
Page 29 Holmes and Professor Moriarty (Eric Porter) at the Reichenbach Falls in *The Final Problem*
Page 33 Bottom: Holmes in disguise, with Irene Adler

SERGEANT CRIBB
Page 38 Right: *Wobble to Death*
Page 39 Top: with Police Constable Thackeray (William Simons)

HERCULE POIROT
Page 43 Bottom: *The Tragedy at Marsdon Manor*
Page 44 Top: *Peril at End House;* bottom: with Captain Hastings (Hugh Fraser)
Page 45 Top: Inspector Japp (Philip Jackson); bottom: *The Mysterious Affair at Styles*
Page 48 Left: *Four and Twenty Blackbirds*
Page 49 Left: *Four and Twenty Blackbirds*
Page 50 Bottom: *Triangle at Rhodes*
Page 52 Left: *Murder in the Mews*

LORD PETER WIMSEY
Page 55 With Harriet Vane (Harriet Walter)
Page 57 Top: *Strong Poison;* middle and bottom: *Gaudy Night*
Page 60 *Strong Poison*
Page 61 *Strong Poison*

ALBERT CAMPION
Page 65 With Magersfontein Lugg (Brian Glover) in *Look to the Lady*
Page 67 Left: *Sweet Danger;* right: with Amanda Fitton (Lysette Anthony) in *Sweet Danger*

INSPECTOR MORSE
Page 71 *The Dead of Jericho*
Page 74 Top: with opera star Nicole Burgess (Frances Barber) in *Death of the Self;* left: pathologist Dr. Grayling Russell (Amanda Hillwood)
Page 75 Top left: with Sergeant Lewis (Kevin Whately); bottom right: car dealer Jeremy Boynton (Patrick Malahide) in *Driven to Distraction*
Page 79 Top: with Colin Dexter; middle: Colin Dexter (to the left of Morse) in one of his Hitchcock-like cameos; bottom: *The Day of the Devil*
Page 80 Middle: with Dr. Russell in *The Secret of Bay 5B*
Page 81 Top: Sir John Gielgud in *Twilight of the Gods;* bottom: *Absolute Conviction*

ADAM DALGLIESH
Page 82 *Unnatural Causes*
Page 83 *The Black Tower*
Page 84 Top: with Susannah York in *Devices and Desires;* bottom: with Mel Martin in *Unnatural Causes*
Page 85 Top left and right: *Devices and Desires;* bottom: *A Mind to Murder*

Page 86 Left: *Shroud for a Nightingale*
Page 88 Bottom: with Ann Lambton in *Unnatural Causes*
Page 90 Top: with Wendy Hiller, left, in *A Taste for Death*
Page 91 Bottom: *The Black Tower*
Page 92 Right: *The Black Tower*

PRIME SUSPECT
Page 98 Top: with Det. Sgt. Bill Otley (Tom Bell), left; bottom: with Det. Ch. Sup. Mike Kernan (John Benfield)

INSPECTOR ALLEYN
Page 106 Inspector Alleyn (Patrick Malahide)
Page 107 Inspector Alleyn (Simon Williams)
Page 108 Top: *Artists in Crime;* bottom: with Inspector Fox (William Simons) in *The Nursing Home Murder*
Page 109 Top: Agatha Troy (Belinda Lang) in *Final Curtain;* bottom: *Final Curtain*
Page 111 Bottom right: *The Nursing Home Murder*

MAIGRET
Page 114 Middle, bottom: with Madame Maigret (Barbara Flynn)

TOMMY AND TUPPENCE BERESFORD
Page 128 Bottom: with Albert (Reece Dinsdale)

CHANDLER & CO.
Page 132 Dee Tate (Barbara Flynn), left, Elly Chandler (Catherine Russell)
Page 133 With Elly's ex-husband Max (Christopher Bowen)
Page 134 Left: Larry Blakeston (Peter Capaldi)

MISS MARPLE
Page 141 *A Caribbean Mystery* (not seen on Mystery!)
Page 142 Top right: *Murder at the Vicarage;* bottom: *The Moving Finger*
Page 143 Left: *Sleeping Murder;* right: *They Do It with Mirrors* (not seen on Mystery!)
Page 144 Top: *Murder at the Vicarage;* bottom: *The Mirror Cracked* (not seen on Mystery!)
Page 145 Right: *Murder at the Vicarage*
Page 146 Right: *The Body in the Library;* left: *A Pocketful of Rye*
Page 147 Top: *The Moving Finger;* bottom: *The Body in the Library*

JEMIMA SHORE
Page 149 Mother Ancilla (Renee Asherson)
Page 150 Top: with Tom Amyas (David Burke)

CHARTERS AND CALDICOTT
Page 154 Left: Charters (Robin Bailey); right: Caldicott: Michael Aldridge

BROTHER CADFAEL
Page 164 With Ellis Peters

BERNARD SAMSON
Page 180 Top: Fiona Samson (Mel Martin); bottom: Gloria Kent (Amanda Donohoe)

HORACE RUMPOLE
Page 186 Left: with Phyllida Trant Erskine-Brown (Patricia Hodge)
Page 187 Top: Hilda Rumpole (Marion Mathie); middle: Hilda Rumpole (Peggy Thorpe Bates)
Page 190 Left: Justice Featherstone (Peter Bowles)

Page 193 Top: with Liz Probert (Abigail McKern)

PARKER PYNE
Page 195 Maria Packington (Gwen Watford) in *The Case of the Middle-Aged Wife*
Page 196 Middle and bottom: *The Case of the Middle-Aged Wife*
Page 197 Top: Lady Noreen Elliot (Cherie Lunghi) and Edward Robinson (Nicholas Farrell) in *The Manhood of Edward Robinson;* bottom: Dermot West (Richard Morant) and Claire Trent (Joanna David) in *The Red Signal*

THE DETECTION CLUB
Page 203 Dorothy Sayers holding Eric

MOTHER LOVE
Page 208 Helena Vesey (Diana Rigg), left, Kit Vesey (James Wilby), center, Angela Turner Vesey (Fiona Gillies), right
Page 209 Top: Alex Vesey (David McCallum)
Page 211 Bottom: Ruth Vesey (Isla Blair), left

DR. JEKYLL AND MR. HYDE
Page 213 Right: with Ann Coggeshall (Lisa Harrow)

A DARK ADAPTED EYE, GALLOWGLASS
Page 216 Faith (Helena Bonham Carter), left, Vera (Celia Imrie), center, Eden (Sophie Ward), right
Page 219 Top: Nina Abbott (Arkie Whitely) and Sandor (Paul Rhys); bottom: Nina with Paul Garnet (John McArdle)
Page 220 Right: Joe Herbert (Michael Sheen)
Page 222 Left: Vera with her son; right: Sandor and Joe with Tilly (Claire Hackett)

DYING DAY
Page 223 Anthony Skipling (Ian McKellan) and Doris Skipling (Gwyneth Powell)

SWEENEY TODD
Page 226 Sweeney Todd (Freddie Jones), left
Page 227 Left: with Charley/Charlotte (Mel Martin); top: Mrs. Lovett (Heather Canning)

PRAYING MANTIS
Page 228 Christian Magny (Jonathan Pryce) and Beatrice Manceau (Cherie Lunghi)
Page 229 Right: Beatrice with Paul Canova (Pinkas Braun)

DARK ANGEL
Page 230 Maud Ruthyn (Beatie Edney) and Uncle Silas (Peter O'Toole)
Page 231 Middle: Madame de la Rougierre (Jane Lapotaire)

THE WOMAN IN WHITE
Page 233 Anne Catherick (Deirdra Morris)
Page 234 Top: Laura Fairlie (Jenny Seagrove); bottom: Frederick Fairlie (Ian Richardson)
Page 235 Top left: Laura and Marian Halcombe (Diana Quick); top right: Count Fosco (Alan Badel)

BRAT FARRAR
Page 236 Brat Farrar (Mark Greenstreet), left, Simon Ashby (Mark Greenstreet), right
Page 238 Left: Simon with Eleanor Ashby (Dominique Barnes)

DIE KINDER
Page 239 Lomax (Frederic Forrest), left, Sidonie Reiger (Miranda Richardson), right

MALICE AFORETHOUGHT
Page 242 Julia Bickleigh (Judy Parfitt), left, Dr. Bickleigh (Hywel Bennett), right
Page 243 Left: Dr. Bickleigh with Madeleine Cranmere (Cheryl Campbell)

Page 244 Top: Dr. Bickleigh surrounded by Madeleine and Denny Bourne (Christopher Guard)

REBECCA, MY COUSIN RACHEL
Page 246 Mrs. de Winter (Joanna David), left, Mrs. Danvers (Anna Massey), right
Page 247 Bottom: Max de Winter (Jeremy Brett) with Mrs. de Winter
Page 250 Top: Rachel Sangalletti (Geraldine Chaplin) and Philip (Christopher Guard)

THE MAN FROM THE PRU
Page 254 Julia Wallace (Anna Massey), left, William Wallace (Jonathan Pryce), center, Amy Wallace (Susannah York), right

CAUSE CÉLÈBRE
Page 257 Alma Rattenbury (Helen Mirren), second from left, George Bowman (David Morrissey), right
Page 258 Alma with Francis Rattenbury (Harry Andrews)

WE, THE ACCUSED
Page 259 Myra Bawne (Angela Down) and Paul Presset (Ian Holm)
Page 260 Top: Elinor Presset (Elizabeth Spriggs) with Paul

THE LIMBO CONNECTION
Page 261 Mark Omney (James Bolam)
Page 262 Top: Annabelle Fraser (Rosalind Ayers), center; left: Clare Omney (Suzanne Bertish)

MELISSA
Page 263 Guy Foster (Peter Barkworth)

MISS MORISON'S GHOSTS
Page 266 Miss Elizabeth Morison (Wendy Hiller), left, Miss Frances Lamont (Hannah Gordon), right
Page 267 Bottom right: Miss Morison and Miss Lamont with some Versailles ghosts

SHADES OF DARKNESS
Page 268 Hartley (Joanna David) in *The Lady's Maid's Bell*
Page 269 Right: *The Lady's Maid's Bell*
Page 270 Left: *Bewitched*; right: Mrs. Rutledge (Eileen Atkins), right, in *Bewitched*
Page 271 Top: Garvin (John Duttine), left, in *The Intercessor;* bottom: Catherine (Francesca Annis) in *The Maze*

SHOW CREDITS

*PROGRAMS MARKED BY AN ASTERISK ARE AVAILABLE ON VIDEO.

ADAM DALGLIESH MYSTERIES

Produced by Anglia Television
Based on the novels by P. D. James
Adam Dalgliesh (Roy Marsden)

Death of an Expert Witness
6 episodes
October 24–November 28, 1985
Writer Robin Chapman
Producer John Rosenberg
Director Herbert Wise
Old Mr. Lorimer (Cyril Cusack)
Dr. Maxim Howarth (Barry Foster)
Brenda Pridmore (Chloe Franks)
Dr. Edwin Lorimer (Geoffrey Palmer)
John Massingham (John Vine)

Shroud for a Nightingale
5 episodes
October 9–November 6, 1986
Writer Robin Chapman
Producer John Rosenberg
Director John Gorrie
Stephen Courtney-Briggs (Joss Ackland)
Mary Taylor (Sheila Allen)
Mavis Gearing (Liz Fraser)
Delia Dettinger (Margaret Whiting)

Cover Her Face
5 episodes
March 26–April 23, 1987
Writer Robin Chapman
Producer John Rosenberg
Director John Davies
Deborah Riscoe (Mel Martin)
Eleanor Maxie (Phyllis Calvert)
Sir Reynold Price (Bill Fraser)
Felix Hurst (Julian Glover)

The Black Tower
6 episodes
April 28–June 2, 1988
Writer William Humble
Producer John Rosenberg
Director Ronald Wilson
Maggie Hewson (Pauline Collins)
Father Michael Baddeley
  (Maurice Denham)
Wilfred Anstey (Martin Jarvis)
Grace Williston (Rachel Kempson)
Julius Court (Art Malik)

A Taste for Death
6 episodes
March 22–April 26, 1990
Writer Alick Rowe
Producer John Rosenberg
Director John Davies
Lady Ursula Berowne
  (Dame Wendy Hiller)
Sir Paul Berowne (Bosco Hogan)
Theresa Nolan (Rebecca Saire)
Stephen Lampart (Simon Ward)

Devices and Desires*
6 episodes

October 3–November 7, 1991
Writer Thomas Ellice
Producer John Rosenberg
Director John Davies
Dr. Toby Gledhill (Harry Burton)
Dr. Alex Mair (James Faulkner)
Alice Mair (Gemma Jones)
Meg Dennison (Susannah York)

Unnatural Causes
2 episodes
January 13–20, 1994
Writer Peter Buckman
Producer Hilary Bevan Jones
Director John Davies
Deborah Riscoe (Mel Martin)
Inspector Reckless (Kenneth Colley)
Digby Seton (Simon Chandler)
Justin Bryce (James Cossins)
Oliver Latham (Bill Nighy)

A Mind to Murder
single 2–hour episode
May 9, 1996
Writer uncredited
Producer Hilary Bevan Jones
Director Gareth Davies
Nurse Ambrose (Suzanne Burden)
Professor Etheridge (Frank Finlay)
Peter Nagle (Jerome Flynn)
Godbolt (David Hemmings)
Dr. Baguley (Christopher Ravenscroft)
Neil Casey (Sean Scanlan)

Original Sin
3 episodes
January 1997
Writer Michael Chaplin
Producer Andrew Benson
Director Andrew Grieve
Gabriel Dauntsey (Ian Bannen)
Detective Inspector Daniel Aron
  (Tim Dutton)
Detective Inspector Kate Miskin
  (Lizzie McInnerny)
Claudia Etienne (Amanda Root)
Gerard Etienne (James Wilby)

AGATHA CHRISTIE'S MISS MARPLE*

Produced by BBC
Based on the novels by Agatha Christie
Miss Jane Marple (Joan Hickson)
Detective Inspector Slack (David
  Horovitch)

SERIES I
5 episodes
January 2–30, 1986
Producer Guy Slater

The Body in the Library
3 episodes
Writer T. R. Bowen
Director Silvio Narizzano

Conway Jefferson (Andrew Cruikshank)
Mark Gaskell (Keith Drinkel)
Chief Constable Melchett
  (Frederick Jaeger)
Josie Turner (Trudie Styler)
Dolly Bantry (Gwen Watford)
Colonel Arthur Bantry (Moray Watson)

The Moving Finger
2 episodes
Writer Julia Jones
Director Roy Boulting
Megan Hunter (Deborah Appleby)
Gerry Burton (Andrew Bicknell)
Edward Symmington (Michael Culver)
Joanna Burton (Sabina Franklyn)
Maud Calthrop (Dilys Hamlett)

SERIES II
5 episodes
December 4, 1986–January 15, 1987

A Pocketful of Rye
2 episodes
Writer T. R. Bowen
Producer George Gallaccio
Director Guy Slater
Lance Fortescue (Peter Davison)
Adele Fortescue (Stacey Dorning)
Miss Henderson (Fabia Drake)
Patricia Fortescue (Frances Low)
Detective Inspector Neele
  (Tim Wilkinson)

A Murder Is Announced
3 episodes
Writer Alan Plater
Producer Guy Slater
Director David Giles
Dora Bunner (Renee Asherson)
Detective Inspector Craddock
  (John Castle)
Miss Hinchcliffe (Paola Dionisotti)
Letitia Blacklock (Ursula Howells)
Miss Murgatroyd (Joan Sims)

SERIES III
6 episodes
December 10, 1987–January 28, 1988
Producer George Gallaccio

Nemesis
Writer T. R. Bowen
Director David Tucker
Archdeacon Brabazon (Peter Copley)
Anthea Bradbury-Scott (Anna Cropper)
Michael Rafiel (Bruce Payne)
Lionel Peel (Peter Tilbury)
Clothilde Bradbury-Scott
  (Margaret Tyzack)

Sleeping Murder
Writer Ken Taylor
Director John Davies
Gwenda Reed (Geraldine Alexander)
Raymond West (David McAlister)
Giles Reed (John Moulder-Brown)
Dr. James Kennedy (Frederick Treves)

At Bertram's Hotel
Writer Jill Hyem
Director Mary McMurray
Chief Inspector Davy (George Baker)
Lady Bess Sedgwick
  (Caroline Blakiston)
Lady Selina Hazy (Joan Greenwood)
Elvira Blake (Helena Michell)
Canon Pennyfeather (Preston
  Lockwood)

SERIES IV
4 episodes
February 9–March 16, 1989
Producer George Gallaccio

Murder at the Vicarage
Writer T. R. Bowen
Director Julian Amyes
Anne Protheroe (Polly Adams)
Mrs. Clement (Cheryl Campbell)
Mrs. Price-Ridley (Rosalie Crutchley)
Reverend Len Clement
  (Paul Eddington)
Lawrence Redding (James Hazeldine)

4:50 from Paddington
Writer T. R. Bowen
Director Martyn Friend
Dr. John Quimper (Andrew Burt)
Emma Crackenthorpe (Joanna David)
Luther Crackenthorpe
  (Maurice Denham)
Lucy Eyelesbarrow (Jill Meager)

AGATHA CHRISTIE'S POIROT

Produced by LWT
Based on the novels and stories by
  Agatha Christie
Producer Brian Eastman
Hercule Poirot (David Suchet)
Captain Hastings (Hugh Fraser)
Chief Inspector Japp (Philip Jackson)
Miss Lemon (Pauline Moran)

SERIES I*
9 episodes
January 18–March 15, 1990

The Adventure of the Clapham Cook
Writer Clive Exton
Director Edward Bennett
Arthur Simpson (Dermot Crowley)
Eliza Dunn (Freda Dowie)
Ernestine Todd (Brigit Forsyth)

Murder in the Mews
Writer Clive Exton
Director Edward Bennett
Major Eustace (James Faulkner)
Jane Plenderleith (Juliette Mole)
Laverton West (David Yelland)

The Adventure of Johnnie Waverly
Writer Clive Exton

Director Renny Rye
Marcus Waverly (Geoffrey Bateman)
Ada Waverly (Julia Chambers)
Jessie Withers (Carol Frazer)

Four and Twenty Blackbirds
Writer Russell Murray (Script
Consultant Clive Exton)
Director Renny Rye
Dulcie Lane (Holly de Jong)
George Lorrimer (Richard Howard)
Harry Clarke (Geoffrey Larder)

The Third Floor Flat
Writer Michael Baker
(Script Consultant Clive Exton)
Director Edward Bennett
Patricia Matthews (Suzanne Burden)
Mildred Hope (Amanda Elwes)
Donovan Bailey (Nicholas Pritchard)

Triangle at Rhodes
Writer Stephen Wakelam (Script
Consultant Clive Exton)
Director Renny Rye
Marjorie Gold (Angela Down)
Valentine Chantry (Annie Lambert)
Pamela Lyall (Frances Low)

Problem at Sea
Writer Clive Exton
Director Renny Rye
Ellie Henderson (Ann Firbank)
General Forbes (Roger Hume)
Colonel Clapperton (John Normington)

The King of Clubs
Writer Michael Baker
Director Renny Rye
Bunny Saunders (Jonathan Coy)
Valerie Saintclair (Niamh Cusack)
Henry Reedburn (David Swift)

The Dream
Writer Clive Exton
Director Edward Bennett
Hugo Cornworthy (Alan Howard)
Joanna Farley (Joely Richardson)
Herbert Chudley (Martin Wenner)

THE INCREDIBLE THEFT
October 4, 1990
Writers David Reid, Clive Exton
Director Edward Bennett
Sir George Carrington (John Carson)
Mrs. Vanderlyn (Carmen Du Sautoy)
Lady Mayfield (Ciaran Madden)
Tommy Mayfield (John Stride)

SERIES II*
10 episodes
January 10–March 14, 1991

Peril at End House
2 episodes
Writer Clive Exton
Director Renny Rye
Challenger (John Harding)
Freddie (Alison Sterling)
Nick (Polly Walker)

The Veiled Lady
Writer Clive Exton
Director Edward Bennett
Lady Millicent (Frances Barber)
Mr. Lavington (Terence Harvey)
Mrs. Godber (Carole Hayman)

The Lost Mine
Writers Michael Baker, David Renwick
Director Edward Bennett
Lord Pearson (Anthony Bate)
Reggie Dyer (James Saxon)
Charles Lester (Colin Stinton)

The Cornish Mystery
Writer Clive Exton
Director Edward Bennett
Jacob Radnor (John Bowler)
Edward Pengelly (Jerome Willis)
Mrs. Pengelly (Amanda Walker)

The Disappearance of Mr. Davenheim
Writer David Renwick
Director Andrew Grieve
Matthew Davenheim (Kenneth Colley)
Charlotte Davenheim (Mel Martin)
Gerald Lowen (Tony Mathews)

Double Sin
Writer Clive Exton
Director Richard Spence
Mary Penn (Elspeth Gray)
Miss Dorritt (Caroline Milmot)
Norton Kane (Adam Kotz)

The Adventure of the Cheap Flat
Writer Russell Murray
Director Richard Spence
Stella (Samantha Bond)
Burt (William Hootkins)

The Mysterious Affair at Styles
2 episodes
Writer Clive Exton
Director Ross Devenish
Evelyn Howard (Joanna McCallum)
Alfred Inglethorp (Michael Cronin)
John Cavendish (David Rintoul)

SERIES III*
8 episodes
February 13–April 2, 1992

The Kidnapped Prime Minister
Writer Clive Exton
Director Andrew Grieve
Sir Bernard (Timothy Block)
Imogen Daniels (Lisa Harrow)
Commander Daniels (David Horovitch)

The Adventure of the Western Star
Writer Clive Exton
Director Richard Spence
Gregory Rolf (Oliver Cotton)
Lady Yardley (Caroline Goodall)
Marie Marvelle (Rosalind Bennett)

How Does Your Garden Grow?
Writer Andrew Marshall
Director Brian Farnham
Katrina Reiger (Catherine Russell)
Mary Delafontaine (Anne Stallybrass)
Henry Delafontaine (Tim Wylton)

The Plymouth Express
Writer Rod Beacham
(Script Consultant Clive Exton)
Director Andrew Piddington
Florence Carrington (Shelagh McLeod)
Mr. Halliday (John Stone)
Rupert Carrington (Julian Wadham)

The Tragedy at Marsdon Manor
Writer David Renwick
Director Renny Rye

Susan Maltravers (Geraldine Alexander)
Miss Rawlinson (Anita Carey)
Jonathan Maltravers (Ian McCulloch)

The Million Dollar Bond Mystery
Writer Anthony Horowitz
Director Andrew Grieve
Miranda Brooks (Lizzy McInnerny)
Philip Ridgeway (Oliver Parker)
Mr. Shaw (David Quilter)

The Double Clue
Writer Anthony Horowitz
Director Andrew Piddington
Bernard Parker (David Bamber)
Marcus Hardman (David Lyon)
Countess Vera Rossakoff
(Kika Markham)

Wasps' Nest
Writer David Renwick
Director Brian Farnham
Claude Langton (Peter Capaldi)
Molly Deane (Melanie Jessop)
John Harrison (Martin Turner)

SERIES IV*
6 episodes
November 19, 1992–January 7, 1993

The ABC Murders
2 episodes
Writer Clive Exton
Director Andrew Grieve
Franklin Clarke (Donald Douglas)
Megan Barnard (Pippa Guard)
A. B. Cust (Donald Sumpter)

The Affair at the Victory Ball
Writer Andrew Marshall
Director Renny Rye
Viscount Cronshaw (Mark Crowdy)
Coco Courtney (Haydn Gwynne)
Chris Davidson (Nathaniel Parker)

The Theft of the Royal Ruby
Writers Anthony Horowitz,
Clive Exton
Director Andrew Grieve
Desmond Lee-Wortley
(Nigel le Vaillant)
Sarah Lacey (Helena Michell)
Colonel Lacey (Frederick Treves)

The Mystery of the Spanish Chest
Writer Anthony Horowitz
Director Andrew Grieve
Marguerite Clayton (Caroline
Langrishe)
Colonel Curtiss (John McEnery)
Major Rich (Pip Torrens)

The Mystery of Hunter's Lodge
Writer T. R. Bowen
Director Renny Rye
Harrington Pace (Bernard Horsfall)
Zoe Havering (Diana Kent)
Roger Havering (Jim Norton)

SERIES V*
8 episodes
November 18, 1993–January 6, 1994

The Adventure of the Egyptian Tomb
Writer Clive Exton
Director Peter Barber Fleming
Rupert Bliebner (Paul Birchard)
Lady Willard (Anna Cropper)
Dr. Ames (Rolf Saxon)

Dead Man's Mirror
Writer Anthony Horowitz
Director Brian Eastman
Gervase Chevenix (Iain Cuthbertson)
Ruth (Emma Fielding)
Liss Lingard (Fiona Walker)

*Jewel Robbery at the Grand
Metropolitan*
Writer Anthony Horowitz
Director Ken Grieve
Ed Opalsen (Trevor Cooper)
Margaret Opalsen (Sorcha Cusack)
Celestine (Hermione Norris)

The Adventure of the Italian Nobleman
Writer Clive Exton
Director Brian Farnham
Margherita (Anna Massotti)
Vizzini (David Neal)
Mr. Graves (Leonard Preston)

One, Two, Buckle My Shoe
2 episodes
Writer Clive Exton
Director Ross Devenish
Alistair Blunt (Peter Blythe)
Mabelle Sainsbury Seale
(Carolyn Colquhoun)
Frank Carter (Christopher Eccleston)

Death in the Clouds
2 episodes
Writer William Humble
Director Stephen Whittaker
Daniel Clancy (Roger Heathcott)
Norman Gale (Shaun Scott)
Jane Grey (Sarah Woodward)

SERIES VI*
4 episodes
November 24–December 29, 1994

The Chocolate Box
Writer Douglas Watkinson
Director Ken Grieve
Virginie Mesnard (Anna Chancellor)
Madame Deroulard (Rosalie Crutchley)
Xavier St. Alard (Geoffrey Whitehead)

Yellow Iris
Writer Anthony Horowitz
Director Peter Barber-Fleming
Stephen Carter (Hugh Ross)
Pauline Weatherby
(Geraldine Somerville)
Barton Russell (David Troughton)

The Underdog
Writer Bill Craig
Director John Bruce
Lady Astwell (Ann Bell)
Charles Leverson (Jonathan Phillips)
Horace Trefusis (Bill Wallis)

The Case of the Missing Will
Writer Douglas Watkinson
Director John Bruce
Violet Wilson (Beth Goddard)
John Siddaway (Terrence Hardiman)
Andrew Marsh (Mark Kingston)

SERIES VII*
4 episodes
October 26–November 23, 1995
Writer Anthony Horowitz
Director Andrew Grieve

Murder on the Links
Marthe Daubreuil (Sophie Linfield)
Bella Duveen (Jacinta Mulcahy)
Jack Renauld (Ben Pullen)

Hickory, Dickory, Dock
Nigel Chapman (Jonathan Firth)
Sally Finch (Paris Jefferson)
Celia Austin (Jessica Lloyd)

SERIES VIII
4 episodes
October 31–November 21, 1996

Dumb Witness
Writer Douglas Watkinson
Director Edward Bennett
Charles Arundel (Patrick Ryecart)
Arabella Tanios (Julia St. John)
Wilhemina Lawson (Norma West)

Hercule Poirot's Christmas
Writer Clive Exton
Director Edward Bennett
Simeon Lee (Vernon Dobtcheff)
Stella (Olga Lowe)
Inspector Sugden (Mark Tandy)

AGATHA CHRISTIE STORIES

Produced by Thames Television
Based on the stories by
Agatha Christie
Producer Pat Sandys

SERIES I
4 episodes
February 17–March 10, 1983

The Manhood of Edward Robinson
Writer Gerald Savory
Director Brian Farnham
Edward Robinson (Nicholas Farrell)
Lady Noreen Elliot (Cherie Lunghi)
Maud (Ann Thornton)

Magnolia Blossom
Writer John Bryden Rodgers
Director John Frankau
Vincent Easton (Ralph Bates)
Richard Darrell (Jeremy Clyde)
Theodora Darrell (Ciaran Madden)

The Red Signal
Writer William Corlett
Director John Frankau
Sir Alington West (Alan Badel)
Jack Trent (Christopher Cazenove)
Mrs. Thompson (Rosalie Crutchley)
Claire Trent (Joanna David)
Dermot West (Richard Morant)

The Girl in the Train
Writer William Corlett
Director Brian Farnham
Elizabeth (Sarah Berger)
George Rowland (Osmund Bullock)
William Rowland (James Grout)

SERIES II
6 episodes
January 31–March 7, 1985

Jane in Search of a Job
Writer Gerald Savory
Director Christopher Hodson

Nigel Guest (Andrew Bicknell)
Jane Cleveland (Elizabeth Garvie)
Pauline, Grand Duchess of Ostravia
(Amanda Redman)

The Mystery of the Blue Jar
Writer T. R. Bowen
Director Cyril Coke
Dr. Lavington (Michael Aldridge)
Jack Hartington (Robin Kermode)
Felise Marchand (Isabelle Spade)

The Fourth Man
Writer William Corlett
Director Michael Simpson
Canon Parfitt (Geoffrey Chater)
Sir George Durand (Michael Gough)
Sir Campbell Clark (Alan
MacNaughtan)
Raoul Letardeau (John Nettles)

In a Glass Darkly
Writer William Corlett
Director Desmond Davis
Matthew Armitage (Nicholas Clay)
Sylvia Carslake (Emma Piper)
Neil Carslake (Shaun Scott)

The Case of the Middle-Aged Wife
Writer Freda Kelsall
Director Michael Simpson
Parker Pyne (Maurice Denham)
George Packington (Peter Jones)
Maria Packington (Gwen Watford)

The Case of the Discontented Soldier
Writer T. R. Bowen
Director Michael Simpson
Parker Pyne (Maurice Denham)
Freda Clegg (Patricia Garwood)
Major John Wilbraham
(William Gaunt)

ARTISTS IN CRIME

see *Ngaio Marsh's Alleyn Mysteries*

THE BLACK TOWER

see *Adam Dalgliesh Mysteries*

BRAT FARRAR

3 episodes
November 13–27, 1986
Produced by BBC
Based on the novel by Josephine Tey
Writer James Andrew Hall
Producer Terrance Dicks
Director Leonard Lewis
Brat Farrar/Simon Ashby
(Mark Greenstreet)
Eleanor Ashby (Dominique Barnes)
Beatrice Ashby (Angela Browne)
Mr. Sandal (Colin Jeavons)
Alec Loding (Francis Matthews)
George Ledingham (Frederick Treves)

CADFAEL*

Produced by Central
Independent Television

Based on the novels and characters
created by Ellis Peters
Producer Stephen Smallwood
Brother Cadfael (Derek Jacobi)
Brother Oswin (Mark Charnock)
Abbot Heribert (Peter Copley)
Prior Robert (Michael Culver)
Brother Jerome (Julian Firth)
Hugh Beringar (Sean Pertwee/
Eoin McCarthy)

SERIES I
Four 90-minute episodes
Director Graham Theakston
January 12–February 2, 1995

The Leper of St. Giles
Writer Paul Pender
Joscelyn (Jonathan Firth)
Iveta (Tara Fitzgerald)
Simon (Jamie Glover)

Monk's Hood
Writer Russell Lewis
Gervase Bonel (Bernard Gallagher)
Abbot Radulfus (Terrence Hardiman)
Richildis (Mary Miller)

The Sanctuary Sparrow
Writer Russell Lewis
Juliana (Rosalie Crutchley)
Susanna (Fiona Gillies)
Liliwin (Stephen Mackintosh)

One Corpse Too Many
Writer Russell Lewis
Adam Courcelle (Christian Burgess)
Godith (Juliette Caton)
Giles Seward (Nigel Hastings)

SERIES II
Three 90-minute episodes
1997

The Virgin in the Ice

The Devil's Novice

St. Peter's Fair

CAMPION

Produced by BBC
Based on the novels by Margery
Allingham
Albert Campion (Peter Davison)
Magersfontein Lugg (Brian Glover)
Inspector Oates (Andrew Burt)

SERIES I
8 episodes
October 12–November 30, 1989
Producer Ken Riddington

The Case of the Late Pig
Writer Jill Hyem
Director Robert Chetwyn
Dr. Brian Kingston (John Fortune)
Hayhoe (Michael Gough)
Sir Leo Pursuivant (Moray Watson)

Police at the Funeral
Writer Jeremy Paul
Director Ronald Wilson
Joyce Blount (Suzanne Burden)
Caroline Faraday (Mary Morris)
William Faraday (Timothy West)

Death of a Ghost
Writer Elaine Morgan
Director Michael Owen Morris
Belle Lafcadio (Jean Anderson)
Lisa (Rosalie Crutchley)
Donna Beatrice (Isabel Dean)

Look to the Lady
Writer Alan Plater
Director Martyn Friend
Professor Cairey (Gordon Jackson)
Mrs. Shannon (Barbara Jefford)
Val Gyrth (Robin Lermitte)

SERIES II
8 episodes
November 15, 1990–January 3, 1991
Producer Jonathan Alwyn

Sweet Danger
Writer Jill Hyem
Director Robert Tronson
Amanda Fitton (Lysette Anthony)
Brett Savanake (Iain Cuthbertson)
Guffy Randall (David Haig)

Mystery Mile
Writer John Hawkesworth
Director Ken Hannam
Judge Lobett (Brian Greene)
Isopel (Lisa Orgolini)
Marlowe (Gary Parker)

Dancers in Mourning
Writer Jeremy Paul
Director Christopher Hodson
Linda Sutane (Pippa Guard)
Jimmy Sutane (Ian Ogilvy)
Eve Sutane (Nina Marc)

Flowers for the Judge
Writer Brian Thompson
Director Michael Owen Morris
Michael Barnabas (Neil Daglish)
Ritchie Barnabas (Barrie Ingham)
John Barnabas (Robert Lang)

CAUSE CÉLÈBRE

2 episodes
October 13–20, 1988
Produced by Anglia Television
Based on the play by Terence Rattigan
Writer Ken Taylor
Producer John Rosenberg
Director John Gorrie
Alma Rattenbury (Helen Mirren)
Francis Rattenbury (Harry Andrews)
T. J. O'Conner (David Suchet)
George Bowman (David Morrissey)
Irene Riggs (Norma West)

CHANDLER & CO.

4 episodes
April 11–May 2, 1996
Produced by Skreba for BBC
Producer Ann Skinner
Elly Chandler (Catherine Russell)
Dee Tate (Barbara Flynn)
Larry Blakeston (Peter Capaldi)
David Tate (Struan Rodger)
Misty (Indra Ove)

On the Job
Writer Paula Milne
Director Renny Rye
Clifford Talbot (William Armstrong)
Carmen Talbot (Julie Peasgood)

Past Imperfect
Writer Paula Milne
Director Renny Rye
Max Chandler (Christopher Bowen)
Paul Dailey (Neil Duncan)
Wendy Dailey (Sian Webber)

Family Matters
Writer Jacqueline Holborough
Director Robert Marchand
Bill Savage (Peter Armitage)
Louise Parsons (Susan Derrick)
Ray Godley (Neil Phillips)

Those Who Trespass Against Us
Writer Paula Milne
Director Robert Marchand
Reverend Ewan Price (Ian Gelder)
Chris (Vincent Regan)

CHARTERS AND CALDICOTT

6 episodes
March 20–April 24, 1986
Produced by BBC
Based on the characters created by
Frank Launder and Sidney Gilliat
Writer Keith Waterhouse
Producer Ron Craddock
Director Julian Amyes
Charters (Robin Bailey)
Caldicott (Michael Aldridge)
Margaret Mottram (Caroline Blakiston)
Inspector Snow (Gerard Murphy)
Jenny (Tessa Peake-Jones)

A DARK-ADAPTED EYE

two 90-minute episodes
January 4–5, 1995
Produced by BBC
Based on the novel by Ruth Rendell
(writing as Barbara Vine)
Writer Sandy Welch
Producer Phillippa Giles
Director Tim Fywell
Faith (Helena Bonham Carter)
Vera (Celia Imrie)
Eden (Sophie Ward)
Helen (Polly Adams)
John (Robin Ellis)
Francis (Steven Mackintosh)

THE DARK ANGEL*

single 2 1/2-hour episode
March 21, 1991
Produced by BBC
Based on the novel *Uncle Silas* by
Sheridan le Fanu
Writer Don MacPherson
Producer Joe Waters
Director Peter Hammond
Uncle Silas (Peter O'Toole)
Maud Ruthyn (Beatie Edney)
Madame de la Rougierre
(Jane Lapotaire)

Austin Ruthyn (Alan MacNaughtan)
Dudley Ruthyn (Tim Woodward)

DEATH OF AN EXPERT WITNESS

see *Adam Dalgliesh Mysteries*

DEVICES AND DESIRES

see *Adam Dalgliesh Mysteries*

DIE KINDER

6 episodes
March 28–May 2, 1991
Produced by BBC in association with
WGBH/Boston
Writer Paula Milne
Producer Michael Wearing
Director Robert Walker
Sidonie Reiger (Miranda Richardson)
Lomax (Frederic Forrest)
Stefan Reiger (Hans Kremer)
Alan Mitchell (Sam Cox)
Karin Muller (Tina Engel)
Crombie (Derek Fowlds)

DOROTHY L. SAYERS' LORD PETER WIMSEY

10 episodes
October 1–December 3, 1987
Produced by BBC
Based on the novels by
Dorothy L. Sayers
Producer Michael Chapman
Lord Peter Wimsey
(Edward Petherbridge)
Harriet Vane (Harriet Walter)
Bunter (Richard Morant)

Strong Poison
3 episodes
Writer Philip Broadley
Director Christopher Hodson
Norman Urquhart (Clive Francis)
Chief Inspector Parker (David Quilter)
Dowager Duchess of Devonshire
(Margaretta Scott)

Have His Carcase
4 episodes
Writer Rosemary Anne Sisson
Director Christopher Hodson
Inspector Trethowan (Ray Armstrong)
Mrs. Weldon (Rowena Cooper)
Henry Weldon (Jeremy Sinden)

Gaudy Night
3 episodes
Writer Philip Broadley
Director Michael Simpson
Dr. Baring (Sheila Burrell)
Miss Devine (Dilys Hamlett)
Miss Hillyard (Charmian May)

DR. JEKYLL AND MR. HYDE

2 episodes
January 6–13, 1981

Produced by BBC and Time/Life Films
Based on the novel by
Robert Louis Stevenson
Writer Gerald Savory
Producer Jonathan Powell
Director Alastair Reid
Dr. Jekyll/Mr. Hyde (David Hemmings)
Ann Coggeshall (Lisa Harrow)
Utterson (Ian Bannen)
Lanyon (Clive Swift)
Kate Winterton (Diana Dors)

DYING DAY

2 episodes
October 19–26, 1982
Produced by Thames Television
Writer John Bowen
Producer Brenda Ennis
Director Robert Tronson
Anthony Skipling (Ian McKellan)
Doris Skipling (Gwyneth Powell)
Mountjoy (Cyril Shaps)

FATHER BROWN

4 episodes
November 2–23, 1982
Produced by ITC Entertainment
Based on the stories by G. K. Chesterton
Writer Hugh Leonard
Producer Ian Fordyce
Father Brown (Kenneth More)
Flambeau (Dennis Burgess)

Three Tools of Death
Director Robert Tronson
Patrick Royce (John Flanagan)
Sir Aaron Armstrong (James Hayter)
Alice Armstrong (Nina Thomas)

The Head of Caesar
Director Robert Tronson
Philip Hawker (Brian Anthony)
Christabel Carstairs (Rosalind Ayres)
Arthur Carstairs (John Normington)

The Eye of Apollo
Director Peter Jefferies
Pauline Stacey (Alison Key)
Kalon (Ronald Pickup)
Joan Stacey (Emily Richard)

The Secret Garden
Director Peter Jefferies
Julius K. Brayne (Peter Dyneley)
Lord Galloway (Cyril Luckham)
Aristide Valentin (Ferdy Mayne)

GALLOWGLASS

3 episodes
October 5–19, 1995
Produced by BBC
Based on the novel by Ruth Rendell
(writing as Barbara Vine)
Writer Jacqueline Holborough
Producer Phillippa Giles
Director Tim Fywell
Paul Garnet (John McArdle)
Sandor (Paul Rhys)
Joe Herbert (Michael Sheen)
Ralph Apsoland (Gary Waldhorn)
Nina Abbott (Arkie Whiteley)
Tilly (Claire Hackett)

GAME, SET AND MATCH

12 episodes
March 23–June 8, 1989
Produced by Granada Television
Based on the novels *Berlin Game*, *Mexico Set*, and *London Match*
by Len Deighton
Writer John Howlett
Producer Brian Armstrong
Directors Ken Grieve, Patrick Lau
Bernard Samson (Ian Holm)
Fiona Samson (Mel Martin)
Bret Rensselaer (Anthony Bate)
Dicky Cruyer (Michael Culver)
Werner Volkmann (Michael Degen)
Gloria Kent (Amanda Donohoe)
Giles Trent (Hugh Fraser)
Erich Stinnes (Gottfried John)
Frank Harrington (Frederick Treves)

HERCULE POIROT

see *Agatha Christie's Poirot*

THE INSPECTOR ALLEYN MYSTERIES

see *Ngaio Marsh's Alleyn Mysteries*

INSPECTOR MORSE*

Produced by Zenith for Central
Independent Television
Based on the novels and characters created by Colin Dexter
Chief Inspector Morse (John Thaw)
Detective Sergeant Lewis
(Kevin Whately)
Chief Superintendent Strange
(James Grout)
Max (Peter Woodthorpe)
Dr. Grayling Russell
(Amanda Hollwood)

SERIES I
6 episodes
February 4–March 10, 1988
Producer Kenny McBain

The Dead of Jericho
Writer Anthony Minghella
Director Alastair Reid
Anne Staveley (Gemma Jones)
Tony Richards (James Laurenson)
George Jackson (Patrick Troughton)

The Silent World of Nicholas Quinn
Writer Julian Mitchell
Director Brian Parker
Monica Height (Barbara Flynn)
Philip Ogleby (Michael Gough)
Dr. Bartlett (Clive Swift)
Dean of Lonsdale College
(Frederick Treves)

Service of All the Dead
Writer Julian Mitchell
Director Peter Hammond
Ruth Rawlinson (Angela Morant)
Reverend Lionel Pawlen (John Normington)
Harry Josephs (Maurice O'Connell)

SERIES II
6 episodes
December 15, 1988–February 2, 1989
Producer Kenny McBain

The Wolvercote Tongue
Writer Julian Mitchell
Director Alastair Reid
Dr. Theodore Kemp (Simon Callow)
Cedric Downes (Kenneth Cranham)
Sheila Williams (Roberta Taylor)

Last Seen Wearing
Writer Thomas Ellice
Director Edward Bennett
Cheryl Baines (Suzanne Bertish)
Craven (Glyn Houston)
Phillipson (Peter McEnery)
Grace (Frances Tomelty)

Last Bus to Woodstock
Writer Michael Wilcox
Director Peter Duffell
Jennifer Colby (Jill Baker)
Dr. Crowther (Anthony Bate)
Clive (Terrence Hardiman)

SERIES III
6 episodes
May 3–June 7, 1990

The Setting of the Sun
Writer Charles Wood
Producer Kenny McBain
Director Peter Hammond
Mrs. Warbut (Avis Bunnage)
Dr. Robson (Anna Calder-Marshall)
Sir Wilfred (Robert Stephens)

Ghost in the Machine
Writer Julian Mitchell
Producer Chris Burt
Director Herbert Wise
Sir Julius Hanbury (Michael Godley)
Lady Hanbury (Patricia Hodge)
John McKendrick (Michael Thomas)

The Last Enemy
Writer Peter Buckman
Producer Chris Burt
Director James Scott
Arthur Drysdale (Michael Aldridge)
Sir Alexander Reece (Barry Foster)
Dr. David Kerridge (Tenniel Evans)

SERIES IV
6 episodes
May 16–June 20, 1991

The Infernal Serpent
Writer Alma Cullen
Producer David Lascelles
Director John Madden
Sylvie (Cheryl Campbell)
Matthew Copley-Barnes
(Geoffrey Palmer)
Jake Normington (Tom Wilkinson)

Deceived by Flight
Writer Anthony Minghella
Producer Chris Burt
Director Anthony Simmons
Anthony Donn (Daniel Massey)
Kate Donn (Sharon Maughan)
Roland Marshall (Norman Rodway)

The Secret of Bay 5B
Writer Alma Cullen
Producer Chris Burt

Director Jim Goddard
Fran Pierce (Marion Bailey)
Rosemary Henderson (Mel Martin)
Edward Manley (Andrew Wilde)

SERIES V
6 episodes
April 9–May 14, 1992
Producer David Lascelles

Masonic Mysteries
Writer Julian Mitchell
Director Danny Boyle
McNutt (Iain Cuthbertson)
Marion Brooke (Diane Fletcher)
Hugo de Vries (Ian McDiarmid)

Driven to Distraction
Writer Anthony Minghella
Director Sandy Johnson
Tim Ablett (Christopher Fulford)
Jeremy Boynton (Patrick Malahide)
Derek Whittaker (David Ryall)

The Sins of the Fathers
Writer Jeremy Burnham
Director Peter Hammond
Linacre (John Bird)
Isobel Radford (Isabel Dean)
Charles Radford (Lionel Jeffries)
Victor Preece (Alex Jennings)

SERIES VI
6 episodes
March 25–April 29, 1993
Producer David Lascelles

Promised Land
Writer Julian Mitchell
Director John Madden
Anne Harding (Rhondda Findleton)
Paul Matthews (Con O'Neill)
Dave Harding (Noah Taylor)

Second Time Around
Writer Daniel Boyle
Director Adrian Shergold
Patrick Dawson (Kenneth Colley)
Frederick Redpath (Oliver Ford Davies)
Terrence Mitchell
(Christopher Eccleston)

Fat Chance
Writer Alma Cullen
Director Roy Battersby
Freddie Galt (Kenneth Haigh)
Hilary Dobson (Maggie O'Neill)
Emma Pickford (Zoe Wanamaker)

SERIES VII
8 episodes
February 24–April 14, 1994

Dead on Time
Writer Daniel Boyle
Producer Deirdre Keir
Director John Madden
Susan (Joanna David)
Marriel (Adrian Dunbar)
Rhodes (David Haig)
Fallon (James Walker)

Happy Families
Writer Daniel Boyle
Producer Deirdre Keir
Director Adrian Shergold
James (Martin Clunes)
Harry (Jonathan Coy)

Who Killed Harry Field?
Writer Geoffrey Case
Producer David Lascelles
Director Colin Gregg
Harry (Trevor Byfield)
Mrs. Field (Geraldine James)
Doyle (John Castle)

Greeks Bearing Gifts
Writer Peter Nichols
Producer David Lascelles
Director Adrian Shergold
Friday (Jan Harvey)
Tuckerman (James Hazeldine)
Rees (Martin Jarvis)
Maria (Elvira Poulianou)

SERIES VIII
5 episodes
February 9–March 9, 1995
Producer Deirdre Keir

Death of the Self
single 2-hour episode
Writer Alma Cullen
Director Colin Gregg
Nicole Burgess (Frances Barber)
Russell Clark (Michael Kitchen)

Absolute Conviction
Writer John Brown
Director Antonia Bird
Alex Bailey (Sean Bean)
Charlie Bennett (Jim Broadbent)
Hilary Stevens (Diana Quick)

Cherubim and Seraphim
Writer Julian Mitchell
Director Daniel Boyle
Marilyn Garrett (Charlotte Chatton)
Dr. Desmond Collier (Jason Isaacs)
Vicky Wilson (Lisa Walker)

SERIES IX
4 episodes
February 1–22, 1996
Producer Chris Burt

The Day of the Devil
Writer Daniel Boyle
Director Stephen Whittaker
John Peter Barrie (Keith Allen)
Humphrey Appleton (Richard Griffiths)
Dr. Esther Martin (Harriet Walter)

Twilight of the Gods
Writer Julian Mitchell
Director Herbert Wise
Chancellor Lord Hinksey
(Sir John Gielgud)
Gwladys Probert (Sheila Gish)
Andrew Baydon (Robert Hardy)

SERIES X
4 episodes
1997
Produced by
Central Television/Carlton UK
Producer Chris Burt

The Way Through the Woods
Writer Russell Lewis
Director John Madden
David Michaels (Neil Dudgeon)
Cathy Michaels (Michelle Fairley)
Dr. Alan Hardinge (Nicholas Le Prevost)
Chief Inspector Johnson
(Malcolm Storry)

Deadly Slumber
Writer Daniel Boyle
Director Stuart Orme
Michael Steppings (Brian Cox)
Wendy Hazlitt (Penny Downie)
John Brewster (Jason Durr)
Claire Brewster (Janet Suzman)

THE LIMBO CONNECTION

3 episodes
March 24–April 7, 1983
Produced by Thames Television
Based on the novel by Derry Quinn
Writer Philip Mackie
Producer Jacqueline Davis
Director Robert Tronson
Mark Omney (James Bolam)
Annabelle Fraser (Rosalind Ayers)
Clare Omney (Suzanne Bertish)
Dr. Walcott Brown (Michael Culver)
Blanche Terraine (Beatrix Lehmann)

LORD PETER WIMSEY

see *Dorothy L. Sayers' Lord Peter Wimsey*

MAIGRET

Produced by Granada Television
Based on the novels by George Simenon
Chief Inspector Maigret
(Michael Gambon)
Mme Maigret (Barbara Flynn/
Ciaran Madden)
Sergeant Lucas (Geoffrey Hutchings)
Inspector Janvier (Jack Galloway)
Inspector Lapointe (James Larkin)

SERIES I
6 episodes
October 8–November 12, 1992
Producer Jonathan Alwyn

The Patience of Maigret
Writer Alan Plater
Director James Cellan Jones
Aline Bauche (Cheryl Campbell)
Monsieur Comeliau (John Moffatt)
Moers (Christian Rodska)

Maigret Sets a Trap
Writer Douglas Livingstone
Director John Glenister
Madame Moncin (Ann Mitchell)
Marthe Jusserand (Catherine Russell)
Marcel Moncin (Richard Willis)

Maigret and the Mad Woman
Writer William Humble
Director John Glenister
Marcel (Mark Frankel)
Emile (Mark Lockyer)
Madame Antoine
(Marjorie Sommerville)

Maigret and the Burglar's Wife
Writer Alan Plater
Director John Glenister
Guillaume Serre
(Christopher Benjamin)
Ernestine (Sandy Ratcliff)
Madame Serre (Margery Withers)

Maigret and the Home Ground
Writer Robin Chapman
Director James Cellan Jones
Dr. Mouchardon (Jonathan Adams)
Jean Metayer (James Clyde)
Father Martin (Daniel Moynihan)

Maigret Goes to School
Writer William Humble
Director James Cellan Jones
Captain Danielou (Adrian Lukis)
Madame Gastin (Joanna David)
Joseph Gastin (Struan Rodger)

SERIES II
6 episodes
October 13–November 17, 1994
Producer Paul Marcus

Maigret on the Defensive
Writer William Humble
Director Stuart Burge
Henri Lautier (John Benfield)
Dr. François Melan (John Salthouse)
Nicole Prieur (Liza Walker)

Maigret and the Nightclub Dancer
Writer Douglas Livingstone
Director John Strickland
Rose (Brenda Blethyn)
Arlette (Minnie Driver)
Freddie (Tony Doyle)

Maigret and the Hotel Majestic
Writer William Humble
Director Nicholas Renton
Charlotte (Nicola Duffell)
Prosper Donge (Michael J. Jackson)
Jean Ramuel (John Kavanagh)

Maigret's Boyhood Friend
Writer William Humble
Director John Strickland
Victor Drouet (Kenneth Haigh)
Concierge (Betty Marsden)
Leon Florentin (Edward Petherbridge)

Maigret and the Minister
Writer Bill Gallagher
Director Nicholas Renton
Auguste Point (Peter Barkworth)
Blanche Lamotte (Sorcha Cusack)
Charles Mascoulin (Jon Finch)

Maigret and the Maid
Writer Douglas Livingstone
Director Stuart Burge
Felice (Susan Lindeman)
Jacques Petillon (Steven Mackintosh)
Ernest Lapie (Tony Rohr)

MALICE AFORETHOUGHT

4 episodes
January 29–February 10, 1981
Produced by BBC and Time/Life Films
Based on the novel by Francis Iles
Writer Philip Mackie
Producer Richard Beynon
Director Cyril Coke
Dr. Bickleigh (Hywel Bennett)
Julia Bickleigh (Judy Parfitt)
Madeleine Cranmere (Cheryl Campbell)
Denny Bourne (Christopher Guard)
Sir Francis Lee-Bannerton
    (Thorley Walters)

THE MAN FROM THE PRU*

single 90-minute episode
May 9, 1991
Produced by
BBC/Scotland and Liverpool FIlms
Writer Robert Smith
Producer Roger Gregory
Director Rob Rohrer
William Wallace (Jonathan Pryce)
Julia Wallace (Anna Massey)
Amy Wallace (Susannah York)
Detective Superintendent Moore
    (Tom Georgeson)
Gordon Parry (Gary Mavers)
Hemmerde K. C. (Richard Pasco)

MELISSA

3 episodes
November 30–December 14, 1982
Produced by BBC
Writer Francis Durbridge
Producer Morris Barry
Director Peter Moffatt
Guy Foster (Peter Barkworth)
Melissa Foster (Moira Redmond)
Paula Hepburn (Joan Benham)
Felix Hepburn (Ronald Fraser)
Don Page (Ray Lonnen)
Detective Chief Inspector Carter
    (Philip Voss)

A MIND TO MURDER

see *Adam Dalgliesh Mysteries*

MISS MARPLE

see *Agatha Christie's Miss Marple*

MISS MORISON'S GHOSTS

single 90-minute episode
March 17, 1983
Produced by Anglia Television
Based on the book *The Adventure* by
Elizabeth Morison and Frances Lamont
Writer Ian Curteis
Producer John Rosenberg
Director John Bruce
Miss Elizabeth Morison
    (Dame Wendy Hiller)
Miss Frances Lamont (Hannah Gordon)
The Reverend Oliver Hodgson
    (Bosco Hogan)
Dr. Hadley (Vivian Pickles)
Lord Kavanagh (Niall Toibin)

MOTHER LOVE

3 episodes
October 25–November 8, 1990
Produced by BBC
Based on the novel by Domini Taylor
Writer Andrew Davies
Producer Ken Riddington
Director Simon Langton
Helena Vesey (Diana Rigg)
Kit Vesey (James Wilby)

Angela Turner Vesey (Fiona Gillies)
Alex Vesey (David McCallum)
George Batt (James Grout)
Ruth Vesey (Isla Blair)

MY COUSIN RACHEL

4 episodes
December 5–26, 1985
Produced by BBC
Based on the novel by
Daphne du Maurier
Writer Hugh Whitemore
Producer Richard Beynon
Director Brian Farnham
Rachel Sangalletti (Geraldine Chaplin)
Philip Ashley (Christopher Guard)
Ambrose Ashley (John Shrapnel)
Rainaldi (Charles Kay)
Louise Kendall (Amanda Kirby)
Nick Kendall (John Stratton)

NGAIO MARSH'S ALLEYN MYSTERIES

Produced by BBC
Based on the novels by Ngaio Marsh
Producer George Gallaccio
Chief Inspector Roderick Alleyn
    (Patrick Malahide)
Inspector Fox (William Simons)
Agatha Troy (Belinda Lang)

Artists in Crime
2 episodes
January 9–16, 1992
Writer T. R. Bowen
Director Silvio Narizzano
Chief Inspector Roderick Alleyn
    (Simon Williams)
Lady Alleyn (Ursula Howells)
Sir Norman Chapple (Edward Judd)
Colonel Pascoe (Reginald Marsh)

SERIES I
6 episodes
October 7–November 11, 1993

Final Curtain
Writer Hugh Leonard
Director Martyn Friend
Millamant Ancred (Eleanor Bron)
Cedric Ancred (Jonathan Cullen)
Fenella Cairnes (Sarah Winman)

The Nursing Home Murder
Writer Kevin Laffan
Director Silvio Narizzano
Ruth O'Callaghan (Anna Massey)
Sir John Philips (David Rintoul)
Harold Sage (David Sibley)
Sir Derek O'Callaghan (John Stride)

A Man Lay Dead
Writer Barbara Machin
Director Sarah Pia Anderson
Sir Hubert Handesley (Julian Glover)
Arthur Wilde (David Haig)
Rosamund Grant (Susan Wooldridge)

SERIES II
two 2-hour episodes
March 30–April 6, 1995

Death in a White Tie
Writer Ken Jones
Director John Woods
Sir Daniel Davidson (John Carlisle)
Lord Robert Gospell (Harold Innocent)
Lady Evelyn Carrados (Diana Quick)

Death at the Bar
Writer Alfred Shaughnessy
Director Michael Winterbottom
Abel Pomeroy (Paul Brooke)
Sebastian Parish (Alex Jennings)
Luke Watchman (Kevin McNally)

OLIVER'S TRAVELS

4 episodes
October 3–24, 1996
Produced by BBC
Writer Alan Plater
Producer David Cunliffe
Director Giles Foster
Oliver (Alan Bates)
Diane Priest (Sinead Cusack)
Baron Farquhar/Kite (Miles Anderson)
Cathy (Charlotte Coleman)
Michael (Morgan Jones)
Baxter (Bill Patterson)
Mrs. Robson (Mollie Sugden)

ORIGINAL SIN

see *Adam Dalgliesh Mysteries*

PARTNERS IN CRIME*

Based on the stories by Agatha Christie
Produced by LWT
Producer Jack Williams
Tuppence Beresford (Francesca Annis)
Tommy Beresford (James Warwick)
Albert (Reece Dinsdale)
Inspector Marriott (Arthur Cox)

SERIES I
5 episodes
November 29–December 27, 1984

The Affair of the Pink Pearl
Writer David Butler
Director Tony Wharmby
Colonel Kingston Bruce
    (Graham Crowden)
Lady Laura Barton (Dulcie Gray)
Lawrence St. Vincent (Tim Woodward)

The House of Lurking Death
Writer Jonathan Hales
Director Christopher Hodson
Lois Hargreaves (Lynsey Baxter)
Miss Logan (Joan Sanderson)
Hannah Macpherson (Liz Smith)

Finessing the King
Writer Gerald Savory
Director Christopher Hodson
Captain "Bingo" Hale (Peter Blythe)
Lady Vere Merivale (Annie Lambert)
Sir Arthur Merivale
    (Benjamin Whitrow)

The Clergyman's Daughter
Writer Paul Annett
Director Paul Annett

Monica Deane (Jane Booker)
Norman Partridge (Geoffrey Drew)
O'Neill (David Delve)

The Sunningdale Mystery
Writer Jonathan Hales
Director Tony Wharmby
Hollaby (Edwin Brown)
Captain Sessle (Denis Lill)
Doris Evans (Emily Moore)

SERIES II
5 episodes
May 1–29, 1986

The Ambassador's Boots
Writer Paul Annett
Director Paul Annett
Cicely March (Jennie Linden)
Randolph Wilmott (T. P. McKenna)
Virna La Strange (Catherine Schell)

The Man in the Mist
Writer Gerald Savory
Director Christopher Hodson
"Bulger" Estcourt (Constantine Gregory)
Gilda Glen (Linda Marlowe)
Mrs. Honeycott (Anne Stallybrass)

The Case of the Missing Lady
Writer Jonathan Hales
Director Paul Annett
Dr. Horriston (Ewan Hooper)
Lady Susan Clonray (Elspeth March)
Gabriel Staransson (Jonathan Newth)

The Unbreakable Alibi
Writer David Butler
Director Christopher Hodson
Peter le Marchant (Michael Jayes)
Montgomery Jones (Tim Meats)
Una Drake (Anna Nygh)

The Crackler
Writer Gerald Savory
Director Christopher Hodson
Major Laidlaw (David Quilter)
Hank Ryder (Shane Rimer)
Marguerite Laidlaw (Carolle Rousseau)

PRAYING MANTIS*

3 episodes
January 10–24, 1985
Produced by Portman Productions
Based on the novel *Les Mantes
Religieuses* by Hubert Monteilhet
Writer Philip Mackie
Producers Ian Warren,
Dickie Bamber
Director Jack Gold
Christian Magny (Jonathan Pryce)
Beatrice Manceau (Cherie Lunghi)
Vera Canova (Carmen Du Sautoy)
Paul Canova (Pinkas Braun)
Gertrude (Anna Cropper)

PRIME SUSPECT*

Produced by Granada Television
Series created by Lynda La Plante
Detective Chief Inspector Jane Tennison
(Helen Mirren)
Detective Chief Superintendent Mike
Kernan (John Benfield)

Detective Sergeant Bill Otley (Tom Bell)
Detective Inspector Tony Muddyman
(Jack Ellis)
Detective Inspector Frank Burkin
(Craig Fairbrass)
Detective Inspector Brian Dalton
(Andrew Woodall)

Prime Suspect
3 episodes
January 23–February 6, 1992
Writer Lynda La Plante
Producer Don Leaver
Director Christopher Menaul
George Marlow (John Bowe)
Michael (Ralph Fiennes)
Moyra Henson (Zoe Wanamaker)
Peter Rawlins (Tom Wilkinson)

Prime Suspect 2
4 episodes
February 11–March 4, 1993
Writer Alan Cubitt
Producer Paul Marcus
Director John Strickland
Detective Sergeant Robert Oswalde
(Colin Salmon)
Jason Reynolds (Matt Bardock)
Esme Allen (Claire Benedict)
Tony Allen (Fraser James)
David Harvey (Tom Watson)
Emmy award for Outstanding
Miniseries
Peabody award

Prime Suspect 3
4 episodes
April 28–May 19, 1994
Producer Paul Marcus
Director David Drury
Vera Reynolds (Peter Capaldi)
Edward Parker-Jones (Ciaran Hinds)
Jake Hunter (Michael J. Shannon)
James Jackson (David Thewlis)
Emmy award for Outstanding
Miniseries
Peabody award

QUIET AS A NUN

3 episodes
December 21, 1982–January 4, 1983
Produced by Thames Television
Based on the novel by Antonia Fraser
Writer Julia Jones
Producer Jacqueline Davis
Director Moira Armstrong
Jemima Shore (Maria Aitken)
Mother Ancilla (Renee Asherson)
Sister Boniface (Sylvia Coleridge)
Tom Amyas (David Burke)
Tessa (Patsy Kensit)

THE RACING GAME

Produced by Yorkshire Television
Based on the novel *Odds Against* by
Dick Francis
Producer Jacky Stoller
Sid Halley (Mike Gwilym)
Chico Barnes (Mick Ford)
Jenny Halley (Susan Wooldridge)
Charles Rowland (James Maxwell)

SERIES I
3 episodes
April 8–22, 1980

Odds Against
Writer Terence Feely
Director Lawrence Gordon Clark
Doria Graves (Rachel Davies)
Howard Graves (Gerald Flood)
Geoffrey Bynge (Peter Land)

Trackdown
Writer Terence Feely
Director Lawrence Gordon Clark
Tom Mansell (Jeremy Clyde)
Trish Latham (Carol Royle)
Jack Beater (Leslie Sands)

Gambling Lady
Writer Evan Jones
Director Peter Duffell
Sylvia Guiccolli (Caroline Blakiston)
Count Guiccolli (Anthony Steel)
Duncan Adams (George Waring)

SERIES II
3 episodes
March 31–April 14, 1981

Needle
Writer Terence Feely
Director Peter Duffell
John Fenby (Davyd Herries)
Peter Dobson (Bert Oxley)
Inspector Kilbride (Andrew Downie)

Horses for Courses
Writer Leon Griffiths
Director John MacKenzie
Archie Hunter (Milton Johns)
Michael Carston (Robert Swann)
Des Cunnington (Simon Thompson)

Horsenap
Writer Trevor Preston
Director Colin Bucksey
Lankester (Iain Cuthbertson)
Hearne (Tommy Wright)
Carol Tomes (Susan Penhaligon)

REBECCA

4 episodes
March 11–April 1, 1980
Produced by BBC
Based on the novel by
Daphne du Maurier
Writer Hugh Whitemore
Producer Richard Beynon
Director Simon Langton
Maxim de Winter (Jeremy Brett)
Mrs. de Winter (Joanna David)
Mrs. Danvers (Anna Massey)
Colonel Julyan (Robert Flemyng)
Jack Favell (Julian Holloway)
Beatrice (Vivian Pickles)

REILLY, ACE OF SPIES*

12 episodes
January 19–April 5, 1984
Produced by Euston Films
for Thames Television
Based on the novel by
Robin Bruce Lockhart
Writer Troy Kennedy Martin

Producer Chris Burt
Directors Jim Goddard,
Martin Campbell
Sidney Reilly (Sam Neill)
Sir Robert Bruce Lockhart
(Ian Charleson)
Count Orlove (Michael Aldridge)
Joseph Stalin (David Burke)
Margaret Thomas (Jeananne Crowley)
Pepita Bobadilla (Laura Davenport)
Eugenie (Eleanor David)
Hill (Hugh Fraser)
Basil Zaharov (Leo McKern)
Tanyatos (John Rhys-Davies)
Reverend Thomas (Sebastian Shaw)
Inspector Tsientsin (David Suchet)

RUMPOLE OF THE BAILEY

Produced by Thames Television
Writer John Mortimer
Horace Rumpole (Leo McKern)
Hilda Rumpole (Peggy Thorpe
Bates/Marion Mathie)
Liz Probert (Samantha Bond/
Abigail McKern)
Claude Erskine-Brown (Julian Curry)
Phyllida Trant Erskine-Brown
(Patricia Hodge)
Samuel Ballard, QC (Peter Blythe)
Henry (Jonathan Coy)
Judge Bullingham (Bill Fraser)
Fiona Allways (Rosalyn Landor)
Mr. Bernard (Denis Lill)
Mr. Justice Featherstone (Peter Bowles)
Lady Marigold Featherstone
(Joanna Van Gyseghem)
Uncle Tom (Richard Murdoch)
Dot Clapton (Camille Coduri)
George Forbisher (Moray Watson)

SERIES I
4 episodes
February 12–March 4, 1980
Producer Irene Shubik

*Rumpole and the
Honourable Member*
Director Graham Evans
Bridget (Elizabeth Romilly)
Ken (Anton Rodgers)

Rumpole and the Married Lady
Director Graham Evans
Tripp (Clifford Parrish)
Norman (Matthew Ryan)

Rumpole and the Learned Friends
Director Graham Evans
Charlie (Ken Jones)
Dickerson (Malcolm Storry)

Rumpole and the Heavy Brigade
Director Herbert Wise
Justice Prestcold (Mark Dignam)
Peter (Stewart Harwood)
Basil (Derek Newark)

SERIES II
6 episodes
February 17–March 24, 1981
Producer Jacqueline Davis

Rumpole and the Man of God
Director Brian Farnham
Reverend Skinner (Derek Farr)

Ida (Rosemary Leach)
Evelyn Skinner (Valerie Lush)

Rumpole and the Case of Identity
Director Derek Bennett
Dave (Martin Fisk)
Angela (Caroline Holdaway)
Betty (Seretta Wilson)

Rumpole and the Show Folk
Director Peter Hammond
Christine (Henrietta Baynes)
Albert (Derek Benfield)
Maggie (Eleanor Bron)

Rumpole and the Fascist Beast
Director Robert Knights
Latif Khan (Lyndham Gregory)
Captain Parkin (Robert Lang)

Rumpole and the Course of True Love
Director Brian Farnham
Francesca (Kate Dorning)
Ransom (Nigel Havers)

Rumpole and the Age for Retirement
Director Donald McWhinnie
Percy (George Hilsdon)
Brush (Struan Rodger)
Nick (David Yelland)

SERIES III*
6 episodes
October 18–November 22, 1984
Producer Jacqueline Davis

Rumpole and the Genuine Article
Director Robert Knights
Pauline (Brenda Blethyn)
Nancy (Sylvia Coleridge)
Harold Ridling (Emlyn Williams)

Rumpole and the Old Boy Network
Director Tony Smith
Napier Lee (Michael Denison)
Lorraine Lee (Dulcie Gray)
Mr. X (Jack Watling)

*Rumpole and the Female
of the Species*
Director Tony Smith
Dianne (Maureen Darbyshire)
April Timson (Mary Maddox)
Detective Inspector Brush (Struan
Rodger)

Rumpole and the Golden Thread
Director Donald McWhinnie
David Mazenze (Olu Jacobs)
Chief Justice Sir Worthington Banzana
(Errol John)
Sir Arthur Remnant (James Villiers)

Rumpole and the Sporting Life
Director Bill Hays
Jonathan Postern (Andrew Burt)
Mr. Justice Twyburne (Roland Culver)
Jennifer Postern (Joanna David)

Rumpole and the Last Resort
Director Stuart Burge
Frank Armstrong (Michael Melia)
Ward-Webster (Richard Morant)
Fig Newton (Jim Norton)

SERIES IV*
6 episodes
March 17–April 21, 1988
Producer Jacqueline Davies

Rumpole and the Old, Old Story
Director Roger Bamford
Hugo Lutterworth (Robin Sachs)
Captain Gleason (David Waller)
Amanda Gleason (Victoria Wicks)

Rumpole and the Bright Seraphim
Director Martyn Friend
Captain Betteridge (Geoffrey Bateman)
Captain Sandy Ransom
(Dominic Jephcott)
Lt. Colonel Hugo Undershaft
(Neil Stacy)

Rumpole and the Blind Tasting
Director Roger Bamford
Hugh Timson (George Innes)
Honoria Bird (Phyllida Law)
Dodo Mackintosh (Ann Way)

Rumpole and the Official Secret
Director Rodney Bennett
Sir Frank Fawcett (Peter Cellier)
Rosemary Tuttle (Judy Cornwell)
Basil Thorogood (Andrew Seear)

Rumpole and the Judge's Elbow
Director Donald McWhinnie
Mr. Addison (David Allister)
Charles Hearthstoke (Nicholas Gecks)
Mrs. Addison (Hazel McBride)

Rumpole's Last Case
Director Rodney Bennett
Dennis Timson (Ron Pember)
Cyril Timson (Michael Robbins)
Peanuts Molloy (David Squire)

SERIES V*
6 episodes
December 7, 1989–January 11, 1990
Producer Jacqueline Davis

Rumpole and the Tap End
Director Julian Amyes
Tony Timson (Philip Davis)
April Timson (Cindy O'Callaghan)
Detective Inspector Brush
(Struan Rodger)

Rumpole and the Bubble Reputation
Director Mike Vardy
Amelia Nettleship (Jennifer Daniel)
Connie Coughlin (Caroline Mortimer)
Machin (Norman Rodway)

Rumpole and the Barrow Boy
Director Julian Amyes
Nigel Timson (Douglas Hodge)
Rosie Japhet (Elizabeth Hurley)
Mark Marcellus (Lucien Taylor)

Rumpole and the Age of Miracles
Director Mike Vardy
Campion (Michael Aitken)
Canon Timothy Donkin (Martin Jarvis)

Rumpole and Portia
Director Roger Bamford
Stanley Culp (Jim Dunk)
"Boxey" Horne (Leslie Phillips)
Cy Stratton (Bob Sessions)

Rumpole and the Quality of Life
Director Roger Bamford
Perdita Derwent (Helen Fitzgerald)
Helen Derwent (Caroline Goodall)
David Inchcape (Michael Grandage)

SERIES VI
6 episodes
May 20–June 24, 1993
Producer Jacqueline Davis

Rumpole at Sea
Director Michael Simpson
Mr. Justice Graves (Robin Bailey)
Howard Swainton (Julian Holloway)
Reverend Bill Britwell
(Benjamin Whitrow)

Rumpole and the Summer of Discontent
Director Julian Amyes
Ernie Elver (Robert Austin)
Lord Chancellor (Preston Lockwood)
Ben Baker (Bryan Pringle)

Rumpole a la Carte
Director Jim Goddard
Everard Wystan (James Maxwell)
Tricia Benbow (Pamela Miles)
Jean Pierre O'Higgins (T. P. McKenna)

Rumpole for the Prosecution
Director Robert Tronson
Gregory Fabian (Geoffrey Chater)
Judge Ollie Oliphant (James Grout)
Christopher Jago (James Simmons)

Rumpole and the Quacks
Director Robert Tronson
Dr. Rachmat (Saeed Jaffrey)
Dr. Cogger (Gary Waldhorn)
Heather Whittaker (Pauline Yates)

Rumpole and the Right to Silence
Director Julian Amyes
Audrey Wystan (Jemma Churchill)
Clive Clympton (Maurice Roeves)
Martin Wayfield (Trevor T. Smith)

SERIES VII
6 episodes
April 13–May 18, 1995
Producer Jacqueline Davies

*Rumpole and the Children
of the Devil*
Director James Cellan Jones
Cary Timson (Paul Bigley)
Roz Timson (Chrisse Coterill)
Mirabelle Jones (Joanna David)

*Rumpole and the
Miscarriage of Justice*
Director Robert Tronson
Chief Superintendent Belmont
(Harvey Ashby)
Detective Superintendent Gannon
(Tony Doyle)
Betty Yeomans (Rosalind March)

Rumpole and the Eternal Triangle
Director Robert Tronson
Elizabeth Casterini (Eleanor David)
Desmond Casterini (Patrick Drury)
Tom Randall (Richard Hawley)

*Rumpole and the Reform
of Joby Johnson*
Director Martyn Friend
Elspeth Dodds (Sara Coward)
Marvel Perkins (Osaze Ehibor)
Joby Johnson (John Simon)

Rumpole and the Family Pride
Director John Gorrie
The Honorable Jonathon Sackbut
(Jackson Kyle)

Dr. Hugo Swabey (John Nettleton)
Lord Richard Sackbut (Patrick Ryecart)

Rumpole on Trial
Director John Gorrie
Mr. Justice Graves (Robin Bailey)
Fred Timson (John Bardon)
Mr. Justice Oliphant (James Grout)

RUMPOLE'S RETURN*
single 2-hour episode
October 11, 1984
Produced by Thames Television
Writer John Mortimer
Producer Jacqueline Davies
Director John Glenister
Horace Rumpole (Leo McKern)
Hilda Rumpole (Peggy Thorpe-Bates)
Phyllida Trant (Patricia Hodge)
Judge Bullingham (Bill Fraser)
Cracknell (John Price)
Frobisher (Moray Watson)

THE SECRET ADVERSARY*
2 episodes
January 22–29, 1987
Produced by LWT
Based on the novel by Agatha Christie
Writer Pat Sandys
Producer Jack Williams
Director Tony Wharmby
Tommy Beresford (James Warwick)
Tuppence Cowley (Francesca Annis)
Whittington (George Baker)
Mr. Carter (Peter Barkworth)
Rita Vandemeter (Honor Blackman)
Sir James Peel Edgerton (Alec
McCowen)
Julius Hersheimmer (Gavan O'Herlihy)

SERGEANT CRIBB
Based on the novels by Peter Lovesey
Produced by Granada Television
Producer June Wyndham Davies
Sergeant Cribb (Alan Dobie)
Police Constable Thackeray
(William Simons)
Inspector Jowett (David Waller)

SERIES I
3 episodes
April 29–May 13, 1980

Wobble to Death
Writer Alan Plater
Director Gordon Flemyng
Erskine Chadwick (Andrew Burt)
Charles Mostyn-Smith
(Kenneth Cranham)
Charles Darrell (Archie Tew)

Swing, Swing Together
Writer Brian Thompson
Director June Wyndham Davies
Percy Bustard (Ron Lacey)
Harriet Shaw (Heather Moray)
Jim Hackett (Brian Rawlinson)

Abracadaver
Writer Brian McIlwraith
Director Julian Amyes
Bella (Valerie Holloway)
Lola (Wendy Holloway)
Buckmaster (Derek Tansley)

SERIES II
5 episodes
April 21–May 19, 1981

Waxwork
Writer Pauline Macauley
Director June Wyndham Davies
Simon Allingham (David Ashford)
Josiah Perceval (Geoffrey Larder)
Miriam Cromer (Carol Royle)

Something Old, Something New
Writers Peter and Jacqueline Lovesey
Director Oliver Horsburgh
Uncle Ezra Winter (Geoffrey Bayldon)
Denise Winter (Alison Glennie)
Daphne Winter (Sally Osborn)

The Horizontal Witness
Writers Peter and Jacqueline Lovesey
Director Alan Grint
Sister Armstrong (Elizabeth Bennett)
Charles Vokins (James Coyle)
James Hepplewhite (John Ringham)

The Detective Wore Silk Drawers
Writer Peter Lovesey
Director Alan Grint
Constable Henry Jago (Barry Andrews)
Robert D'Estin (David Hargreaves)
Isabel Vibart (Norma West)

A Case of Spirits
Writer Arden Winch
Director Bill Gilmour
Winifred Probert (Georgine Anderson)
Alice Probert (Emma Jacobs)
Dr. Probert (Clive Swift)

SERIES III
5 episodes
January 13–February 10, 1983

The Last Trumpet
Writers Peter and Jacqueline Lovesey
Director Brian Mills
Mrs. Pennycook (Joyce Carey)
William Newman (Garrick Hagan)
Abraham Bartlett (Geoffrey Keen)

Mad Hatter's Holiday
Writer Bill McIlwraith
Director June Wyndham Davies
Inspector Pink (Kevin Brennan)
Zena Prothero (Fenella Fielding)
Albert Moscrop (Derek Fowlds)

The Choir That Wouldn't Sing
Writers Peter and Jacqueline Lovesey
Director Mary McMurray
Joshua (Alan Downer)
Mr. Jessop (Barry McGinn)
Mrs. Gurney (Elizabeth Spriggs)

Murder Old Boy
Writers Peter and Jacqueline Lovesey
Director George Spenton-Foster
Russell Haygarth (John Carson)
Matron (Petra Davies)
Headmaster (Terence Edmond)

Invitation to a Dynamite Party
Writer Arden Winch
Director Alan Grint
Devlin (Charles Keating)
Malone (Anthony Scott)
Colonel Martin (James Taylor)

SHADES OF DARKNESS*

7 episodes
April 12–May 24, 1984
Produced by Granada Television
Producer June Wyndham Davies

Bewitched
Based on a short story by
Edith Wharton
Writer Alan Plater
Director John Gorrie
Mrs. Rutledge (Eileen Atkins)
Saul Rutledge (Alfred Lynch)
Owen Bosworth (Gareth Thomas)

The Intercessor
Based on a short story by May Sinclair
Writer Alan Plater
Director Peter Smith
Garvin (John Duttine)
Mrs. Falshaw (Maggie Ford)
Mr. Falshaw (David Hargreaves)

Seaton's Aunt
Based on a short story by
Walter de la Mare
Writer Ken Taylor
Director Brian Parker
Seaton (Paul Hertzberg)
Seaton's Aunt (Mary Morris)
Withers (Peter Settelen)

The Lady's Maid's Bell
Based on a short story by
Edith Wharton
Writer Ken Taylor
Director John Glenister
Hartley (Joanna David)
Mrs. Brympton (Norma West)

Afterward
Based on a short story by
Edith Wharton
Writer John Shaughnessy
Director Simon Langton
Mary Boyne (Kate Harper)
Edward Boyne (Michael J. Shannon)

The Maze
Based on a short story by
C. H. B. Kitchin
Writer Ken Taylor
Director Peter Hammond
Catherine (Francesca Annis)
Arthur Frode (James Bolam)
Daisy (Sky McCaskill)

Feet Foremost
Based on a short story by
L. P. Hartley
Writer Ken Taylor
Director Gordon Flemyng
Lady Elinor (Samantha Gates)
Charles Ampleforth (Jeremy Kemp)
Maggie Winthrop (Carole Royle)
Mildred Ampleforth
(Joanna Van Gyseghem)

SHE FELL AMONG THIEVES

single 90-minute episode
February 5, 1980
Produced by BBC
Based on the novel by Dornford Yates

Writer Tom Sharpe
Producer Mark Shivas
Director Clive Donner
Vanity Fair (Eileen Atkins)
Chandos (Malcolm McDowell)
Mansel (Michael Jayston)
Virginia (Sarah Badel)
Jenny (Karen Dotrice)

SHERLOCK HOLMES MYSTERIES

Based on the stories by Sir Arthur
Conan Doyle
Produced by Granada Television
Developed for television by
John Hawkesworth
Sherlock Holmes (Jeremy Brett)
Dr. John Watson
(David Burke/Edward Hardwicke)
Inspector Lestrade (Colin Jeavons)
Mrs. Hudson (Rosalie Williams)

THE ADVENTURES OF SHERLOCK HOLMES*
Producer Michael Cox

SERIES I
7 episodes
March 14–April 25, 1985

A Scandal in Bohemia
Writer Alexander Baron
Director Paul Annett
Irene Adler (Gayle Hunnicutt)
Godfrey Norton (Michael Carter)
King of Bohemia (Wolf Kahler)

The Dancing Men
Writer Anthony Skene
Director John Bruce
Elsie Cubitt (Betsy Brantley)
Hilton Cubitt (Tenniel Evans)
Abe Slaney (Eugene Lipinski)

The Naval Treaty
Writer Jeremy Paul
Director Alan Grint
Percy Phelps (David Gwilym)
Annie Harrison (Alison Skilbeck)
Joseph Harrison (Gareth Thomas)

The Solitary Cyclist
Writer Alan Plater
Director Paul Annett
Carruthers (John Castle)
Woodley (Michael Siberry)
Violet Smith (Barbara Wilshere)

The Speckled Band
Writer Jeremy Paul
Director John Bruce
Dr. Grimesby Roylett (Jeremy Kemp)
Helen Stoner (Rosalyn Landor)
Julia Stoner (Denise Armon)

The Crooked Man
Writer Alfred Shaughnessy
Director Alan Grint
Nancy Barclay (Lisa Daniely)
James Barclay (Denys Hawthorne)
Henry Wood (Norman Jones)
Miss Morrison (Fiona Shaw)

The Blue Carbunkle
Writer Paul Finney

Director David Carson
James Ryder (Ken Campbell)
Henry Baker (Frank Middlemass)
Peterson (Frank Mills)

SERIES II
6 episodes
February 6–March 13, 1986

The Greek Interpreter
Writer Derek Marlowe
Director Alan Grint
Wilson Kemp (George Costigan)
Mycroft Holmes (Charles Gray)
Mr. Melas (Alkis Kritikos)

The Resident Patient
Writer Derek Marlowe
Director David Carson
Dr. Percy Trevelyan (Nicholas Clay)
Blessington (Patrick Newell)
Inspector Lanner (John Ringham)

The Norwood Builder
Writer Richard Harris
Director Ken Grieve
Jonas Oldacre (Jonathan Adams)
Mrs. McFarlane (Helen Ryan)
John Hector McFarlane
(Matthew Solon)

The Copper Beeches
Writer Bill Craig
Director Paul Annett
Jephro Rucastle (Joss Ackland)
Violet Hunter (Natasha Richardson)

The Red-Headed League
Writer John Hawkesworth
Director John Bruce
Professor Moriarty (Eric Porter)
Jabez Wilson (Roger Hammond)

The Final Problem
Writer John Hawkesworth
Director Alan Grint
Professor Moriarty (Eric Porter)
Minister (Claude LeSache)
Louvre Director (Olivier Pierre)

THE RETURN OF SHERLOCK HOLMES*
Producer June Wyndham Davies

SERIES I
7 episodes
February 5–March 19, 1987

The Empty House
Writer John Hawkesworth
Director Howard Baker
Colonel Moran (Patrick Allen)
Sir John Hardy (Richard Bebb)
Countess Maynooth (Naomi Buch)

The Abbey Grange
Writer T. R. Bowen
Director Peter Hammond
Lady Mary Brackenstall
(Anna Louise Lambert)
Sir Eustace Brackenstall
(Conrad Phillips)
Captain Crocker (Oliver Tobias)

The Musgrave Ritual
Writer Jeremy Paul
Director David Carson
Sir Reginald Musgrave (Michael Culver)

Richard Brunton (James Hazeldine)
Rachel Howells (Johanna Kirby)

The Second Stain
Writer John Hawkesworth
Director John Bruce
Lord Bellinger (Harry Andrews)
Lady Hilda Trelawney Hope
(Patricia Hodge)
Right Honorable Trelawney Hope
(Stuart Wilson)

The Man with the Twisted Lip
Writer Alan Plater
Director Patrick Lau
Mrs. St. Clair (Eleanor David)
Neville St. Clair (Clive Francis)
Inspector Broadstreet (Denis Lill)

The Priory School
Writer T. R. Bowen
Director John Madden
Dr. Huxtable (Christopher Benjamin)
James Wilder (Nicholas Gecks)
The Duke of Holdernesse
(Alan Howard)

The Six Napoleons
Writer John Kane
Director David Carson
Venucci (Steve Okytas)
Horace Harker (Eric Sykes)
Beppo (Emile Wolk)

SERIES II
6 episodes
October 27–December 8, 1988

The Sign of Four
Writer John Hawkesworth
Director Peter Hammond
Inspector Athelney Jones (Emrys James)
Thaddeus/Bartholomew Sholto
(Ronald Lacey)
Mary Morstan (Jenny Seagrove)
Jonathan Small (John Thaw)

The Devil's Foot
Writer Gary Hopkins
Director Ken Hannam
Reverend Roundhay (Michael Aitken)
Leon Sterndale (Denis Quilley)
Mortimer Tregennis (Damien Thomas)

Silver Blaze
Writer John Hawkesworth
Director Brian Mills
Colonel Ross (Peter Barkworth)
Edith Baxter (Amanda-Jayne Beard)
John Straker (Barry Lowe)

The Bruce Partington Plans
Writer John Hawkesworth
Director John Gorrie
Mycroft Holmes (Charles Gray)
Inspector Bradstreet (Denis Lill)
Cadogan West (Sebastian Stride)
Violet (Amanda Waring)

Wisteria Lodge
Writer Jeremy Paul
Director Peter Hammond
Inspector Baynes (Freddie Jones)
Henderson (Basil Hoskins)
Miss Burnett (Kika Markham)

The Hound of the Baskervilles
Writer T. R. Bowen
Director Brian Mills
Stapleton (James Faulkner)
Barrymore (Ronald Pickup)
Sir Henry Baskerville (Kristoffer Tabori)

THE CASEBOOK OF SHERLOCK HOLMES*
6 episodes
November 14–December 19, 1991
Producer Brian Eastman

The Illustrious Client
Writer Robin Chapman
Director Tim Sullivan
Violet de Merville (Abigail Cruttenden)
Baron Gruner (Anthony Valentine)

The Creeping Man
Writer Robin Chapman
Director Tim Sullivan
Professor Presbury (Charles Kay)
Jack Bennett (Adrian Lukis)
Edith Presbury (Sarah Woodward)

The Problem of Thor Bridge
Writer Jeremy Paul
Director Michael Simpson
Bates (Niven Boyd)
Gibson (Daniel Massey)
Grace Dunbar (Catherine Russell)

The Boscombe Valley Mystery
Writer John Hawkesworth
Director June Howson
James McCarthy (James Purefoy)
Alice Turner (Joanna Roth)
John Turner (Peter Vaughan)

Shoscombe Old Place
Writer Gary Hopkins
Director Patrick Lau
Sir Robert Norberton (Robin Ellis)
John Mason (Frank Grimes)
Lady Beatrice (Elizabeth Weaver)

*The Disappearance of
Lady Frances Carfax*
Writer T. R. Bowen
Director John Madden
Lady Frances Carfax (Cheryl Campbell)
Albert Shlessinger/Henry Peters
(Julian Curry)
Mrs. Peters (Mary Cunningham)

SHERLOCK HOLMES

SERIES I*
2 episodes
March 11–18, 1993
Producer June Wyndham Davies

The Master Blackmailer
Writer Jeremy Paul
Director Peter Hammond
The Dowager (Gwen Frangcon-Davies)
Charles Augustus Milverton (Robert
Hardy)
Bertrand (Nickolas Grace)
Diana, Lady Swinstead (Norma West)

SERIES II*
4 episodes
January 27–February 17, 1994

The Last Vampyre
Writer Jeremy Paul
Director Tim Sullivan
Dolores (Juliet Aubrey)
Reverend Merridew (Maurice Denham)
John Stockton (Roy Marsden)

The Eligible Bachelor
Writer T. R. Bowen
Director Peter Hammond
Lady Helena/Agnes Northcote (Anna
Calder-Marshall)
Flora Miller (Joanna McCallum)
Robert St. Simon (Simon Williams)

**THE MEMOIRS OF
SHERLOCK HOLMES***
6 episodes
November 30, 1995–January 25, 1996
Producer June Wyndham Davies

The Dying Detective
Writer T. R. Bowen
Director Sarah Hellings
Victor Savage (Richard Bonneville)
Adelaide Savage (Susannah Harker)
Culverton Smith (Jonathan Hyde)

The Cardboard Box
Writer T. R. Bowen
Director Sarah Hellings
Susan Cushing (Joanna David)
Sarah Cushing (Deborah Findlay)
Jim Browner (Ciaran Hinds)

The Three Gables
Writer Jeremy Paul
Director Peter Hammond
Isadora Klein (Claudine Auger)
Mary Maberley (Mary Ellis)
Langdale Pike (Peter Wyngarde)

The Red Circle
Writer Jeremy Paul
Director Sarah Hellings
Inspector Hawkins (Tom Chadbon)
Enrico Firmani (Joseph Long)
Mrs. Warren (Betty Marsden)

The Golden Pince-Nez
Writer Gary Hopkins
Director Peter Hammond
Professor Coram/Serguis (Frank Finlay)
Mycroft Holmes (Charles Gray)
Inspector Hopkins (Nigel Planer)

The Mazarin Stone
Writer Gary Hopkins
Director Peter Hammond
Agnes Garrideb (Phyllis Calvert)
Count Silvius (Jon Finch)
Mycroft Holmes (Charles Gray)
John Garrideb (Gavan O'Herlihy)

**SHROUD FOR A
NIGHTINGALE**

see *Adam Dalgliesh Mysteries*

SWEENEY TODD

single 90-minute episode
October 12, 1982
Produced by Thames Television
Based on the play by George Dibdin Pitt
Writer Vincent Tilsey
Producer Reginald Collin
Director Reginald Collin
Sweeney Todd (Freddie Jones)
Mrs. Lovett/Molly (Heather Canning)
Crumbles/Dr. Fogg/Dr. Makepeace
(Russell Hunter)
Charley/Charlotte (Mel Martin)
Brogden/Mundel/Hopkins (Peter Sallis)

A TASTE FOR DEATH

see *Adam Dalgliesh Mysteries*

UNNATURAL CAUSES

see *Adam Dalgliesh Mysteries*

WE, THE ACCUSED

5 episodes
April 14–May 12, 1983
Produced by BBC
Based on the novel by Ernest Raymond
Writer Julia Jones
Producer Jonathan Powell
Director Richard Stroud
Paul Presset (Ian Holm)
Myra Bawne (Angela Down)
Elinor Presset (Elizabeth Spriggs)
Detective Inspector Boltro
(Iain Cuthbertson)

THE WOMAN IN WHITE

5 episodes
May 2–30, 1985
Produced by BBC
Based on the novel by Wilkie Collins
Writer Ray Jenkins
Producer Jonathan Powell
Director John Bruce
Walter Hartright (Daniel Gerroll)
Laura Fairlie (Jenny Seagrove)
Anne Catherick (Deirdra Morris)
Count Fosco (Alan Badel)
Marian Halcombe (Diana Quick)
Frederick Fairlie (Ian Richardson)
Sir Percival Glyde (John Shrapnel)

APPENDIX B
RESOURCE LIST

HERE IS A REPRESENTATIVE SAMPLING OF WHAT IS
AVAILABLE FOR MYSTERY! BUFFS WHO WANT TO
LEARN MORE ABOUT THEIR FAVORITE PROGRAMS,
BOOKS, AND AUTHORS.

VIDEO

Those Mystery! programs that
are for sale on video (as we go to
press) are noted within in
Appendix A. Because new programs are made available on
video regularly, while others are
pulled from distribution, it is
important to check with major
video outlets about specific titles.
Cassettes of some Mystery! programs are also available for rental
at some public libraries and
video stores and for sale through
Videofinders, 800-343-4727.

BOOKSTORES

Most mainstream bookstores
have extensive mystery sections
and also will special order any
in-print books (and in some
cases videos as well). The following are special-interest bookstores in the U.S. that focus on
the mystery genre.

ARIZONA

CLUES UNLIMITED
123 S. Eastbourne
Tuscon, AZ 85716
520-326-8533
fax: 520-326-9001
E-mail: clues@azstarnet.com
Web site:
http://www.tdigital.com/clues

THE POISONED PEN
7100 E. Main St.
Scottsdale, AZ 85251
602-947-2974
fax: 602-945-1023
E-mail: sales@poisonedpen.com
Website: www.poisonedpen.com

CALIFORNIA

BOOK'EM MYSTERIES
1118 Mission Street
S. Pasadena, CA 91030
818-799-9600
fax: 818-799-9605
E-mail: mystbooks@aol.com
Web site:
http://www.gbm.net/bookem

**GREEN DOOR MYSTERY
BOOKSTORE**
31878 Del Obispo
San Juan Capistrano, CA 92675
714-248-8404

GROUNDS FOR MURDER
3858 5th Street
San Diego, CA 92103
619-299-9500; 800-WHODUNIT
fax: 619-225-8580

MYSTERIES BY MAIL
Box 8515
Ukiah, CA 95482-8515
800-722-0726
E-mail: scp@sodacreekpress.com

**MYSTERIOUS BOOKSHOP
WEST INC.**
8763 Beverly Blvd.
Los Angeles, CA 90048
310-659-2959; 800-821-9017
fax: 310-659-2962
E-mail:
mysteriousbookshp@msn.com

THE MYSTERY ANNEX
1407 Ocean Front Walk
Venice, CA 90291
310-399-2360

**THE SAN FRANCISCO
MYSTERY BOOKSTORE**
4175 24th Street
San Francisco, CA 94114
415-282-7444

THE SILVER DOOR
P.O. Box 3208
Redondo Beach, CA 90277
310-379-6005

COLORADO

BOOK SLEUTH
2501 W. Colorado
Colorado Springs, CO 80904
719-632-2727

MURDER BY THE BOOK
1574 S. Pearl Street
Denver, CO 80210
303-871-9401

THE RUE MORGUE
946 Pearl Street
Boulder, CO 80302
303-443-8346; 800-356-5586

FLORIDA

**SNOOP SISTERS MYSTERY
BOOKSHOPPE**
566 N. Indian Rocks Road
Belleair Bluffs, FL 33770
813-584-4370

GEORGIA

**THE SCIENCE FICTION
AND MYSTERY
BOOKSHOP, LTD.**
2000F Cheshire Bridge Road NE
Atlanta, GA 30324
404-634-3226

ILLINOIS

CENTURIES & SLEUTHS
743 Garfield
Oak Park, IL 60304
708-848-7243

SCOTLAND YARD BOOKS
556 Green Bay Road
Winnetka, IL 60093
847-446-2214
fax: 847-446-2210

INDIANA

MURDER AND MAYHEM
6411 Carrollton Avenue
Indianapolis, IN 46220-1614
317-254-8273
E-mail: jsyrk@aol.com

KANSAS

THE RAVEN BOOKSTORE
8 East 7th Street
Lawrence, KS 66044
913-749-3300

MAINE

DUNN & POWELL BOOKS
The Hideaway
Bar Harbor, ME 04609
207-288-4665
E-mail: dpbooks@acadia.net
Web site:
http://www.dpbooks.com

MARYLAND

**MYSTERY BOOKSHOP
BETHESDA**
*Home of Masterpiece Murder and
Collectible Crime*
7700 Georgetown Road
Bethesda, MD 20814
301-657-2665; 800-572-8533

MYSTERY LOVES
COMPANY
1730 Fleet Street
Baltimore, MD 21231
410-276-6708

MASSACHUSETTS

KATE'S MYSTERY BOOKS
2211 Massachusetts Avenue
Cambridge, MA 02140
617-491-2660
E-mail: katesmysbk@aol.com

SPENSER'S MYSTERY
BOOKSHOP
314 Newbury Street
Boston, MA 02115
617-262-0880

MICHIGAN

DEADLY PASSIONS
BOOKSHOP
157 S. Kalamazoo Mall
Kalamazoo, MI 49007
616-383-4402
fax: 616-383-4403

MINNESOTA

ONCE UPON A CRIME
604 W. 26th Street
Minneapolis, MN 55405
612-870-3785

UNCLE EDGAR'S
MYSTERY BOOKSTORE
2864 Chicago Avenue S
Minneapolis, MN 55407
612-824-9984
E-mail: unclehugo@aol.com

MISSOURI

BIG SLEEP BOOKS
239 N. Euclid
St. Louis, MO 63108
314-361-6100

NEW HAMPSHIRE

MYSTERY LOVERS INK
8 Stiles Road
Salem, NH 03079
603-898-8060

NEW MEXICO

MURDER UNLIMITED—
A MYSTERY STORE
2510 San Mateo Place NE
Albuquerque, NM 87110
505-884-5491

NEW YORK

BLACK ORCHID
BOOKSHOP
303 E. 81 Street
New York, NY 10028
212-734-5980
E-mail: borchid@aol.com

MURDER INK
2486 Broadway
New York, NY 10025
212-362-9805
fax: 212-877-0112

MURDER INK II
1467 Second Avenue
New York, NY 10021
212-517-3222

MYSTERIOUS BOOKSHOP
129 W. 56 Street
New York, NY 10019
212-765-0900; 800-352-2840
fax: 212-265-5478

OCEANSIDE BOOKS, INC.
Corner of Routes 97 and 55
P.O. Box 248
Barryville, NY 12719
914-557-3434

PARTNERS & CRIME
44 Greenwich Avenue
New York, NY 10011
212-243-0440
fax: 212-243-4624
E-mail:
partners@crimepays.com
Web site: http://www.crime-
pays.com

SCIENCE FICTION,
MYSTERIES AND MORE!
140 Chambers Street
New York, NY 10007
212-385-8798

OHIO

FICKES CRIME FICTION
1471 Burkhardt Avenue
Akron, OH 44301
330-773-4223

FOUL PLAY
6072 Busch Boulevard
Columbus, OH 43229
614-848-5583

GRAVE MATTERS—
MYSTERIES BY MAIL
P.O. Box 32192
Cincinnati, OH 45232
513-242-7527 (phone/fax)
E-mail: gravematrs@aol.com

MYSTERIES FROM THE
YARD
253B Xenia Avenue
Yellow Springs, OH 45387
513-767-2111

OREGON

ESCAPE BOOKS
488 Willamette
Eugene, OR 97401
541-484-9500

MURDER BY THE BOOK
7828 SW Capitol Highway
Portland, OR 97210
503-293-6507
E-mail: cave@teleport.com
Web site:
http://www.thecase.com/mbtb/

PENNSYLVANIA

MYSTERY BOOKS
916 N. Lancaster Avenue
Bryn Mawr, PA 19010
610-526-9993
fax: 610-526-1620
E-mail: mystrybk@op.net

THE MYSTERY LOVER'S
BOOKSHOP
514 Allegheny River Boulevard
Oakmont, PA 15139
412-828-4877; 888-800-6078
(toll free)
fax: 412-828-6470
E-mail: 71652.2654@com-
puserve.com
Web site:
http://www.ourworld.com-
puserve.com/homepages/mys-
teryloversbookshop

WHODUNIT?
1931 Chestnut Street
Philadelphia, PA 19103
215-567-1478

TEXAS

MURDER BY THE BOOK
2342 Bissonet
Houston, TX 77005
Web site:
http://www.neosoft.com/~mrdr-
bybk

THE MYSTERY
BOOKSTORE
6906 Snider Plaza
Dallas, TX 75205
214-265-7057
fax: 214-265-8101
E-mail: mystery@onramp.net

VIRGINIA

MAGNA MYSTERIES
P.O. Box 5732
Virginia Beach, VA 23471
804-464-5861

WASHINGTON

SEATTLE MYSTERY
BOOKSHOP
117 Cherry Street
Seattle, WA 98104
206-587-5737
E-mail: susan@eskimo.com
Web site:
http://www.wolfe.net/~netwerks/
smbshome.html

MYSTERY BOOKS
1715 Connecticut Avenue
Washington, D.C. 20009
202-483-1600
fax: 202-387-8252
E-mail: boris1@arols.com
Web site: http://www.killer-
books.com

WISCONSIN

BOOKED FOR MURDER,
LTD.
2701 University Avenue
Madison, WI 53705
608-238-2701
Web site: http://www.infohi-
way.com/way/booked

REFERENCE BOOKS

A Catalog of Crime: Reader's Guide to the Literature of Mystery, Detection and Related Genres. Jacques Barzon and Wendell Hertig Taylor, Harper and Row (New York) 1989.

Crime and Mystery: 100 Best Books. H. R. F. Keating, editor, Carroll & Graf (New York) 1987.

Detectionary: A Biographical Dictionary of Leading Characters in Detective and Mystery Fiction. Otto Penzler et al., compilers, Overlook Press (Woodstock, New York) 1977.

The Fine Art of Murder: The Mystery Reader's Indispensable Companion. Ed Gorman et al., editors, Carroll & Graf (New York) 1993.

Murder Ink: The Mystery Reader's Companion. Dilys Winn, Workman Publishers (New York) 1977 (revised 1984).

Murderess Ink: The Better Half of the Mystery. Dilys Winn, Workman Publishers (New York) 1979.

The New Bedside, Bathtub and Armchair Companion to Agatha Christie. Dick Riley and Pam McAllister, editors, Ungar Press (New York) 1986.

A Reader's Guide to the Classic British Mystery. Susan Oleksiw, G. K. Hall & Co. (Boston) 1988.

PERIODICALS

ALFRED HITCHCOCK MYSTERY MAGAZINE
1540 Broadway
New York, NY 10036
New stories of mystery and suspense published monthly.

THE ARMCHAIR DETECTIVE
129 W. 56th Street
New York, NY 10019
Quarterly publication of mystery and crime fiction.

ELLERY QUEEN'S MYSTERY MAGAZINE
Dell Magazines
1540 Broadway
New York, NY 10036
Monthly compendium of mystery and suspense fiction.

MYSTERY SCENE
P.O. Box 669
Cedar Rapids, IA 52406
Bimonthly journal of reviews, news, and events.

THE THIRD DEGREE
17 East 47th Street
6th Floor
New York, NY 10017
The official newsletter of the Mystery Writers of America, published 10 times/year.

ORGANIZATIONS

MYSTERY WRITERS OF AMERICA
236 W. 27th Street
New York, NY 10001
Their annual Edgar Award is the most prestigious in the genre.

PRIVATE EYE WRITERS OF AMERICA
330 Surrey Road
Cherry Hill, NJ 08002
Gives out Shamus awards for writing..

SISTERS IN CRIME
P.O. Box 442124
Lawrence, KS 66044-8933
Open to anyone specially interested in mystery writing and combatting discrimination against and promoting awareness of women in the mystery field.

CONVENTIONS

Up-to-date information about dates and locations appears regularly in periodicals such as *The Armchair Detective* and *Mystery Scene.*

BOUCHERCON, THE WORLD MYSTERY FAN CONVENTION
(1997 convention to be held in Monterey)
P.O. Box 26114
San Francisco, CA 94126
The largest mystery fan convention (named for critic Anthony Boucher). Traditionally held over Columbus Day weekend in a different location every year; presents the Anthony Awards and Private Eye Writers of America's Shamus Awards.

LEFT COAST CRIME
(1997 convention to be held in Seattle)
c/o 8616 Linden Avenue

North Seattle, WA 98103
Alternates annually between northern and southern West Coast locations, held over Presidents' Day weekend.

MID-ATLANTIC MYSTERY BOOK FAIR & CONFERENCE
Deen and Jay Kogan
c/o Detecto Mysterioso Books at Society Hill Playhouse
507 S. 8th Street
Philadelphia, PA 19147
Regional convention held in Philadelphia each November.

MALICE DOMESTIC
P.O. Box 701
Herndon, VA 22070
Annual celebration of the "cozy" mystery; held each May near Washington, D.C., where the Agatha Awards are presented.

OF DARK AND STORMY NIGHTS
MWA Midwest
P.O. Box 8
Techny, IL 60082
Annual one-day June mystery writing workshop with guest speakers, sponsored by Midwest branch of the Mystery Writers of America.

MISCELLANEOUS

THE SHERLOCK HOLMES MEMORABILIA COMPANY
230 Baker Street
London NW1 5RT, England
01144-171-935-0522
Fax: 01144-171-935-0522
Handcrafted gifts, books, posters celebrating the great detective.

SIGNALS-
WGBH Educational Foundation
P.O. Box 64428
St. Paul, MN 55164-0428
800-669-9696
Catalog for fans of Public Television that offers many Mystery!-related items from Edward Gorey lithographs to videotapes to coffee mugs.

CREDITS

ILLUSTRATIONS AND PHOTOGRAPHS

All of the illustrations in this book (except for the pens and masks on the author and actor pages) are © Edward Gorey, taken from *Amphigorey* (Berkley Publishing Group), *Amphigorey Too* (Harcourt Brace Jovanovich), and *Amphigorey Also* (Berkley Publishing Group), and used with permission of the artist.

Animation stills on the following pages are © Derek Lamb (with Eugene Fedorenko, Janet Perlman, and Rose Newlove), done in the style of Edward Gorey, and used with permission: pages XIV, 20, 204, 272.

Photographs on the following pages are used by permission of British Broadcasting Corporation:16-19; 54-57; 59-67; 68 (top middle, middle right, bottom right); 106-111; 132-138; 140-147; 154-157;198-201;208-222; 230-244; 246-251; 254-256; 259-260; 263-264; 277-281.

Photographs on the following pages are used by permission of Carlton Television: backcover (right); 68 (bottom middle); 70-76; 78-81; 158-165.

Photographs on the following pages are used by permission of Granada Television: backcover (left and far right); 24-29; 32-40; 68 (top left, middle left); 94-98; 100-105; 112-116; 178-182; 268-271; 274; 275 (right).

Photographs on the following pages are used by permission of London Weekend Television: backcover (far left); 42-53; 124-131.

Photographs on the following pages are used by permission of Thames Television—A Pearson Television Company: 68 (top right, bottom left); 148-152; 172-177; 184-197; 223-224; 226-227; 261-262; 276.

Photographs on the following pages are used by permission of Channel 4: 68 (middle middle); 228-229.

Photographs on the following pages are used by permission of International Television Enterprises: 82-85; 87-93; 257-258; 265-266; 275 (left).

Photographs on the following pages are used by permission of Polygram: 166-170.

Photographs on the following pages are used by permission of Yorkshire Television Company: 118-120; 122-123.

Photographs on the following pages are courtesy of WGBH: 3; 4; 10-14.

Photographs on the following pages are used by permission of Popperfoto: 30; 48 (top); 50 (top); 58; 203; 252.

Photographs on pages 8-9 © Derek Lamb.

Images on page 31 used by permission of The Sherlock Holmes Memorabilia Company, London.

Photograph on page 40, top right, by Valerie Cooper.

Photograph on page 77 courtesy of Macmillan Publishing.

Photograph on page 86, top, © Nigel Parry, courtesy P. D. James, used with permission.

Photograph on page 99 © Brian Aris.

Photograph on page 110, top, by Pamela Chandler.

Photograph on page 115, top left, by Yves Debraine, courtesy of Administration de l'Ouevre de Georges Simenon.

Photograph on page 121, left, by Adrian Houston/Idols.

Photograph on page 170, top, courtesy of William B Eerdmans Publishing Co.

Photograph on page 181, top left, by Joe Partridge.

Photograph on page 189, top, © Rosemary Herbert.

REPRINTED MATERIALS

The following excerpted material is used by kind permission of the publishers or authors.

Page 26 Top: excerpted from the *New York Times*. Reprinted with permission.

Page 29 Bottom: © 1987 Time, Inc. Reprinted with permission.

Page 46 Top: excerpted from *Agatha Christie's Poirot: A Celebration of the Great Detective* by Peter Haining, Boxtree, London. Reprinted with permission.

Pages 53 and 146 Excerpted from *Agatha Christie: An Autobiography*, by Agatha Christie. Reprinted with permission.

Page 57 Excerpted from "Dying in Style" by Celia Brayfield in the *London Daily News*. Reprinted by permission of Mirror Group, London.

Page 72 Excerpted from "As the World Turns" by John Leonard in *New York*. © 1988 Los Angeles Times. Reprinted with permission.

Page 81 Excerpted from "British Actor Cracks the Morse Code" by Kay Gardella in the *Daily News*. © New York Daily News, L.P. Reprinted with permission.

Page 85 Excerpted from "Blood and Brains" by John Leonard in *New York*. © 1985 Los Angeles Times. Reprinted with permission.

Page 88 Bottom: excerpted from "The Lady Has a Taste for Murder" by Gayle Kidder in the *San Diego Union*. Reprinted with permission from the author.

Page 99 Excerpted from "Lynda La Plante, Author of *Prime Suspect*, Has A New Heroine" by Elsa Burt, from the December 1995 issue of *At Random*. © 1995 by Random House, Inc. Reprinted by permission of *At Random*.

Page 102 Excerpted from "The Prime of Helen Mirren" by David Ansen in *Newsweek*, May 16 1994. © 1994, Newsweek, Inc. All rights reserved. Reprinted with permission.

Page 103–105 Interview excerpted from *Helen Mirren: Prime Suspect* by Amy Rennert, © 1995 KQED Books. Reprinted with permission.

Page 103 Bottom: excerpted from "The Prime of PBS" by Robert Sullivan in *Vogue*. Reprinted with permission from the author.

Page 104 Bottom: excerpted from "Mirren and Middlemarch" by Christopher Hitchens in *Vanity Fair*, May 1994. Reprinted with permission from the author.

Page 105 Bottom: excerpted from "Acting Tough with Intent" by David Lister in the *Independent*. Reprinted with permission.

Page 121 Excerpted from "Two Outsiders Who Became a Winning Double" by Romany Bain in *TV Times*. Reprinted with permission.

Page 130 Francesca Annis quoted in "5 Oh-So-Elegant Christie Tales" by Bart Mills in the *Philadelphia Inquirer*. © Bart Mills. Reprinted with permission.

Page 131 Excerpted from "The Moving Finger" by Nancy Banks-Smith in the *Guardian*. © the *Guardian*. Reprinted with permission.

Pages 142 and 145 Excerpted from "Diversionary Devices" by Peter Kemp in the *Times Literary Supplement*. Reprinted with permission.

Page 144 Excerpted from "Murder Most Tidy" by John Mortimer in the *New York Times Magazine*. Reprinted with permission.

Page 153 Excerpted from "Who Dunit? The Mysterious Appeal of the Mystery" by Carolyn Heilbrun, aka Amanda Cross, in *Harper's Bazaar*, November 1995. Reprinted with permission of the author.

Page 156 Excerpted from "Car Chases? Not For These Gentlemanly Sleuths" by John J. O'Connor in the *New York Times*. Reprinted with permission.

Page 165 Excerpted from "Catching the Crime Habit" by Simon Says in the *Daily Mirror*. Reprinted by permission of Mirror Group, London.

Page 180 Excerpted from "Seduction and Betrayal" by John Leonard in *New York* magazine. © 1989 Los Angeles Times. Reprinted with permission.

Page 182 Top: excerpted from "Game, Set: Espionage Anyone?" by Howard Rosenberg in the *Los Angeles Times*. © 1989 Los Angeles Times. Reprinted with permission.

Pages 187 and 192 Excerpted from *Murderers and Other Friends: Another Part of Life* by John Mortimer, Viking 1995. Reprinted with permission.

Page 197 Top: excerpted from *Agatha Christie: The Woman and Her Mysteries* by Gillian Gill. © 1990 by Gillian Gill. Reprinted with permission of The Free Press, a division of Simon & Schuster.

Page 218 Excerpted from "Thrilling In The Best Sense" by Julian Symons in the *Sunday Times*. © Julian Symons. Reprinted with permission.

Page 219 Ruth Rendell quoted by Anwer Bati in the *Times Saturday Review*, September 7, 1991. © Anwer Bati. Reprinted with permission.

INDEX

NOTE:
*PAGE NUMBERS IN BOLDFACE TYPE INDICATE
PRINCIPAL REFERENCES.*

A

Abbey Grange, The, 295
ABC Murders, The, 287
Abracadaver, 38, 294
Absolute Conviction, 290
Adam Dalgliesh Mysteries. See Dalgliesh,
  Commander Adam
Adams, Polly, 216, 286, 289
Adventure of Johnnie Waverly, The, 286-287
Adventure of the Cheap Flat, The, 287
Adventure of the Clapham Cook, The, 286
Adventure of the Egyptian Tomb, The, 287
Adventure of the Italian Nobleman, The, 287
Adventure of the Western Star, The, 277, 287
Adventures of Sherlock Holmes, The, 15, **25-
35**, 173, 294. *See also Sherlock Holmes*
Affair at the Victory Ball, The, 280, 287
Affair of the Pink Pearl, The, 126, 127, 291
Afterward, 268, **270,** 294
Agatha Christie's Miss Marple, 6, 15, 22, 48,
  51, 68, 99, 139, **141-147,** 152, 153, 156,
  167, 201, 275, 276, 277, 281, 286
Agatha Christie's Poirot, 15, 22, 25, 41, **43-
53,** 55, 71, 77, 87, 109, 141, 142, 144, 165,
  173, 182, 206, 275, 276, 277, 279, 286-288
Agatha Christie Stories, 15, 48, 156, 183,
  195-197, 279, 280, 288
Aitken, Maria, 149, 292. *See also Quiet
As a Nun*
Aldridge, Michael, 155, 156, 173, 288, 289,
  290, 292
Alleyn, Inspector Roderick. *See Ngaio
Marsh's Alleyn Mysteries*
Allingham, Margery, 63, 64, **66-67,** 107, 288
Ambassador's Boots, The, 131, 292
Amyes, Julian, 286, 289, 293, 294
Anderson, Miles, 199, 291
Andrews, Harry, 257, 258, 288, 295
Anglia Television, 83, 84, 101, 257, 266, 286,
  288, 291
Annis, Francesca, 125, 127, 130, 270, 291,
  293, 294. *See also* Beresford, Tommy and
  Tuppence
Artists in Crime, 15, 107, 108, 275, 288, 291
Asherson, Renee, 149, 286, 292
At Bertram's Hotel, 286
Atkins, Eileen, 16, 17, 18, **19,** 268, 278, 294
Awards
  for *Malice Aforethought,* 242
  for *Mother Love,* 208, 209
  for *Prime Suspect,* 95, 99, 101, 102, 103
Ayers, Rosalind, 261, 290

B

Badel, Alan, 233, 234, 235, 288, 295
Badel, Sarah, 16, 294
BAFTA award, 99, 102, 103, 208, 209, 242
Bailey, Robin, 155, 156, 289, 293
Baker Street Irregulars, 27, 275
Bannen, Ian, 212, 286, 289
Barkworth, Peter, 263, 291, 293, 295
Barnes, Dominique, 236, 288
Bate, Anthony, 179, 180, 287, 289, 290
Bates, Alan, 199, 201, 280, 291
Bates, Peggy Thorpe, 185, 292
Bates, Ralph, 196, 288
BBC (British Broadcasting Corporation),
  16, 55, 56, 63, 100, 107, 133, 138, 141, 145,
  155, 199, 208, 212, 216, 222, 230, 233, 235,
  236, 239, 240,
  242, 246, 248, 254, 259, 263, 286, 288, 289,
  291, 292, 294, 295
Becton, Henry, 2, 3, 9
Bell, Tom, 95, 292
Benfield, John, 95, 291, 292
Benham, Joan, 263, 291
Bennett, Edward, 286, 287, 288, 290
Bennett, Hywel, 242, 291
Beresford, Tommy and Tuppence, 6, 48, 51,
  88, 108, 117, **125-131,** 168. *See also
Partners in Crime; Secret Adversary, The*
Berkeley, Anthony, 202. *See also* Iles, Francis
Bertish, Suzanne, 261, 290
Bewitched, **268,** 294
Beynon, Richard, 242, 243, 244, 248,
  291, 292
Bickleigh, Dr. Edmund. *See Malice
Aforethought*
Black Tower, The, 15, 83, 84, 274, 286, 288
Blair, Isla, 208, 291
Blakiston, Caroline, 155, 286, 289, 292
Blue Carbunkle, The, 294
Blythe, Peter, 185, 287, 292
Body in the Library, The, 141, 142, 286
Bolam, James, 261, 290, 294
Bond, Samantha, 185, 287, 292
Bookstores, mystery-oriented, 296-298
Boscombe Valley Mystery, The, 295
Bowen, John, 223-224, 289
Bowen, T. R., 286, 287, 288, 291, 295
Bowles, Peter, 185, 292
Bowman, George, 257, 258
Brat Farrar, 15, 225, **236-238,** 279, 288
Braun, Pinkas, 228, 292
Brett, Jeremy, 25-27, 28, 29, **33-34,** 68, 165,
  246, 248, 292, 294. *See also Sherlock
Holmes*
Brown, Father. *See Father Brown*
Browne, Angela, 236, 288
Bruce, John, 287, 291, 294, 295

Bruce Partington Plans, The, 295
Burgess, Dennis, 167, 289
Burke, David, 25, 26, 28, **32,** 68, 149, 173,
  292, 294. *See also* Watson, Dr. John
Burt, Andrew, 63, 286, 288, 293

C

Cadfael, 15, 139, **159-165,** 275, 277, 288
Caldicott, Giles Evelyn. *See* Charters and
  Caldicott
Campbell, Cheryl, 242, 286, 290, 291, 295
Campion, 15, 22, 41, **63-67,** 68, 107, 108,
  278, 281, 288
Canning, Heather, 226, 227, 295
Capaldi, Peter, 133, **135,** 138, 287, 288, 292
Cardboard Box, The, 275, 295
Carmichael, Ian, 2
Carter, Helena Bonham, 216-217, 289
Casebook of Sherlock Holmes, The, 15, **25-35,**
  295. *See also Sherlock Holmes*
Case of Spirits, A, 38, 294
Case of the Discontented Soldier, The, 195,
  196, 288
Case of the Late Pig, The, 63, 64, 281, 288
Case of the Middle-Aged Wife, The, 195, 288
Case of the Missing Lady, The, 292
Case of the Missing Will, The, 287
Cause Célèbre, 15, 52, 206, 245, **257-258,**
  280, 288
Central Independent Television, 71, 159,
  288, 289, 290
Chandler & Co., 15, 22, 114, 117, **133-138,**
  277, 288-289
Chandler, Raymond, 153, 255
Chandos, Robert, 16, 17, 18
Chaplin, Geraldine, 246, 250, 251, 291
Chapman, Robin, 83-84, 286, 291, 295
Charnock, Mark, 159, 162, 288
Charters and Caldicott, 15, 139, **155-157,**
  275, 289
Cherubim and Seraphim, 290
Chesterton, G. K., 167, 168, 169, **170,** 190,
  202, 203, 289
Chocolate Box, The, 287
Choir That Wouldn't Sing, The, 294
Christie, Dame Agatha, **48-51,** 66, 67, 107,
  153, 156, 168, 195, 197, 202, 244, 278, 280
  Agatha Christie's Miss Marple, 6, 15, 22,
    48, 51, 68, 99, 139, **141-147,** 152, 153, 156,
    167, 201, 275, 276, 277, 281, 286
  Agatha Christie's Poirot, 15, 22, 25, 41, **43-
53,** 55, 71, 77, 87, 109, 141, 142, 144, 165,
    173, 182, 206, 275, 276, 277, 279, 286-288
  Agatha Christie Stories, 15, 48, 156, 183,
    195-197, 279, 280, 288
  Partners in Crime, 6, 15, 48, 117, **125-131,**
    168, 278, 291-292

Secret Adversary, The, 15, 48, 117, **125-131**, 276, 293
  See also Beresford, Tommy and Tuppence
Chronology, 15
Clergyman's Daughter, The, 128, 130, 292
Coleman, Charlotte, 199, 291
Coleridge, Sylvia, 149, 150, 292, 293
Collins, Wilkie, 206, 218, **233-235**, 295
Copley, Peter, 159, 286, 288
Copper Beeches, The, 294
Cornish Mystery, The, 287
Cover Her Face, 15, 83, 84, 86, 87-88, 142, 286
Cox, Anthony Berkeley. *See* Iles, Francis
Cox, Arthur, 125, 291
Cox, Sam, 239, 289
Coy, Jonathan, 185, 287, 290, 292
Crackler, The, 292
Creeping Man, The, 295
Cribb, Sergeant. *See* Sergeant Cribb
Crooked Man, The, 28, 294
Cropper, Anna, 228, 286, 287, 292
Crowley, Jeananne, 173, 292
Culver, Michael, 159, 162, 179, 261, 262, 286, 288, 289, 290, 295
Curry, Julian, 185, 187, 292, 295
Curtain, 44, 46, 51
Curteis, Ian, 267, 291
Cusack, Sinead, 199, 201, 291
Cuthbertson, Iain, 259, 287, 288, 290, 292, 295

D
Dalgliesh, Commander Adam, xiii, 22, 25, 68, 69, **83-90**, 91-93, 107, 110, 142, 276, 277, 279, 281, 286
Dancers in Mourning, 288
Dancing Men, The, 28, 294
Daniel, Jennifer, 187, 293
Danvers, Mrs., 246, **247-248**, 249, 270
Dark-Adapted Eye, A, 15, 202, 206, 207, **216-218**, **221-222**, 277, 289
Dark Angel, The, 15, 206, 225, **230-232**, 277, 289
Daughters of Cain, The, 81
David, Joanna, 74, 114, 196, 246, 248, 269, 286, 288, 290, 291, 292, 293, 294, 295
Davies, Andrew, 210, 211, 291
Davies, June Wyndham, 29, 293, 294, 295
Davison, Peter, 63, 68, 286, 288. *See also* Campion
Day of the Devil, The, 277, 290
Deadly Slumber, 290
Dead Man's Mirror, 287
Dead of Jericho, The, 71, 72, 80, 289
Dead on Time, 74, 290
Death at the Bar, 291
Death in a White Tie, 109, 291
Death in the Clouds, 28
Death of a Ghost, 288
Death of an Expert Witness, 15, 69, **83-84**, 92, 286, 289
Death of the Self, 74, 75, 81, 290
Deceived by Flight, 71, 290
Degen, Michael, 179, 180, 289

Deighton, Len, 179-180, **181-182**, 202, 280, 289
De la Mare, Walter, 268, 269, 294
Denham, Maurice, 195, 286, 288, 295
Detection Club, **202-203**, 244
Detective Wore Silk Drawers, The, 38, 294
Devices and Desires, 15, 83, 84, 277, 286, 289
Devil's Foot, The, 29, 295
Devil's Novice, The, 288
Dexter, Colin, 50, 71, 75, **77-79**, 80, 289-290
Dickens, Charles, 233
Dinsdale, Reece, 125, 127, 291
Disappearance of Mr. Davenheim, The, 45, 287
Disappearance of Lady Frances Carfax, The, 295
Dobie, Alan, 37, 39, 293. *See also* Sergeant Cribb
Donner, Clive, 17, 18, 294
Donohoe, Amanda, 179, 289
Dorothy L. Sayers' Lord Peter Wimsey, 2, 15, 22, 41, **55-61**, 63, 66, 87, 107, 108, 110, 278, 279, 289
Dors, Diana, 212, 289
Dotrice, Karen, 16, 17, 294
Double Clue, The, 287
Double Sin, 45, 47, 287
Down, Angela, 259, 287, 295
Doyle, Sir Arthur Conan, 22, 23, 25-29, **30-31**, 32-35, 37, 43, 48, 55, 156, 159, 169, 270, 279, 294-295. *See also* Sherlock Holmes
Dream, The, 287
Driven to Distraction, 68, 72, 73, 75, 290
Dr. Jekyll and Mr. Hyde, 11, 15, 206, 207, **212-215**, 276, 280, 289
Du Maurier, Daphne, 3, 246-251, **252-253**, 270, 291, 292
Dumb Witness, 46, 288
Durbridge, Francis, 263-264, 270, 291
Du Sautoy, Carmen, 228, 229, 287, 292
Duttine, John, 268-269, 294
Dying Day, 15, 207, **223-224**, 280, 289
Dying Detective, The, 295

E
Eastman, Brian, 44, 46, 286, 287, 295
Eaton, Rebecca, 3, 12, 13, 97, 180
Edney, Beatie, 230, 231, 289
Eligible Bachelor, The, 295
Ellis, Jack, 95, 292
Ellis, Robin, 216, 289, 295
Emmy award, 95, 96, 101
Empty House, The, 294
Engel, Tina, 239, 289
Euston Films, 292
Exton, Clive, 286, 287, 288
Eye of Apollo, The, 167, 289

F
Fairbrass, Craig, 95, 97, 292
Fair, Vanity, 16, 17, 18, **19**
Family Matters, 134, 289
"Fantods," 4, 6
Farnham, Brian, 250, 287, 288, 291, 293
Farrar, Brat. *See* Brat Farrar

Farrell, Nicholas, 196, 288
Fat Chance, 74, 290
Father Brown, 15, 139, 159, **167-170**, 280, 289
Feet Foremost, 268, **270**, 294
Final Curtain, 109, 291
Final Problem, The, 35, 294
Finessing the King, 292
Firth, Julian, 159, 162, 288
Fleetwood, Susan, 138
Flemyng, Robert, 246, 292
Flowers for the Judge, 288
Flynn, Barbara, 113, 114, 133, **135**, 138, 288, 289, 290
Ford, Mick, 119, 120, 292
Forrest, Frederic, 239, **240**, 289
Foster, Melissa. *See* Melissa
4:50 from Paddington, 286
Fourth Man, The, 196, 288
Four and Twenty Blackbirds, 287
Fowlds, Derek, 239, 289, 294
Francis, Dick, 2, 119-120, **121-123**, 153, 202, 292
Fraser, Bill, 185, 286, 292, 293
Fraser, Hugh, 43, 44, **47**, 109, 173, 179, 286, 289, 292
Fraser, Lady Antonia, 149, 150, **151-152**, 270
Fraser, Ronald, 263, 291
Friend, Martyn, 286, 288, 291, 293
Fywell, Tim, 216, **222**, 289

G
Gallaccio, George, 107-108, 286, 291
Galloway, Jack, 113, 290
Gallowglass, 15, 202, 207, **216**, **219-222**, 276, 289
Gambling Lady, 292
Gambon, Michael, 113-114, 290
Game, Set and Match, 15, 68, 171, **179-182**, 279, 280, 289, 292
Gaudy Night, 55, 58, 60, 87, 278, 289
Georgeson, Tom, 254, 291
Gerroll, Daniel, 233, 234, 295
Ghost in the Machine, 75, 290
Gilliat, Sidney, 155, 289
Gillies, Fiona, 208, 291
Girl in the Train, The, 196, 288
Glenister, John, 290, 293, 294
Glover, Brian, 63, 64, **65**, 67, 288
Goddard, Jim, 290, 292, 293
Golden Pince-Nez, The, 295
Good guys as bad guys, 68
Gordon, Hannah, 266, 267, 291
Gorey, Edward, 3, **4-8**, 9
Gorrie, John, 286, 288, 293, 294, 295
Granada Television, 25, 37, 95, 97, 100, 101, 113, 179, 268, 289, 290, 292, 293, 294
Gray, Cordelia, 88, 142
Greek Interpreter, The, 294
Greeks Bearing Gifts, 290
Greenstreet, Mark, 236, 237, 288
Grieve, Andrew, 286, 287, 289
Grout, James, 71, 72, 208, 288, 289, 291, 293
Guard, Christopher, 242, 243, 246, 250, 251, 291
Gwilym, Mike, 119, 120, 121, 122, 123, 292

H

Halley, Sid. *See Racing Game, The*
Hammett, Dashiell, 153
Hammond, Peter, 231, 289, 290, 293, 294, 295
Happy Families, 290
Hardwicke, Edward, 25, 27, 28, **32**, 34, 294. *See also* Watson, Dr. John
Harrow, Lisa, 212, 214, 287, 289
Hartley, L. P., 268, 270, 271, 294
Hastings, Captain Arthur, 43, 44, **47**, 109, 280
Have His Carcase, 55, 57, 289
Hawkesworth, John, 63, 288, 294, 295
Hayes, Helen, 141, 143, 146
Head of Caesar, The, 167, 289
Hemmings, David, 212, 213, 214, 286, 289
Hercule Poirot. See Agatha Christie's Poirot
Hercule Poirot's Christmas, 288
Hickory, Dickory, Dock, 44, 45, 288
Hickson, Joan, 6, 141, 143-144, **146-147**, 286
Hiller, Dame Wendy, 266, 267, 286, 291
Hillwood, Amanda, 71, 74, 289
Hitchcock, Alfred, 77, 155, 196, 237, 242, 247-248
Hodge, Patricia, 185, 290, 292, 293, 295
Hodson, Christopher, 288, 289, 291, 292
Hogan, Bosco, 266, 286, 291
Holloway, Julian, 246, 292, 293
Holm, Ian, 51, 68, 179, **182**, 259, 289, 295
Holmes, Sherlock. *See Sherlock Holmes*
Horizontal Witness, The, 294
Horovitch, David, 141, 142, 286, 287
Horsenap, 292
Horses for Courses, 292
Hound of the Baskervilles, The, 29, 32, 270, 274, 295
House of Lurking Death, The, 126, 291
How Does Your Garden Grow?, 287
Howlett, John, 179, 289
Humble, William, 286, 287, 290, 291
Hunter, Russell, 226, 295
Hutchings, Geoffrey, 113, 290
Hyde, Mr. *See Dr. Jekyll and Mr. Hyde*

I

Iles, Francis, 202, 242-243, **244**, 291
Illustrious Client, The, 295
Imrie, Celia, 216-217, 289
In a Glass Darkly, 196, 288
Incredible Theft, The, 15, 287
Infernal Serpent, The, 290
Inspector Alleyn Mysteries. See Ngaio Marsh's Alleyn Mysteries
Inspector Morse, 15, 22, 25, 37, 68, 69, **71-81**, 83, 91, 162, 175, 206, 274, 275, 276, 277, 278, 289-290
Intercessor, The, **268-269,** 294
Invitation to a Dynamite Party, 294
ITC Entertainment, 167, 289

J

Jackson, Philip, 43-44, 286
Jacobi, Sir Derek, 159, 160, **165**, 288
James, P. D., xiii, 22, 25, 69, 83-85, **86-90,** 91-93, 107, 110, 142, 144, 145, 202, 276, 279, 286
Jane in Search of a Job, 196, 288
Japp, Chief Inspector, 43-44, 45
Jayston, Michael, 16, 17, 294
Jeavons, Colin, 25, 236, 288, 294
Jekyll, Dr. *See Dr. Jekyll and Mr. Hyde*
Jenkins, Ray, 235, 295
Jewel Robbery at the Grand Metropolitan, 287
John, Gottfried, 179, 289
Jones, Julia, 150, 286, 292, 295
Jones, Morgan, 199, 291
Jones, Freddie, 226, 227, 295

K

Kay, Charles, 246, 250, 291, 295
Kemp, Jeremy, 270, 294
Kidnapped Prime Minister, The, 287
Kinder, Die, 15, 136, 138, 206, 225, **239-241,** 275, 279, 289
King of Clubs, The, 287
Kirby, Amanda, 246, 291
Kitchin, C. H. B., 268, 270, 294
Kremer, Hans, 239, 289

L

Lady's Maid's Bell, The, 268, **269,** 294
Lamb, Derek, 3, 4, 6, **9**
Lamont, Miss Frances. *See Miss Morison's Ghosts*
Lang, Belinda, 47, 107, 108, **109,** 291
Langton, Simon, 210, 248, 291, 292, 294
Lansbury, Angela, 141, 143, 153
La Plante, Lynda, 95, 96, **99-101,** 105, 292
Lapotaire, Jane, 230, 231, 289
Larkin, James, 113, 290
Last Bus to Woodstock, 77, 78, 290
Last Enemy, The, 290
Last Seen Wearing, 290
Last Trumpet, The, 294
Last Vampyre, The, 29, 68, 295
Launder, Frank, 155, 289
Lear, Peter. *See* Lovesey, Peter
Le Fanu, Sheridan, 230-231, **232,** 289
Lehmann, Beatrix, 261, 262, 290
Leonard, Sandy, 12
Leper of St. Giles, The, 162, 288
Lewis, Detective Sergeant, 25, 71, 72, 73, 75, **76,** 78, 79, 162, 274, 275
Limbo Connection, The, 15, 206, 245, **261-262,** 281, 290
Liverpool Films, 254
London Weekend Television, 43, 101, 125, 286, 291, 293
Longrigg, Roger. *See* Taylor, Domini
Lonnen, Ray, 263, 291
Look at the Lady, 288
Lord Peter Wimsey. See Dorothy L. Sayers' Lord Peter Wimsey
Lost Mine, The, 287
Lovesey, Peter, 3, 37, **40,** 293-294
Lugg, Magersfontein, 63, 64, **65**
Lunghi, Cherie, 68, 196, 228, 229, 288, 292

M

MacDonald, Ross, 153
Mackie, Philip, 290, 291, 292
Mackintosh, Elizabeth. *See* Tey, Josephine
Mackintosh, Steven, 216, 288, 289, 291
Macnaughton, Alan, 230, 288, 289
Madden, Ciaran, 113, 114, 196, 287, 288, 290
Mad Hatter's Holiday, 294
Magnolia Blossom, The, 196, 288
Maigret, 15, 69, **113-116,** 276, 278, 290-291
Maigret and the Burglar's Wife, 114, 290-291
Maigret and the Home Ground, 291
Maigret and the Hotel Majestic, 291
Maigret and the Mad Woman, 290
Maigret and the Maid, 291
Maigret and the Minister, 114, 291
Maigret and the Nightclub Dancer, 291
Maigret Goes to School, 291
Maigret on the Defensive, 276, 291
Maigret's Boyhood Friend, 291
Maigret Sets a Trap, 114, 135, 290
Malahide, Patrick, 68, 75, 107, 108, 110, 290, 291
Malice Aforethought, 15, 156, 202, 225, **242-244,** 278, 291
Man from the Pru, The, 15, 206, 245, **254-256,** 281, 291
Manhood of Edward Robinson, The, 68, 196, 288
Man in the Mist, The, 168, 292
Man Lay Dead, A, 109, 291
Man with the Twisted Lip, The, 295
Marple, Miss Jane. *See Agatha Christie's Miss Marple*
Marsden, Roy, 68, 83, 84, 85, **91-93,** 286, 295. *See also* Dalgliesh, Commander Adam
Marsh, Dame Ngaio, 15, 47, 69, 107, **110-111,** 153, 291
Martin, Mel, 84, 179, 226, 227, 281, 286, 287, 289, 290, 295
Martin, Troy Kennedy, 174, 292
Masonic Mysteries, 76, 290
Massey, Anna, 246, 247, 248, 249, 254, 256, 291, 292
Mathie, Marion, 185, 292
Matthews, Francis, 236, 288
Maxwell, James, 119, 120, 292, 293
Mazarin Stone, The, 34, 279, 295
Maze, The, 268, **270,** 294
McArdle, John, 216, 219, 289
McBain, Kenny, 80, 289, 290
McCallum, David, 208, 209, 279, 291
McCarthy, Eoin, 159, 161, 288
McDowell, Malcolm, 16, 17, **18,** 294
McEnery, John, 43, 287
McKellan, Ian, 223, 289
McKern, Abigail, 185, 193, 292
McKern, Leo, 68, 173, **177,** 185, 188, 191, **192-193,** 292, 293
Melissa, 15, 206, 245, **263-264,** 270, 274, 291
Memoirs of Sherlock Holmes, The, 15, **25-35,** 275, 279, 295. *See also Sherlock Holmes*
Mercer, Cecil William. *See* Yates, Dornford

Million Dollar Bond Robbery, The, 279, 287
Milne, Paula, 133, 135, **136-138**, 239-241, 288, 289
Mind to Murder, A, 15, 83, 84-85, 87, 90, 277, 286, 291
Minghella, Anthony, 80, 289, 290
Miriam, Sister, 149-150, 275
Mirren, Helen, 95, 96, 101, **102-105**, 257-258, 288, 292. *See also* Tennison, DCI Jane
Miss Marple. See Agatha Christie's Miss Marple
Miss Morison's Ghosts, 15, 206, 265, **266-267**, 276, 291
Monk's Hood, 159, 161, 288
Monteilhet, Hubert, 228, 229, 292
Moran, Pauline, 43, 286
Morant, Richard, 55, **60**, 196, 288, 289, 293
More, Kenneth, 167, 289. *See also Father Brown*
Moriarty, Professor James, **35**, 294
Morison, Miss Elizabeth. *See Miss Morison's Ghosts*
Morris, Deirdra, 233, 234, 295
Morris, Mary, 269, 284, 288
Morrissey, David, 257, 288
Morse, Chief Inspector. *See Inspector Morse*
Mortimer, John, 2, 50, 185, 186-188, **189-191**, 192, 292, 293
Mother Love, 13, 15, 206, 207, **208-211**, 274, 279, 291
Moving Finger, The, 286
Murder at the Vicarage, 28
Murder by the Book, 51, 182
Murder in the Mews, 286
Murder Is Announced, A, 201, 286
Murder Old Boy, 294
Murder on the Links, 288
Murphy, Gerard, 155, 156, 289
Musgrave Ritual, The, 295
My Cousin Rachel, 15, 136, 206, 245, **246, 250-251**, 252, 253, 279, 291
Mysterious Affair at Styles, The, 43, 47, 49, 287
Mystery, attraction of, x, xi
Mystery!, chronology of, 15
Mystery Mile, 288
Mystery of the Blue Jar, The, 156, 196, 288
Mystery of the Hunter's Lodge, The, 287
Mystery of the Spanish Chest, The, 43, 287

N
Naval Treaty, The, 294
Needle, 292
Neill, Sam, 173, **176**, 292. *See also Reilly, Ace of Spies*
Nemesis, 145, 286
Newton, Madelaine, 76
Ngaio Marsh's Alleyn Mysteries, 15, 25, 47, 68, 69, **107-111**, 275, 291
Norwood Builder, The, 294
Nursing Home Murder, The, 111, 291

O
Odds Against, 119, 123, 292
Oliver's Travels, 15, 183, **199-201**, 280, 291
One Corpse Too Many, 288

One, Two, Buckle My Shoe, 287
On the Job, 288
Original Sin, 15, 83, 85, 89, 286, 291
O'Toole, Peter, 230-231, 289

P
Parfitt, Judy, 242
Pargeter, Dame Edith. *See* Peters, Ellis
Partners in Crime, 6, 15, 48, 117, **125-131**, 168, 278, 291-292. *See also* Beresford, Tommy and Tuppence
Pasco, Richard, 254, 291
Past Imperfect, 289
Patience of Maigret, The, 114, 290
Patterson, Bill, 199, 291
Paul, Jeremy, 288, 294, 295
Peabody award, 95, 292
Peake-Jones, Tessa, 155, 289
Peril at End House, 287
Pertwee, Sean, 159, 161, 288
Peters, Ellis, 159-160, 161, 163, **164**, 288
Petherbridge, Edward, 55, 56, 57, 114, 289, 291
Pickles, Vivian, 246, 266, 291, 292
Pitt, George Dibdin, 226-227, 295
Plater, Alan, 199, 201, 286, 288, 290, 291, 293, 294, 295
Plymouth Express, The, 287
Pocketful of Rye, A, 68, 142, 145, 286
Poirot, Hercule. *See Agatha Christie's Poirot*
Police at the Funeral, 288
Porter, Eric, 35, 294
Portman Productions, 228, 292
Powell, Gwyneth, 223-224, 289
Powell, Jonathan, 212, 213, 235, 289, 295
Praying Mantis, 15, 68, 225, **228-229**, 281
Price, Vincent, 6, **11-12**, 14, 147
Priest, Diane. *See Oliver's Travels*
Prime Suspect, 3, 15, 22, 69, **95-105**, 278, 292, *See also* Tennison, DCI Jane
Prime Suspect 2, 15, 95, 96, 97-98, 99, 101, 279, 292
Prime Suspect 3, 15, 96, 97, 99, 101, 103, 293
Prime Suspect: The Lost Child (Prime Suspect 4), 96, 101
Priory School, The, 295
Problem at Sea, 287
Problem of Thor Bridge, The, 295
Promised Land, 81, 290
Pryce, Jonathan, 228, 254, 255, 256, 291, 292
Pyne, Parker, 183, **195-197**, 279

Q
Quick, Diana, 233, 234, 290, 291, 295
Quiet As a Nun, 15, 68, 139, **149-152**, 270, 275, 292
Quinn, Derry, 261-262, 290
Quiz, 274-285

R
Rachel. *See My Cousin Rachel*
Racing Game, The, 2, 3, 15, 117, **119-123**, 275, 292
Rattenbury, Alma. *See Cause Célèbre*
Rattigan, Terence, 257-258, 288
Raymond, Ernest, 259, **260**, 295

Rebecca, 3, 15, 25, 68, 206, 245, **246-249**, 251, 252, 253, 270, 274, 292
Red Circle, The, 276, 295
Red-Headed League, The, 35, 294
Redmond, Moira, 263, 291
Red Signal, The, 196, 288
Reid, Alastair, 80, 213, 289, 290
Reilly, Ace of Spies, 15, 17, 32, 52, 68, 156, 171, **173-177**, 192, 280, 292
Rendell, Ruth, 50, 90, 107, 202, 216, 218, 219, **221-222**, 289. *See also* Vine, Barbara
Resident Patient, The, 294
Resource list, 296-298
Return of Sherlock Holmes, The, 15, **25-35**, 294-295. *See also* Sherlock Holmes
Rhys, Paul, 216, 219, **220**, 289
Richardson, Ian, 233, 234, 235, 295
Richardson, Miranda, 239, 241, 289
Riddington, Ken, 63, 288, 291
Rigg, Dame Diana, **13-14**, 147, 208, 209, **210-211**, 247, 249, 279, 291
Riscoe, Deborah, 84, 87-88
Robinson, Edward, 68, 196
Rodger, Struan, 133, 288, 291, 293
Rodway, Norman, 187, 290
Rosenberg, John, 84, 286, 288, 291
Rumpole, Horace. *See Rumpole of the Bailey*
Rumpole a la Carte, 293
Rumpole and Portia, 293
Rumpole and the Age for Retirement, 293
Rumpole and the Age of Miracles, 293
Rumpole and the Barrow Boy, 293
Rumpole and the Blind Tasting, 293
Rumpole and the Bright Seraphim, 293
Rumpole and the Bubble Reputation, 187, 293
Rumpole and the Case of Identity, 293
Rumpole and the Children of the Devil, 293
Rumpole and the Course of True Love, 293
Rumpole and the Eternal Triangle, 293
Rumpole and the Family Pride, 293
Rumpole and the Fascist Beast, 187, 293
Rumpole and the Female of the Species, 187, 293
Rumpole and the Genuine Article, 293
Rumpole and the Golden Thread, 293
Rumpole and the Heavy Brigade, 292
Rumpole and the Honourable Member, 292
Rumpole and the Judge's Elbow, 293
Rumpole and the Last Resort, 293
Rumpole and the Learned Friends, 292
Rumpole and the Man of God, 293
Rumpole and the Married Lady, 292
Rumpole and the Miscarriage of Justice, 274, 293
Rumpole and the Official Secret, 293
Rumpole and the Old Boy Network, 293
Rumpole and the Old, Old Story, 293
Rumpole and the Quacks, 293
Rumpole and the Quality of Life, 293
Rumpole and the Reform of Joby Johnson, 293
Rumpole and the Right to Silence, 293
Rumpole and the Show Folk, 293
Rumpole and the Sporting Life, 293

Rumpole and the Summer of Discontent, 293
Rumpole and the Tap End, 293
Rumpole at Sea, 293
Rumpole for the Prosecution, 293
Rumpole of the Bailey, 2, 3, 15, 68, 173, 183, **185-193**, 276, 281, 292-293
Rumpole on Trial, 293
Rumpole's Last Case, 293
Rumpole's Return, 15, 187, 188, 293
Russell, Catherine, 114, 133, **135**, 287, 288, 290, 295
Rutherford, Margaret, 6, 141, 143, 146
Rye, Renny, 287, 288, 289

S
Sallis, Peter, 226, 295
Samson, Bernard. *See Game, Set and Match*
Sanctuary Sparrow, The, 159, 162, 288
Sandor. *See Gallowglass*
Sangalletti, Rachel. *See My Cousin Rachel*
Savory, Gerald, 213, 288, 289, 292
Sayers, Dorothy L., 2, 15, 22, 41, 55-57, **58-59**, 63, 66, 86, 87, 107, 110, 153, 202, 203, 244, 254, 255, 289
Scandal in Bohemia, A, 26, 32, 294
Scent of Darkness, 96
Schmertz, Herb, 2
Seagrove, Jenny, 233, 234, 295
Seaton's Aunt, 268, **269**, 294
Second Stain, The, 295
Second Time Around, 290
Secret Adversary, The, 15, 48, 117, **125-131**, 276, 293. *See also* Beresford, Tommy and Tuppence
Secret of Bay 5B, The, 74, 290
Secret Garden, The, 167, 289
Sergeant Cribb, 3, 15, 22, 23, **37-40**, 280, 293-294
Service of All the Dead, 72, 73, 289
Setting of the Sun, The, 290
Shades of Darkness, 15, 206, 265, **268-271**, 274, 294
Shalit, Gene, 3, **10**, 11, 16, 37, 247, 249
Shaps, Cyril, 223, 224, 289
Sharpe, Tom, 16, 17, 294
Sheen, Michael, 216, 219, 289
She Fell Among Thieves, 3, 15, **16-19**, 278, 294
Sherlock Holmes, 3, 15, 22, 23, **25-35**, 37, 43, 44, 47, 55, 68, 156, 159, 169, 206, 270, 279, 294-295
Sherlock Holmes: The Master Blackmailer, 15, 295
Shore, Jemima. *See Quiet As a Nun*
Shoscombe Old Place, 295
Show credits, 286-295
Shrapnel, John, 233, 234, 246, 250, 291, 295
Shroud for a Nightingale, 15, 83, 84, 87, 286, 295
Sign of Four, The, 29, 34, 37, 68, 295
Silent World of Nicholas Quinn, The, 72, 73, 75, 135, 289
Silver Blaze, 295
Simenon, Georges, 113, **115-116**, 290
Simons, William, 37, 107, 108, 291, 293

Simpson, Michael, 288, 289, 293, 295
Sinclair, May, 268-269, 294
Sins of the Fathers, The, 75, 290
Six Napoleons, The, 295
Skreba, 133, 288
Sleeping Murder, 143, 286
Smith, Robert, 254-256, 291
Solitary Cyclist, The, 294
Something Old, Something New, 294
Speckled Band, The, 294
Spriggs, Elizabeth, 259, 295
Stevenson, Robert Louis, 212, 213, **215**, 289
Stoller, Jacky, 120, 122, 123, 292
St. Peter's Fair, 288
Stratton, John, 246, 291
Strickland, John, 96, 291, 292
Strong Poison, 55, 57, 59, 61, 108, 289
Suchet, David, xiii, 43, 44, 46, **52-53**, 173, 257, 258, 286, 288, 292. *See also Agatha Christie's Poirot*
Sugden, Mollie, 199, 291
Sunningdale Mystery, The, 126, 129, 130, 292
Sweeney Todd, 15, 225, **226-227**, 277, 295
Sweet Danger, 288
Swift, Clive, 212, 289, 294
Swing, Swing Together, 280, 294

T
Taste for Death, A, 15, 83, 87, 280, 286, 295
Tate, Dee. *See Chandler & Co.*
Taylor, Domini, 208, **211**, 234, 291
Taylor, Ken, 286, 288, 294
Temple, Paul. *See* Durbridge, Francis
Tennison, DCI Jane, 22, 25, 69, 83, 95, **96-98, 99-101,** 102, 103-105, 275, 278. *See also Prime Suspect*
Tey, Josephine, 236-237, **238**, 288
Thames Television, 149, 173, 185, 188, 195, 223, 226, 261, 288, 289, 290, 292, 293, 295
Thaw, John, 68, 71, 75, 78, **80-81**, 191, 289, 295. *See also Inspector Morse*
Theft of the Royal Ruby, The, 287
Third Floor Flat, The, 287
Those Who Trespass Against Us, 134, 289
Three Gables, The, 32, 295
Three Tools of Death, 167, 289
Time/Life Films, 212, 242, 289, 291
Todd, Sweeney. *See Sweeney Todd*
Toibin, Niall, 266, 291
Trackdown, 292
Tragedy at Marsdon Manor, The, 287
Treves, Frederick, 179, 236, 286, 287, 288, 289
Triangle at Rhodes, 287
Trivia quiz, 274-285
Tronson, Robert, 261-262, 288, 289, 290, 293
Twilight of the Gods, 71, 81, 290

U
Unbreakable Alibi, The, 129, 292
Undergod, The, 287
Unnatural Causes, 15, 83, 84, 278, 286, 295

V
Vane, Harriet, 55, 56-57, 59, **61**, 108, 278, 279
Van Gyseghem, Joanna, 185, 292, 294
Veiled Lady, The, 276, 287
Vesey, Helena. *See Mother Love*
Videos, 296
Vine, Barbara, 202, 216, 218, 219, **221-222**, 234, 289. *See also* Rendell, Ruth
Virgin in the Ice, The, 161, 288
Voss, Philip, 263, 291

W
Walker, Robert, 241, 289
Waller, David, 37, 293
Walter, Harriet, 55, 56, 61, 289. *See also* Vane, Harriet
Walters, Thorley, 242, 291
Ward, Sophie, 216-217, 289
Warwick, James, 125, 127, 130, 291, 293. *See also* Beresford, Tommy and Tuppence
Wasps' Nest, 287
Waterhouse, Keith, 155, 289
Watson, Dr. John, 25, 26, 28, 30, 31, **32**, 34, 68, 109
Waxwork, 38, 40, 294
Way Through the Woods, The, 81, 290
West, Norma, 257, 288, 294, 295
We, the Accused, 15, 68, 182, 245, **259-260**, 279, 295
WGBH, 2-3, 97, 240, 289
Wharmby, Tony, 291, 292, 293
Wharton, Edith, 268, 269-270, 271, 274, 294
Whately, Kevin, 71, 75, **76**, 78, 275, 289. *See also* Lewis, Detective Sergeant
Whiteley, Arkie, 216, 219, 289
Whitemore, Hugh, 246, 248, 291, 292
Who Killed Harry Field?, 290
Wilby, James, 208, 286, 291
Williams, Rosalie, 25, 294
Williams, Simon, 107, 108, 291, 295
Wilson, Joan, 2, 3, 6, 9, 11, 12, 25, 34
Wimsey, Lord Peter. *See Dorothy L. Sayers' Lord Peter Wimsey*
Winter, Maxim de. *See Rebecca*
Wise, Herbert, 84, 286, 290, 292
Wisteria Lodge, 295
Wobble to Death, 37, 40, 293
Wolvercote Tongue, The, 290
Woman in White, The, 15, 206, 225, **233-2235**, 274, 279, 295
Woodall, Andrew, 95, 292
Woodthorpe, Peter, 71, 289
Woodward, Tim, 230, 231, 289, 291
Wooldridge, Susan, 119, 120, 291, 292

Y
Yates, Dornford, 16, **17**, 18, 294
Yellow Iris, 287
York, Susannah, 254, 255, 286, 291
Yorkshire Television, 119, 122, 123, 292

Z
Zaharov, Basil, 68, 173, **177**, 192
Zenith, 71, 289

SUPPORT YOUR LOCAL PUBLIC BROADCASTING STATION!

EVERY COMMUNITY ACROSS AMERICA IS REACHED BY ONE OF THE 346 memberstations of the Public Broadcasting Service. These stations bring information, entertainment, and insight for the whole family.

Think about the programs you enjoy and remember most:

Mystery! . . . *Masterpiece Theatre* . . . *Nova* . . . *Nature* . . . *Sesame Street* . . . *Reading Rainbow* . . . *Baseball* . . . *The Civil War* . . . *The NewsHour with Jim Lehrer* . . . *Three Tenors* . . . *Great Performances* . . . *The American Experience* . . . *Washington Week in Review* . . . and so many more.

On your local PBS station, you'll also find fascinating adult education courses, provocative documentaries, great cooking and do-it-yourself programs, and thoughtful local analysis.

Despite the generous underwriting contributions of foundations and corporations, more than half of all public television budgets come from individual member support.

For less than the cost of a night at the movies, less than a couple of months of a daily paper, less than a month of your cable TV bill, you can help make possible all the quality programming you enjoy.

Become a member of your public broadcasting station and do your part.

PUBLIC TELEVISION. YOU MAKE IT HAPPEN!

CONTRIBUTORS

AUTHOR RON MILLER IS THE NATIONALLY SYNDICATED TELEVISION COLUMNIST for Knight Ridder Newspapers and television editor of the *San Jose Mercury News.* He's a former national president of the Television Critics Association and has served as a national judge for the CableAce Awards. His columns earned a 1994 National Headliner Award. Miller's articles and short fiction have appeared in a wide variety of publications across the country. He wrote the foreword to Les Brown's third edition of *The Encyclopedia of Television* and conducted and wrote all the interviews for *Masterpiece Theatre* (1995). A native of Santa Cruz, California, Miller lives with his wife, Darla, in Los Altos, California.

KAREN SHARPE HAS BEEN AN EDITOR AND WRITER FOR MORE THAN 25 years, working for and contributing to a variety of publishing companies, publications, and organizations. At KQED Books she seems to have the British beat, having been the editor for the bestselling *Are You Being Served?* and *Masterpiece Theatre.* Prior to that she was publisher of Vanstar Books, a line of computer titles. She has also worked in television, as a producer, writer, director. She lives in Berkeley, California.

ELLEN BASKIN IS A WRITER LIVING IN SANTA MONICA, CALIFORNIA. She has been a creative executive in the motion picture and television industries and is the author of *Filmed Books and Plays* (Ashgate, 1993) and *Serials on British Television* (Ashgate, 1995). She also worked on the predecessor to this book, *Masterpiece Theatre.*

DISEÑO IS AN AWARD-WINNING GRAPHIC DESIGN STUDIO IN SAN FRANCISCO whose clients include Chronicle Books, the San Francisco Art Institute, Autodesk, Aetna Health Insurance, the San Francisco AIDS Foundation, and KQED Books, for which they designed *Are You Being Served?.* Diseño has been published widely in *Graphis,* the Japanese compendium New Typo Graphics, several publications of the American Center for Design, and other publications. Diseño's principal, Raul Cabra, is a member of the faculty at the California College of Arts and Crafts.